KU-187-940

THEATRE AND HUMANISM
English Drama in the Sixteenth Century

WITHDRAWN FROM STOCK

This book examines the hundred years of drama preceding Shakespeare in the light of a critical problem: English drama at the beginning of the sixteenth century was allegorical, didactic, and moralistic; but by the end of the century theatre was censured as emotional and even immoral. How could such a change occur? Kent Cartwright suggests that some theories of early Renaissance theatre – particularly the theory that Elizabethan plays are best seen in the tradition of morality drama – need to be reconsidered. He proposes instead that humanist drama of the sixteenth century is theatrically exciting – rather than literary, elitist, and dull as it has often been seen – and socially significant, and he attempts to integrate popular and humanist values rather than setting them against each other. Taking as examples plays by writers from Medwall and Heywood to Marlowe, Lyly, and Greene, as well as many by lesser-known dramatists, the book demonstrates the contribution of humanist drama to the theatrical vitality of the sixteenth century.

KENT CARTWRIGHT is Associate Professor of English at the University of Maryland, College Park. He has published on Shakespeare, Renaissance drama, and American fiction. His previous books are *Shakespearean Tragedy and its Double: The Rhythms of Audience Response* (1991) and *Othello: New Perspectives* (1991), which he edited with Virginia Mason Vaughan.

THEATRE AND HUMANISM

English Drama in the Sixteenth Century

KENT CARTWRIGHT

CAMBRIDGE
UNIVERSITY PRESS

PUBLISHED BY THE PRESS SYNDICATE OF THE UNIVERSITY OF CAMBRIDGE
The Pitt Building, Trumpington Street, Cambridge CB2 1RP, United Kingdom

CAMBRIDGE UNIVERSITY PRESS
The Edinburgh Building, Cambridge, CB2 2RU, UK http://www.cup.cam.ac.uk
40 West 20th Street, New York, NY 10011-4211, USA http://www.cup.org
10 Stamford Road, Oakleigh, Melbourne 3166, Australia

© Kent Cartwright 1999

This book is in copyright. Subject to statutory exception and to the provisions of relevant collective licensing agreements, no reproduction of any part may take place without the written permission of Cambridge University Press.

First published 1999

Printed in the United Kingdom at the University Press, Cambridge

Typeset in Baskerville 11/12.5 pt [wv]

A catalogue record for this book is available from the British Library

Library of Congress cataloguing in publication data
Cartwright, Kent, 1943–
Theatre and humanism : English drama in the sixteenth century / – Kent Cartwright.
p.   , cm.
ISBN 0 521 64075 X (hardback)
1. English drama – Early modern and Elizabethan, 1500–1600 – History and criticism.
2. Theater – England – History – 16th century. 3. Renaissance – England.
4. Humanists – England. I. Title.
PR646.C37   1999
822'.309 – dc21   98-37229 CIP

ISBN 0 521 64075 X hardback

To
my brother Jerry

Contents

Acknowledgments

In the six and a half years that I spent writing this book I tugged on many sleeves. Demands for brevity do not permit me to identify in detail the substantial and varied contributions of the owners of those sleeves, but I list their names now with a deep sense of gratitude: Catherine Belsey, Thomas Berger, David M. Bevington, Theresa Coletti, Robert Coogan, Jane Donawerth, Donna B. Hamilton, William M. Hamlin, Grace Ioppolo, Erin Kelly, Bernice Kliman, Robert S. Knapp, Theodore B. Leinwand, Maynard Mack Jr., Laurie Maguire, Nancy Klein Maguire, Robert Miola, Alan H. Nelson, Elihu Pearlman, Joseph A. Porter, Lois Potter, Martha Tuck Rozett, William H. Sherman, Virginia Mason Vaughan, Paul Whitfield White, Gary Williams, and Georgianna Ziegler. In spring 1996 I was privileged to participate in a semester-long Folger Institute seminar led by J. W. Binns on "Books, Learning, and the Academy in the English Renaissance." I am obliged to Professor Binns's seminar for greatly increasing my understanding of sixteenth-century neo-Latin literature in England. I owe subsequent debts to the two anonymous readers, for their perceptive comments, and to Sarah Stanton of Cambridge University Press, for her efficient editorship. Immeasurable thanks are also due to the Folger Shakespeare Library for providing the venue for most of the research and writing of the manuscript. The drafting of several chapters was facilitated by a semester research fellowship from the Graduate Research Board of the University of Maryland.

I also express my gratitude for opportunities to present parts of this project at meetings of the Modern Language Association, South Atlantic Modern Language Association, Central Renaissance Conference, Southeastern Renaissance Conference, Shakespeare Society of America, and International Shakespeare Conference. An early version of chapter 1 was published in *Studies in the*

Literary Imagination; portions of chapter 3 appeared in *Renaissance Papers*; and chapter 6 first saw light in *Comparative Drama*, to all of which, for their permission to reprint material here, I register my appreciation.

I save several special thanks for last. When I began working on this project I profited greatly from numerous conversations about Tudor drama with my graduate student, Victoria Plaza. This book still reflects many of the interests that surfaced in those discussions, and I remain grateful to Victoria for her perspicacity. Later, when I was beginning to wonder if I would ever finish, my friend Mike Casey coached me for eight months through the drafting of a large share of the manuscript. It was one of the most productive periods of my life, and this book would not be appearing now without his help. As I was preparing the manuscript for submission and printing, Mary Tonkinson, copy-editor *extraordinaire* for *Shakespeare Quarterly*, helped me to sharpen and tighten it sentence by sentence. Finally, I express my gratitude and love to my wife, Pam, whose encouragement and support are without end.

Introduction

English drama at the beginning of the sixteenth century registers as allegorical, didactic, and moralistic, yet by the end of the century theatre would be censured as emotional, fantasy-arousing, and even immoral. How could such a change occur? How does it happen that drama, which enters the century as a vehicle of spiritual enlightenment, becomes, by the 1590s, itself an object of emotion? To address such questions requires exploring the ways that Tudor drama engages feelings and sensibilities, the ways that it creates the Renaissance experience of being "moved";[1] it requires exploring, that is, dramaturgy and theatrical effect. Such an inquiry will suggest that influential theories of early Renaissance theatre – particularly the theory that Elizabethan plays are viewed best through the tradition of morality drama – need reconsidering to explain theatre's affective power. The excitement of the Tudor stage derives partly from a humanist dramaturgy that embroils feelings and emotions in the creation of meaning.

An overarching issue continues to be troubling: how to account for England's high tide of drama in the sixteenth century. Prior to the explosion of commercial theatre in Elizabeth's reign, plays had already taken firm hold. In the Tudor humanist educational program at grammar schools and universities, for example, students studied and performed plays to a degree difficult to explain. Critics have developed various reasons for the burgeoning of drama during the century: the pedagogical interest in classical literature; the value of playacting as academic training for eloquence; the usefulness of theatre for religious and political argument; the efficacy of spectacle in confirming power; the broad social receptiveness to theatre; the importance of representation to nascent capitalism; the capacity of drama to accommodate different traditions and interests. To such ideas, one can give

1

considerable assent. Yet few analyses provide an adequate understanding of certain values that pulse through Tudor drama, particularly its sense of lively play and unpredictability, manifested
in linguistic exuberance, parody, physicality, virtuosic acting, and
teasing enigma. A mixture of surprise and elusiveness animates
Tudor theatre: the meaning of a play can be left suddenly open to
an actor's choice, as in *The Foure PP* (*c.* 1520s); or a play can
unexpectedly challenge its own stereotypes, as in *Gammer Gurton's
Needle* (*c.* 1553); or it can set confusion seductively against ideas,
as in *Gallathea* (*c.* 1584). The seemingly spontaneous or expansive
conjoins with the patterned; in humanist dramaturgy something
vivid and unanticipated can arise as a formal possibility. That hos-
pitality to the striking, surprising, and enigmatic contributes cru-
cially to Tudor theatre's ability to engage spectatorial feelings and
emotions in the midst of a complex and changing culture and can
help us to understand how drama exerted its magnetism upon the
age.

1

In recent decades many of sixteenth-century drama's virtues have
been attributed to the influence of a lively popular theatre, as
opposed to the influence of a more formal academic and humanist
theatre. The argument would seem to find perfect embodiment in
the comments of a particular Elizabethan dramatist. In 1592 one
of the most celebrated playwrights of the English stage set forth
a prefatory defense of his new tragicomedy – an impure form frequent in Renaissance drama yet divergent from the rules of Aristotle and Horace. Addressing an imagined carping critic, our playwright justifies his mongrel tragicomedy, saying, "For, just as in
living, so in writing my method is somewhat free and relaxed, of
a sort which pleases the learned less than the unskilled ... For
my part, I have produced this tragedy, or play, or historical narrative, or whatever it is right and proper to call it, not according to
the exacting standards of the *Art of Poetry* employed as some sort
of goldsmith's balance, but rather measured according to the
exacting standards of popular taste, and I have poured it forth
rather than composed it." These remarks celebrate popular
theatre: the assertion of a freedom and spontaneity in writing
similar to lived experience; the standards of popular taste in

contrast to codified rules about form; the sense of writing as inspiration ("poured forth"), in which the poet warbles his native woodnotes wild; and finally the carefree generic vagueness, recalling the itinerant acting troupe memorialized by Polonius that is ready to play any combination of tragedy, comedy, history, and pastoral. In sum, our playwright's comments sound like the anthem of popular theatre and would seem to confirm those critics who have looked to plebeian taste and morality drama as the shaping forces of the sixteenth-century stage.

The problem with this conclusion is that the passage in question was written not by a "popular" dramatist but by the premier academic playwright of the Elizabethan age, William Gager.[2] The address to the critic comes as a preface to Gager's *Ulysses Redux*, a drama strictly classical in theme, adapted from Homer, composed in Latin hexameters, and performed, as the title page declares, "at Christ Church, Oxford in the presence of the academic community."[3] We have here the curious case of a quintessential neoclassical, Latin, humanist academic play justified according to the tastes of "unskilled" audiences. That apparent contradiction invites a few simple observations: first, the separation that we moderns make between learned and popular drama may not have been drawn so sharply by Elizabethans, for whom the invocation of the popular may sometimes be as much a rhetorical ploy as a real distinction; more important, the humanist theatre that criticism has treated as formalistic and enervated may be far richer theatrically than we have allowed, and rich exactly in the virtues that we attribute to popular theatre.

2

Much recent Elizabethan dramatic criticism argues that the signal tradition of sixteenth-century theatre is that of the medieval morality play, which Marlowe, Shakespeare, and their contemporaries adapt with brilliant results. The "morality theory" arose as a reaction to criticism that interprets Elizabethan drama through the lens of sixteenth-century humanist learning, particularly classical strictures for dramatic construction, neo-Aristotelian poetics, humanist rhetoric, and literary formalism.[4] In rebuttal, David Bevington's seminal *From* Mankind *to* Marlowe (1962) turned to the "popular," "national," and "native" tradition of morality drama, whose influence, Bevington argues, permeates the sixteenth century from early Tudor plays to those of the University Wits.[5] Against humanist values of "unity, correspondence, subordination, and the like," Bevington considers morality drama to be defined by structural principles of "coordination," "repetitive effect, multiplicity, episode, and progressive theme."[6] Those features reflect the limited size of professional acting companies – "four men and a boy" – and their doubling of acting parts.[7] Complementing Bevington's study was Robert Weimann's materialist *Shakespeare and the Popular Tradition of the Theater* (1978).[8] Weimann emphasizes a plebeian and folk tradition of drama, which he investigates particularly in relation to the morality Vice figure. With his physicality, his topsy-turvy folk humor, and his signature ability to move between *locus* and *platea*, players and spectators, illusion and actuality, the Vice represents, for Weimann, a triumphantly vital theatrical figure. Likewise extolling the morality theory, Alan Dessen, in a series of studies, finds the theatrical conventions of Marlowe and Shakespeare deriving from the morality stage practices of the 1570s.[9] Those and a host of related works have invoked the moralities to understand Elizabethan dramatic construction, acting, characterization, staging practice, and audience reception.

But the valorizing of morality drama has entailed not only the dismissal of humanist theatricality but also the devaluing of other medieval forms, such as the saints' plays, civic mystery plays, and folk drama. Howard Norland has recently insisted on the complexity of the medieval dramatic inheritance, noting that if the morality was the foremost model of popular drama, its reign was during the first four Tudor decades.[10] By that argument, the claim that the morality tradition held sway as a "dominant mode of popular dramatic expression for about a century" becomes less tenable than was previously thought.[11] From 1531 to the early 1580s, the moralities account for only twenty to twenty-five percent of identified plays.[12] Partly because they "appealed more to the intellect than to the emotions," the moralities found their "most significant role" as they became "incorporated into the rediscovered forms of tragedy and comedy" or combined with the popular saints' plays into the history play.[13] In the parishes of England before 1540, furthermore, the seminal popular form may have been not Corpus Christi cycles or morality plays but folk drama.[14] Current scholarship thus makes positing morality plays as a definitive Tudor influence problematic.

The morality thesis has profited from some blurring of the term *popular*. Used to mean "native" by some and "plebeian" by others, and also connoting "broadly appealing," *popular* acquires an aura of approval and tends to triumph *de facto* in any set of opposing binaries, such as "popular versus humanist" or "popular versus elite" or "popular versus learned." Native dramaturgy, however, can show its spirit through innovations on forms that are imported and classical; audiences for plebeian drama might include aristocrats;[15] and the appealing repertories of the sixteenth century contain works of humanist provenance. Thus, as the term *popular* conflates differences, it institutes a questionable category.[16] For Bevington, "popular" correlates with "indigenous" but contrasts with "elite," even though the appeal of the "popular" crosses class boundaries. The implication here is that "elite" (i.e., humanist) drama cannot attract broad audiences; accordingly, "popular" would exclude by definition the possibility of an exciting humanist theatricality.[17] In addition, the notion that morality drama radiates a certain plebeian or native consciousness squares awkwardly with the apparent mixture of learned and folk elements in a prototypical morality play such as *Mankind*: "If it was *for* the folk the play was certainly not *by* the folk, and one is tempted to see it as the Shrovetide *jeu d'esprit* of a group of Cambridge clerks."[18] The morality theory stumbles, as well, on certain of its claims. Repetitive effect and multiplicity of detail, for example, cannot be ascribed exclusively to morality dramaturgy, as Doran's discussion of "multiple unity" and humanist *copia* suggests.[19] Nor is the practice of alternating different sets of characters scene by scene exclusive to morality drama, for Terence and Plautus often rely on competing lines of character and action. Likewise, Senecan tragedy can undertake an exploration of emotional states suggestive of the "coordinated" dramaturgical structure of the morality tradition.[20] Indeed, Seneca demonstrates how congenial humanist drama can be to exploratory and cumulative effects as well as to climactic ones. While Bevington rightly points to the appearance of the rounded human character in morality drama, that emergence can be seen in the light of Tudor humanism and its dramaturgical influence, not just in terms of a new interest in chronicle history (itself encouraged by humanism). For the development in drama of realistic human representations, in fact, the morality theory accounts rather poorly. While the critical emphasis on doubling in the moralities constitutes a significant insight, doubling can also operate in nonmorality plays, such as *Gammer Gurton's Needle*, which derives from the world of humanist academics. (Terence, the ancient dramatist most often used as a Renaissance model, seems also to have employed doubling.) Finally, in claiming that the stage romances of the 1570s belong exclusively to the morality tradition, the morality theory oversteps.[21] While romances such as *Clyomon and Clamydes* (c. 1570) contain Vice-like figures and episodic action, those plays also unfold humanist themes, values, and characterizations. To state these objections differently, the distance between the moralities and humanist drama is not nearly so great as the morality theory proposes.

Most important, the morality theory elides humanist theatricality. It does so by discussing humanist drama in terms of classical models, five-act structures, Aristotelian unities, and intellectual and philosophical themes.[22] Contained by such terms, humanist drama becomes something arid, literary, elitist, and rule-bound – incapable of the liveliness, energy, expansiveness, and high theatricality that Bevington, Weimann, and others associate with popular morality drama. Although those critics would do justice to humanist plays, a certain privileging of the popular seeps in: "Nor did the writers of school or courtly plays reject the *humor and freedom* of indigenous drama ... England's glory came ultimately from the fact that its courtly drama could *borrow life and vitality* from its humble brother" (emphasis mine).[23] To put that argument less circumspectly, popular theatricality redeems humanist artificiality and dullness. Likewise, Weimann portrays humanist dramaturgy as concerned with the unities and the rules of five-act structure in his suggestion that Elizabethan playmaking reached its zenith when popular theatrical energy finally converged with humanist unity and coherence. According to Weimann, the history of the sixteenth-century stage is the ever-expanding introduction into humanist, courtly, and Reformation plays of popular morality dramaturgy: vice characters, psychomachia, folk language, and audience address.[24] "In this way," Weimann summarizes, "the learned tradition of rhetoric and the humanist concern for form and symmetry were accommodated, however crudely, to the practical requirements of popular theatre with its greater capacity for action, spectacle, and low comedy."[25] Thus do efforts to make room for humanist plays in accounts of sixteenth-century drama end up confirming their deficient theatricality. But the interpretation of humanist drama as literary and readerly lacks the subtlety to differentiate Fulke Greville's closet drama *Mustapha* (pub. 1609) from the theatrically engaging *Gammer Gurton's Needle* or *Roister Doister* (c. 1553) or *Damon and Pithias* (1564) – all of which exude "action, spectacle, and low comedy." Some morality theorizing even confines humanist drama to the "élite" plays associated with Sir Thomas More early in the century.[26] To similar effect, the investigation of stage conventions at the commercial playhouses tends to leave out dramaturgical practices, including those by humanist playwrights, from decades before the 1570s, even though, to take one example, a seminal property of the commercial stage, the mirror, makes its first active appearance in the academic *Wit and Science* in the 1530s. In such ways a lively humanist theatricality – from Henrician plays to school and university drama to Inns of Court shows to works of the University Wits – tends to vanish.

What I have argued so far might give the impression that I wish to privilege the "humanist tradition" at the expense of the "morality tradition." Not so. The work of Bevington, Weimann, Dessen, and others on morality theatre constitutes a luminous contribution of twentieth-century scholarship to the understanding of Tudor drama. I would, however, redress the devaluing of humanist dramaturgy, a side-effect of the morality thesis perhaps not fully intended. To a large extent, of course, the morality theorists have only perpetuated the argument-by-opposites inherited from their predecessors, who dismiss the popular tradition in favor of classically influenced drama. But even if one were to contend that humanist drama ought to be preferred once again over the morality tradition – a proposition that I do not believe – the case would not be worth making, for it would merely preserve a formulaic, binarial, see-saw criticism.[27] Instead, I propose that humanist dramaturgy be explored for its own theatrical experiments, innovations, discoveries, and virtues. Such an effort will reveal in humanist theatre qualities of performance, structure, characterization, and auditorial experience that parallel or complement the theatrical virtuosities prized by the morality theory.

The contention risks overemphasis, obliging one to bear in mind the argument that a great virtue of early Tudor drama is its capacity to absorb and refashion a range of influences. A new sense of humanist dramaturgy, then, will help criticism move away from the binarial model itself and toward a conception of Tudor drama's triumphant mingling, balancing, and negotiating of sources and interests.

3

Any examination of humanist dramaturgy must consider a second-generation attack on humanism that reformulates the earlier "popular versus humanist" binary: the charge of "essentialism" leveled by cultural materialism and new historicism. "[M]aterialist theory," one proponent says, "rejects ... the humanist belief in a unified, autonomous self" – that is, an "essential" self of unchanging human characteristics.[28] According to this critique, essentialism coalesced in "sixteenth-century Christianity and its stoic and humanist derivatives" and stresses such qualities as man's reason, his soul's immortality, and his free will.[29] That essentialist humanist model presumably receives a radical "interrogation" in Renaissance tragedy, which draws on "estimates of human nature which were largely outside, or even in opposition to, these dominant forms and their internal strains."[30] Another influential critique of humanism sees Renaissance tragedy as indeterminate in meaning because it expresses a transition between a medieval conception of the self and a post-Enlightenment, liberal humanist one.[31] The hero of the medieval moralities is "a transitory configuration of fragments, of states of being over which he has only the most minimal control."[32] By contrast, "Liberal humanism proposes that the subject is the free, unconstrained author of meaning and action, the origin of history[,] ... [u]nified, knowing and autonomous."[33] Here Renaissance drama expresses the unresolved contest for meaning between two views of humankind, the fragmented being of the medieval moralities and the autonomous, empirical individual. But that Foucauldian distinction between two epistemes may be overdrawn, for, argues Norland, saints' plays attest to the possibility of heroic human endeavor, and both the saints' and mystery plays evoke a medieval belief in human efficacy at odds with the moralities' view of feckless mankind.[34] The complex dramatic representations of humans in the mysteries and saints' plays, along with the historical belatedness of the moralities, cast doubt on any neat medieval episteme and the resulting binarial opposition of the medieval to the humanist.

From a Marxist perspective, essentialism implies an idealized, static concept of a homogeneous self located outside history and social experience. While Renaissance humanism does invoke a sense of human nature – for example, in the premise that reason is a distinguishing feature of mankind – anti-essentialism makes something of a hobgoblin of that view by overidealizing it.[35] Humanist thinkers such as Erasmus and More reject what they consider the stultifying idealizations and abstractions of scholasticism. To that end, the humanists argue that people could speak about God only "metaphorically . . . and of invisible things only through the visible things of this world."[36] Knowledge of reality, they claimed, is bounded by material experience and mediated by language.[37] Erasmus, More, and their colleagues emphasize a person as a social and historical being – not some ideal, ahistorical phantasime – and make historical contextualization and philology central to their exegetical work. In the *Ciceronianus*, for example, Erasmus lampoons linguistic anachronisms resulting from an orator's idealization of Ciceronian style; in the "Letter to Martin Dorp," he defends his own New Testament translation and commentary against scholastic criticism of its historical and philological grounding. Likewise, Erasmus typically reorients controversies toward questions of the lived life and extols the exemplary careers of Socrates, Cicero, Paul, Jerome, and, of course, Christ – as he does in the *Antibarbarorum liber*, the *Moriae encomium*, and the *Enchiridion militis christiani*, for example. Similarly, one cannot read Erasmus's educational writings without feeling his revulsion at the brutalizing of children and his sensitivity, compassion, and innovative playfulness toward children as learners. Erasmus consistently rejects theological hair-splitting so as to attend to the immediate, even pragmatic, exigencies of living a pious, ethical, and useful life – the kind of attitude that made him refuse to jump instantly on the anti-Luther bandwagon. And Erasmus, of course, writes with wit, energy, ironic understatement, and sly parody. Terms such as *idealist* and *essentialist* utterly miss the Erasmian ethos, so central to English humanism, as such terms similarly miss the

historical and social consciousness of his fellow humanists More,
Colet, and Elyot.[38]

If we approach the Renaissance as not just a transitional phase
caught between two philosophical paradigms or epistemes but a
complex culture with its own integrity, the anti-essentialist critique further weakens. The opposition between the (allegedly
medieval) view of human beings as rudderless and the (allegedly
liberal humanist) image of them as autonomous could then be
understood to reflect creative tensions at the heart of sixteenth-
century humanism itself, which posits a dynamic, unstable
relationship between human potential and performance. Rejecting
the idea of a dominant orthodox ideology and a marginalized sub-
versiveness, Debora Shuger has recently envisioned the Renaissance in terms of an ideology that was itself pluralistic and contradictory: "radical questioning, alternate voices, and perception of
contradiction manifest themselves *within* supposedly orthodox
texts."[39] Where the epistemic or Marxist critiques interpret
Renaissance drama as indeterminate in meaning or as "subversive," Shuger sees the pluralistic habits of thought of the English
Renaissance itself. A central "problematic" then becomes the
"placement of boundaries." Shuger describes a dialectic between
a "sacramental/analogical" thinking that "tends to deny rigid
boundaries; nothing is simply itself, but things are signs of other
things and one thing may be inside another," and a more rationalistic thought that distinguishes rigorously between "conceptual
and national territories."[40] The problem of boundaries and their
"thickness" suggests why the term *essentialism*, as it fences off and
idealizes a supposedly humanist self, distorts Renaissance habits
of thought. Humanist educators, for example, could contemplate
a human "essence," but one that is inchoate, corruptible or
improveable, requiring a kind of performance to be fully realized –
an essentialism with permeable boundaries. Richard Mulcaster,
writing in *Positions* (1581), offers one example of this neo-
Aristotelian contrast between potential and performance. After
finding in Plato, Xeno, and Aristotle agreement that "nature" has
given women "vertues" equivalent with those of men, Mulcaster
proceeds:

That as naturally euery one hath some good assigned him, whervnto he
is to aspire, and not to cease vntill he haue obtained it, onlesse he will
by his owne negligence reiect that benefit, which the munificence of

nature hath liberally bestowed on him: so there is a certaine meane, wherby to winne that perfitly, which *nature* of her selfe doth wish us franckly. This meane they call *education*, whereby the naturall inclinations be gently caryed on . . . [Y]oung *maidens* deserue the traine : bycause they haue that treasure, which belongeth vnto it, bestowed on them by *nature, to be bettered in them by nurture.*[41]

Everyone, male or female, possesses a potential for good, a "vertue," which he or she must realize, bring to performance, while society's responsibility is to provide through education the opportunity for such performance. Nurture can actually "better" nature. Essential human identity occurs here not as something fixed, static, or rigid but as a potential, an immanence, a possibility; nor does Mulcaster define a unitary, monolithic, homogeneous "good" that all will ideally achieve. Essentialism, as the materialists have used it, fails to account for the permeability of the humanist self and the indeterminate unfolding of its possibilities. "Why did I write this book?," asks Dollimore in introducing the second edition of *Radical Tragedy*. The main reason, he tells us, was that the aspiration " 'to write' . . . helped keep me going on an arduous and damaging journey from being a miserable 15-year-old school-leaver chained to a lathe in a car factory to becoming – well, someone else."[42] One could hardly find a modern statement that corresponds better to the humanist spirit of Mulcaster, Elyot, and Erasmus.

Despite the impact that anti-essentialism and the morality theory have made on our understanding of sixteenth-century plays, other approaches have still flourished. Diverging from the morality argument, Joel Altman enlarges the sense of humanist dramaturgy by proposing that much early Tudor and Elizabethan playmaking is structured according to the humanist rhetorical practice of arguing *in utramque partem*, on both sides of the question.[43] In Altman's view, humanist theatre allows explorative thought to weave itself into the ebb and flow of dramatic action and emotion in a way that defuses the humanist stereotype of arid unities and five-act formulas.[44] Differently, David Bevington can be credited with reviving interest in the topical political signals of Tudor drama.[45] That approach has been pursued by, among others, Greg Walker in his detailed study of early Tudor plays composed, he contends, to infuence the politics of Henry's court.[46] In the domain of religious politics, Paul Whitfield White has recently demonstrated that drama from the early 1530s to the early 1580s was used extensively for Protestant propaganda, from the Cranmer-inspired, anti-Papist theatre of John Bale through the mid-century reformers and their Marian resistance and continuing halfway into Elizabeth's reign.[47] In a material vein, Jean-Christophe Agnew maintains that early drama must be understood as deriving from, and expressing the problems of, a nascent market economy.[48] Many of those critics would likely agree that a special characteristic of early Tudor drama is not its adherence to a single line but its capacity to incorporate a variety of influences, including those from topical politics, religion, and the market, as well as those from saints' plays, civic mystery plays, moralities, folk drama, Roman comedy and tragedy, and humanist poetics.[49] The principle of inclusiveness deserves underscoring because it resists the tendency to exaggerate any particular influence under consideration. Likewise, both Walker and White show uneasiness with the popular-versus-something-else binary, and all the recent perspectives just mentioned pay tribute to the boldness, ingenuity, and vitality of sixteenth-century drama. Alongside the recognition of Tudor drama's richness, a general reconsideration of humanism is also underway, from the politics of advocacy, to the relationship between humanism and capitalism, or between humanism and empirical science, to humanism's bearing on early modern subjectivity.[50] The overall effect of these appraisals is to recreate the importance of humanism to the political and cultural dialogue of the sixteenth century.[51]

4

My opening question asked how drama, a vehicle for spiritual knowledge in the morality plays, becomes during the sixteenth century itself an object of interest.[52] An answer, I suggested, can help us to understand the burgeoning of drama through the century, a growth, in the case of school theatricals, far out of proportion to the instructional value claimed for the genre.[53] The dramaturgy of vernacular humanist plays provides a path toward some answers. Vernacular plays constitute the truest crucible in drama for the medieval, humanist, political, and religious interests of the century that we have been discussing. Accessible to more than a coterie audience, they offer the best opportunity for gauging a humanist theatricality comparable to that of the moralities. *Wit and Science* and *Gammer Gurton's Needle*, for example, began as school plays for specific audiences but managed to achieve influence or appeal beyond their initial confines. The itinerant acting company in *The Book of Sir Thomas More* (*c.* 1590) lists the humanist *Foure PP* as well as *The Marriage of Wit and Wisdom* (*c.* 1570), derived from *Wit and Science*, in its repertory. Such interludes suggest the capacity of academic plays to appeal to popular theatrical tastes. On the other hand, recent studies and translations have reawakened us to the substantial and rich body of university drama written in Latin.[54] Humanist plays in English share a relationship with that tradition of neo-Latin work, and the present study will make reference to academic playwrights such as Nicholas Grimald, George Buchanan, Thomas Legge, and William Gager.

To mention school plays is to recall that, from early in the sixteenth century, humanists used drama to teach. Humanism, of course, takes men and women as creatures of "undetermined nature" (in Pico della Mirandola's famous phrase) and focuses on the capacity of people to transform themselves by education. Here drama, like other forms of literature, offers images of virtue for neo-Platonic inspiration and likenesses of vice for rejection: "to show virtue her feature, scorn her own image" (*Hamlet*, III.ii.22–23).[55] Thus pedagogues could quarry ethical philosophy and rhetorical examples by excavating Terence. Proposing a series of steps for teaching a classical author such as Terence or Virgil, Erasmus concludes: "Finally he [the teacher] should turn to philosophy and skillfully bring out the moral implication of the poets' stories, or employ them as patterns, for example, the story of Pylades and Orestes to show the excellence of friendship, that of Tantalus the curse of avarice."[56] For their moral wisdom as well as their eloquence, classical speeches, sentences, and adages could be memorized, and, says Erasmus, in proverbs "almost all the philosophy of the Ancients was contained."[57] His *Adages* draw not only from Homer, Plutarch, Virgil, Cicero, and Jerome (among many others), but also from playwrights such as Sophocles, Euripides, Aristophanes, Seneca, Terence, and Plautus. Playacting, in particular, saturated humanist education because, as it occasioned learning in language, diction, gesture, attitude, and sententia, it modeled the "[m]imetic assimilation ... fundamental to all humanist pedagogy."[58]

During the sixteenth century, humanist drama maintains its connection with learning, but the nature of that connection changes. The change might be understood best in terms of the dialogue between knowledge and experience. Morality drama often employs an authoritative stage figure – Charity, Mercy, the Doctor – to enunciate the lessons of the play. Thus, while a work such as *Everyman* makes the hero experience estrangement from God, the play does not depend exclusively on the hero's experience to drive its truths home. Humanist drama grapples noticeably with the relationship between experience and knowledge. *Wit and Science*, for example, dilates on Wit's experience of his fall into error and on the stages of his transformation, while emphasizing the doubts of Wit's would-be bride, Lady Science, about her groom. The play's didactic figures assume social rather than soteriological roles, and the value of learning is transmitted metaphorically. A tension between quotidian life and eschatological wisdom infiltrates medieval drama,[59] of course, but as Renaissance theatre showcases secular experience, that tension becomes varied, complex, and urgent.

Knowledge and experience are linked throughout the sixteenth century, but precept increasingly falls short in explaining life. For Erasmus the breech between monistic truth and multivalent reality is capable of a mysterious accommodation, as in the case of the adage: "Erasmus maintains that ... a combination of the antiquity of the adage (often an authority spoken through a sequence of different voices) and its metaphorical resistance to any simple or singular interpretation ... gives it a special status – multivalence enhances the practical utility of an authority supposedly grounded in another kind of authority."[60] Later English humanists pursue a less gnomic relationship between the ideal and the practical. In a mid-century letter to Johann Sturm, Roger Ascham says of books of rhetoric, "I always look for rhetorical principles to be carefully linked to examples" from historians or orators, "so that whatever there is of splendor and equity in virtue, of foulness and fraud in vice, of seasonable opportunity in wisdom, and of unexpected good luck in fortune can be observed and collected."[61] Humanists animate the rules of art or of life with abundant examples drawn from history or literature, and that concreteness releases an immediacy, energy, and delight felt to be crucial: "this conjunction of art and imitation produces a new sweetness and pleasure in studies and makes the fruit useful."[62] Thus, in the art of imitation, as in religion, "one ought to join examples from life to points of doctrine."[63]

But eighteen years later, in 1568, Ascham has pulled back from the vivifying equilibrium between precept and illustration: "For just as in one's philosophy of life and morals, so also in the philosophy of learning and education, examples are far more beneficial than rules."[64] Ascham no longer implies that experience and practice conform wholly to maxims; in arts or crafts learned through imitation, for example, "rules have no place, or at least a very small one."[65] The urge for examples has perhaps opened awareness to the untidiness of existence, so that the magisterial Erasmian accommodation now seems unavailable. In a prefatory epistle to the reader of *Thesavrvs Oeconomiae* (1597), the Oxford philosopher John Case ruminates on these matters: "I had previously written (diligent reader) a few observations on Aristotle's *Economy*; but then I wrote as a reader or spectator of the play, not as an actor. Now, in truth, after having sat for twenty years in the stern of a private ship, I have reviewed those jottings, which, when I wrote them, I had tested but little or not at all: *So much does wise maturity differ from witty youth, so much does long experience differ from art and simple thought.*"[66] Case's terms may refer ironically to the famous humanist dicta that "Learning teacheth more in one yeare than experience in twentie," as Ascham himself puts it in *The Scholemaster* (1570).[67] Twenty years of private experience have revealed to Case the glibness of his youthful precepts. Rather than attempting to harmonize precept with practical life, Sir Philip Sidney finds it necessary sometimes to transcend history, which is "captived by the truth of a foolish world" and "many times ... an encouragement to unbridled wickedness."[68] The relationship between experience and preceptual knowledge goes to the heart of humanism; its initial, optimistic version releases "sense, feeling, profit,"[69] and energy – and even confidence in a mysterious harmony – but its later version struggles with the intractability of experience. The sixteenth century begins with Europe's preeminent scholar, Erasmus, undertaking to reform the world through humanist education: "Nature is an effectuall thynge, but

education, more effectuall, ouercommeth it," wrote Erasmus in
1529.[70] But the century ends, we might say, with Europe's arche-
typal melancholy student, Hamlet, immobilized by the failure of
knowledge to reform or even elucidate experience.[71] As the century waned, the humanist dream of perfectability through learning
began to fail: "What became increasingly clear, ... as the sixteenth century proceeded through expansion, war, religious persecution and reformation, and expansion once again, was that the
human value preached from a classical past when aligned with
Christianity could not always account for subsequent observation
and experience."[72] As we shall see, the dialectic between knowledge and experience registers itself variously in drama, as a sense
of play or even a subtle uncertainty – emotional doubt, confusions
in language, conflicts between ethics and feelings, even theatrical
self-awareness.

The humanists' attraction to the experiential and empirical was
concomitant with their concern for education and human improve-
ment. Erasmus justifies the liberal arts experientially, for
example, when he claims that "though they are not virtues in
themselves, they prepare the mind for virtue by making it gentle
and pliable instead of savage and cruel."[73] For an intellectual such
as Juan Luis Vives – and Erasmus as well – knowledge and education are valuable as they enhance a mental and subjective attitude of piety. Overall, Renaissance humanism contributed to a
new sense of the conditions and limits of human knowledge, as
well as a sense of the possibilities and problems of understanding
the external world, the human mind, and the nature of God, all
in relation to each other.[74] In its efforts to rediscover a universal
knowledge, the humanists grappled in a primary way with tensions
and oppositions, such as those between human nature and education, fate and free will, passive and active life, individuality and
community, history and timeless truth, empiricism and idealism,
and knowledge and experience. Even a humanist romance, such
as Sidney's *Arcadia*, becomes on one level a vast acknowledgment
of the slippery, endless permutations of the conflict between passion and reason. That exploratory, dialectical, and expansive quality of humanism deserves stressing, for it complements the notion
of a "crisis of authority" in the sixteenth century, most visible in
the Protestant Reformation.[75] The view of humanism as dynami-
cally engaged with problems of truth departs from the "anti-

essentialist" caricature of humanism as complicitous with repressive authoritarianism. According to the negative critique,
humanism "offered everyone a model of true culture as something
given, absolute, to be mastered, not questioned – and thus fostered
in all its initiates a properly docile attitude towards authority."[76]
Weimann similarly sees humanism as embracing a "concept of
interdependence between linguistic order and political stability,"
a view that allows him to contrast presumed humanist authoritarianism with drama's "volatile and divided" view of authoriz-
ation.[77] But if humanists granted authority to writing, their own
works were alive to the problems of legitimization. New studies of
"margins" and marginalia allow us to understand the printed page
itself as "a territory of contestation upon which issues of political,
religious, social, and literary authority are fought."[78] From a philosophical perspective, moreover, humanism advances an effect
opposite to the implicit charge of oppression: "The reaction
against traditional scholastic authorities had grown into a questioning of all authorities, even the classical ... [T]he principal
lesson from the various Renaissance conceptions of philosophy ...
was the need to jettison pre-established truths, to re-evaluate constantly all doctrinal and methodological choices and to respect
the perpetual newness of the problems with which philosophy and
scientific research have to deal."[79] That description of Renaissance
philosophy could be taken as a virtual gloss on a comparable statement by Vives: "it is far more profitable to learning to form a
critical judgment on the writings of the great authors, than to
merely acquiesce in their authority."[80] Likewise Erasmus, in
rejecting a formulaic imitation of Cicero or any other author,
insisted that differences among individual minds and rhetorical
styles must be respected, for "A speech comes alive only if it rises
from the heart."[81] Humanism endeavored to acknowledge the
multiplicity and contradictoriness of life and yet to reconcile those
qualities with the oneness of God.

The tension between knowledge and experience thus constitutes
one reason why humanist drama might have thrived. Drama tests
the scripted and the felt, the conceived and the experienced,
against each other. All drama depends, of course, on the actor's
voice, gesture, and body to authenticate the written dialogue; early
plays, moreover, repeat *sententia* that their characters' fortunes
may or may not confirm. With the secularized interludes emerging

from the More-circle playwrights – Medwall, Rastell, Heywood, Redford – drama emphasizes its engagement with the social and quotidian world. A sense of material reality was already present in the civic pageant plays, of course, such as the on-stage banquet in *The Chester Play of the Shepherds* or the wooden cross with its misaligned holes over which the carpenters painfully stretch the body of Christ in *The York Play of the Crucifixion*. Humanist drama picks up that fascination with the materiality of theatre. John Heywood's *The Foure PP* delights in the physical objects displayed by Pardoner, Pothecary, and Pedlar, and the play as a whole draws attention to the actors' physicality, to acting itself. Dirt, tatters, excrement, bruises, and injuries spread among the characters of *Gammer Gurton's Needle*. Its *mise-en-scène* is a world of the soiled, and the play returns repeatedly to the experiences of the human body, as the song "Back and sides go bare, go bare" indicates. Spectacle gains increased theatrical importance in the 1560s – witness the flaying in *Cambises* and the near beheading in *Damon and Pithias* – a trend augmented by the works of Lyly, Marlowe, and Greene. Like popular theatre, humanist plays redound with an exploratory interest in acting, human physicality, material existence, and spectacle. In that respect, drama offers a remarkably apt and stimulating vehicle for humanist exploration of the problems of knowledge and human experience.[82] Attention to the physical, furthermore, can heighten a spectator's sense of theatricality. At some point, the more one scrutinizes the acting, the more one becomes aware of the paradoxical relationship between actor and character, in which the spectator sees not exactly one or the other but the "actor-as-character."[83] Emphasis on physicality in the theatre comes to reveal drama's capacity for a mysterious doubleness.

The search for knowledge and the exploration of the physical thus find their counterpart in a sense of theatrical enigma, a feeling of elusiveness. Enigmatic possibilities arise in the "humanist acting" of the More circle playwright John Heywood. Likewise the university play *Gammer Gurton's Needle* can create a buffoonish, stereotypical character only to develop him against that caricature into a surprisingly rich, peculiarly realistic, even sympathetic, persona. In the second half of the sixteenth century, humanist drama explores theatre's power to move spectatorial emotions in ways, as in *Gorboduc* (1562), that render a straightforward statement of political meaning difficult. Indeed, Lyly's *Gallathea* has the distinction of making a theatrical value of intellectual confusion – an argument that can help to redeem Lyly's plays from their derogation as "dramas of ideas." Greene illustrates the scope of the enigmatic in Tudor theatre as his *Friar Bacon and Friar Bungay* (1589) echoes within its narrative other plays and outside events in a manner that complicates meaning. Such a theatre makes extracting a simple message difficult; rather, the thematics of the play come to reside in the experience of its multiform relationships. That humanist reticulation, we shall discover, fits admirably the commercial conditions of fixed-venue theatre in the late 1580s. Thus to the desire for knowledge, Tudor humanist drama comes to offer the seductiveness of experience. It grasps that feelings, memories, emotions, sensate and psychological experiences, and language itself constitute our imperfect but only vehicles for approaching the nature that surrounds and includes us. Identifying humanist drama by its complex relationship between knowledge and experience helps to explain drama's power in the sixteenth century and invites consideration of the knowledge and experience of the play itself, of its dramaturgy and theatricality, of its spectatorial emotions, ideas, and effects. Certain terms for those experiences will recur in our discussions: *enigma, doubt, empathy, spectacle, confusion* – for those terms hint at the vitality and creative tension released into humanist theatre.

To speak favorably of qualities such as "confusion" in humanist drama, however, may seem to offer another theory of "indeterminate" meaning. The proponents of "indeterminacy" wish to locate Renaissance tragedy on the cusp of a Foucauldian epistemic change that renders fixed meaning impossible; I would emphasize instead the Renaissance desire to place experience and knowledge in a proximate relationship. After almost a hundred years of Terence in Tudor schools, Richard Bernard in his bilingual Latin-English *Terence in English* (1598) is still moralizing about characters and displaying flowers of Latin learning after every scene. Didacticism continues to occupy a site along the continuum of knowledge and experience in drama. As the sixteenth century ends, pedagogues still affirm proverbial wisdom, although the academician John Case has begun to explore truth in Sidneyan poetic terms.[84] Renaissance drama derives productive tension from its mutual commitments to an enriched sense of human experience and to the possibility of knowable truths, a commitment different from postmodernism's fascination with indeterminacy. From the perspective of humanist drama, confusion and its associated values function to make meaning complex, even dynamic – and thereby stimulating and moving. In John Lyly's *Gallathea*, the two maidens, Gallathea and Phillida, enjoy pleasurable confusion – a blushing, physical confusion as well as a mental confusion about each other's identity – that facilitates their relationship. The play works an analogous pleasure upon the spectators as it entangles them in wondering about the conclusion and even about their own perplexity. Evoking self-conscious confusion and engagement from material that is remote, mythological, and rhetorically artificial constitutes part of *Gallathea*'s mastery. Humanist dramaturgy puts feelings and emotions in productive tension with ideas, apothegms, and intellectual certainties, so that what emerges is a complex matrix of experience and understanding. The effect of doubt, confusion, and their sister values will be to intensify and personalize the engagement with drama and to open its meaning to increased possibilities.

Humanist dramaturgy may now be seen as complementing or paralleling morality dramaturgy in two major respects: audience engagement and dynamic tension. For Bevington and Weimann, as we have noted, the moralities stir spectators with panoramic grandeur while also establishing a conspiratorial intimacy with them, in contrast to humanist drama's alleged formalist aridity and intellectualism. But humanist drama, we can say, explores its own creative tensions between knowledge and experience, and does so in ways that reveal corresponding methods of engaging the audience. Humanist drama may evolve toward a self-contained world, but with its play of enigma, empathy, suspense, and pleasurable confusion, humanist theatre draws spectators inside that environment as participants, respondents, and even fellow creators who incriminate themselves emotionally or imaginatively in the illusion. Thus, to the audience engagement celebrated by Weimann in the moralities and their creative tension admired by Bevington, humanist dramaturgy adds its own analogous virtues.

5

I have already hinted at some of the arguments in this study. The first chapter contends that John Heywood's *The Foure PP* presents the unusual theatrical possibility that, at a crucial moment in the play, the actor might reveal either of two opposite intentions or hide his intentions entirely. Such enigmatic acting reflects the sense of play in humanist pedagogy, embodied in that definitive, protean humanist persona, Erasmus's Folly. The enigmatic also appears in other Heywood plays and in those of his fellow More-circle writers, including Medwall and Rastell. Chapter 2 argues that John Redford's school play, *Wit and Science* (*c.* 1530–47), show-cases new humanist interests in emotional experience, mirrored identities, and doubt. The play's orientation toward emotional experience reflects its metaphorical argument, that a student's progress in humanist education is like that of the morality hero toward salvation. Related theatrical values can be seen in a host of early plays permeated with educational concerns, from Palsgrave's translation of *Acolastus* (1540) to *Nice Wanton* (1547–53), *The Disobedient Child* (*c.* 1560), and *Misogonus* (*c.* 1570). Chapter 3 finds a dramaturgy of empathy emerging in the mid-century Cambridge play *Gammer Gurton's Needle* through the character Hodge, who evokes schoolboy fears and hopes as he develops against his early stereotype. Applying Roman comedic form and the theories of Donatus and Melanchthon, the play yet reveals possibilities of sympathetic involvement not implicit in Terence and Plautus. Chapter 4 suggests that the "popular" *Cambises* and the humanist *Gorboduc*, despite their apparent differences, share common psychological and emotional effects that characterize early Elizabethan drama's responses to tyranny and that crystallize in the emergence of suspense as a dramaturgical strategy in *Damon and Pithias*. Chapter 5 turns to a range of plays emphasizing women characters – from *Fulgens and Lucres* (*c.* 1490) and *Godly Queene Hester* (*c.* 1527) to *Mary Magdalene* (*c.* 1558) and *Patient Grissell* (*c.* 1559) to *Clyomon and Clamydes* and *The Rare Triumphs of Love and Fortune* (1582) – and argues that "alternative" female values are evident across the century and take inspiration from those expansive views on women promoted by Tudor humanists. The chapter culminates with an illustration of female empowerment in the seldom-discussed stage romances of the 1570s. Chapters 7, 8, and 9 turn to the University Wits, with an interest in confusion in Lyly's *Gallathea*, bearing witness in Marlowe's *Tamburlaine* (*c.* 1587), and intertextuality in Greene's *Friar Bacon and Friar Bungay*. Those discussions of the University Wits suggest the adaptability of humanist dramaturgy to the emergent popular and commercial theatre of London. *Gallathea* and other Lyly plays share features with the widely appealing stage romances of the previous decade. *Tamburlaine*'s innovations with the choric function reflect the dramaturgy of neo-Latin academic plays, such as Legge's *Richardus Tertius* (1579) and Gager's *Meleager* (1582). *Friar Bacon and Friar Bungay* gains its theatrical resonance by adapting the practice of humanist allusion, as it recalls humanist sonnets, refers to works of Lyly and Marlowe, and advances its own action through a system of internal parallels and contrasts. Greene's play suggests the construction of the sophisticated, knowing playgoer on which success at the fixed-venue playhouses will depend. Another feature of humanist dramaturgy emerges here in the idea of community, with plays not only recreating communities onstage but using the theatre to create an implicit community among playgoers. Structurally, the chapters of this study proceed in a roughly chronological fashion, but they do not presume to demonstrate any step-by-step development of affective dramaturgy. Rather, they suggest the recurrence of an affective dimension in humanist drama, its exploratory range, and its contribution to the vitality of sixteenth-century English theatre. Although I began this introduction by suggesting that during the sixteenth century drama moves from didacticism toward emotionalism, I can now qualify that assertion. While a fantasy-arousing and affective drama gains ground, didacticism by no means disappears – and its presence as an impulse is central to the tension in humanist dramaturgy. Instead of linear development, sixteenth-century plays reflect irregular oscillations along a continuum of theatrical possibilities.

The essays here endeavor generally to locate plays in their historical circumstances, from the fertile intellectual activity around Sir Thomas More, to the production of school drama for convincing aristocrats of the value of humanist learning, to the demographic changes of mid-century Christ's College students, to the marriage politics of the early Elizabethan court, to the need for repeat customers at fixed-venue playhouses. They seek to read specific plays from the perspective of dramaturgy and audience effect.[85] I should acknowledge the speculative aspect of such analysis: one cannot prove, for example, that Cambridge schoolboys actually felt empathy for Hodge at the first performance of *Gammer Gurton's Needle*. Such responses can only be inferred, and they attain credibility solely on the basis of the analysis behind them. That analysis cannot be certain, moreover, because it can never escape the obscurities inherent in fishing for sixteenth-century responses through the muddy waters of previous centuries and from the particular shore of our own modernism. It would be most accurate to state, therefore, that the essays investigate the potential of humanist dramaturgy to evoke certain audience effects. Yet even that potential forwards the present argument, for it suggests the way that humanist plays make themselves open to new explorations of theatrical experience.[86] I should acknowledge another danger in the following essays: the problem of defining Renaissance humanism. While certain features of humanism, such as its pedagogical orientation, command consensus, humanism is notoriously fuzzy at the edges, as intellectual historians acknowledge. For the present purposes, difficulty arises when claiming certain plays as humanistic, as I will, for example, with the stage romances of the 1570s. Indeed, few of the plays under discussion are exclusively humanist: even *Wit and Science* and *Gammer Gurton's Needle* combine various dramatic traditions, yet it would be misguided to deny the humanism of those two plays because of their other influences. The humanist dimension that I claim for most plays, such as *Gorboduc*, *Damon and Pithias*, and *Gallathea*, will, I hope, admit of general agreement. Otherwise, where necessary, I undertake to demonstrate a humanist provenance. A larger purpose, furthermore, will be to see humanist drama working not exclusively but in a mix of traditions. I should add, as well, that the present approach, even with its reference to social issues and its orientation toward theatrical performance, possesses an aesthetic dimension. The aesthetic perspective treats the art object, in a basic sense, as not entirely comprehensible by the political, religious, or didactic statements that it might reflect.[87] That stance easily gravitates toward identifying and valuing opaqueness in its object, a tendency susceptible to preciocity and hinting of a disconcerting circularity. It leads necessarily to exaggerations and omissions, some works accorded a surprising importance and other worthy objects scanted, so that the methodology maintains bad faith with any presumption that it will yield a "history." Thus the present study cannot claim to be exhaustive.

It does claim, however, that humanism's voice, method, and philosophical spirit introduce doubt into Renaissance drama and that humanist doubt enriches the affective dimension of sixteenth-century theatre. Writing at the end of that period, Shakespeare, in a play such as *Twelfth Night*, can convert maxims for moral behavior into experiential mysteries; that penchant for theatricalizing knowledge suggests a kinship with his predecessors, from Heywood to Lyly. *Twelfth Night* – like other Shakespearean works – plays on moments of dissonance between symbol and evidence, definition and event, language and object, like slippage in a weak magnetic field. In John Lyly's *Gallathea* Shakespeare may have found one model for the ambivalent energy by which his own comedy haunts the minds of his playgoers; yet the tension between knowledge and experience in *Twelfth Night* reaches farther back through the sixteenth century, even to the More circle interludes, with their own witty corrupters of words. In that respect, Shakespeare's plays lend themselves to interpretation as the most recent and rewarding embodiments of humanist dramaturgical values that help define the theatre of an age.

The humanism of acting: John Heywood's
The Foure PP

To the extent that medieval morality plays reproduce a system of allegorical correspondences, they depend on straightforward acting: Good Deeds must demonstrate her name. Even when a work's meaning may signify in political or social rather than in exclusively religious terms, the moralities favor clarity of representation.[1] But sixteenth-century drama's shift toward humanist and secular subjects privileged ambiguity in a character's presentation, evident in the enigmatic acting of both the Pardoner and the Palmer in John Heywood's *The Foure PP* (*c.* 1520s).[2] That ambiguity invades the lying contest that forms the play's climactic action, for there the script obscures whether the victor has spoken falsely or truly. With acting and audience perception an implicit theme, *The Foure PP* manifests an unusual complexity in the representation of truth and its didactic effect. Ambiguity of acting in secular humanist drama produces an unexpected openness of meaning, an effect with implications for English sixteenth-century theatre[3]

While the protagonist of medieval dramatic allegory represents every man, Renaissance theatre inches away from fixed correspondences; interpretive possibilities begin to derive, at least partly, from the nature of theatrical experience itself. Sixteenth-century England, of course, struggled increasingly with the conflict between its habits of categorical thinking and the vagaries of experience, conscience, and historical fact. Against what they considered scholastic abstractionism, the humanists launched a return to historical context in philology, rhetoric, and biblical exegesis. Led by Erasmus, they advocated a learning oriented toward practical experience, just as early Tudor interludes aimed their didacticism at personal behavior and specific abuses of power.[4] To that end, Erasmus invented a rhetorical persona,

10123996

epitomized in Folly, a presumably authoritative but sly, playful, and enigmatic figure who foreshadows Heywood's own personages. Folly's demand to be understood in a complicated, almost moment-by-moment way chafes against the age's inherited tendency toward apothegmatic wisdom. Likewise, *The Foure PP* puts didacticism in friction with theatrical experience. In doing so, Heywood's play anticipates the creative energy of later sixteenth-century drama, as it grapples with the dilemma of explaining life proverbially while presenting it complexly.

1

Humanist pedagogy offers a crystallizing perspective on early Tudor interludes. I would emphasize here, first, the humanist educators' interest in personal experience and, second, their belief in humanity's unlimited potential – matters embedded in *The Foure PP*'s enigmatic acting. Erasmus's pedagogy implies a tension between authority and experience.[5] The humanists criticized scholastic grammar and dialectic for their artificial abstractness and promoted instead a discourse paralleling life experience.[6] Folly notes that "The apostles refuted pagan philosophers and the Jews . . . more by the example of their way of life and their miracles than by syllogisms."[7] Likewise, Socrates, because he validated his philosophy by the life he lived, became a humanist hero. In Erasmus's *Apophthegms*, an important sixteenth-century school text, Socrates earns first position for "not onely so framyng and ministryng his doctrine, that he might effectually persuade unto menne vertue & perfecte honestee, but also directyng ye exaumple and paterne of all his life and dooynges to the same ende, effecte and purpose."[8] The precept convinces through its embodiment, a strategy that valorizes experience. Thus, Erasmus peppers his own educational writings with personal anecdotes about the shaping of his pedagogical theories, particularly his abhorrence for corporal punishment.[9] While the humanists taught by imitating classical authority, they added, according to Kristeller, a new seriousness toward individual feeling and experience: "An air of subjectivity pervades all humanist literature."[10]

An emphasis on subjective experience – particularly play and delight – constitutes a humanist pedagogical innovation.[11] Erasmus and Vives stress "allurements to learning: kindness, praise, judicious recreation; play and games as methods of teaching; stories, fables, and jokes to spice uninteresting facts; and graphic devices of many kinds."[12] Erasmus contends that pictures impart a wealth of information "in a most instructive yet delightful manner" and that "Brightness, attractiveness, these make the only appeals to a boy in the field of learning," and he further reminds us that "excellence in true learning" can only "be attained by those who find pleasure in its pursuit; and for this cause the liberal arts were ... called 'Humanitas.'"[13] He recommends giving children "letter-shapes" so that they can learn letters by holding them, handling them, pinning them to their clothes; he even promotes baked goods made in letter-shapes so that when a child identifies one, "his reward is to eat it!"[14] Because it releases a special reservoir of childhood energy, play figures centrally in Erasmian pedagogy. The most effective learning, according to Erasmus, engages the child actively or imaginatively in play, a godly energy felicitous to the training of free men.[15] But play does more than "serve" learning; rather, its creative, liberating power manifests the spirit of learning itself.

Later humanists followed Erasmus in making experience a part of formal education and thereby revealed tensions that help clarify *The Foure PP*. Elyot emphasizes delight in *The Gouernour* (1531), and Ascham in his preface to *The Scholemaster* (1570) echoes Socrates, saying that "the schoolhouse should be indeed, as it is called by name, the house of play and pleasure [*ludis literarum*]."[16] Pushing beyond the heuristic of play, Juan Luis Vives urges learning by direct observation, reminding young scholars that "we very rarely attain actual knowledge; or rather we get none, as long as so-called knowledge consists of people's views of it."[17] But that is the road to skepticism. Against it, the more conservative Erasmus insists ultimately on authority: experience can benefit only those who "by the wisdom of learning have acquired an intelligent and informed judgment. Besides, philosophy teaches us more in one year than individual experiences can teach us in thirty."[18] In *The Foure PP*, experience confirms by surprise the wisdom of authority. The play thus expresses the crucial but potentially troublesome relationship between direct observation and doctrinal learning in early humanist epistemology.

A related humanist tenet, the belief in man's potential, also reaches the stage in *The Foure PP*'s enigmatic acting. Pico della

Mirandola, one of the Florentine neo-Platonists who influenced Erasmus, had, of course, declared man "a work of indeterminate form," dislodged from the medieval hierarchy, capable of becoming earthly or heavenly by his own free will.[19] Erasmus likewise defends man's free will against Luther's denial of it. Erasmus's moral view of the human condition and his belief in man's perfectibility and powers of self-determination grant mystery and unpredictability to human action and psychology. That mystery reverberates rhetorically in Folly's ambiguities or the wryness of Erasmus's *Colloquies* – and later in the enigmatic mode of Heywood's Palmer. Folly's voice can veer from high-spirited Erasmian self-parody to a certain graveness, to an authorial earnestness, to a melancholy irony about life.[20] The relationship between Folly and Erasmus sometimes blurs, as if the character suddenly speaks for the divided soul of the author, an effect also apparent in Erasmus's *Colloquies*.

Much of the power of *The Praise of Folly* lies in its narrator's engaging and vacillating presence. As Altman observes, "Folly pursues a decorum that is consistently inconsistent, and this makes it impossible for the reader, too, to respond consistently, since one never knows whether at any given moment she is to be taken seriously."[21] That enigmatic voice, as much as the tract's ideas, may account for the sometimes outraged responses from scholastic theologians toward *The Praise of Folly*. In his "Letter to Martin Dorp," Erasmus takes pains to defend his tone, his voice, and the reformative power of satire.[22] Folly, self-consciously oratorical, focuses attention on her immediate presence and, paradoxically, on her mystery receding before analysis. Folly, that is, dramatizes herself.[23] *The Praise of Folly* employs the metaphor of drama to suggest man's "indeterminate form" and potential; Heywood takes the next step, into the Tudor playing space. By no accident did Erasmus dedicate the *Moriae encomium* to Heywood's patron, Sir Thomas More. Erasmus notes More's delight in Folly's brand of humor, and he adjures More to champion his namesake, Folly.[24] More practiced a wry, enigmatic, even dramatic style – perhaps of necessity, given the cultural and political paradoxes he faced – noted in some famous incidents. Roper, of course, reports More's jumping into Cardinal Morton's Christmastide plays and improvising the wittiest part.[25] According to Harpsfield, More had to dissemble his merry wit at court so that he would not be sent for so often; conversely, at a dinner once, More hid his identity to create amusement by astonishing a foreign pedant with his reasoning.[26] The university student Messenger in *A Dialogue Concerning Heresies* tells More that "ye vse (my mayster sayth) to loke so sadly whan ye mene merely y^t many times men doubte whyther ye speke in sporte whan ye mene good ernest"[27] It would be false to suggest that humanism had a particular dramatic persona (especially since many scholars view humanism as preeminently an educational movement[28]), yet if we could say that a certain persona served some humanists well, it would be the witty enigmaticness lived by More, fictionalized by Erasmus, and staged by Heywood.

2

The Foure PP unfolds, principally, by shifting the spectator's attention from theology to character and performance, and, secondarily, by allowing the Ps to parody spiritual values with material ones. In pursuing those interests the play creates an ongoing sense of surprise and unpredictability, with the individual voice taking centerstage.[29] *The Foure PP* may be divided into three segments: (1) from the beginning through the Pedler's first recommendation of partnership in sending souls to heaven (1–403); (2) from the Potycary's and the Pardoner's reactions against cooperation through their competitive displays and the lying contest (404–1033); and (3) from the subsequent reactions of the contest losers until the end of the play (1034–1234). The first section states theological issues; the second section reduces those issues to comedy; and the third section mediates the opening theological concerns. Parody operates as a principle of structure. The play's activating debate about the best path to salvation, for example, degenerates in the second section into a competition for mastery in the world: "To one of you thre[,] twayne must obey" (429). Likewise, rivalry over spiritual riches in the initial section descends in the next to boasting about material riches. Again, the debate over truth in the first section devolves in the second into the contest of lying. The first section emphasizes virtue; the second section, virtuosity – in merchandizing and prevaricating. Overall, Heywood stages both Socrates' critique of the sophists

and the humanists' critique of the schoolmen by reducing the
search for reasoned truth to artful lying.[30]

The spirit of surprise sometimes registers in Heywood's precari-
ous transitions – as when the Potycary enters in a farcical mode
discontinuous with the comedy he interrupts. Because such tran-
sitions-by-disruption can seem gratuitous, Heywood lubricates
them with puns and multivalent words – "nought," "hope,"
"rychesse," "honest," "mervell" – that set up an engaging play of
ideas that parallels the action. The Potycary's "By the masse, I
holde us nought all thre" (202), for example, uses "nought" in a
spiritual sense. But the Pedler misinterprets that "nought" as a
reference to penury (203, 215). The pun helps sway the action
toward the material and physical, further exaggerated moments
later when the presumably harmless "pyncases" (242) unleashes
a rain of puns about female sexual voracity and male impotence.
Similarly, following the Pedler's phrase, "eche of you may hope to
wyn" (461), the Potycary performs a pun, hoping/hopping
(another confusion of the spiritual and physical), by suddenly hop-
ping about (at 467), adding, "Upon whiche hoppynge, I hope and
nat doute it, / To hop so that ye shall hope without it" (472–73).
Riches, too, go the way of hope. With the Palmer defending a
spiritual "quietnesse" as sufficient "rychesse" (474–82), the
multivalent *richesse* affords Heywood a comic interlude about
materiality, as Pardoner and Potycary boast unquietly and com-
petitively about whose pack carries the greater riches (483–643).
Later Renaissance drama will struggle with the disconcerting
proximity of the spiritual to the economic; Heywood grasps that
confusion early and creates with it a volatile atmosphere of aesthetic play.[31]

With the Palmer's "honestie," Heywood moves beyond confusions about verbal meaning to confusions about a speaker's
intention. The uncertainties here (655–97) foreshadow the epistemological quandary of the ending. Challenged to proceed with
the lying contest, the Potycary replies to the Palmer, "Forsoth ye
be an honest man" (655), to which the Palmer agrees. Believing
that the Potycary had meant to praise the Palmer for honesty, the
Pardoner interjects that they both lie – whereupon the Potycary
declares that he was really lying himself. The Pardoner's misper-
ception hints at the dramaturgical problem that the ending will
exploit: the possibility of not knowing whether a character offers

prevarication or honesty. The action now halts to sort out who speaks the truth about the Palmer: "But who tolde true or lyed in dede, / That wyll I knowe or we procede" (666–67). The episode lodges a question on which the play will later capitalize: is the Palmer an honest man or not? From spiritual issues the dialogue glides toward doubtful matters of intention and character. Truth, likewise, takes on the subjective aura of marvelousness. Marvelousness and improbability will win the lying contest, declares the Pedler, as he invites the other Ps to "telleth most mervell / And most unlyke to be true" (701–02). "Mervell" emerges as a spectatorial value for the Ps. The Potycary makes claims of "mervalynge" and "a mervaylouse thynge" (704–05) about his story; likewise, the Pedler praises the Pardoner's adventure as wondrous (977). But when the Palmer comments on the Pardoner's narrative, he complicates the language of the marvelous by linking it to a truth-claim: "This in effect he tolde for trueth, / Wherby muche murvell to me ensueth, / That women in hell suche shrewes can be / And here so gentyll as farre as I se" (989–92; see also 982). Correspondingly, the Palmer's own truth-claim is now received as marvelous. The Pedler, for example, declares the Palmer victorious for his "incredyble" assertion that he has never seen a woman "out of paciens" (1061, 1003).[32] Surprise and confusion persist as a pattern: "Richesse" takes on multiple meanings; the intention behind the word "honestie" becomes opaque; what is claimed as truth registers as "mervaylouse." That pattern invites spectatorial doubts about what and how one knows in *The Foure PP*.

3

Thus, structurally, *The Foure PP* evolves from a focus on theological issues to a focus on character and acting,[33] a movement that foregrounds epistemological confusion. Heywood inherited from medieval morality plays a rhetoric whereby different modes of characterization battle for the power to define values. In an allegory, characters express a "relationship rhetorically constructed and controlled," manifest a set of conflicting theological definitions, and achieve a final configuration revealed as doctrine.[34] Such allegorical drama depends on unambiguous acting to define virtues.[35] With Corpus Christi plays, similarly, "Overall, characterisation is strong and can be subtle, but is generic, not individual," so that

"Character is always subordinate to narrative."[36] Because plays such as the mysteries are "extremely intellectual," the actor is obliged to emphasize "content" rather than "motivation and the emotion behind it."[37] In folk drama, by contrast, the playful relationship that apparently prevailed between playgoers and stage tricksters suggests that those characters fashioned not intellectual representation but a more emotionally based theatrical enigmaticness. Robert Weimann links the folk-inspired Vice, for example, to plebeian social satire, game, and topsy-turvydom, the Vice standing ambiguously at the intersection of the serious and the comic.[38] Although folk drama does not survive, its wily deceivers probably help to make credible *The Foure PP*'s more cultivated beguilers; Heywood may be reworking a value deriving from folk theatre to serve the interests of humanist thematics. In cycle drama, nonetheless, even the folkloric and elusive Mak of *The Second Shepherd's Play* must be rendered recognizeable, his disguises stripped away as the play progresses. An opposite process occurs in Heywood's interlude; there opaque acting evolves toward an epistemology of doubt: how do we know what truth a character represents?

Posing the problem of truth, *The Foure PP* demands from its spectators increasing sophistication in discerning its characters' qualities and meanings. The play's attention to character and acting complements its structural and linguistic drive toward the marvelous. Although the Palmer wins the lying contest by claiming, against the Pardoner's and Potycary's misogyny, that he has never seen "any one woman out of paciens," he may intend no lie at all. Because the play never defines his intentions, its most important moment coincides with inscrutability in a character's scripted meaning. Here the actor may choose between opposed interpretations or may choose a reading that could include the possibility of either interpretation. The choice identifies an acting dimension explored in the Renaissance that will lead from Heywood to Marlowe, Shakespeare, and beyond. More than any early humanist playwright, Heywood anticipates the modern, because among its allegorical figures, his stage interjects characters who begin to stand for an irreducible theatricality.[39] Enigmatic acting not only induces audience doubt but also can reveal the *absence* of a definitive frame of reference to explain a character's meaning. In a Shakespearean example, Benedick says to Leonato, "Your answer, sir, is enigmatical" (*Much Ado About Nothing*, v.iv.27),[40] to describe a possibility beyond Benedick's understanding: namely, that the Prince, Claudio, and Leonato have engineered his falling in love. Enigmatic acting conveys not irony but ambiguity; it desta-bilizes spectatorial assumptions and emphasizes the spectator's position as a reader of theatrical signals; it encourages specu-lation. In *The Foure PP*, doctrine may propose truth, but theatri-cality must mediate it.

Criticism traditionally lumps the Palmer, Pardoner, and Potycary together as scalawags: "con-men," "quacks," and "char-latans."[41] But the Ps form a group partly by their contrasts, and each occupies a different moral and satirical domain. The Palmer and Pardoner provide opposing approaches to salvation, the one through travail, the other through ease. The Palmer, frequently addressed as "father," is the eldest P and resembles a friar in his penury and probably his habiliments (283–84). While the others display their worldly wares, the Palmer lists holy shrines. He speaks the least, the most tactfully, and the most disarmingly, his modesty illustrating his spirituality. At the other extreme, the Potycary comes closest to the Vice figure by attempting to subvert the play's morality and seriousness. He enters on a drinking joke, "Sende ye any soules to heven by water?" (151), and acts period-ically tipsy (579). His path to salvation is theologically farcical. He leads the others in singing, hops around the stage, lavishes kisses on a relic presumed to intoxicate, attempts to bribe the judge, and dances mock curtsies around the Palmer. His role is the most physical of the four (the Palmer's is the least), and his activity is complemented by the most scatological humor, particu-larly jokes about excremental functions and the Gargantuan size of female parts. He stands for the carnivalesque body, exuberant, extrusive, and bawdy. The Potycary bears a generic resemblance to the hard-drinking, womanizing quack Doctor Brundyche in *The Croxton Play of the Sacrament*, and that likeness may suggest a shared folk provenance. As a festive outsider – a recurrent figure in Heywood's plays[42] – the Potycary does not occupy the same ethical or ontological ground as the others. He is the parody to their *topos*. The Pardoner, on the other hand, asserts an outsized egoism; he begins by optimizing physical comfort over pain. More theologically fraudulent than the Palmer and more subtle than the Potycary, charming and dangerous in his hubris, like his

Chaucerian ancestor, the Pardoner offers a juicy and complex role.[43] By the conclusion of his fabliau, he becomes a slightly uncanny presence in *The Foure PP*, priming the audience for the Palmer's enigma. The Pedler, finally, both encourages and arbitrates the play's different rhetorical directions. He sells goods and jokes with the Potycary and Pardoner about women and liquor but remains independent of their perspectives; he judges the lying contest but also participates in its misogyny.[44] The Pedler sometimes speaks for the play, sometimes not, and his changeable taffeta of homily and expressionism demands both thespian authority and malleability.[45]

In terms of acting, the Palmer's part calls for sincerity and reserve, the Potycary's for hyperbole and slapstick, the Pardoner's for presumptuous confidence, and the Pedler's for versatility in negotiating the improvisational and the authoritative.[46] A common acting problem arises, however, when the Potycary and Pardoner each display their wares. How should they speak: deadpan, pretending seriously to hawk their bogus junk, or ironically, acknowledging its humor: the con-man or the unconned hearer? That local problem of voice again shows *The Foure PP* moving from its opening issues of religion toward those of character and acting, as if in a slow barrel roll. The Potycary's inventory implies a heavily tongue-in-cheek acting:

> It pourgeth you clene from the color
> And maketh your stomake sore to walter,
> That ye shall never come to the halter.
> (599–601)

> A lytell thynge is inough of this,
> For even the weyght of one scryppull
> Shall make you stronge as a cryppull.
> (613–15)

The extravagant joke, that the Potycary's medicines are poisons, calls for a winking, comic presentation, with speaker and hearers in cahoots. That style recollects the boy Colle's farcical praise of his master Dr. Brundyche: "He seeth as wele at noone as at nyght, / And sumtyme by a candelleyt / Can gyff a judgyment aryght– / As he that hathe noone eyn" (537–40).[47]

By contrast, the Pardoner's role offers a more subtle, less winking attack. To be sure, his vaudevillian stage properties are immense and grotesque, like a clown's shoes: a swollen great-toe of the Trinity, All-Hallow's stinking jawbone, a smelly slipper, Pentecost's buttock-bone, a huge eyetooth from the Great Turk (as a Christian relic). Reducing a saint's life to absurdity, the Pardoner's relics recall those in Erasmus's satirical colloquy "A Pilgrimage for Religion's Sake," where, on a visit to the shrine of Our Lady of Walsingham in England, a pilgrim is invited to kiss a giant-sized joint from a human finger that his guide claims belonged to the apostle Peter.[48] The Pardoner's sly speeches, however, play against the clownish visuals: "Here is a relyke that doth nat mys / To helpe the leste as well as the moste. / This is a buttocke bone of Pentecoste" (519–21). Heywood creates the speech's subtlety by burying the irony of the first two lines inside the third's rise toward climactic visual display. The performer's success will depend on that flicker of irony, whatever acting attack he chooses, from that of a streetvendor to something Brechtian.

Indeed, different choices invest the Pardoner's dialogue now, perhaps more than on any occasion so far. The script even invites the performer to shift from voice to voice: The Pardoner's persuasion to kiss one of the tongue-twisting Seven Sleepers' slippers ("For all these two dayes it shall so ease you / That none other savours shall displease you" [528–29]), for example, sounds more subtly wry than his boast about the Turk's eyetooth ("Whose eyes be ones sette on thys pece of worke / May happely lese parte of his eye syght, / But nat all, tyll he be blynde outryght" [539–41]).[49] Such implied acting recollects Folly's shifting decorum and enigmaticness. But the Pardoner's properties always resist the speeches describing them. The props are cruder, grosser, and more insistent in humor, and their physical presence registers a productive tension between visual overstatement and verbal understatement. An actor could hold up a bulbous toe yet boast straightfacedly of its healing powers: "[Who] ones may role it in his moueth, / All hys lyfe after, I undertake, / He shall be ryd of the toth ake" (511–13). Unlike the Potycary's farce, the Pardoner's comedy increases if he affects sincerity as a counterpoint to the objects.

During the Pardoner's relic speeches the Potycary makes overt the comedy of the Pardoner's claims, so that when the Pardoner coaxes that if you kiss the slipper, then for two days "none other savours shall displease you" (529), the Potycary completes the

joke with, "For all the savours that may come here / Can be no
worse" (531–32). Toward the play's end, the Pedler praises the
Potycary for such responses to the relics, saying, "Ye are well
beloved of all thys sorte, / By your raylynge here openly / At par-
dons and relyques so leudly" (1198–1200). That tribute to the
Potycary's railings confirms the comedy-team acting implicit in
the dialogue, with the Pardoner as a kind of slick carnival barker
and the Potycary a witty rube, the former acting as the straight-
man who sets up the latter's punch lines.[50] This "marketplace"
style of acting underscores, moreover, how the play's spiritual
interests can be bootlegged into a domain of materialistic connotations. The Pardoner's speeches require the audience to scrutinize gestures, to listen carefully for nuances of voice, to revise
impressions – in short, to attend to the acting more closely than
before; the spectatorial position loses stability. Understanding in
The Foure PP becomes not just a dimension of reason but also of
close observation, contextual looking and listening, experience.

The Pardoner's fabliau further destabilizes spectatorial
interpretation in a way that anticipates the Palmer's later defense
of women. Generations of readers have found the Pardoner's tale
engaging, delightful, surpassing anything else in the play.[51] But
what creates its appeal? The Potycary's misogynistic and scatological fabliau simply extends his role as Vice; his tale is predictable.
But the Pardoner's story surpasses predictability. The Potycary's
crude humor cloaks a fear of female sexuality, and the expansiveness of his tale registers in a fictional female body that is mon-
strously carnivalesque, as the enema's ballistic effect shows. The
expansiveness of the Pardoner's tale, however, appears in its *mise-
en-scène*, its largeness of environment rather than of anatomy. The
Pardoner's story sparkles with ornamental details well beyond
those needed for his narrative: the souls curtseying to him in Purgatory; the one sent to Heaven for blessing his sneeze; his
acquaintance with the devil-doorkeeper from Corpus Christi plays
at Coventry; the elaborately worded safe-conduct pass; the trust
between Pardoner and devil, who walk "arme in arme" (872); the
appearance of the devils on their festival day and their merry
game of rackets; the description of Lucifer, so frightful that the
Pardoner flatters him as "O plesant pycture" (904); the Pardoner's self-promotion before Lucifer as he claims himself to be a
"controller" of souls (918); the image of Margery turning her spit;

the celebratory joy of the devils as the two pass out of hell; and the parting on Newmarket Heath. The Pardoner's self-satisfied rehearsal of narrative minutiae reveals him as a seductive incarnation of Pride. His travelogue is really the landscape of his dazzling, imaginative egoism; the objective details expose hauntingly the subjective interior architecture. The story is engaging as a projection not simply of social role, doctrine, or rhetoric but of mind and will, of an aura or presence exceeding role, doctrine, or rhetoric. The fabliau inspires an uncommon delight, less from its action than the ego it represents, and, reciprocally, the Pardoner's exhibition blazons his theatricality, his pleasure in being watched. His narrative's energy derives from his solipsism, as outsized, in its own way, as the eyetooth of the Great Turk. The passage challenges the spectator's assumptions about what and how the narrative will reveal; it demands, like the Pardoner's relic-speeches, a close, adaptable looking and listening.

4

The Foure PP spoofs the Palmer but also cloaks him with a certain moral opaqueness, shifting him away from a doctrinal or allegorical ontology to more theatrical grounds. Overall, the play distinguishes the Palmer for his honesty, even when it satirizes his profession. Before the lying contest he alone speaks truthfully and seriously; the play discusses his honesty (and only his) as a real possibility; he makes his "lie" as a brief rebuttal (to another's traducing of women), bracketed from the preceding narratives. The Palmer launches the play with disarming humility and straightforwardness; the humor about him arises indirectly through his catalog of shrines. Having entered first, looked at the audience, and discovered himself in high company, the Palmer apologizes for his homespun pilgrim's appearance. This father figure speaks devoutly and sincerely throughout his monologue; his comedy emerges not in his manner of speech or preposterous logic but in his busyness. The parody in the Palmer's inventory of shrines (he names some forty-two, mostly in Britain) rests on a humanist critique of excessive pilgrimages and phony relics shared by Erasmus, More, Colet, and other reformers.[52] The inventory proceeds, like the play as a whole, according to a process of parodic reduction. The Palmer begins with an authentically miraculous locale, Jerusalem and its sites of Christ's passion (13–16) – though some church reformers discouraged visits even there. His humility – "My rewdnes" (4), "good intent" (12) – helps to deflect criticism, and his experiences in Jerusalem honor Christ's suffering. But as he describes Rome and Saint Peter's shrine (21–23), the Palmer betrays self-satisfaction about his superior knowledge of holy places (23–28). Eventually, the sheer density of the Palmer's almost consumerist itemizing diminishes his spirituality: "On the hylles of Armony where I see Noes arke, / With holy Job and Saynt George in Suthwarke" (33–34).[53] From Jerusalem the trajectory of parodic reduction descends finally to the trivial "Our Lady that standeth in the oke" (50), apparently a statue of the Virgin in the forest on Hampstead Heath.[54]

The list of shrines becomes saturated with locales of secondary and dubious veneration, as much associated with popular superstition as with the Bible or sainthood. Saint Tronion (31) may have been a medieval burlesque phallic saint; by mid-century Geoffrey Fenton derided his site as an example of French Papist idolatry.[55] The Cross of Waltham (34) involved a fantastical story of dream visions, pseudo-stigmata, and a sometimes miraculously immovable slab of marble with healing powers.[56] Walsingham, a favorite of the upper classes, was notorious enough that Erasmus lampoons its excesses in his colloquy on pilgrimages.[57] Concerning the Palmer's "Saynt James in Gales" (37), Erasmus satirizes his own pilgrim for having departed festooned foolishly with straw necklaces, shells inlaid with lead images, and snake eggs adorning his arms.[58] Saint Patrick's Purgatory (40) earned Erasmus's mockery more than once,[59] and Hazlitt observes of this old, apparent coal-pit that "The popular tradition concerning it is as ridiculous as is to be found in any legend of the Romish Martyrology."[60] The dissolvers of the monasteries exposed the blood of Hailes (41) as a trick of colored water and light.[61]

Thus the Palmer's inventory of shrines degenerates into a list of well-known regional sites ridiculed by humanists and reformers. Many such locales were notorious for their great crowds, crass commercialism, dubiously miraculous healing powers, and Marian cultism.[62] Such associations taint the Palmer's piety. To some degree the progressive debasement of Christian sites in the Palmer's inventory recalls the loss of early Christian vision and experience for which Erasmus faults the schoolmen. But while the audience might laugh at the catalog, the Palmer rehearses it with naive sincerity: he has labored barefoot (18), sweated "[m]any a salt tere" (19), observed diligently (26–27), prayed devoutly (52), and undertaken "dayly payne" (55). For an age that anticipated the agonies of Purgatory even for the righteous, the intercession of the saints had real importance.[63] Toward the end of his opening speech, however, the Palmer manifests the self-love that Erasmus's Folly makes her theme. Going "for love of Chryst" (1143) will be the play's grounds for approving pilgrimages, and the Palmer claims to seek saints "for Crystes sake" (59). Yet he also asserts that pilgrims who "punyshe thy frayle body – / Shall therby meryte more hyely / Then by any thynge done by man" (61–63). In his self-abasement the Palmer takes a certain pride, the comic insight hinted in the lines' quick brush-strokes. Even with this first speech, Heywood begins to train the audience to attend carefully for nuance and complexity. The Palmer emerges as comically tinged but, unlike the others, as neither hypocritical nor insincere; rather, he poses a subtle paradox of manner and matter. This opening figure initiates the kind of complex dialectic the More circle enjoyed: a figure who is humanly sympathetic, in pursuit of an excess that is ridiculous. The irony at work here helps to distinguish *The Foure PP* from the moralities, where the audience is seldom asked to make subtle judgments of character. The Palmer's complexity is an effect of theatre, of, particularly, the spectators' discrepant awareness.

The Palmer's role is the shortest in *The Foure PP* and requires the most straightforward acting, a difference from all the other parts and a sign that his praise of women could be performed as sincere. The Palmer explains simply, for example, that he began the pilgrim's life "To rydde the bondage of my syn" (78), beseeching the mediation of the saints upon his "humble submyssion" (86). He sincerely invites someone to present a surer means to salvation (103–05) but rehearses the popular wisdom in distrusting pardoners (107–14). The Palmer becomes, in fact, the play's temporary spokesman: "Ryght selde is it sene or never / That treuth and pardoners dwell together" (109–10). He notes that pardoners often exaggerate their claims; that his own authentic suffering makes for more certain remission than does a dubious pardon; and that God will respect the labor of each person. Indeed, the Palmer's claim "So by his [i.e., God's] goodnes all is rewarded" (126) anticipates the final sentiments of the play. Only the Palmer consistently takes others seriously. When the Pedler and Potycary joke about women's pincases, the Palmer alone remains silent. To the Pedler's proposal of the lying contest, the Palmer replies that, though he can fib, he is "loth for to goo to it" (453). The Pedler's answer implicitly treats the Palmer as more honest than the others (454–55). To the Potycary's comic preening before the lying contest, the Palmer responds moderately:

> Syr, I wyll neyther boste ne brawll,
> But take suche fortune as may fall,
> And yf ye wynne this maystry
> I wyll obaye you quietly.
> And sure I thynke that quietnesse,
> In any man is great rychesse
> In any maner company
> To rule or be ruled indifferently.
>
> (474–81)

The Palmer defends the dignity of quietness, a value that his part has come to demonstrate. In that same spirit, after he wins the contest, he immediately releases the others from serving him.

Although the Palmer wins the lying bout, *The Foure PP* portrays him as a truth-teller and leaves his intentions in the competition open to doubt. The Pardoner has just told his ornamented tale of redeeming his friend Margery Coorson from Hell, with the devils relieved to shed themselves of a typically troublesome woman. Margery gains renewed life because of her unruliness; the Pardoner claims also to have subsequently sent ten women to Heaven for every man, pursuant to Lucifer's request.[64] The Palmer then declares the Pardoner's tale "mervaylous" (982) in the part

> ... where he sayde the devyls complayne
> That women put them to such payne
> By theyr condicions so croked and crabbed,
> Frowardly fashonde, so waywarde and wrabbed,
> So farre in devision and sturrynge suche stryfe
> That all the devyls be wery of theyr lyfe.
> This in effect he tolde for trueth,
> Wherby much murvell to me ensueth,
> That women in hell suche shrewes can be
> And here so gentyll as farre as I se. (983–92)

The deictic "here" of the last line invites the Palmer-actor to include the gentlewomen of the audience in his assessment, looking out at them "as far as I see." The Palmer's overall scripting suggests straightforward delivery here. Indeed, an audience of aristocratic women would make the Palmer's description, "gentyll," demonstrably true. The Palmer attributes to the Pardoner's tale depredations about women that the devils never uttered, but in so doing, the Palmer only amplifies the Pardoner's real attitude. True in spirit if false in fact: the Palmer tells a "true" lie, whose enigma anticipates his own praise of women.

The Palmer proceeds to claim that in his travels, among all the "fyve hundred thousande" (998) women he has known and with whom he has "long time [taried]" (999),[65] "I never sawe nor knewe, in my consyens, / Any one woman out of paciens" (1002–03). That statement prompts convulsive charges of gross lying from his fellow Ps, producing the Palmer's victory. But the Palmer never acknowledges a lie, nor does he offer the appropriate "tale" like the two preceding, nor does he announce his "entry" in the contest as the other two have done (704–05, 742, 797). The play separates the Palmer from the misogynistic jokes and prejudices of the other Ps. One can imagine a pilgrim who might not have viewed women as "out of paciens" – since the claim is subjective – and his "conseyns" need not dismiss them with the misogynist term "shrewes."[66] While critics often assume that the Palmer prevaricates, Jill Levenson has recently claimed that the Palmer does not participate in the lying contest and wins "unintentionally" in an effort to correct a falsehood.[67] The Palmer, of course, *could* be lying, but he also *could* be telling the truth: the script as a blueprint to performance leaves the issue suspended in doubt. An actor might make either choice, or he might remain inscrutable; moreover, unless he indicates by inflection, facial expression, or stage business that he prevaricates, the audience *cannot* know his state of mind. If an actor, that is, plays the lines straight his intentions will be unknowable on stage. That the Potycary, Pardoner, and Pedlar react to the Palmer's comments with such immediate outrage makes sincerity more likely than winking irony in the Palmer's delivery. *The Foure PP* raises at a critical juncture the horror and delight of secular drama: there is no authority, beyond an equivocal misogynism, capable of settling meaning. Just as *The Foure PP*'s epistemology shifts from theology to theatricality, its lying contest also mirrors the performance: actors – professional

liars – imitating professional lying, so that the play hints at a
complicated, proto-modern self-reflexivity.

The Palmer does not win just for telling a lie; rather, he wins
for telling the biggest lie, the one most marvelous and most
"unlyke to be true." Put differently, the Palmer triumphs solely
because of the misogyny of the other characters, who cannot
imagine speaking well of women. The Pedler offers "evidence"
more absurd and offensive by far than the Palmer's praise of
women:

> But hys boldnes hath faced a lye
> That may be tryed evyn in thys companye.
> As yf ye lyste to take thys order
> Amonge the women in thys border,
> Take thre of the yongest and thre of the oldest,
> Thre of the hotest and thre of the coldest,
> Thre of the wysest and thre of the shrewdest,
> Three of the cheefest and thre of the lewdest,
> Thre of the lowest and thre of the hyest,
> Thre of the farthest and thre of the nyest,
> Thre of the fayrest and thre of the maddest,
> Thre of the fowlest and thre of the saddest;
> And when all these threes be had a sonder,
> Of eche thre two justly by nomber
> Shall be founde shrewes – excepte thys fall,
> That ye hap to fynde them shrewes all.
>   (1066–80)

If "evyn in thys companye" and "in thys border" invite an inclusive
gesture toward the women in the Tudor aristocratic audience,
then the Pedler's empirical test would hardly have sounded convincing[68] – especially in the More circle with, for example, its commitment to women's education. The Pedler's "proof," that is, can
produce the opposite effect, for its flagrancy makes the Palmer's
encomium to women that much more credible. Indeed, the Pedler's deictic language – "thys companye," "thys border" – sets
itself up specifically against the Palmer's "here so gentyll." The
two speeches would seem to draw the audience's female members
into the play, and the Pedler's crude abuse might actually pull
response in the other direction. The Pedler's attack virtually
guarantees that post-performance conversation will consider
whether or not women are shrews. *The Foure PP* invites the audience's play in creating its truth, and play, Erasmus proposed,

expresses the spirit of learning by another name.[69] *The Foure PP* refuses to affirm that the Palmer really lies; this Tudor interlude about honesty and falsehood leaves the spectator's perception unstable.

Although the Palmer succeeds by speaking well of women, we should note the ambiguity as he stresses his closeness to them: "Yet have I sene many a myle / And many a woman in the whyle" and "And oft with them have longe tyme [taried]" (993–94, 999). Do such lines carry innuendoes of sexual foraging along the pilgrim's way, as with Chaucer's travellers? Much earlier the Pedler has teased the Palmer: "Have ye nat a wanton in a corner / For your walkyng to holy places? / By Cryste, I have herde of as straunge cases!" (228–30). And why does the Palmer, when examining the Pardoner's fetid relics, step forward eagerly to kiss the bumble-bees "That stonge Eve as she sat on her knees / Tastynge the frute to her forbydden" (547–48)? Seeing the Palmer as a philanderer refashions him also as a religious hypocrite, especially given his guise of ascetic suffering. But dalliance can also lend his defense of women's patience a kind of credibility, one that emanates from a dallier's determination to be pleasing and to be pleased. Such puzzling over the Palmer merely enhances the inscrutability toward which his broader rhetorical scripting leads. Ultimately, we cannot tie the Palmer at the play's climax to any particular doctrine about women. It is not just that the available positions fail to do justice to the Palmer; rather his mode of being is *other* than a position. We might say that in some sense he exists dramatically, that our impression of him now arises ineluctably from the theatrical circumstances of his performance.

5

Although the play anticipates the productive tensions between theatricality and doctrinal knowledge that will characterize much Renaissance humanist drama, delight actually supports instruction in *The Foure PP*. The enigma of the Palmer amplifies the play's advice about how to discover the truth, for received authority gets its strongest boost from empirical observation's inconclusiveness. That relationship recalls the problems of authority and observation treated by Erasmus and Vives. To the rivalry over religious practices, the play proposes three successive answers: mutual

cooperation, respect for hierarchy, and wise tolerance. Concluding
the play's first section, the Pedler proposes mutual cooperation:
the other Ps should "contynue togyther all thre" (393), united in
a common will in which each shares (388–96). But that idea of
Utopian cooperation ends up only rearranging, not ending, the
rivalry. The Potycary proposes hierarchy. For "good order," he
says, "Twayne of us must wayte on a thyrde. / And unto that I do
agree, / For bothe you twayne shall wayt on me" (414–17). But
hierarchical self-glorification fails, too, as the Potycary and Pardoner resist serving the Palmer after he wins, and he wisely
declines to force them. Pride has defeated the first solution and
intransigence the second: "Now be ye all evyn as ye begoon"
(1137).

With the opening aversions returned, the Pedler advises the Ps
to amend their spirits by following their occupations "for love of
Chryst" (1143) or for love of their neighbors "in God onely"
(1150). "[E]very vertue . . . / Is pleasaunt to God" (1171–72), but
despising another's virtue is proof of ungodliness, "lyke as the
syster might hange the brother" (1186). But this mutual tolerance falters, too, for the Potycary claims to have no virtue and
insists on the Pardoner's phoniness (the Palmer has disappeared
as an object of satire). Perforce the Pedler refines his case: you
may reject the obvious fraud, but where you cannot know the
truth, believe the best, or preferably, follow the church's judgment
(1203–16). Spiritual attitude now looms as the secret to social
order. A proper spirit, though preferring to think better of someone rather than worse, recognizes that the limits of human understanding necessitate the authority of doctrine: "where ye dout, the
truthe nat knowynge, / . . . as the churche doth judge or take
them, / So do ye receyve or forsake them" (1207–14).

That advice verges on self-combusting, for *The Foure PP* has just
cast doubt on both religious practices and empirical observations.
The play has cloaked the Pardoner and climactically the Palmer
in enigma and marvelousness, as truth has moved from the obvious to the complex. By shifting focus from theology to character
and acting, *The Foure PP* has demanded ever-closer observation
from its participants and spectators, only to demonstrate that such
attentiveness will not settle its epistemological disputes. The Pardoner's speeches invite a scrutiny that leaves him all the more
uncanny; the Palmer's "lie" invites a questioning before which his

intentions only recede: if the Pedler offers a convincing politics, he does so on grounds aesthetic as much as political. We must think the best of others or trust the prior authority of the church because our keenest empirical judgments fall prey to error and presumption, a stance somewhere between Erasmus and Vives. The inscrutability of the actor validates the Pedler's argument experientially. Though *The Foure PP*'s performance values support its sentence of wise ignorance, that conjunction seems rather fortuitous. From the larger perspective of Tudor drama, *The Foure PP* demonstrates that the claims of theatrical experience have begun to rival those of authority. Doubleness, duplicity, depth of space: theatricality at its extreme tends to undercut narrative certainty. The emergence of secular, nonallegorical plays in the sixteenth century manifests an energy latent in performance and surely familiar in folk drama. No matter, then, whether Heywood "intended" an enigmatic Palmer or not. Judging from its mention by the itinerant actors in *The Book of Sir Thomas More*, *The Foure PP* had an active stage life for fifty years after its publication in the 1540s. If so, during that time the ambiguity scripted in the Palmer's role surely underwent exploration.

The opacity hinted regarding the Pardoner and realized climactically with the Palmer expresses a quality present elsewhere in early Tudor drama. Other Heywood plays contain moments similar to the Palmer's "lie," moments that surprise formal expectations, suddenly offering characters in a new light of seriousness, pathos, or realism. At the end of *The Pardoner and the Frere*, for example, the two eponymous, self-aggrandizing scalawags, who have been shouting over each other's voices for most of the play, finally fall to fisticuffs. The Parson and Neighbor Pratt enter at this commotion and undertake to haul the two off to the stocks. Instead, the Friar and the Pardoner pummel their would-be policemen and stroll off the stage under their own steam, threatening to return: "Than adew, to the devyll, tyll we come agayn" (640). These two comic figures disappear suddenly tinged with dangerousness. In *A Play of Love*, the character No lover nor loved occupies the most Stoic position in the debate over love's sufferings. But toward the play's end, No lover nor loved rushes onstage as "the Vice" with a pail of exploding squibs on his head. The switch from high Roman philosophy to low-humor high-jinks gives No lover nor loved a newly compelling stage presence.[70] *Johan Johan* also changes tone unexpectedly. A cuckolded husband, angry and defiant when alone but hen-pecked and submissive before his wife, apparently rises at the end of the play to beat her and her lover out the door. But this victory snatched from the jaws of defeat turns just as abruptly into despair, as Johan imagines the two gone off to cuckold him. Heywood increases the poignancy of this ending over its French original: "Although he [i.e., Johan] now triumphs physically, the victory is both momentary and empty."[71] In these cases, Heywood sets new twists of behavior against the characters' previous rhetorical identities so as to give the audience a sudden, climactic impression of the enigmatic.[72] *The Play of the Wether*'s Mery Report shows, too, a Folly-like ambivalence: though serving as authorial voice, Mery Report also "reflects the petty vices around him and enlarges them to the highly visible proportions of caricature."[73] Thus, Mery Report pursues a double function that invites audience discrimination. In such examples, Heywood transgresses the boundaries of allegorical identity to give us an experience of character that must be understood in theatrical terms.

Although Heywood's dramaturgy ventures beyond that of Henry Medwall or Heywood's father-in-law, John Rastell, the three playwrights share affinities. In Rastell's *The Nature of the Four Elements* (*c.* 1517) the Taverner's puns create transitions and disruptive surprises in a way that may have influenced Heywood, and Rastell even devises an incident where spectatorial response seems to shape meaning. Yngnoraunce encourages Humanyte to dance, sing, and make merry, "And so shalt thou best please / All this hole company" (1296–97).[74] Yngnoraunce obviously means the audience members, since he adds, "For all they that be nowe in this hall, / They be the most parte my servauntes all" (1301–02). Yngnoraunce's insult invites the audience to resist his blandishments to Humanyte; the deictic gesture is in danger of provoking a moral backlash. That speech works remarkably like the Pedler's long, outrageous diatribe naming every two out of three women "in this border" as shrews, a diatribe that invites a moral resistance from the audience confirming the Palmer's view of women. In *Calisto and Melebea* (*c.* 1527) the heroine Melebea angrily resists Calisto's wooer-by-proxy, the bawd Celestina, but Celestina hits finally on the metaphor of a knight sick with "the toth ake"(835) and begs remedy from Melebea's holy girdle. At this plea Melebea softens in pity toward Calisto. Is she suddenly enticed sexually, or is she duped into innocent sympathy by the old toothache routine? The metaphoric dialogue renders Melebea's intentions temporarily ambiguous, as with Heywood's characters; only ensuing events make her susceptibility clear.

Medwall's *Fulgens and Lucres* (*c.* 1490) offers the characters A and B as audience members who step into the drama, deploying the two as sometimes wise, sometimes utter fools.[75] Beyond those confusions of character, the play also concerns itself with the enigmatic relationship between play and earnest. At the beginning of Part II, A enters as prologue, reminds spectators of the first half's action, and reflects that "there was / Dyvers toyes mengled yn the same / To styre folke to myrthe and game . . . / The which tryfyllis be impertinent / To the matter principall" (II.21–26).[76] Those irrelevant trifles are apparently the doings in Part I between Lucres's maid, Joan, and the two males A and B, when Joan, sent as a messenger from her mistress, encounters B, who attempts to woo her. Joan refuses him, with the business turning ribald, upon which A enters and offers himself as a rival wooer. Joan declares that she will choose the one "that can do most maystry" (I.1095). Following inconclusive singing and wrestling contests, A and B engage in a parody of a chivalric joust, apparently involving sticks and anatomical targets. The two fight ridiculously, with B finally knocking down A, only to have Joan declare triumphantly that she is already engaged to another man. Joan makes fools of the two and escapes uncompromised and saucy. In comparison, the main plot of *Fulgens and Lucres* involves the competition between the aristocrat Publius and the self-made man Gayus for the hand of Lucres, to be decided according to which man is "most honorable" (I.454). Is the episode of A, B, and Joan an impertinent trifle to that principal matter? Although the central plot could proceed without it, the episode parodies the main business – with its burlesque marriage contest concerned more with money than honor, with Joan outwitting pernicious suitors, as does Lucres, and with the forms of chivalry reduced to bawdy pranks so as, possibly, to reflect on Publius's aristocratic presumptions or the cockfighting potential of both principal suitors. Such trifles may be deliciously pertinent. While A in the prologue to Part II claims, tongue-in-cheek, that the qualities of mad and sad, trifle and matter, amusement and instruction, coexist independent of each other, the experience of *Fulgens and Lucres* suggests the opposite. *The Foure PP*'s confusion of earnest and game, its enigmatic moments, its audience engagement, even its puns and surprises, enlarge upon possibilities hinted in earlier or contemporaneous drama.

From the perspective of the 1590s, Heywood-style acting may look vaudevillian, artificial, fixed in a narrow range of low comedy.[77] But *The Foure PP* and other interludes suggest that, while each acting role would carry a rough "line," the actor might be called on to exercise several voices – honest, ironic, clownish, authorial, ribald – contrasting realism with playfulness and culminating in the enigmatic. Heywood employs a humanist-inflected theatrical dynamic that will migrate to *Gammer Gurton's Needle*, to the Vice drama of the 1560s and 1570s, to Marlowe's ambiguous protagonists, and beyond. In recent years we have learned to talk about subjectivity. "The human subject, the self, is the central figure in the drama which is liberal humanism," argues Catherine Belsey.[78] But the "self" of *The Foure PP* does not tend toward the attributes – autonomy, knowledge, unity – that Belsey finds in liberal humanism. Rather, Heywood's subject emerges as an aspect, as something reticulated in the acting and auditorial relationships of the performance event. In early humanist drama, we might consider that "self" identifies not so much an autonomous subjectivity as a theatrical ontology.

2

Wit and Science
and the dramaturgy of learning

In the early sixteenth century, humanist pedagogues discovered in drama a useful vehicle to promote their educational ideals. While print helped humanist reformers to stimulate controversy and public interest,[1] drama served well for countering resistance to humanist education and for shaping students to humanist values. Plays, of course, were widely read and performed in schools in England and across Renaissance Europe:[2] Terence and Plautus were translated and morally explicated, and play-acting offered students practice in language, oratory, gesticulation, public presentation, and even boldness and discretion. Mid-century statutes at Eton, for example, memorialize the practice of teaching oratory and gesture through dramatic presentation,[3] and Richard Mulcaster's Merchant Taylor's School in the 1570s and 1580s was remembered for instilling "'good behaviour and audacitye"' through acting.[4] Besides being heuristic, school theatre revealed itself as apt for promoting the humanist educational vision. That vision shapes John Redford's *Wit and Science* (c. 1530–47), and learning as a theme permeates numerous other plays, such as Henry Medwall's *Nature* (c.1495), *Youth* (c. 1513), John Rastell's *The Nature of the Four Elements* (c.1518), John Skelton's *Magnificence* (1519), *Nice Wanton* (1547–53), *Lusty Juventus* (c. 1550), Thomas Ingelend's *The Disobedient Child* (c. 1560), William Wager's *The Longer Thou Livest the More Fool Thou Art* (c. 1568), and *Misogonus* (c. 1570).[5] What about early drama makes it so appealing to humanist learning?[6]

For humanist reformers, drama promised to encourage the spectators' emotional embrace of the transformative vision of education through their engagement with the protagonist's self-discovery. To suggest auditorial excitement for pedagogical plays runs aslant of much recent criticism of Tudor drama, which honors

49

the dramatic vitality, panoramic power, and audience-engaging theatrics of the medieval morality tradition. In the "two-traditions" paradigm, humanist drama suffers as classically imitative, artificial, and limited by rules of genre, unity, and decorum. But just as John Heywood's *The Foure PP* reveals a capacity in humanist dramaturgy to excite audience engagement with enigmatical acting, so Redford's *Wit and Science* reveals how pedagogical drama integrates theatrical conventions from morality, romance, and prodigal-son plays to make the pilgrimage of learning emotionally compelling. From morality theatre, *Wit and Science* refashions the allegory of Everyman's salvation into the metaphor of transformation through academic study, with secular knowledge replacing divine grace as the goal. From the romance tradition, *Wit and Science* feminizes knowledge, making Lady Science into the object of chivalric desire. From the prodigal-son drama, the play elaborates the process of self-recognition and contrition. Altogether Redford's generic remodeling shows how pedagogical plays could develop an affective power aimed at winning audiences – and overcoming aristocratic opposition – to the humanist educational agenda. Learning – its imagery, language, and experience – saturates Tudor and Elizabethan drama, from children's plays to neo-Latin university dramas, to comedies such as Gascoigne's *The Glasse of Government*, to University Wit plays such as *Campaspe*, *Doctor Faustus*, and *Friar Bacon and Friar Bungay*, and finally to Shakespeare's comedies of learning and even his tragedy of a student prince. The legacy of pedagogical drama for the century can hardly be overestimated.

1

Written for his pupils by John Redford, master of the choir school of St. Paul's Cathedral, the text of *Wit and Science* indicates that it was performed before the "Kyng and Quene" (1101), "ther honorable Cowncell" (1102), and other aristocrats.[7] Henry VIII was much interested in education, of course, as evidenced by Wolsey's edict in 1529 ordering the academic use of Lily's *Grammar*, preceding only slightly *Wit and Science*'s composition.[8] Like his fellow humanist playwright John Heywood, Redford fashions learning into play: *Wit and Science* employs popular genres to make the educational pilgrimage familiar, while it adds prodigal-son

conventions to answer the affective needs of the humanist argument. Modern criticism has explored various influences on *Wit and
Science*, particularly those of the romance and morality play.[9] As
Edgar Schell puts it, the play welds together a morality thesis (the
need for Reson and Instruction to guide Wyt) with a chivalric
romantic fable (the knight slaying the giant Tediousness and
thereby winning the hand of Lady Science), with, finally, a deeper
Platonic myth of "the intuitive yearning of the mind to realize its
potentiality."[10] To the morality and romance influences, we can
add that of the prodigal-son play, a narrative form that helps to
illuminate the political circumstances and affective design of *Wit
and Science*.[11] While not a formulaic prodigal-son narrative, the play
echoes and sometimes repeats prodigal-son motifs.[12] Pleased with
the company of Honest Recreacion, for example, Wyt rebuffs the
father-figure Reson, falls to dancing, and attempts dalliance, all
in the spirit of the prodigal-son plays, which often include the vices
of drinking, gluttony, dicing, and concupiscence, as in *Acolastus* and
Misogonus. When Wyt returns to Reson's fold, he receives new garments, a prodigal-son convention found also in the clothing-anew
motif of the moralities.[13] Most important, *Wit and Science* adapts
from the prodigal-son tradition the protagonist's process of self-
recognition and remorse, a process that becomes a crux of humanist dramaturgy. While the prodigal-son fable's attention to self-
knowledge, repentance, and contrition will attract later Protestant
writers, early humanist interest in the story precedes and may
even facilitate its subsequent appropriation.[14]

The prodigal-son story proved useful to humanists in defending
their new studies against parents and aristocrats who distrusted
education.[15] Erasmus spends considerable energy in *De pueris instituendis* (1529) arguing for the importance of education and criticiz-
ing parents who neglect the early training of their children. Some
"actually think that children should be kept from education as
though it were a poison."[16] The rich particularly suspected learning: "It seems to be customary that the wealthier a person is, the
less he cares for the education of his children," presumably from
the belief that wealth and good lineage suffice.[17] In the humanist
vision aristocratic parents miss the key to their children's happiness, which is "founded upon a good upbringing and education,"
for "while nature is strong, education is more powerful still."[18]
Likewise, Sir Thomas Elyot in *The Boke named the Gouernour* (1531)

criticizes parents who "without shame, dare affirme, that to a great gentilman it is a notable reproche to be well lerned," and he similarly warns against "These persones that so moche contemne lernyng, that they wold that gentilmen's children shulde haue no parte or very litle therof, but rather shulde spende their youth alway ... playeng at dice, and other games named unlefull."[19] That the alternative to education can only be dissipation reveals how dialectical and strongly urged is the humanist polemic.

Juan Luis Vives's *Linguae latinae exercitatio*, or *School Dialogues*, (1539) and Roger Ascham's *The Scholemaster* (1570) urge impressing learning upon children early and avoiding the pride that besets aristocratic youths. Vives's *School Dialogues*, widely read in Renaissance grammar schools,[20] offer witty Latin conversations about school habits and learning, suitable for student oral presentation. In an ongoing attack on aristocratic opposition, one of Vives's fictional teachers observes that the "conviction has taken hold of the stupid nobles that nothing is more mean or vile than to pursue knowledge in anything."[21] Likewise in a wry dialogue, "Education," Vives satirizes a noble youth who has been brought up to be haughty, proud, condescending, and quarrelsome. Vives insists that humbleness is "the solid and special foundation of the best education, and truly of society."[22] Early bad exposure will ruin children, worries Roger Ascham, as he recalls a gentleman's home "where a yong childe, somewhat past fower yeare olde, cold in no wise frame his tonge, to saie, a litle shorte grace: and yet he could roundlie rap out, so manie vgle othes ... and that which was most detestable of all, his father and mother wold laughe at it."[23] Throughout the century, humanist pedagogues struggled against parental and aristocratic indifference, opposition, and contempt toward "grammar and these Latin lessons."[24]

Aristocratic philistinism bedeviled the royal schoolmaster, John Palsgrave. Palsgrave, whose important translation of *Acolastus* by Gnapheus (or Fulonius) appeared in 1540, served Henry VIII as the first tutor to his illegitimate son Henry Fitzroy, duke of Richmond, in the mid-1520s. Palsgrave and his successor as tutor, Dr. Richard Croke, each complained of courtiers around the adolescent duke who thought learning a hindrance to a nobleman and attempted to divert the boy with hunting, hawking, and other pleasures.[25] Those courtiers resemble the foolish counselor Morobulus in Vives's *School Dialogues*, who argues that a young prince should "chat with the daughters of your august mother, dance, learn the art of bearing arms, play cards or ball, leap and run. Such, you see, are the studies in which young nobles most delight."[26] Palsgrave's experience with those attitudes helps to explain his attraction to the contemporary neo-Latin, prodigal-son play *Acolastus*, which he published, with a translation, as a school text to accompany Lily's *Grammar*. Palsgrave's translation, with its repetitive, multiple renderings of phrases and sentences, makes difficult reading, but as a textbook it was frequently used in the sixteenth century, so much so that Shakespeare may have meant to satirize its redundancies in the speeches of Holofernes. Palsgrave found in *Acolastus* not only a popular Continental school text and an interesting play but also an instructive story of a prodigal son who rejects the moral authority and good counsel of his father, falls into the bad company of sycophants, and squanders his money in feasting, womanizing, and gambling. That narrative seems neatly attuned to the struggles for youthful souls between teachers such as Palsgrave and those who held " 'that lerning ys a great hyndrance and displeasure to a nobyll man.' "[27]

Many pedagogical plays condemn feckless parents who indulge their children's resistance to education or who dismiss education's value. Xantippe, the foolish mother of *Nice Wanton*, refuses to discipline two of her children or to enforce their learning: "Poor souls, they sit a-school all day / In fear of a churl; and if a little they play, / He beateth them like a devil" (109–10).[28] As a result her two pampered children are "[i]dle, disobedient, proud, wanton, and nice" (90). The daughter turns prostitute and dies of the pox; the son commits murder and dies on the gallows, for which fates the play insists on the mother's responsibility. Likewise, Ingelend's *The Disobedient Child* offers a father whose son's "chyldhood with me so easely dyd slyde, / Full of all pastime and delectacyon," that the son refuses learning's hard work, to his ruination.[29] In *Misogonus*, the father, Philogonus, admits that, out of indulgence and aristocratic pride, he has spoiled his son and scorned his learning: "I esteem[ed] not grammar and these Latin lessons" (I.i. 75). Rather than cultivating a gentleman, he has produced a swaggerer, gambler, roisterer, and bully, such that Philogonus now realizes poignantly that "[e]ducation is the best thing that can be" (II.i.242).

Humanists were attracted to drama for its instrumentality in defending their educational mission, evident particularly in drama's potential for suasion and emotional effect, a capacity that takes us to the heart of *Wit and Science*. David Bevington criticizes the play as "refined," "genteel," and "intellect[ual]," associating it with a classical, rule-conscious, literary drama opposed to the lively, episodic, and panoramic popular dramatic tradition.[30] But *Wit and Science* has affective strategies comparable to, if different from, those of morality drama. Wyt receives wise counsel from Reson (who takes the place of the morality figure Mercy or Charity); he falls through pride, indolence, and deception but finally achieves self-knowledge and triumph. In the morality play, when the Mankind figure returns to Charity, he thereby folds himself into God's grace. Medieval morality drama is allegorical in the strictest sense: it represents the manifest truth of God's omnipotence and mercy, which needs no justification. In consequence, the conversion and reconciliation of the Mankind figure seem brief and undernourished by modern standards, as if unmotivated by character or immediate action. In *Mankind*, as Mercy bemoans the hero as "flexible" (747), "wanton," and "frail" (765), Mankind himself re-enters suddenly already ashamed of his unworthiness (806); their ensuing conversation explores God's assurance of forgiveness.[31] Mankind undergoes virtually no onstage process of self-recognition and shame; his transformation comes to us as having already happened, occurring instantaneously. Likewise in *Youth*, the eponymous hero changes heart with striking alacrity: hard upon his promise to Riot, "I will follow thy mind in everything / And guide me after thy learning" (692–93), he is ready, after hearing a few brief speeches on God's mercy, to "be ruled" by Charity so as "My soul to save" (727, 728).[32] In the later morality *Lusty Juventus* (*c.* 1550), Good Counsel reads to Juventus a list of his abominations (whoredom, pride, envy, oaths) and threatens him with "terrible fire" (1007), upon which Juventus collapses on the ground with a one-line repentance and an appeal for God's mercy.[33] In these morality plays, the Mankind figure undergoes a sudden transformation, and his greatest concern thereafter is God's willingness to receive him despite his sins. The Continental and Catholic *Everyman* emphasizes contrition and good works, of course, and lengthens Everyman's steps toward salvation, but the play lacks the struggle for self-knowledge that will infuse humanist and Protestant drama. As Paula Neuss observes, "the sudden reformation of the hero without any apparent internal motivation is common in moral interludes."[34] Morality plays presume a disposition toward salvation in its characters, who are easily made mindful of their sins and who acknowledge the balm of God's grace even if they doubt his mercy towards them. The characters' transformations lack the hallmarks of personal struggle because, as Catherine Belsey has suggested, their soteriological end is to be enfolded into the consuming grace of God rather than to become individuals: "In the Middle Ages ... to know God was not to differentiate oneself from the objects of knowledge but, on the contrary, to become absorbed in total presence, to be transformed, and ultimately dissolved."[35] Thus the knowledge at issue in *Everyman* differs from the objective kind associated with humanism: in *Everyman* and other moralities, "Knowledge is not instrumental but constitutive; it is a condition of being."[36]

Unlike the morality play, the pedagogical interlude cannot claim an incontrovertible truth; scholastic knowledge is not grace. To compensate, humanist drama seeks to heighten the audience's emotional engagement with the protagonist in his struggle for self-knowledge. Given that strategy, such terms as "refined," "genteel," and "intellect[ual]" may underestimate humanist dramaturgy. In appropriating morality structure, pedagogical drama faces an immediate challenge, for it attempts to evoke the aura of religious salvation in order to argue that learning is something like grace. Pedagogical drama, that is, would convince its spectators that humanist knowledge resembles divine grace, that the story of learning repeats the story of redemption.[37] The pedagogical interlude thus endeavors to enact a *metaphor* rather than an allegory – a crucial shift. Indeed, the humanist argument for learning might be understood as so deficient in obviousness that it must exercise multiple metaphors, multiple genres: learning is like morality play salvation or like a chivalric quest or like the return of the prodigal son. Lacking the authority of an incontrovertible truth, the humanist narrative must convince its audience to embrace its metaphor. Medieval drama fits humanist argumentative ends because its allegory of fall and redemption commands cultural assent. But the extremity of humanist polemics and the added burden of persuasion due to the shift from allegory to metaphor demand that drama maximize its affective power. A characteristic of pedagogical interludes, then, will be an urgency for engaging and moving the audience.

From these rhetorical circumstances several implications arise. In Belsey's analysis, Renaissance humanism represents the subject as aspiring not to a new "condition of being" (the sense of presence in God) but to empirical knowledge, so that humanist drama emerges as concerned less for ecstatic union with God and more for detached and analytical truth. Yet humanist plays often prefer personal, emotional experience over intellectual knowledge, and Renaissance humanism itself cannot be comprehended fully as ratiocinative system.[38] Humanist plays will seek spectatorial assent to their educational program by blessing the protagonist's personal transformation with a pathos that engages interest, sympathy, and agreement. The rhetorical problem of humanist drama creates the occasion for audience-affecting scenes of self-recognition and heroic triumph. Thus theatricality colors its philosophical values. Humanist drama's commitment to emotional effect suggests, moreover, that humanist learning seeks an experience akin to a sense of "being" rather than a strictly empirical knowledge. Indeed, the emphasis by Vives and others on the student's attitude – humbleness, responsiveness, piety – argues how much early humanism sought to associate itself with a certain psychological perspective. The humanist mission fastens on pedagogical drama's affective power.

2

Wit and Science employs compelling, often popularist, theatrical values that promote audience engagement. Drama possesses abundant resources – speech, gesture, song, music, dance, disguise, mimicry, costume, properties, and color – to move its audience, and *Wit and Science* uses them with elegant clarity. Honest Recreacion, Cumfort, Quyckness, and Strenght [*sic*] awaken the defeated Wyt's senses with singing; Wyt and Honest Recreacion dance a comic galliard; Idlenes makes a triumphant theatrical exit "bles[sing]" (592) the weak-brained Wyt with a folk-dance "skyp or twayne" (590); Fame, Favour, Riches, and Worship play viols and serenade Lady Science on her first entrance; at the dénouement, Wyt with his party and Lady Science with hers converge on each other from opposite sides of the stage singing alternating verses of "Wellcum, my nowne"; and in a grand betrothal finale, all the cast members gather onstage as a chorus, accompanied by the viols, to lift their voices in "Remembreance" and file off the platform curtseying and singing. Broadway could admire such theatrics. The show skillfully deploys properties and costumes: for props, Reson's mirror, Wyt's portrait, Shame's whip, and Science's sword of comfort; for costumes, Tediousness's visor, rusty chain mail, and funny nose, along with Ingnorance's motley, Idlenes's blackface, and Wyt's lost and new academic gowns. The detailing here is vivid, efficient, and broadly appealing. Redford even calls upon some stock comedy routines and other winning set-pieces: Tedious imitates a ranting Herod; Honest Recreacion and Idlenes engage in a female flyting; Idlenes orchestrates the hilarious classroom send-up of Ingnorance's spelling lesson; and Reson as audience-guide declaims patrician wisdom. While the characters are largely abstractions, Redford also gives them enlivening touches: Studye is timorous; Confydence enters breathless from pursuing Wyt; Lady Science has doubts; and Wyt displays the kinetic attributes – speed and lightness – of his name. This humanist play levitates on devices of popular theatre.

Wit and Science's multiple genres also add a layering and depth comparable to the sweeping world view of medieval drama. The morality plays have been justly admired by Bevington for "panoramic" scope: their universal themes, their alternating episodes of virtue- and Vice-characters, and their profusely populated world evoked by the doublings of "four men and a boy." Such panoramic effect, argues Bevington, confers on the moralities a theatrical energy and resonance. The point is well taken, and one would be ill-advised to claim quite the same elements in *Wit and Science* – which doubles the roles of only four supporting actors.[39] But *Wit and Science* displays its own peculiar resonance, a sense of layering, texture, and multiple perspective from its overlapping of morality, romance, and prodigal-son paradigms. In *Wit and Science*, the medieval morality tradition anchors the narrative in Christian reality; chivalric-romance motifs introduce the domain of wish-fulfillment, desire, and fantasy; while the prodigal-son narrative conveys the synthesizing presence of an individual consciousness. Those different dimensions – Christian, fantastical, personal – give Wyt's final winning of Lady Science, for example, a special spectatorial satisfaction. Such generic layering is not typical of the medieval

morality play, whose structure must be limpid even if its implications are multivalent. Thus, *Wit and Science*'s self-contained
metaphoric world, appealing through several paradigms of action,
offers a compelling counterpart to the panoramic vistas of good
and evil available in the morality.

Since spectators do not necessarily identify with Wyt as they
would with a morality protagonist, the play employs other strategies to make the message engaging.[40] To that end, Redford
exploits the youth of his schoolboy performers by emphasizing
farce, play, and game. Wyt's pursuit of Science is structured as a
game, with objectives, obstacles, resources, and rules; Wyt engages
Tediousness in a mock chivalric combat;[41] and game turns into
self-parody with Idlenes's spelling lesson. The game motif continues as Idlenes disguises Wyt unbeknownst to him, and Science
herself seems to be engaged in a game of pretending not to recognize Wyt. While morality drama locates play and game around the
Vice-characters, *Wit and Science* uses these motifs frequently and
expansively and even structures the narrative as a game. They
help to make agreeable the interlude's tendentious values – discipline, obedience, study – by lodging them inside the pleasure of
heightened play, so that *Wit and Science* provides an object lesson
in humanist pedagogy. The interlude can even orchestrate the
kind of complex audience awareness and delight that will characterize the best Elizabethan drama, as Lady Science's first appearance demonstrates. Idlenes has blackened Wyt's face, dressed him
in Ingnorance's garments, and left him sleeping on the ground so
transformed that not even his anxious servant Confidence recognizes him (612–13). Fame, Favour, Riches, and Worship bustle in
to serenade Lady Science, arriving for her meeting with Wyt. She
refuses to be cheered by the music and embarks, with her mother,
Experience, on a denunciation of the "waverying" (674) and
"scorne[ful]" (679) Wyt, who has not appeared for their rendezvous despite his vehement protestations of love (677–92). Experience confirms these judgments with the appropriate senten-
tiousness:

> . . . it is true, thys proverbe old:
> 'Hastye love is soone hot and soone cold.'
> Take hede, dowghter, how you put youre trust
> To lyght lovers to hot at the furst.   (699–702)

Mother Experience concludes ominously, "Wyt hath set hys love

... another way" (709–10). The delight of this episode is its complex discrepant awareness. The audience recognizes what the
women do not, that Wyt lies nearby as empirical evidence for their
hypothesis about his behavior. Redford juxtaposes the serious with
the farcical, for while Science speaks earnestly and Experience
disapprovingly, their example, Wyt, remains comic. The juxtaposition of earnestness and play disarms the danger of moral pom-
posity, establishes an engaging richness of tone, and confirms the
audience's pleasurably superior relationship to the characters
onstage. If *Wit and Science* arises from humanist pedagogical concerns, it yet melds genres, treats learning as play, orchestrates
audience response, and otherwise deploys popular devices to
create theatrically astute effects.

3

After his defeat by Tediousness, his baffling by Idlenes, and his
folly before Science, Wyt finally triumphs by passing through the
stages of self-regeneration. That process displays a heightening of
empathy and emotional effect characteristic of the prodigal-son
plays. In the last installment of his downfall, Wyt behaves like a
coarse and bullying fool before Lady Science and Experience; his
blindness to his appearance and behavior earns him the clothing
and figurative identity of Ingnorance. Wyt must undergo a transformation, accomplished in stages of reflection, shame, and
communal penance. In that process, the prodigal-son play shows
its hand. A characteristic of the prodigal-son parable is that
"instead of concentrating on God's active role in seeking the 'lost,'
Jesus here emphasizes the development of repentance in the heart
of the sinner."[42] In that emphasis prodigal-son plays differ from
moralities, the latter stressing God's mercy and the former exploring man's remorse. Palsgrave, translating the prodigal play *Acolastus*, pauses at a turning-point late in the action to marvel at
three ensuing scenes in which the author "bryngeth in Acolastus,
to make his moone."[43] In the first of these scenes, Palsgrave notes,
Acolastus laments his "sodayn mysery," "misordred lyfe," and
"noughty governa[n]ce"; in the second, he endures "penury,"
"hunger," and "cold" in contrast to his recent sensual pleasures;
and in the third, Acolastus expresses "repentaunce of his myser-
able lyfe, with a hope to haue forgyueness of his mercyfull father,

whervpon is grounded the catastrophe of this comedye."[44]
Palsgrave praises Acolastus's speeches for a rhetoric "most mete
and conuenient for a person that in delyberatyng with hym selfe,
falleth in maner into extreme desperation: and therfore to moue
the audience unto commiseration."[45] Palsgrave emphasizes two
features of these transformation scenes: first, their emotional
intensity and credibility, and, second, their resultant capacity "to
moue the audience" to "commiseration" and "compassion."[46] The
passage deserves critical attention because Palsgrave offers here
an early Tudor statement on the theory of audience-effect in
humanist pedagogical drama.

Like *Acolastus*, English pedagogical plays emphasize the pathos
of the hero's recognition, shame, and contrition. In so doing, they
encourage audience engagement – commiseration and compassion – with the hero of the humanist metaphoric narrative.
Nice Wanton helps identify these features. After the interval, the
once-beautiful daughter Dalilah, who has given herself to prosti-
tution, enters "Full of pain and sorrow, crooked and lorn: / Stuff'd
with diseases" (263–64). Her "sinews be shrunken," her "flesh
eaten with pox," leaving her "bones full of ache and great pain"
(265–66); her gorgeous yellow hair has fallen out; her eyesight
has turned dim and her stomach queasy:

> Now am I foul and horrible to see;
> All this I have deserved for lack of grace;
> Justly for my sins God doth plague me.
> . . .
> I fell to naught, and shall die with shame.
> Yet all this is not half of my grief and pain.
> The worm of my conscience, that shall never die,
> Accuseth me daily more and more.   (274–82)

Dalilah, like Wyt, has undergone a degradation in stage appearance, and her insight about the source of this change, "All this I
have deserved for lack of grace," might touch both characters.
Dalilah's recognition of physical corruption induces her awareness
of moral corruption, followed by "shame," a key emotional value.
Dalilah repeatedly draws audience attention to her shame (279,
291, 306, 318). Eventually a character named Worldly Shame will
enter to gloat over Dalilah and Ismael and to plague their mother.
The motif of shame captures how Dalilah's visual transformations
provoke psychological and moral ones. Her soliloquy is followed by

the entrance of her brother Barnabas, the displaced figure of the father in the prodigal-son paradigm. Even before he recognizes his sister, Barnabas invites her to "Confess the truth ... Repent and amend" (287–90). They join in a touching reunion, and Barnabas takes Dalilah home to heal her soul, if not her body. The spectacle of Dalilah's suffering, shame, and forfeited worldly bliss solicits the audience's "compassion" and "commiseration" on her behalf.

Parallel features occur comically in *Wit and Science*. After Lady Science and Experience exit disgusted, Wyt holds the stage in soliloquy, still wearing the blackface applied by Idlenes and dressed in Ingnorance's coat, coxcomb, hood, and ears – a comic spectacle. Wyt's parodic physical transformation is as complete in its own way as Dalilah's, and Wyt has further altered in behavior by blustering like Tediousness and retorting in ignorance. Despite his self-justifications, however, Wyt questions himself enough that he brings forth the mirror given him by Reson: "Am I so fowle as those drabes wold make me? / Wher is my glas that Reson dyd take me? / ... Hah! Goges sowle! What have we here? A dyvyll?" (801–05). Shocked by what he sees, Wyt tests the mirror by reflecting it on the audience, only to discover that the spectators look "fayre and cleere they, evry-chone" (813), while he alone is "[d]eckt ... lyke a very asse" (817). Wyt's distress at his appearance allows him to recognize his corrupted behavior and present shame and to acknowledge his foolish forfeiture of Lady Science: "Evrye man I se lawhe me to scorne. / Alas, alas, that ever I was borne! / ... Alas, that lady I have now lost / ... I have woone Hatred, Beggry, and Open Shame" (827–42). Those ideas and feelings have their parallel in *Nice Wanton*, as does Wyt's commenting on himself as spectacle; they suggest a shared dramaturgy for moral regeneration in the prodigal figure.[47] With the entrance of the character Shame (a precursor of *Nice Wanton*'s Worldly Shame), followed by Reson, the tone of *Wit and Science* darkens surprisingly. Reson calls on Shame to whip Wyt: "Upon hym, Shame, wyth stryppes inow smitten, / While I reherce his fawtes herein wrytten" (845–46). Reson proceeds to read a kind of formal indictment of Wyt's broken promises and transgressions, concluding, "Wherfore, spare him not, Shame! Bete him well there! / He hath deservyd more than he can beare" (859-60). By all indications, Shame actually does beat Wyt onstage, since Wyt "knelith downe" (s.d. at 860) and cries out that "Alas, thes strypes of Shame will undo mee" (862) – upon which Reson commands Shame to cease.[48] Reson later declares that Wyt's willingness to accept punishment gives evidence of his reformable nature (891–900), a proof needed to make Wyt's change credible. The rapid movement from parodic folly to pained self-recognition, to shame and physical humiliation, and finally to amendment is remarkable. Behind Wyt's comedy stands a serious narrative of self-discovery and expiation. Even the light-hearted Wyt must be humiliated, and the shaming must be experienced by the audience as realistic, emotional, and embarrassing. The presence of beating in a play built upon a school-room analogy raises a highly charged issue in Renaissance pedagogy. Rebecca Bushnell argues that humanists expressed ambivalence about corporal punishment: on the one hand, it instilled discipline designed to fashion a self-reliant citizen; on the other hand, it broke the youthful spirit so as to induce servility.[49] Likewise the humanist attack on education's opponents aims to replace aristocratic pride with humility, as Vives's *School Dialogues* illustrate, while, simultaneously, pedagogical writers such as Erasmus express outrage at the excessive thrashing of school children. Although *Everyman* stages a self-flagellation, beating looms as an emotional flash-point in Tudor pedagogical plays. The children in *Nice Wanton* fear being beaten, and the Son in *The Disobedient Child* anxiously fabricates a tale about a schoolboy being thrashed to death by a vicious schoolmaster. Wyt's onstage punishment seems chosen to arouse complicated audience "affections": Redford, like the author of *Nice Wanton*, takes pains to create spectacle and pathos, mediated by Reson, around Wyt's transformation.

The vital instrument of Wyt's self-recognition is a stage property, the mirror that Reson gives Wyt in the opening section of the play: "Thys glas of Reason shall show ye all: / Whyle ye have that, ye have me, and shall" (7–8). The mirror of reason symbolizes the special sense of self-recognition on which humanist drama capitalizes. *Wit and Science* contains the first known use of a mirror as a significant physical property on the English stage. In the 1500s, Venetian glassmakers began to produce hand mirrors made of flat, uncolored glass, backed by a silvery tin amalgam and giving off a clear, sharp, realistic image.[50] This new mirror, its glass called "crystal," constituted a radical technological advance over the medieval mirror's polished metal or stone or its cloudy green glass.[51] Because of that technological breakthrough, the Venetian mirror industry underwent an economic explosion in the sixteenth century. European demand was insatiable, and pocket mirrors, such as the four-by-two-inch mirror, sometimes worn in the girdle or even disguised as a prayer book and carried in the breeches pocket, rapidly became "an essential part of dress."[52] It must be a version of this fashionable Venetian mirror that Wyt lifts from his belt or pocket, since its virtue as a stage property depends on a trueness in the glass when turned to the audience (813). Dramaturgy now shapes the idea of humanist self-recognition: because of new technology, a property can embody that idea graphically, achieving a humorous theatrical moment. Indeed, the mirror will become one of the most important stage properties, visual images, and metaphors of Renaissance drama. The physical property enhances the dramatic argument and identifies the play with the humanist values of reason, clarity, and emotional credibility. The crystalline mirror confirms *Wit and Science*'s eschewing of the morality protagonist's sudden change and manifests its commitment to a more elaborate humanist self-recognition.[53] In a virtuosic balancing act, the emotional is grounded in the clear-sighted.

Although no other Tudor pedagogical play contains the spectacular mirror of *Wit and Science*, many move toward a pathos capable of evoking audience compassion and commiseration. In *Magnificence*, the eponymous hero emphasizes his own shame: "Alasse that ever I sholde be so shamed!" (1982; see also 2054, 2279, 2444, 2565).[54] Toward the end of *The Disobedient Child*, the prodigal son recapitulates the stages of transformation etched by Acolastus, Wyt, and Dalilah. At first he blames his wife for his hunger, menial work, and misery (pp. 44–45), but subsequently the Son acknowledges in detail his transgressions. Introduced by the stage direction *"Here he confesseth his noughtynes, uttring the same with a pitifull voice"*(p. 50), the Son's soliloquy constitutes a set piece inviting audience compassion and commiseration. The Son acknowledges his wantonness, willfulness, and resistance to good counsel, and he does so in terms that recall *Wit and Science*: "The thynge that was good I greatly hated, / As one which lacked both wytte and reason; / . . . I coulde not abyde of the schole to heare; / Masters and teachers my harte abhorred" (p. 50). With several

pathetic "alases," the Son arrives at the emotional and moral
shame of the earlier plays: "now I am fayne a cote that is rent, /
Alas! to weare for verye shame" (p. 51). The soliloquy here, like
those in the previous works, brings to climax the process of self-
recognition, acceptance of responsibility, and shame. The Son proceeds to a reunion with his father, the play's audience-surrogate,
who has lamented to the spectators repeatedly over his child:
"Howe great griefe it is, and hevynes, / To every man that is a
father, / To suffre his chylde to folowe wantonnes" (pp. 14–15).
Thus audience commiseration and compassion are re-enforced
from a double perspective. Likewise the figure of the suffering
father commands sympathy in *Acolastus* and *Misogonus*. While the
fragmentary *Misogonus* breaks off just when the protagonist's reconciliation with his father, Philogonus, begins, so that we do not
know the workings of the transformation, the first scene does
establish Philogonus as heartbroken (I.i.51) at his son's "lewd-
ness" (94). His good friend, Eupelas orchestrates audience sympathy: "Alas, good Philogonus! It pitieth me sore / To see you, my
dear friend, in this heavy plight" (97–98). In such ways, *Misogonus*
directs audience attention toward the pathos of the father as
another lure to compassion and commiseration. The persona
present in Tudor pedagogical drama registers as different from
the humanist-as-empiricist of the "anti-essentialist" model, for
humanist knowledge requires a metamorphosis characterized by
self-recognition, shame, humility, and contrition. That transformation evolves in emotionally charged stages, all calculated to move
the sympathies of the audience in concert with the passions of the
protagonist. Humanist drama explores thematically its capacity to
move, engulf, and (to use Elyot's term) "inflame" its audience.[55]
In the process of dramatic transformation, moreover, the hero –
Acolastus, Wyt, Dalilah – surrenders pretensions to autonomy and
truth and accepts communal wisdom and discipline, in *Wit and
Science* the discipline of learning as a way of being.

4

Self-knowledge comes to Wyt not from his defeat by Tediousness
but from his resemblance to Ingnorance. That fact again extends
Wit and Science beyond the morality tradition and marks the
emergence of a seminal strategy in humanist dramaturgy: the

deployment of characters of converging identity, characters who are discovered to be simulacra, doubles. Since morality heroes all stand for humankind, the morality tradition has no need for doubles. While the morality plays may externalize a character's attributes – such as Beauty or Five-Wits – a protagonist never assumes an individuality that distinguishes him from his fellow man. A fascinating element of humanist dramaturgy, however, is its melding of – as the modern mind would consider it – two versions of the individual, one as a private and unique identity, the other communal and shared. A recurrent strategy of humanist dramaturgy, from *Wit and Science* to *Doctor Faustus* and *Hamlet*, is to posit a character as a separate self and then to reveal progressively his or her shared identity with others. The discovery of that mutuality often defines the protagonist's self-discovery and change, as in *Wit and Science*. Wyt finds himself by recognizing in a mirror his doubleness with Ingnorance. For Renaissance dramaturgy, such a strategy of correspondences possesses enormous significance. It demonstrates the kinship of humanist drama with its medieval forebears, since the experience of corporate identity descends from that tradition; simultaneously it demonstrates humanist drama's distinctness from the moralities, since the latter preclude an interest in individuality.

Redford, for example, establishes the converging identities of Honest Recreacion and Idlenes, evidence that the motif resonates beyond Wyt's experience alone. The shift from medieval allegorical figures to humanist doubles virtually charts itself. After Tediousness knocks Wyt unconscious, Honest Recreacion enters with a singing chorus of other allegorical attributes, Cumfort, Quycknes, and Strenght – much as similar attributes arrive to sustain Everyman. If characters at first reflect medieval allegorizing, they next betray a dramaturgy of semblance. Against Reson's urgency, Wyt insists on lingering with Honest Recreacion and will turn again to Science only "at leyser" (277). The flirting Wyt offers Honest Recreacion marriage, then sheds his academic gown (sent to him by Science) and dances with her, whereupon Idlenes mysteriously appears: *"Here they dawnce, and in the mene-whyle Idellnes cumth in and sytth downe"* (s.d. at 330). Wyt soon collapses in Idlenes's lap and, to Honest Recreacion's shock, cannot distinguish between "thes damselles" (334), who launch into a humorous flyting. Idlenes claims that she is "[a]s honest a woman as ye be"

(338) and that Honest Recreacion does the greater corrupting: "Mark her dawnsyng, her maskyng and mummyng. / Where more concupyscene then ther cummyng?" (373–74). Idlenes here scores a point difficult to answer, for when Wyt first awakened, he began to bandy with Honest Recreacion and she entertained his advances, albeit modestly. Honest Recreacion will agree to marry Wyt if he can prove his love for her (307–12), an arrangement of which Reson would hardly approve. When does Honest Recreacion drift into Idlenes? The action muddles distinctions between the two: Honest Recreacion dallies inappropriately with Wyt; Idlenes claims her adversary's honesty for herself; the two level the same accusations of license; and Wyt cannot tell one from the other, until he finally embraces the arguments of Idlenes. While on one level Honest Recreacion and Idlenes are opposed qualities, on another they are surprisingly the same. In fuzzing these boundaries, the play makes a point about how a virtue can become a vice before one knows it. Dramaturgically *Wit and Science* moves away from medieval allegorical figures and toward the humanist semblable identities of Renaissance theatre.

Wyt initiates his transformation by recognizing himself as Ingnorance. *Wit and Science* establishes three different identities or simulacra for Wyt at the beginning of the play: Wyt the onstage personage; Wyt the mirror of Reson; and Wyt the portrait, given to Lady Science, that Confidence displays: "Now wyll ye see a goodly pycture / Of Wyt hym-sealfe, hys owne image sure" (49–50). Science loves Wyt for his "gyftes of graces" (17), for Wyt is "[y]oong, paynefull, tractable, and capax" (19). From the first, then, the play broadcasts several versions of Wyt. When Science encounters him, she will recognize the image of Ingnorance rather than the "well faverde" (55) image from the portrait shown by Confidence. The play sets in motion a dialectic that will echo through *Hamlet* and beyond: a protagonist must face the challenge of living up to his best image, which resides in the hands of someone else. Wyt has shed his academic gown in dancing with Honest Recreacion, a signal of his devolution, and as a further signal, he falls asleep in Idlenes's lap, figuratively sliding back toward the condition in which Tediousness had left him. Idlenes orchestrates the hilarious spelling lesson with Ingnorance, a parody of the humanist heuristic of partitioning a task and learning the parts through mnemonic associations. Redford cleverly gives Ingnorance a seminal humanist shortcoming. The sound of *hiss* propells Ingnorance into a joyful imitation of the goose rather than the enunciation of his name: the idiot boy becomes regularly lost in a figure's vehicle rather than returning to its tenor; he lacks the capacity for metaphor. That failing assumes a certain playfulness, given that *Wit and Science* labors to make a metaphor irresistibly true.

Idlenes confers on Wyt the attributes of Ingnorance, most obviously his blackened face, motley coat, hood, ears, and coxcomb (816–17) and explains the change of appearance: Wyt "shall soone scantlye knowe hym sealfe" (570). Ingnorance's garments fit disconcertingly well: "Heere is a cote as fyt for this elfe / As it had bene made evyn for this bodye" (571–72). The disguise – or transformation – is complete, since no one seems to recognize Wyt. As he changes clothing, Wyt alters behavior, thereby expressing another motif of character transformation in Renaissance drama, as, for example, when female characters assume masculine traits with male clothing. Although Wyt speaks to Science and Experience with a "trym" (724) tongue beyond Ingnorance's capacity, his behavior has degenerated. He lies to Lady Science about his absence; abruptly demands a kiss, as he had of Honest Recreacion; swears oaths as he grows angry toward the ladies; blocks their way; blusters at their assertions that he does not resemble his portrait; calls Experience a "fowle, ugly whoore" and Science a "drab"; and finally threatens violence (713–804). If Wyt looks like Ingnorance, he behaves as a combination of Idlenes's son and the monster Tediousness, to whom Wyt has earlier succumbed and who has called Lady Science a "drab" (163) and accused Wyt of "lust" (164). Science thus scores an important point in saying that Wyt is not a natural fool but a "nawghty vycious" (789) and "arrogant" (791) fool who has been "Browght up wyth Idellnes in her scoole" (790). Wyt has gained his viciousness cumulatively, from his earlier misadventure with Tediousness, from his choice of Idlenes, and only lastly from the disguise-trick. Wyt thus illustrates another important humanist principle that will haunt Renaissance drama, that "use" – behavior – "almost can change the stamp of nature" (*Hamlet* III.iv.168).[56] Finally, of course, Wyt recognizes himself as Ingnorance, and in that ironic discovery of metaphor, similitude, or even shared identity, the possibility of transformation begins. To become "himself," in the sense of his portrait and public image, Wyt must embrace the knowledge that he also resembles Ingnorance, and he must surrender his willfulness to Reson.

I would claim the process under discussion – the protagonist's transition from presumed individuality toward the discovery of shared identity – as a contribution of humanist drama to sixteenth-century theatre. I can do little more here than sketch out such a notion. The boundaries of Renaissance thought have come to appear thin and permeable,[57] and sixteenth-century drama characteristically toys with the transgression of boundaries: actors as characters, men as women, commoners as lords, Globe as globe. Drama here gathers impetus from a strain in humanism, its love of metamorphosis, its sense that something – man – can become something else – a beast or a god,[58] the kind of metamorphosis that occurs in the humanist plays of John Lyly.[59] Renaissance humanism may express a certain sense of "self," but the modern term "self" is misleading, since early humanism perceives character as a permeable locus of choice and action rather than an impenetrable object. Accordingly, in English Renaissance drama, protagonists often discover that they share identity with the people around them. The idea of doubleness haunts even early Renaissance plays. The Continental *Acolastus*, for example, contains characters who seem both separate from, and doubled versions of, other characters: the bad counsellor Philautus exaggerates the prodigal and prideful aspects of Acolastus; the parasitic wastrels Pamphagus and Pantolabus serve as further reductions of Philautus. Likewise, toward the end of *Acolastus* father and son join in a preternatural onstage duet (v.v), even though they abide in different locales, as if, for the moment, they shared a consciousness. The cowardly husband in *Tom Tyler and his Wife* (*c.* 1560) employs a vaguely demonic double to beat his wife, and Jenkin in *Jacke Jugeler* (*c.* 1553) suffers the comic epistemological nightmare of having his identity stolen from him by Jacke. The permeability of the self shapes the Renaissance sense of friendship, which descends from Cicero: "When a man thinks of a true friend, he is looking at himself in the mirror."[60] That view of the friend as "another I" appears recurringly, as in Richard Edwards's *Damon and Pithias* (1564), where the two friends have difficulty telling which of them is which. The motif has its obverse in *John a Kent and John a Cumber* (*c.* 1587–89), where each of the duelling wizards disguises himself as the other, so that their opposition finally hints at a distinction without a difference.

In *Hamlet*, argues Francis Barker, the hero's identity seems to be doubled across the play in other characters who function as simulacra.[61] Hamlet, we might add, moves from an apparent separateness and autonomy toward the discovery that he is deeply implicated in the lives of others, as are they in his, that he is, in a sense, everyone else.[62] That pattern, discernable also in Renaissance comedies, is pronounced in the tragedies, where selves sometimes become refracted into other characters or absorbed into generalized roles. In Marlowe's plays, for example, the hero's individuality, celebrated at the beginning, can dissolve into his assumed role. Tamburlaine comes to live within the contours of the mythic identity that he has donned, and Barabas, who commences with a gigantic individuality, recedes into the role of comedic avenger, leaving in his wake Ithamores, parodic, doubled traces of himself. Similarly in *Doctor Faustus* Mephistophilis functions as a strange simulacrum of Faustus himself. Robert Greene, too, deploys doubled characters, such as Orlando and Sacripant in *Orlando Furioso*, and resolves the problems of individuals and their relationships, in part, by subsuming them into a larger ceremonial and ritualistic order, as he does in *Friar Bacon and Friar Bungay*.[63] Katharine Eisaman Maus notes that in *Measure for Measure* "characters are confused, exchanged, or substituted for one another."[64] Maus argues that the problem of "inwardness" in English Renaissance drama reveals "the fantasy, or romance, or fear of a common, unindividuated corporeality, an embodiment that is both part of the self, and outside of or distinct from it."[65] I take the discovery of shared identity – a process that requires a correlative, nonmedieval sense of individuality – to be a humanist feature of Renaissance dramaturgy, and one that, in the later drama of the age, can achieve a powerful, affecting, almost uncanny quality on stage.

Early humanists such as Erasmus used epistolary, manuscript, and print culture to create a supportive community of like-minded thinkers. The image of an international, itinerant fraternity of intellectuals, educators, and reformers woven together in a furious exchange of manuscripts, books, and letters typifes humanism and its combination of antiquarianism and activism. But drama, more than other literary genres, is entangled with the idea of community and thus ripe for humanist expression.

Inherently imitative, drama invites explorations of similitude:
shared fates, paralleled characters, mistaken identities, disguises,
simulacra. Under humanist influence drama can discover resemblances where differences – separate physical bodies – had
appeared. With its unstable sense of identity, drama likewise
showcases the malleability of the individual. For the early humanists, drama creates communal assent to the idea of academic
learning as a process of transformational discovery because drama
can represent a fictive community sharing just such an experience.
Community, discovery, resemblance, transformation: the values
toward which Renaissance theatre gravitates echo humanist education and culture.

5

Despite his renovation and his triumph over Tediousness, Wyt
closes the play still dogged by public "dowte," particularly the
doubt of Lady Science, a quality foreign to the morality tradition.
Redford introduces the idea of Science's doubt almost from the
first line, when Reson hands Wyt the mirror, saying, "when ye /
Cum neere my dowghter, Science, then see / That all thynges be
cleane and trycke abowte ye, / Least of sum sloogyshnes she myght
dowte ye" (3–6). "Sloogyshnes" sounds akin to "tediousness" and
"idleness," the qualities that will later overwhelm Wyt. Against
"sloogyshnes" Reson has given Wyt the mirror "in remembrance
of Reson" (1), and not accidentally, *Wit and Science* closes with the
choral song "Remembreance" (s.d. at 1104). Memory constitutes
one aspect of the ongoing process of learning. Memory fails
Ingnorance because acquired learning is an instrument of reason,
a stay against "sloogyshnes," and one of the "gyftes of graces."
Wyt is cautioned that his best defense "[f]rom the mysuse of Science" will be his "remembrance" of the endpoint of their lives
(1093–94). Remembrance thus assumes not only pedagogical but
eschatological significance. But Science's "dowte" lingers.

The lady's skepticism plays a motivating role in the action, for
Wyt must not only defeat the monsters before him but also allay
Science's uncertainty. Reson returns to the problem of Lady
Science's doubt after Wyt's shaming: "but all the dowte now is to
thynke how / My dowghter takth this" (901–02). Contrition
through ritual is one thing, but absolution from the lady is

another: guessing that Science has recognized Wyt in their earlier
interview (904–5), Reson ponders whether Wyt's "mysbehaver
perchance evyn strykyng / Her hart agaynst him, she now mysly-
kyng, / As women oft tymes wylbe hard hartyd" (907–09). Yet,
Reson concludes, if he can take Wyt's part with Science, "I dowght
not to ioyne them to-gether" (915).[66] Reson lends Lady Science a
touch of enigma. After Wyt slays Tediousness, she approaches him
across the stage, apparently reconciled; although Science acknowledges that Wyt has "dowghtles" (1026) won her, the betrothal is
as much a warning as a celebration:

> For I, Science, am in this degree
> As all, or most part, of woomen bee –
> Yf ye use me well in a good sorte,
> Then shall I be youre ioy and comfort;
> But yf ye use me not well, then dowt me,
> For, sure, ye were better then wyth-out me.
>
> (1039–44)

The language of "dowte" now bursts into the dénouement: "What
neede these dowtes" (1052), interjects father Reson, while Experience retorts, "This dowgt our dowghter doth well to gather"
(1054[67]). The answer will be for Wyt to use Science for "Godes
honor" (1059) and for his own and his neighbor's profit but not
for "evyll effects" (1067).[68]

Lady Science has doubts about Wyt because knowledge, once
gained, can still be misused, turned to evil effects. Learning alone
does not assure virtue, a tension that Belsey notes: "a humanist
text naturally claims that there is a connection between knowledge and virtue. But the nature of the connection is slightly elusive . . . Science does not self-evidently lead to duty and salvation."[69]
Science's doubt points to a dualism in the humanist representation of knowledge. In Belsey's view, humanism defines knowledge as empirical. Yet, however true in part, that ascription does
not exhaust the humanist sense of knowledge, for humanism
treats learning as a process as well as an object, as *Wit and Science*
illustrates. Knowledge as a thing or a possession can be misused,
but in this drama, learning as an ongoing process works to good
rather than ill effect. What Wyt "learns" in the process of transformation is to abandon pride and willfulness, so that learning
implies a certain frame of mind. Wyt reaches Mount Parnassus by
humbly embracing the communal wisdom and sanctions of Reson

and by gathering around him a community of virtues: Confydence with Science's sword of comfort, Instruction with his stratagems, and Study and Dyligens with their collaborative ploys. The process of learning calls forth humility, obedience, discipline, and communal engagement, and those qualities suggest a knowledge that is not simply empirical but, in some degree, constitutive of being.

An irresolvable tension persists, however, in this two-dimensional concept of knowledge. If knowledge as an object remains capable of misuse, then learning as a process of transformation will never be completed. Wyt may fortify his defenses with reason, experience, information, and memory, but all his promises of virtue will remain vulnerable to Lady Science's doubt. In morality drama, when the play ends, the action of life is over, but when humanist drama ends, the action suggests an afterlife, the possibility of further challenges, triumphs, and failures. Inside the broad arc of *Wit and Science*'s dénouement – its stress on Science's warning, its climactic betrothal, and its celebratory singing – resides a recurrent, provocative seed of doubt. In that sense, Science's doubt has dramaturgical voltage, the hint of unexpended energy propelling the play beyond farce and toward seriousness. The tensions in learning displayed in *Wit and Science*, moreover, reflect the larger tension in humanism between the contemplative life and the active life, acknowledged by a host of Tudor authors. Renaissance humanism yokes the antiquarian study of classical culture with a commitment to exercise its insights on present social problems. Humanism thus points both backward toward the realm of intellectual archaeology and forward toward the realm of imminent civic action. The tension resembles that of learning conceived as something to be possessed or as something to be undertaken. Drama can address the humanist strains of learning because it will always construe ideas through the media of sensation and visceral experience. It can celebrate knowledge as distant, permanent, and Platonic, while also celebrating learning as immediate, vicissitudinous, and kinetic. Thus the contradictions of humanism do not necessarily constitute fatal flaws; such oppositions can be both useful and productive. The suspicion that one's learnedness does not guarantee one's virtue, for example, may have encouraged humanist thinkers such as Elyot to stress the importance in imaginative literature of inspirational models that could enflame the student reader to emulation. Likewise, the doubtful link between knowledge and virtuous action may have prompted humanists to encourage the exercise of specific virtues – humility, discipline, perseverance, tractability – in the process of learning, as in *Wit and Science*. Uncertainty about knowledge's effects arguably inspired humanist thinkers to configure learning in ways suited to produce personal virtue. As answer to our question, what about early drama makes it appealing to humanist education, we can now reply that drama turns a humanist paradox – that learning can be both object and process – into something rich and creative.

Lady Science and her doubt accomplish a further business that will echo through humanist and sixteenth-century drama: the gendering of knowledge as feminine. In Reson's view, Lady Science needs to be explained to the audience, and her behavior cannot be predicted, because "women oft tymes wylbe hard hartyd." As women and knowledge converge, as humanist education and chivalric romance intersect, two attributes arise: enigmaticalness and desirability. Knowledge acquires a certain elusiveness as a chivalric lady; that unpredictability is captured in the doubts of the romance heroine, Lady Science, with surprising effects. Reson can negotiate with Science, but he cannot dominate or manipulate her. Once knowledge is feminized and granted doubt, humanism, at least in this play, registers a limit to patriarchal authority. Lady Science's doubt, furthermore, suggests a mysteriousness, even an impossibility in the quest for knowledge (terrain that *Doctor Faustus* will make its own). The transformation of the enigmatic and unattainable into the desirable happens easily. One of the interesting developments in humanist dramaturgy is the way that women, portrayed as whores and virgins at the beginning of the sixteenth century, become objects of knowledge by its end. As we will see later, Robert Greene's *Friar Bacon and Friar Bungay* invokes a pun on women as "books" and turns his heroine into an object of study. Humanism feminized knowledge so as to make it attractive, to bathe it in the longing of the romance quest. Thus the need to make education metaphorically inspirational may have, in return, enlarged the possibilities for the representation of women in drama.[70]

Humanism called forth the affective capacities of drama and thus helped to shape sixteenth-century theatre. While such scholars as Bevington and Robert Weimann have taught us to appreciate the conventions of audience contact and engagement in the medieval morality tradition, the humanist pedagogical interlude requires its own special engagement from spectators: their assent to the metaphoric action of the play. That need, in turn, produces effects in *Wit and Science* that can be seen radiating through the drama of the century, effects such as the heightening of compassion and commiseration toward the protagonist, the lengthening of his transformation, the movement of the hero from individuality toward a sense of mirrored identity, the irresolvability of doubt in the paradox of knowledge, and the unveiling of new possibilities in the dramatic representation of women. While first and last a delightful and amusing schoolboy farce, *Wit and Science* also outlines the affective power of humanist dramaturgy.

3

Playing against type:
Gammer Gurton's Needle

"Prove your invention! Write a Terentian comedy about a trifle!"
Thus, scholars sometimes imagine, "Mr. S. M[aster] of Art" came
to write *Gammer Gurton's Needle* (*c.* 1553), rising to a challenge by
a fellow teacher at Christ's College, Cambridge.[1] If *Gammer Gurton's Needle* was born in the admiration of Terence, all schoolboys
have not felt that reverence, as a student of a later generation
avers: "Terence, this is stupid stuff!" With Terence as explicated
by Donatus, and Terence and Donatus as explicated by Melanchthon, thrummed and drummed into his brain, a young Tudor
grammarian might have wondered: "Is life really like classical
comedy?" To link Tudor experience and ancient art, Mr. S. infuses
Terentian structure with adolescent anxiety, confusion about
agency, and satire on academic rationalism: in humanist dramaturgy a formalist model becomes saturated with playful contradictions. Against the critique that humanist plays drift toward intellectualism, while popular morality drama accounts for early
theatre's energy, immediacy, and sense of game, *Gammer Gurton's
Needle* reveals humanist playmaking's under-appreciated theatrical
vitality and inventiveness.[2]

One virtue of *Gammer Gurton's Needle* is its open-endedness, a
feeling of unpredictable possibility, even a burgeoning sense of
emotional life and magic – qualities manifested in its impish
sabotagings of form, expectation, logic, and stereotype. In *Wit and
Science*, as we have seen, humanist drama develops its metaphoric
richness and emotional voltage to advance rhetorical ends; in
Gammer Gurton's Needle, didacticism now turns playfully ironic as
the play explores theatre's emotional life. Like other mid-
entury comedies, the drama signals an interest in empathy, and
here Hodge the bumpkin corners a major role. By inventing a
character who stands in for Everyschoolboy, Mr. S. creates a form

of spectatorial identification – composed of both attraction and repulsion – that shapes moral insight, an effect outside Roman comedic norms as analyzed by Donatus and Melanchthon. The play's open-endedness extends in other directions. Questions of dramatic agency expose how stereotyping seems to cause action and how green-world fantasticality subverts the action's superficially mechanistic logic. The play also instructs, but unexpectedly so: *Gammer Gurton's Needle* teaches the utility of error, the pervasiveness of bodily experience, and the importance of community over rationalism, satiric thrusts that seem to critique the atmosphere of conflict bedeviling mid-century Cambridge.

Mr. S. displays one of the most interesting Tudor dramaturgical imaginations prior to Shakespeare. He shows particular skill in producing ambiguity by playing a character against its stereotype, a ploy important for the dramatugy of subjectivity. He also extends the playworld with offstage life, induces spectators to infer action imaginatively, charts complex physical movement through dialogue cues, and creates a *mise-en-scène* of dirt and tatters that eventually engulfs characters. In these respects, the playwright develops what might be called "dramaturgical realism." We tend perhaps to picture a Tudor schoolmaster as drilling students in Latin declensions, rhetorical *copia*, and the ethical dicta of every literary passage that floats his way – a kind of humanist Gradgrind. But Mr. S. overturns stereotypes. From behind the parodic form of *Gammer Gurton's Needle* peeks a dramaturgy of emotional engagement; from behind the logic of causation, a crypto-Catholic marvelousness; from behind the tribute to humanist rationality, the benevolence of error. Within this play about noisy, chaotic, animalistic villagers, a curious Utopianism hums with delight.

1

By eluding Renaissance pedagogical rules for comedy, *Gammer Gurton's Needle* generates emotional engagement in the interstices of Roman form.[3] Of extant early Tudor plays, *Gammer Gurton's Needle* explores most interestingly the possibilities of the audience's identification with a character (Hodge), the kind of engagement that can lead toward empathy. In Roman comedy, the slave, such as Davos in the *Andria*, offers the play's "conduit for empathic understanding."[4] Yet Plautus and Terence show little interest in sustaining such response. Plautus settles for clichéd characters; Terence pairs off stereotypes to make moral distinctions; both maintain an air of detachment. By contrast, some vernacular academic plays of mid-century – *Jacke Jugeler* (*c.* 1550), Nicholas Udall's *Roister Doister* (*c.* 1552) – introduce sympathy for the victims. *Roister Doister*'s Christian Custance displays model virtues in an embattled position.[5] An unwilling victim of Rafe's amorous attentions, Custance emerges as the play's most sensible and sympathetic character, while the priggish males who ought to show confidence in her, including her fiancé Gawain Goodluck, too willingly doubt her honesty. *Jacke Jugeler*'s Jenkin Careaway achieves a certain comic pathos, as well, as he struggles with the predicament of having his identity stolen from him by Jacke.[6] *Gammer Gurton's Needle*, however, would hardly seem to inspire much identification. Its characters suggest English updates of Roman stereotypes: the bullying coward Hodge, the trickster Diccon, the good-natured but dim Gammer, the irascible neighbor Chat, the venal Doctor Rat. The village *mise-en-scène*, furthermore, repels with squalor. Characters are stupid, poor, hungry, and alcoholic; they speak like bumpkins, threaten violence, crawl around on the floor, and trick one another into handling animal feces; Hodge enters caked with clay and exposing his buttocks; later he befouls himself and stinks; women fight each other and tear clothes; a cleric receives a gash on the head; Hodge almost reaches into a cat's anus. These villagers behave like animals.

Gammer Gurton's Needle satirizes the village life that mid-century students at Christ's College might have known all too well and from which they might have wished to distance themselves.[7] In 1506, Godshouse College, originally created to educate school teachers, was refounded as Christ's College, under the benefaction of Lady Margaret Beaufort. The new Christ's College took as its mission "to produce an improved clergy"[8] (a goal that privileges the satire on Doctor Rat). Its forty-seven pupils, mostly from rural northern counties – as was apparently Mr. S. himself – "were chosen from poor boys who knew Latin and were preparing for Holy Orders."[9] The image of lower-class students from unsophisticated villages aspiring to a better life and essaying to improve upon their manners describes exactly the original audience, performers, and perhaps even author of *Gammer Gurton's Needle*.

The epitome of village crudeness, of course, is Hodge. The stage

rustic with his southwestern dialect was apparently "already a
matter of established convention" at the time of *Gammer Gurton's
Needle*.[10] But the play gives Hodge an especially brutish cast. His
entrance speech about "dablynge in the durt" (I.ii.1)[11] seems calculated to recall another barnyard bearer of his name: the spelling
"Hoge" occurs in John Pikeryng's *Horestes* (1567), for example, as
a variant not only for its own bumpkin Hodge but also for a farm
hog. In *Gammer*, Hodge's crawling around on hands and knees and
his battles with Gib the cat enforce the association. Yet Hodge
will also invite reappraisal, a clue to which may be found in a
later rustic character possibly based on him. In *Respublica* (1553),
attributed to the erstwhile Oxfordian Nicholas Udall, People, like
Hodge, speaks in southwestern dialect and suffers the contempt
of the Vice figures.[12] Yet People never seems as despicable as the
Vices would have him appear, and he demonstrates a noticeable
persistence – like that of Hodge – as well as a plebeian canniness
that makes the regal and trusting Respublica look naive. Hodge,
too, constitutes a formulaic yet surprisingly dynamic character,
and toward him *Gammer Gurton's Needle* develops an unanticipated
sympathy. He has always attracted attention: "This superstitious,
hard-driven, ill-fed, coarse-tongued but cheery yokel is the best
observed figure in the play, and gives the impression of having
been drawn from life."[13] Hodge's number of lines trails Diccon's
by few, and he appears in more scenes than any other character.
He also permeates the villagers' minds; like a magnet, he attracts
their ridicule, anger, and emotion; he provides a persistent object
of feeling. Hodge looms as central to the drama, that effect deriving, first, from his evocation of strong student anxieties, and,
second, from the play's reversal of perspective towards him.

Aelius Donatus, the fourth-century commentator on Terence
whose theories helped to shape Renaissance comedy, conceived of
action in three stages – protasis, epitasis, and catastrophe – the
whole driven by error.[14] The protasis explicates background and
constitutes the first act. The epitasis marks the launching of a
plot, trick, or conspiracy in the second act, which leads, in Acts III
and IV, to complications, reversals, "turbations," the entire "knot
of error."[15] The catastrophe comes in Act V with affairs suddenly
salvaged from near-disaster to happiness.[16] "Error" drives Donatus's three stages. For example, Terence's *Andria*, a Renaissance
favorite, employs an overarching social "error" about the girl

Glycerium's identity and a series of local mistakes as the slave Davos and the father Simo battle wits – all solved in the catastrophe. *Gammer Gurton's Needle* employs Donatus's system. As T. W. Baldwin describes it, the first act provides the preparation and argument, "that the needle is lost" (the protasis).[17] The second launches Diccon's trickery – the epitasis. The third develops "'the sequence of turbations . . . and the stirring of all the difficulties,'"[18] in this case, the fight between Gammer and Dame Chat. The fourth act brings the epitasis to near tragedy with the braining of Doctor Rat, while the fifth act catastrophe solves the initial problem, unravels various tricks and confusions, and restores the community to harmony.[19]

But how would one account for Hodge within Donatus's influential system? Donatian analysis fails to place him, to explain his presence in the play. While the protasis explicates the "error" of the lost needle, Hodge figures here only in absentia. In addition, his gulling – when Diccon convinces Hodge that he is raising Lucifer to find the needle, thus terrifying Hodge into soiling himself – falls exactly between the protasis and epitasis. Only after Diccon humiliates Hodge does the epitasis begin: "Is not here a clenly prancke? / . . . A man I thyncke myght make a playe" (ii.ii.3–10). In the last act, Diccon recalls the trick to embarrass Hodge, but the catastrophe leaves the deception unrevealed, providing Hodge neither recognition nor retribution. The "clenly prancke" against him stays outside the official Donatian action. While error drives Donatus's system, Hodge accounts for little motor power there either. True, his gulling aids Diccon's device; he also mistakes Gib's eyes for fire, erroneously encourages Gammer to fight with Chat and to seek Doctor Rat, and almost rakes the cat. But Hodge never makes a crucial misjudgment; the action could proceed without his mistakes. His only essential role in the plot is to be stabbed in the buttocks, because that last insult brings about the catastrophe. Donatus's dramaturgical structure fails to account for Hodge, whose storyline pursues its own life.

The Melanchthonian approach hardly fits better. Philip Melanchthon, the sixteenth-century Wittenberg scholar, replaced Donatus's emphasis with a focus on the moral imperilment that arises from error. Thus Melanchthon favors Pamphilus as the *Andria*'s principal character, because error puts him in moral danger of breaking his marriage promise to Glycerium.[20] Melanchthon also conceives of Donatus's three-part system rhetorically: protasis becomes the play's proposition; epitasis becomes *intensio*, the moment of "highest intensity."[21] Melanchthon's interpretation of Terence carried enormous authority with sixteenth-century English academics, for his ethical pedagogy, like that of Erasmus, went to the heart of the humanist educational mission.[22] Melanchthon's system echoes through *Gammer Gurton's Needle*. The first scene, for example, offers the proposition, a short rehearsal of the whole play-matter. Act III, scene iii provides a textbook example of *intensio*: the mock-epic battle between Gammer and Dame Chat.[23] Similarly, v.ii contains a precise moment of catastrophe when Diccon accidentally drives the needle into Hodge. But whom does the crucial error, the needle's loss, imperil morally? Gammer's jeopardy arises only as an intermittent, phallic double entendre – "My fayre longe strayght neele that was myne onely treasure" (I.iv.5). Act IV certainly imperils Doctor Rat with a blow to the head, yet that danger is quickly exhausted. But hazards to Hodge saturate the play. His buttocks exposed embarrassingly by his torn breeches, Hodge further suffers the loss of his dinner. Worse, he will not have mended breeches when he greets Kirstian Clack, for whom he harbors romantic hopes. Hodge's peril increases as Diccon's trick causes him to soil himself, leaving him more foul than before. Later, Hodge's reputation takes a beating, as Diccon secretly accuses him to Dame Chat of intending to steal her hens, and she reviles him. If *Gammer Gurton's Needle* parodies Gammer's loss of a trifle, it makes Hodge's dangers comically real. He thus holds the principal part, even though, oddly, he is largely irrelevant to the plot.

For Melanchthon, a parodic character could hold the central moral position. Concerning *The Eunuch*, an apparent source for *Gammer Gurton's Needle*, Melanchthon identifies Thraso, the absurd *miles gloriosus*, as most imperiled since the action jeopardizes his dishonorable lust for Thais. Because Thraso represents the moral inversion of a parodic play, he occupies the main role.[24] Does Hodge likewise represent a moralism in reverse? He behaves superstitiously and irascibly; he swaggers only to cower; filth clings to him like a bad angel. A Renaissance pedagogue could harvest some morals out of all that: "Be brave"; "Distrust cow's tails as divine signifiers." But Hodge's aims represent no moral inversion comparable to Thraso's "brothel loves." His endangerment pre-

cedes his follies, and he even displays virtues as well as "deformit-
ies": Boas calls him "honest of hand and true of tongue," neither
dishonest like Diccon nor thieving as Diccon depicts him;[25] rather,
Hodge expresses an appealing, ingenuous delight at finding the
needle for Gammer. But, most important, moralizing about Hodge
cannot unravel his emotional effect. Hodge's "imperilment,"
hardly moral at all, gestates in a domain of feeling shared by other
characters and vicariously by spectators: anger, shame, fear, and
distress. If Hodge's career demonstrates a lesson, it must take
meaning beyond the typical pedagogical apothegms for living.[26]
Mr. S.'s imitation of Terence and Plautus presents a central
character who eludes Renaissance methods of explication. Similarly, *Roister Doister* steps beyond the formulas of Roman comedy
to offer Christian Custance as a sympathetic character who "has
no counterpart in the *Eunuchus* or elsewhere."[27] Hodge – like Custance, Jenkin Careaway, or People – may stand for a dramaturgical
value important at mid-century.

2

Despite his cartoonlike simplicity, Hodge activates enough spectatorial involvement that he acquires a heightened reality or dramaturgical realism. Although the play introduces him as a negative
stereotype, the later acts build sympathy for him. He travels from
"braggart soldier" to "prodigal son," from object of disgust to
source of joy, an action independent of, but parallel to, the needle-
plot. Hodge presents a threat that the play ridicules, then displaces (onto Doctor Rat), and finally dissolves. Criticism lacks the
ideal term to describe his emotional effect. *Empathy* suggests an
untroubled connection between spectator and character, in which
playgoers temporarily vest themselves in the perspective of the
stage figure. Hodge's presence seems too vexed to command
empathy; we might find more suggestive language in *identification*
or *engagement*, allowing those words to encompass both repulsion
towards Hodge and a later good will[28] – for the character poses a
moral and emotional dilemma that the audience must solve.[29]

The play introduces Hodge, almost confrontationally, as the
object of the playgoers' gaze. His first word – "See" – calls attention to his squalid appearance: "See so cham arayed with dablynge
in the durt" (I.ii.1). After Diccon the bedlam begins the action by

describing the uproar in Gammer's house, Hodge enters, assailing the spectators' sight with his filth and raggedness and displaying his "shamefull hole" (7), either pointing to it or flapping his torn breeches. If Diccon launches a narrative, Hodge plants a physical eyesore; Diccon's entrance informs, but Hodge's provokes. The play renders Hodge powerfully "there" but also disgustingly so. His signs are dirt, clay, and particularly excrement. By his second line, Hodge is willing diarrhea upon Gammer (2); he then exposes his buttocks (7–8). He imagines an omen in a cow's "ars" (33), and he later lambasts Gammer with "I thenk you wold loes your ars, and it were loose"(i.iv.16).[30] The first act ends with Cock tricking Hodge into breaking open a stinking "Cats tourd" (i.v.53), whereupon Hodge threatens to make the lad "eate it" (54). Hodge's excremental aura would be hilariously repellent to a university audience of fifteen- and sixteen-year-old boys eager to disassociate themselves from an infantile failure to master bodily elimination and from the function's emblem, excrement.[31] A youthful sensibility must reject Hodge here; empathy would endanger its fantasy of self. Hodge asserts in the first scenes of *Gammer Gurton's Needle* a physical and emotional quality far beyond the main plot's demands.[32]

In the first act, characters become either the agents or the victims of extreme and unexplained aggression. Tib enters blamed, beaten, lamed, and hungry; she and Cock have felt Gammer's frenzy on their bones (i.iii.4–8, 13–14). And Tib cares no more for Gammer's suffering than Gammer does for hers: to Hodge's wish that Gammer had "broke her rumpe" (20), Tib replies, "we wold not greatly care / For bursting of her huckle bone or breakyng of her Chaire" (21–22). Such farcical brutishness is amplified in the first act into a subplot of anger. If Gammer tyrannizes in her anxiety, Hodge especially betrays an anger run wild. He enters upset about his soiled tatters and becomes agitated at the thought of mischance at home, guessing preternaturally that Gammer has lost her needle. Hodge flairs at Tib (i.iii.9–10), upbraids Gammer repeatedly over the needle (27–28, 40–41, i.iv.8–7, 15–18, etc.), and excoriates her for folly, incompetence, and idleness. He frets about his breeches for the next day: "Gogs deth how shall my breches be sewid, shall I go thus to morrow" (i.iv.18, cf. i.iii.38). He would beat the boy Cock but for Gammer's intervention (i.iv.49). Hodge's excessive and growing anger organizes the emotional action of scenes ii through v. This subplot creates its own mystery: what provokes his extreme intemperateness?

Hodge's anger generates responses that confirm his emotional significance. The opening act ends with Hodge banging his shins and making a fool of himself chasing after Gib the cat (whose eyes he mistakes for fire) and with Cock deceiving Hodge into handling cat feces (Gib's revenge). As Cock and Tib guffaw at Hodge, Gammer expresses the play's paradoxical scorn and pity towards her fieldhand: "See here is all the thought that the foolysh Urchyn [i.e., Cock] taketh, / And Tib me thinke at his elbowe almost as mery maketh / This is all the wyt ye haue when others make their mone" (I.v.28–30). The last line, directed to Tib and Cock, reprimands them for the kind of laughter that the first two lines, directed toward the audience, encourage among spectators. Although Gammer herself next becomes exasperated with Hodge, the play introduces complexity as its emotional subplot begins to pit laughter at him against a certain pathos. Diccon initiated the first act by celebrating food and drink, but the next act counters with a song of sadness: hunger, sickness, poverty, exposure. The song distances physical suffering through the conviviality of inebriation and singing. Diccon appropriates its spirit: "One fresh pot of ale . . . / Agaynst this colde wether, my naked armes to defende" (II.i.3–4). As if conjured, Hodge enters hungry: "Neyther butter cheese, mylke onyons fleshe nor fyshe / Saue thys poor pece of barly bread" (13–14). His missing daintrels and remaining crumbs display the play's signature concreteness. *Gammer Gurton's Needle* thus sounds the note of desperate pleasure and distress and echoes it in the speeches of Diccon and Hodge (whose rumbling stomach recalls the weak belly in the song[33]). Nonetheless, a pseudo-stage direction – "*Which bacon Diccon stole, as is declared before*" (at II.i.30) – insists that the reader laugh, and exaggerated acting of Hodge's misery would heighten the humor of his suffering. The play takes care to induce sympathy but contain its pathos.

An ambivalent spectatorial distance weaves through *Gammer Gurton's Needle*. The play raises, like Diccon's demon, those fears that particularly plague youth: fears of uncontrollable bodily functions, of sexuality, of personal odors and bad breath, of omens and demons, of hunger and poverty, even the fear of losing things. These dangers bedevil Hodge, who stands for Everyschoolboy. The play's squalid village *mise-en-scène* signifies the world from which

Everyschoolboy of Christ's College might wish to distance himself. Inside its farce, *Gammer Gurton's Needle* hides a pedagogical allegory. That half-buried pedagogical play, as the humanists developed it in *Wit and Science* (*c.* 1530–47) and its successors, outlines the transformation of an uncivilized rube into a vessel of learned grace; it shows diligence and good instruction (and good language) overcoming the body's slothfulness to achieve as prize the beautiful maiden, wisdom. Hodge exhibits the brute part of Everyschoolboy that must be mocked and ostracized. The mixture of pathos and comedy beginning Act II reflects the "underdistancing" – that is, the uncomfortable closeness to the audience – that certain emotional perils can evoke and the laughter that surmounts them.

Mr. S. also makes humor of superstition. Hodge lives by omens, premonitions, and luck, which he discovers everywhere. In the spirit of Renaissance pedagogy, we could say that Diccon teaches us to laugh at the gullibility and vacillation of the superstitious – a good moral lesson. Such ridicule promotes the attack by mid-century Cambridge Protestants on Catholic superstition. Thus in the mock conjuring of the devil, Diccon demeans Hodge by extracting servile promises, by tricking Hodge into swearing upon and kissing Diccon's breeches, and by terrifying him into bursting his "ars stryngs" (II.i.108).[34] For a Renaissance schoolboy, forced to live at close quarters with numerous other adolescents, seeing a crude, unkempt, stupid, Catholicized blusterer snivel in subservience might have been extremely satisfying.[35] Indeed, dialogue cues build up expectation for Hodge's loss of excretory control, as if to prolong audience delight. Diccon shames and embarrasses Hodge. As a staple of comedy, embarrassment has the advantage of exorcising through shared laughter the audience's latent anxieties about its parallel embarrassments. Hodge as Everyschoolboy becomes a communal scapegoat. Yet his gulling episode preserves some sympathy for him. It solves, for example, the mystery of Hodge's excessive anger in Act I. Hodge desperately needs his breeches mended by tomorrow: "Kirstian Clack Tom simsons maid, bi the masse coms hether to morow / Chamnot able to say, betweene vs what may hap, / She smyled on me the last sonday when ich put of my cap" (II.i.62–64). Although romance lives for Hodge as a version of superstition, a reading of signs and omens, his amiable ingenuousness makes him sympathetic: "She smyled on me"! Everyschoolboy's hopes soar with the same charming –

and embarrassing – ridiculousness that will become the bread and butter of Renaissance romantic comedy.

Hodge's shaming itself may generate sympathy, too. Embarrassment can make the spectator cringe; it threatens, signals danger. Hodge's broadness as a character will keep the threat of underdistancing at bay – for a while. But how far will spectators maintain their complicity in humiliating a character? However the Renaissance may have delighted in ridicule, mid-century drama also suggests a limit. *Roister Doister*'s MeryGreeke, a figure like Diccon, gulls the rather helpless Rafe into full blusterdom. As Rafe's forces gather for the climactic battle, MeryGreeke exasperates Rafe by misunderstanding his "stomake" so persistently that Rafe strikes him (at IV.vii.1637).[36] Udall may intend the moment as satisfaction for his audience: MeryGreeke's humor is not so charming as he thinks; this trickster deserves to have at least one device redound against him. Likewise in *Gammer Gurton's Needle*, the gulled Doctor Rat finally provides the audience the pleasure of seeing Diccon struck (at V.ii.214–15). Diccon's superciliousness, after Hodge exits shamed, may mark the threshhold of audience complicity: "Fy shytten knaue, and out vpon thee / Aboue all other loutes fye on thee, / Is not here a clenly prancke?" (II.ii.1–3). How much contempt and self-satisfaction has Diccon earned? His very boasting might dim his charm; after all, vainglory garners reproof in this play – as Hodge demonstrates.

Diccon invents a narrative for Hodge's identity (as a "shytten knaue") and his utility (for a "clenly prancke"). Yet to the extent that Hodge wins sympathy, he slips the net of Diccon's story. Hodge's eluding of that fiction exposes something about him that might be called "dramaturgical realism." We consider "realistic" characters to be lifelike, verisimilitudinous, close to people in everyday experience. But we might also identify a narrower version of realism. The philosopher Robert Nozick maintains that people experience themselves as more "real" in some circumstances than in others, or consider different individuals as more and less real, just as some literary characters – or works of fiction and visual art – seem more real than others.[37] Accordingly, we could call a character realistic for projecting something beyond life's ordinary presences: "The reality of these characters consists in their vividness, their sharpness of detail, the integrated way in which they function toward or are tortured over a goal ... They

are intensely concentrated portions of reality."[38] Hodge possesses
such a realism, a vividness that exceeds accounts of him such as
Diccon's. Dramaturgical realism, I would argue, activates the playgoer's speculative, inventive, and often sympathetic powers on the
character's behalf, a reciprocal response to the energy concentrated before us.[39] Hodge, that is, comes to partake of the *audience's* reality, as Mr. S. enmeshes spectators in imagining him.
Hodge also keeps turning up; his greatest virtue is persistence –
an aspect of his vividness.[40] He enters II.iii in clean but still torn
breeches, glad to find Diccon alive, and fixated on discovering the
needle. In the next act, the irrepressible Hodge appears with a
thong and awl to stitch up his pants;[41] his lines point up his jubi-
lation, his resourcefulness, and his gratitude to Sym Glover
(III.i.1–10). Hodge's good-natured persistence anchors a narrative
about him quite different from Diccon's. By the end of the play,
Hodge's amiability will finally triumph over the parasite's contempt.

To enhance Hodge's dramaturgical realism, Mr. S. confers on
him an offstage life unusual in Tudor drama at this time.[42] Hodge,
we discover, was privy to stage events even when in the wings:
After running offstage soiled and terrified, he yet overhears
Diccon's conversation with "the devil," actually Dame Chat.
Hodge avouches to Diccon, "Durst swere of a boke, chard him
rore, streight after ich was gon" (II.iii.17), and he tells Gammer,
"O the knaue creyed ho, ho, he roared and he thundred" (III.ii.13).
Indeed, Dame Chat had been roaring and thundering "Oh"
(II.ii.49, 67), and Diccon had even asked her to quiet down after
she exclaimed, "a pestlence & a mischeefe / . . . o that my nails be
short" (48–49). With the phrase "many a hoked nayle" (III.ii.20),
Hodge's description recalls Dame Chat's wish for long nails. The
play thus induces the audience twice to remember the Diccon-
Chat scene and to recognize it distorted in Hodge's fevered brain.
Hodge also embroiders the past, claiming that he has seen the
devil and describing him with details from painted tapestries of
Friar Rush (III.ii.18–22) – probably ones familiar to Christ's College students. Hodge's theatrical life transcends his actual
moments on the boards, as his imagination swallows the scenes of
other characters. His vividness grows as he evokes associations,
comparisons, and recollections in the audience. No other character
lives in the same way. Such dramaturgy makes Hodge less a sacri-

ficial scapegoat for our embarrassments and more an inexplicable theatrical presence attracting attention, pleasure, and engagement.

The third act develops another aspect of Hodge, the *miles gloriosus*, the village (or school) bully – but just as quickly, the action qualifies that view.[43] Hodge recalls the stereotype of the braggart soldier in Plautus and in English dramas such as *Roister Doister*, but his effect on the play differs from the conventional. With Plautus, Terence, and Udall, the *miles gloriosus* play generally reaches its climax, or summa epitasis, in the fourth act (rather than *Gammer*'s third), when the braggart soldier marches his comic, toss-pot forces to battle (with women) only to run away at the offered engagement (sometimes beaten on the way), thereby revealing the risible deformity of his cowardice compared to his vaunts.[44] Fight scenes in most early Tudor plays proceed improvisationally, with undiscriminating stage directions for actors: *They fight*. The dialogue of *Gammer Gurton's Needle*, by contrast, cues a fight scene (III.iii) more complex and choreographed than those in Plautus, Terence, or any Tudor play to date, another sign of Mr. S.'s attention to dramaturgy. The ebb and flow of action includes Hodge, who first holds the stage with Gammer as she approaches Dame Chat's house; then stands at the fight's periphery and shouts encouragement to Gammer as Chat drubs her (III.iii.28–31); next retreats into Gammer's house at Chat's menacing (at 32); re-enters through the audience swinging a staff and threatening Chat (35–38); looks back anxiously, in the face of Chat's advance, as Cock starts to close Gammer's door for safety (41); and finally dashes into the house as Chat pursues him (41–43).

Dame Chat's attack renders Hodge a blusterer and a coward. Why then would a critic such as Boas say "Yet he comes lustily to his mistress's aid with his staff when she is being worsted by Dame Chat"?[45] Unlike the typical epitasis for the *miles gloriosus*, the action here concedes something to Hodge: he does interject himself to save Gammer, and he does distract Chat so that Gammer can recover and jump on her from behind. Hodge boasts falsely, yet a smidgen truthfully: "By the masse Gammer, but for my staffe Chat had gone nye to spyl you" (III.iii.53). Although Hodge continues his comic vainglory (expressing fear that he might kill someone [58]), he also encourages the battered and downcast Gammer to "plucke vp your hart, and leue of al this

glo[m]mi[n]g" (80). The action diverges from the typical thrashing of the swaggering soldier. While the pretensions of the *miles
gloriosus* to sexual desirability justify his pummelling by women,
Hodge lacks such presumptions, so that his exposure in the epitasis does not require the conventional intensity and revenge. Hodge
emerges as weak-spined, but he also voices real sympathy for
Gammer – voices it partly on behalf of the audience – responding
to, just as he has helped to inscribe, the play's subtext of distress.

In the next scene, Hodge, at his most disgusting, confirms his
spectatorial charm. In this comic coda to the fight, his violent
impulses focus on Gib, the cat: "By the masse dame Chat hays me
so moued, iche care not what I kyll, ma god a vowe" (III.iv.16).
Hodge threatens to reach his hand into Gib's fundament ("holde
vp her tayle" [17]), or attempts to peer into it ("Chil see what
deuil is in her guts" [18]), actions renewing his excremental
associations. Lowered to his buffoonish nadir, Hodge still does not
evoke the vengeance traditionally aimed at the braggart soldier.
The episode emphasizes his comic crudity and, simultaneously,
the wonderful obsession with finding the needle that guides it.
Also showcased is a rare live-animal passage in Tudor drama. Tib
holds the cat (surely the college cat[46]) throughout, although
Gammer handles it and Hodge gropes at it repeatedly. The stand-
off of dialogue and unpredictable cat responses must make the
scene hilarious; the play scripts its own violation of the border
between the written and the improvisational. Dramaturgical
realism invests such moments, not because they are so lifelike but
because they appropriate the lifelike so vividly and engagingly for
the audience.

As part of his dramaturgical recuperation, Hodge now receives
a virtuosic exit, as he takes center stage for a plot-summarizing
speech requiring the actor to repeat (and vary) "see now" twenty-
four times in as many lines (IV.ii.5-28)

> My Gammer gurton heare see now,
>   sat her downe at this doore, see now:
> And as she began to stirre her, see now,
>   her neele fell in the floore, see now . . . .

Here the fourteeners split, and the speeding phrases of narrative
constantly play against the blocking "see now." The speech
demands an actorly *tour de force*. If Hodge first presented himself

on "See" (I.ii.1), he likewise takes a bow on "see now." Hodge's history also reinvents the play: he introduces Dame Chat's "blacke cup" (IV.ii.14) and reiterates his own heroic intervention (25), all of which Gammer avouches as true (29). Hodge's speech emphasizes the "wondrous" (12, 20, 24), a word that captures, like an intersection, his palpable innocence, the play's farcical events, and the virtuosity of the speaker's performance. The pleasure of the acting enhances the charm of Hodge's dramaturgical realism.

Playing against type helps to distinguish mid-century perspectives on character before the advent of figures possessing inner lives.[47] It reveals, likewise, an interest in emotional complexity. In *Gammer Gurton's Needle*, the first three acts create Hodge in terms of a stereotype, increasingly qualified, but the last two acts arouse audience sympathies for Hodge against that stereotype. The defeat of the *miles gloriosus* usually dominates the fourth act as the epitasis of the braggart-soldier play, but Hodge is baffled in the third act instead and vanishes from the fourth. To the extent that he represents the play's most imperiled character, in the Melanchthonian system, Hodge's disappearance surprises doubly. Even as a subplot, the Hodge line diverges here from the model as Donatus or Melanchthon would have understood it, for with Terence the subplot usually gathers steam in the fourth act rather than halting. What effect does Hodge's excision create?

Like Terence, who contrasts characters in similar situations to reveal moral differences – as Erasmus and Melanchthon noted[48] – Mr. S. arrays his figures in matched sets: Tib and Cock, Gammer and Chat, Diccon and Baylye, Hodge and Rat. Doctor Rat acts as Hodge's double and enters the play virtually as the antidote to Hodge's confustications (III.iii.21), but the bumpkin improves in relation to the vicar: Mr. S. rehabilitates Hodge by means of Doctor Rat. As the play progresses, Hodge's former gullibility and bluster come to look more and more like naivete, sincerity, and even innocence. Doctor Rat enters in the position of a rational outsider, but he quickly taints himself with venality and hypocrisy, as he complains that he must flatter his parishioners for their tithes and Christmas gifts (IV.i.1–16). Now Doctor Rat takes up Hodge's role as the butt of Diccon's japes: immediately after divulging his duplicity to Doctor Rat (V.ii.41–49), Diccon deceives him with lies, disinvests him symbolically, and induces him to crawl ferretlike through the hole in Dame Chat's wall and take a beating. Rat commits trespass and, metaphorically, sexual assault; his fall from rationality flatters Hodge by comparison.

Hodge also gains from Diccon's and Dame Chat's false accusations and invective. Diccon fictionalizes Hodge as a stalking Senecan avenger who, bent on retribution for being exposed as a coward, has vowed to murder Dame Chat's hens: "like a mad man he farde, / And sware by heauen and hell, he would a wreake his sorowe" (IV.ii.87–88). Chat calls him "great knaue" (72), "dirty dastard" (76), and "horsen dolt" (82). Although at first she doubts that Hodge would dare venture onto her ground (92), her desire to thrash him gets the better of her, and she rises to the prospect of swingeing him and landing him in "scalding water" (103). *Gammer Gurton's Needle* revels in vituperative excess, but this dialogue caricatures Hodge beyond the impression he has just registered. The gap between such vilification and the audience's changing view of Hodge culminates in Act v.

Bitterly refusing to forgive, Doctor Rat himself fulfills, in the final act, the comic image of implacable avenger that Diccon had assigned to Hodge. The words used to traduce Hodge might serve well now as stage directions for Doctor Rat: "starte and flyng" (IV.ii.85), "moyling" (86), "mad man," "sware by heauen and hell, he would a wreake his sorowe." By replacing Hodge with Rat in the fourth act (and placing Hodge's epitasis in the third), Mr. S. redirects contempt toward Rat and allows Hodge to assume a new dramaturgical position. Hodge himself dimly grasps that Rat has succeeded him as object of derision: "Was not wel blest ga[m]mer, to scape y scoure, & chad ben there / The[n] chad ben drest be like, as ill by the masse, as gaffar vicar" (V.ii.196–97). To underline his changed position, the dialogue stresses Hodge's innocence and his incapability of the crimes of which Chat accuses him. Chat repeats her invective against Hodge from Act IV (e.g. 45, 50–51, 53, 68), but Gammer insists on Hodge's honesty (67, 74), and Hodge himself gets his moment of righteous indignation: "Ich defy them al that dare it say, cham as true as the best. / . . . Take[n] there? no master chold not dot, for a house ful of gold" (88–90).[49] Now the curate displays irrationality, anger, and failed self-awareness as Baylye reiterates Rat's culpability and Rat persistently fails to understand it.

The last act completes the recuperation of Hodge, from superstitious, dim-witted, irascible, bragging coward to honest, indignant, endearing defender of his gammer. Mr. S. accomplishes that feat not by changing Hodge so much as by manipulating his dramaturgical position and thereby the audience's relationship to him. Interestingly, Diccon alludes to Hodge's incontinence (253–55) but does not explain the episode: it hangs in the air suddenly as a moment of anxiety that the audience might share with Hodge.[50] Nothing comes of it; nothing *can* come of it. Because Hodge has changed position in the play, his humiliation now would be dramatically unacceptable. Almost like a prodigal son, Hodge leads the rejoicing at the found needle: "Cham I not a good sonne gammer, cham I not" (311). As Duncan argues, Rat incarnates pride, but Hodge (whom Duncan associates with Adam) achieves approval through humility: "by the end of the play, and chiefly through the contrast with Rat, his [i.e., Hodge's] humility has been tacitly approved: the slow-dawning delight he shares with his mistress when the needle is found endears him to the audience."[51] Duncan notes the partially realized sense that Hodge acquires moral stature, that his career plays out a progress from bluster to humility, from imperilment to propriety. Hodge's persistence becomes a virtue – a deft schoolmasterish gesture worthy of *Wit and Science*. The analytical systems of the Terentian commentators cannot quite comprehend Hodge, whose movement recalls the prodigal son. But Hodge achieves redemption not so much from narrative as from dramaturgy, which confers on him a special, engaging realism and reveals his good nature. By the end, *Gammer Gurton's Needle* transforms the anxiety and excessive emotion continually aimed at Hodge into a joy shared with him. Hodge, for whom the embedded needle recapitulates and transforms his humiliations and suffering, achieves a relationship with the audience very close to the empathic.

3

I want to turn now from playing against type in the arena of character to playing against expectations in the arenas of agency and rationalism. Hodge's dramaturgical vitality obviates categories and materializes possibilities against the grain of assumptions, putative truths, and classical form. In so doing, he defines a strategy that can be generalized to other aspects of the play, for

instance, its treatment of the large question of causation. What Hodge embodies at the level of character, Diccon portrays at the level of agency. *Gammer Gurton's Needle* exhibits two contradictory etiologies that intersect in Diccon and that lead us into the disputatious environment of mid-century Cambridge. On one hand, Diccon demonstrates a logical, mechanistic, stimulus-and-response version of causation. He presents himself as a playwright and stage manager, vents his cynical rationalism by manipulating others, and justifies his acts of false witness by claiming that he merely exposes characters as the fools they already are. When Baylye accuses him of having caused all the trouble, Diccon replies that he has merely revealed the true "madnes" of these characters (v.ii.229–233; see also II.iii.4). This version of agency imagines people as fools, baffles them, and orchestrates them for predictable results. Here various currents converge in Diccon: besides the manipulating Roman parasite and the conspiratorial medieval Vice, Diccon also bears traces of polemical Protestantism, for he reveals in Hodge a superstition condemned by reformists.[52]

In fact Diccon behaves as more than a social engineer; he also acts as a demon, one conjured from the language of popular interjection. To some degree, he functions as the satirist of lingering Catholic behavior under attack by the early Anglican Church: superstition, exorcism, invocation of saints, elaborate self-blessing, lighting of mass candles, indolent tavern-loitering by the clergy.[53] Yet Diccon also gives off a whiff of sulfur. Echoing the devil, he fathers lies and capitalizes on human vanities. *[D]ickon* and *dikkon*, according to the *Oxford English Dictionary*, are variants of the interjection *dickens*, as in "I cannot tell what the dickens his name is" (*Merry Wives of Windsor*, III.ii.19–20),[54] where *dickens* substitutes for *devil*. That form of expression Diccon himself invokes: "I can not tel where ye devil he was kept" (II.ii.41), he cries impatiently. More than any other character, Diccon uses devil-interjections.[55] The word *dickens* commonly expresses astonishment and impatience; it invokes demonism to explain something surprising or inexplicable: "What the dickens!" we exclaim. The word arises, too, in phrases such as "play the dickens," meaning "to cause mischief or havoc." Trickster and mischief-maker, Diccon incarnates these slang notions of the devil. He wears the aura of a folk-demon, like Friar Rush, expressive of the play's village provenance and idiom. Just as *dickens* is a rhetorical interjection,

Diccon is a quasi-demonic interjection in the playworld. In that respect, he justifies something of the Catholic superstition that he would seem to ridicule.

As a causal agent, Diccon the demon creates results more astonishing than Diccon the rationalist appreciates. With the mock-conjuring that Diccon performs for Hodge, Mr. S. links Diccon early with the devil. Thereafter "Dyccons deuill" (III.iii.65) haunts Hodge's memory.[56] Diccon's conjuration also furthers his devices unintentionally. What Diccon alleges the devil to have said, for example, becomes grounds, through Hodge's inventive memory, for the fieldhand's agitating of Gammer to confront Chat and his encouraging of Gammer to solicit Doctor Rat's help, developments independent of Diccon's stratagems. Diccon's tricks even threaten to spin out of control. The humbling of Doctor Rat ("And Doctor Rat shall thus catch, some good" [IV.ii.65]) goes far beyond what Diccon intended, and Diccon runs offstage fearing Rat's murder: "Gogs bread, I am afraide, they wil beate out his braine" (IV.ii.149). Finally, of course, Diccon's unprovoked swatting of Hodge in the buttocks unexpectedly brings home the lost needle.

In this second, demonic version of causation, things happen beyond orchestration, by chance and fortune, by magic. Diccon's second agency supports the superstitiousness that Diccon himself ridicules in Hodge. Mr. S. delivers a delicious irony in having the puckish Diccon play upon Hodge's belief in omens, conjurations, and hovering sprites so that Diccon-the-rationalist can sneer in triumph. The play installs two etiologies, one mechanistic, the other metaphysical. They both claim some truth: Gammer's needle resides where logic would lead one to look, yet it can be discovered only through fortune. The play ridicules irrationality but solves its dilemma through a madcap gesture. Did Mr. S. intend that auditors should recognize these contraries? The model of Roman comedy suggests "yes." Donatus's treatment of error, as in the *Andria*, recognizes characters' local misjudgments, as well as a different order of error, the social mislabeling of children separated catastrophically from their parents. Terentian comedy celebrates human ingenuity and, simultaneously, a Providence beyond it. Mr. S. gives such dualism a sixteenth-century coloration as he honors Hodge's good-natured persistence ("Ich knew that ich must finde it, els choud a had it neuer" [v.ii.313]) along with the meddlings of a rather mischievous (and dangerous)

Providence. Critics generally view a farce such as *Gammer Gurton's Needle* as remote from Shakespearean romance, but one might argue that Mr. S. interweaves richly the two worlds of Athens and the woods elaborated later by Shakespeare.

The rational and irrational again knit as etiology in the characters' penchant for stereotyping, a form of communal agency that Diccon encourages. *Gammer Gurton's Needle* exposes the short-sighted and vain assumptions by which people act. Indeed stereotyping itself functions as a kind of causation. To deceive Dame Chat, Diccon paints Hodge as a blusterer: "like a mad man he farde, / And sware by heauen and hell, he would a wreake his sorowe / And leue you never a hen on liue, by viii. of the clock to morow" (IV.ii.87–89). At first Dame Chat does not believe Diccon (92), apparently because, moments earlier, a blustering Hodge has collapsed before her onslaught. But Diccon's mention of the hole behind the stove, whereby a "crafty knaue, may crepe in" (95), brings Chat around. Diccon convinces her by a stereotype (Hodge will bluster but play the sneak) believable to her, a stereotype, moreover, that she *wants* to believe: "O christ that I were sure of it, in faith he shuld haue his mede" (98). Dame Chat typecasts herself as the scourge and avenger of pusillanimous bragging knaves. Diccon's lie works because it activates compelling images: a character's self-righteous vanity encouraged by the stereotype she has of another character. Similarly Diccon engenders Chat's anger towards Gammer by means of a second easy target, Tib, whom he stereotypes as the gossiping maid (II.ii.42). Diccon likewise limns his lie to Gammer, that Chat stole the needle, by mimicking Chat as a haughty scold (II.iv.30–31). While humanist pedagogues treated literary exemplars of virtue and vice as Platonically inspiring, Mr. S. implicitly cautions against idealization's deluding excesses.

Ironically, as characters act on the stereotypical images they hold, they make themselves more and more like rats, hens, cats, foxes, and bandogs. Doctor Rat, of course, who pities himself for a dog's life, creeps like a rat through a hole and is taken for a fox in a henhouse. In such manner the characters make themselves more and more like each other; the more sharply they stereotype one another, the more they efface their own differences. Gammer and Chat, as their flyting escalates, can only sound increasingly redundant:

CHAT	Mary fy on thee, thou old gyb ...
GA[M]MER	Nay fy on thee yu rampe, thou ryg ...
CHAT	A vengeaunce on those lips ...
GA[M]MER	A vengeance on those callats hips ... (III.iii.17–20)

Amid the internal rhymes, the stock epithets, and the shouting, everyone sounds – and acts – the same. Likewise, as the play progresses, characters come to look more and more alike. The action wraps them in clay, filth, mud, and tatters, just as it causes them to behave like animals. The villagers become Mud Creatures, and their compounded errors render them stunned, baffled, and amazed.[57] The Mud World exposes a degenerate sameness based on illogic and pretensions to superiority; it is the mid-century counterpart to Shakespeare's dew-drenched Athenian wood in which identities converge, and it inspires a similar bafflement and wonder.

The satire of stereotyping in *Gammer Gurton's Needle* complements the play's mix of humanist, Protestant, Catholic, and morality-drama perspectives. Although Protestant humanists had gained ascendency in mid-century Cambridge, the university was still a gallimaufry of theological positions – Catholic, Lutheran, Calvinist, Zwinglian – a hotbed of old and new. Issues such as justification, the Real Presence, and even vestments occasioned scholastic disagreement, accusations, and label-mongering. In matters of theology, Cambridge masters seemed to have indulged in a certain contentiousness, even an easy recourse to name-calling and stereotyping.[58] Yet some voices also sought a middle way, as in the first *Book of Common Prayer* or the efforts of the celebrated Protestant conciliator Martin Bucer, who lived his last two years at Cambridge, 1549 to 1551.[59] Likewise, Mr. S.'s etiology combines various perspectives complexly, even ironically, and exposes the errors of a stereotyping mentality as so much human – and perhaps intellectual – mud.

Gammer Gurton's Needle seems to invite schoolmasterish aphorizing for the edification of Cambridge students: work hard, as if your efforts shall have results, but trust to Providence.[60] In such a formulation the indefatigable Hodge emerges again as the moral surprise. But *Gammer Gurton's Needle* holds many didactic surprises. Some critics regard the play's educational values as illustrated negatively: how not to reason, how not to argue.[61] Tib's "we myght it [i.e., the needle] fynd if we knew where it laye" (I.v.9), for example, makes humor from what students would recognize as a logical tautology. Yet *Gammer Gurton's Needle* turns the tables on any auditorial complacency, because the play establishes a case for benign misunderstanding. In doing so, Mr. S. makes communal goals more important than rationalistic ones; additionally, yielding oneself to the good of the whole suggests a further valorizing of "identification." Emotionalism, sensate responses, and class values all derail rationality. No character shows perfect thinking, and full disclosure, the prerequisite of understanding, also eludes them. Even the clear-headed Baylye can jump to a conclusion and fall into error: when Dame Chat makes her accusation against the absent Hodge, Baylye, impatient over Chat's dilations, leaps well ahead of any evidence: "Cal me the knaue hether, he shal sure kysse the stockes. / I shall teach him a lesson, for filching hens or cocks" (v.ii.54–55). Nor do all the play's knots come unraveled: the smug Diccon never learns that Hodge's imaginary witness of the devil facilitates the parasite's lies, just as Hodge never recognizes the conjuring as false, and the other villagers never discover his soiling of himself.[62] *Gammer Gurton's Needle* denies the possibility, and perhaps desirability, of a perfectly rational settlement.

Bodily experience also blocks reason. Indeed, the character most schooled in logic offers its most sensate response. Mr. S. emphasizes Doctor Rat's injured head: stage directions thrice call for Rat to show his broken pate (at v.i.21, v.ii.24, 29), demonstrations requiring a highly visible head wound. Only a substantial, ugly insignia would justify Diccon's fear for Doctor Rat's life and the curate's explosive rage in the last scene. Such concreteness has appeared earlier in the play in references to hunger, cold, sickness, and exposure. Not surprisingly, then, Rat's broken head proves incontrovertibly – to him – that Dame Chat has notoriously wronged him: "This profe I trow may serue, though I no word spoke" (v.ii.24). Rat casts himself, furthermore, in his favorite paradigms and images: "a poore man . . . spoyled: and beaten among theeues" (v.i.4), "an honest learned Clarke" (15). Baylye spotlights Rat's failed logic as he insists on the vicar's culpability (v.i.1–2, 7–13, 16–20). For the Tudor pedagogue, Doctor Rat might illustrate how physical pain or pleasure threaten reason. After all, the Renaissance academy routinely cautioned against the beguilements of sensate experience.[63] But Mr. S. has more than that up his sleeve. Doctor Rat cannot *grasp* Baylye's accusation. The head wound does not exactly drive out Rat's rational powers (although it does function symbolically); rather, the wound establishes the physiological premises from which Doctor Rat will reason: "Is not this evill ynough, I pray you as you thinke?" (v.i.21). The body claims its own logic, and *Gammer Gurton's Needle* has already showcased movingly the power of physical concerns – about clothing, food, drink, elimination – to direct action. No appeal to reason convinces Doctor Rat; angry almost to the end, he agrees to forgo revenge against Diccon exclusively on the grounds of communal identification: "My part is the worst, but since you al here on agree. / Go euen to master Bayly, let it be so for mee" (v.ii.266–67). *Gammer Gurton's Needle* suggests that only something beyond rationality, a strongly felt sense of community, can mediate the imperatives of our physical being.

In another reversal, class privilege also takes a beating. Doctor Rat argues not only from his broken head but also from his curatorial position. He represents himself as an honest, learned clerk, as if honesty were inseparable from learning; Dame Chat, conversely, devolves into a "queane" of dark corners (v.ii.18–19). His social position, Rat contends, guarantees his innocence and integrity, an argument from hierarchy and even patriarchy (as Baylye's rejoinder implicitly recognizes at v.i.22–24). In convincing Rat to remove his frock before crawling into the hole, Diccon demonstrated that Rat's voyeurism exceeded his standing as curate. Master Baylye dismisses Rat's superiority with the communitarian and commonsense assertion that all are equal in the dark (and "in the dark" pretty much describes village life here). Thus the audience of prospective curates is invited to identify with those who laugh at the presumptions of a village pastor. Against rule by class, Baylye achieves a negotiated solution, sorting conflicting testimony, rejecting extreme punishment, acknowledging the humor of Diccon's trick as well as the insult, and offering to forego his fee in return for mutual agreement.[64] The underlying values of the academic *Gammer Gurton's Needle* turn out to be aligned with the kind of village principles it ostensibly satirizes.

Intellectually, *Gammer Gurton's Needle* achieves its ultimate moment with the "penaunce" (v.ii.259) that Baylye imposes on Diccon (270–87). Penance for trickery, however, constitutes a trick of its own, because Baylye's "sentence" sounds like tasks and

restrictions but really instructs Diccon to take honest advantage
of the villagers: for example, "To goodwife chat thou shalt be
sworne, euen on the same wyse / If she refuse thy money once,
neuer to offer it twise" (278–79). The humor derives from Baylye
and Diccon enjoying the superfluousness of these promises, while
the villagers revel in the satisfaction of vindication. "Come on
fellow Diccon chalbe euen with thee now" (288), crows Hodge in
a moment of proto-Dogberrian exhilaration that Diccon shall
"neuer take him, for fine gentleman" (287). Error reigns. While
Plautus and Terence unravel and exorcise error, achieving
communal knowledge as the expression of amity, Mr. S. reestab-
lishes it, as if social harmony needs the lubricant of some benevolent deception. Donatian error, in the form of slippages in meaning, works to reknit the community rather than to create
imperilment. Baylye's sentence insists that binding a community
together in fellowship and good humor surpasses rationality as a
social goal and class privilege as a social value. As Gammer
gathers the whole company for the ritual of drinking together,
Diccon highlights the achieved mutuality: "Soft syrs, take vs with
you, the company shalbe the more, / As proude coms behind they
say, as any goes before" (330–31).[65]

The ambiguous language of the ending invites comment on a
final aspect of the play: its purple epithets, its rich plebeian voice,
its sheer linguistic profusion. We have noted this profusion in the
flyting between Dame Chat and Gammer: "doting drab, avaunt";
"bawdie bitche"; "A bag and a wallet"; "A carte for a callet";
"Thou slut, y^u kut, y^u rakes, y^u iakes"; "Thou skald, thou bald,
thou rotten, yu glotton" (III.iii.5, 21–26). *Gammer Gurton's Needle*
delights in the fecundity and superfluity of language. A similar
quality marks *Roister Doister* – for example, in the numerous epithets that MeryGreeke hurls against Rafe, disproportionate to
Rafe's actual behavior. That love of language – colorful invective,
plebeian coinages, alliteration, rhyme, *copia* – finds a counterpart,
as we have noted, in the rolling thunder of Hugh Latimer's preaching. The play may be aiming another barb at Cambridge academic
disputes. Mid-century humanists, such as John Cheke, Thomas
Smith, Nicholas Udall, Thomas Wilson, and Roger Ascham, took
a new interest in English vernacular, and *Gammer Gurton's Needle*,
with its transmutation of comic Roman form into English village
life, matches that interest. The Cambridge humanists promoted

a plain style: "we never affect any strange inkhorn terms but so speak as is commonly received, neither seeking to be overfine nor yet living overcareless, using our speech as most men do."[66] They sought an orderly, controlled, denotative language reflective of a Ciceronian purity and authority.[67] Again, *Gammer Gurton's Needle* provides both the rationalist model and its refutation. The play excels in the vernacular style, demonstrating its fertility, artfulness, and often its aptness; simultaneously, the language produces more confusion than could any inkhorn Latinisms, quaint proverbs, blind allegories, or dark words. Characters believe their excessive invective out of sheer love; in the paradigmatic flyting, communication collapses and confusion reigns. *Gammer Gurton's Needle* appears to satirize the search for pure and authoritative vernacular, just as it satirizes the rationalist dream that inspires it.

Gammer Gurton's Needle fashions delight from its ambivalences, its sense of openness and ironic possibility. While mocking stupidity, superstition, bravado, and brutality, it forges spectatorial identification with its satirical objects – particularly with Hodge, through the pathos and triumph of his comic persistence. Likewise, the play calls into question rationalist logic about agency, didactic wisdom, even language. By the end, though truth and intelligence largely prevail, they do so only to the extent that they serve a greater communal good. *Gammer Gurton's Needle* does not lend itself well to narrow, aphoristic moralizing of the kind we might too willingly expect of a mid-sixteenth century schoolmaster. Rather the play challenges a simple-minded didacticism by means of audience identification and delight, and it demonstrates the remarkable suppleness and vitality of academic humanist dramaturgy. Its sense of engagement flows outward, finally, as logic gives way to that greater object of humanist desire, the commonweal.

4

Time, tyranny, and suspense in political drama of the 1560s

The early 1560s mark a watershed in Tudor drama, when both popular and humanist theatre exploit an affective, psychological dramaturgy. In 1531, Sir Thomas Elyot, in *The Boke named the Gouernour*, argued that literary images of virtue can so inflame the heart as to stir readers to moral emulation. By the 1580s, however, antitheatricalists such as Stephen Gosson could charge that drama's excitement of spectators' passions outstrips its influence upon their ethics. That new distrust of drama's emotive power may have been well founded, for English playwrights in the 1560s elaborated audience-arousing strategies: variety; fantasy; wish fulfillment; spectacle; and, not least, time-related devices such as anticipation, retrospection, and expansion or compression of action – leading to a new quality of suspense. Emotional and psychological effects become increasingly important to theatrical meaning, a change that includes both popular and humanist drama and suggests that these presumably separate traditions may share affective common ground.

The 1560s, of course, mark a watershed in Tudor history: Elizabeth's ascension; the reinstitution of Protestantism; the end of religious burnings; the Marian exiles' return; the expansion of humanism; and the emergence of political, religious, and intellectual leaders of a new generation. These realignments encouraged political reconsiderations on the stage. Thus one common theme of early Elizabethan plays – including *Cambises* (*c.* 1561), *Gorboduc* (1562), *Appius and Virginia* (*c.* 1564), *Damon and Pithias* (1564), *Jocasta* (1566), *Gismond of Salerne* (*c.* 1566), and *Horestes* (S.R. 1567) – is tyranny.[1] With the exploration of tyranny comes a collateral dramatic interest in court counsellors, trials, executions, and moral dilemmas about civic responsibility in a monarchy. Released from Mary's regime, Elizabethans embraced a new sense of history. If writers of the 1580s endeavored to remake the national culture, the humanists of the 1560s reshaped England's consciousness of historical processes. Translations of Continental histories enlarged historiographic and political self-awareness, a development coincident with the recognition of a generational and philosophical change in the country's leadership. Not surprisingly, a sense of historical narrative registers upon the decade's drama, with its dynastic upheavals and questions of cultural, cosmic, and personal causation.

England also adopted a Protestantism that sought evidence of salvation in subjective experience. Gosson himself bears witness to redemption's equation with inner fervor: "The worde of God is liuelie, and mightie in operation: being liuelie, if it doe not quicken and stirre vs vp to a newenesse of life, it is a token that we haue no life, but are alreadie stone deade, in the workes of darkenes."[2] Thus the language of personal religious transformation comes to overlap with the humanist language of aesthetic effect, of awe and inspiration, captured in Elyot's image of learning as fire in the heart: "the childes courage, inflamed by the frequent redynge of noble poetes, dayly more and more desireth to have experience in those thinges, that they so vehemently do commende."[3] But Gosson argues that drama overstimulates audiences dangerously with sights and sounds, and *Playes Confuted* is alive with depictions of spectators amazed, agog, almost inebriated with drama's delights. In the theatre, wonder takes on a demonic power, unmoored from God's "newenesse of life." Twenty years earlier, notwithstanding theatre's potential "to moue any manne ... to that which is euil," William Bavande had concluded that spectators could turn play-acting to good use by applying their own moral imaginations.[4] But such optimism hardly squares with the Protestant fear of romantic comedy a few decades later. Something changed.

In the 1560s, dramatic effect spills beyond didacticism to emphasize narrative complexity, psychological agitation, and Senecan sensationalism. That last element deserves comment. Early Tudor plays range in tone from comic to tragic and in character from liminal Vice to allegorical Mankind – so that, in Nicholas Grimald's words, "variety may be opposed to satiety."[5] Those values blossomed as Inns of Court playwrights imported Senecan form and its principle of amplitude, whereby tragedy

explores a central problem from a variety of perspectives not logically or emotionally consistent. In *Medea*, argues Joel Altman, "our
attention is continually being diverted from one focus of interest
to another," so that the play "encourages the most widely differentiated kinds of reaction – horror, compassion, nostalgia, fear,
admiration, even wry amusement – in what seems to be a deliberate attempt to keep us continually responding anew."[6] Likewise
early Elizabethan tragedy delivers a cacophony of emotion; according to Bruce Smith, its thrilling speeches, ornate spectacle, music,
choruses, and dumb shows generate inconsistencies but little
tension.[7]

Yet 1560s plays do develop tension, one that arises in relation
to stage time: narrative sequence, proximity of events, anticipation and retrospection, temporal expansions and contractions,
and ultimately suspense. The sequence and time-span of dramatic
events influence the impressions that can be drawn from action;
the way in which plays present the truth shapes the truth presented. For political drama, that realization is momentous.
Cambises, *Gorboduc*, and *Damon and Pithias* show early Elizabethan
theatre exploring the dramaturgy of proximity, chronology, and
suspense. Thomas Preston's *Cambises* reflects the morality tradition; it virtually defines "popular" theatre, from its doubled roles
to its sensationalist violence. Sackville and Norton's *Gorboduc* looks
like *Cambises*'s opposite: a humanist Inns of Court play with Senecan characters, long rhetorical speeches, offstage action, and
scores of performers. Richard Edwards's *Damon and Pithias* splits
the difference as an Oxford playwright's court tragicomedy
employing both popular and learned elements and winning broad
acclaim.[8] If we can determine that these plays share an affective
dramaturgy, then we will not only have identified the emotional
values, intertwined with political concerns, that shape a generation of dramatists; we will also have revealed a theatricality that
washes across both humanist and popular traditions.

1

Cambises's theatrical pleasure, critics agree, conflicts with its
political message: Ambidexter's audience-delighting highjinks, in
particular, seem irrelevant to the chronicle plot, which records a
tyrant's cruelty and self-degradation.[9] But ambidexterity, I would

argue, defines a principle of emotional structure. The play derives theatrical energy from its dynamic swings, its changes of fortune and reversals of emotion, so that *Cambises* trains the audience in expectation and surprise. Even more, it trains the audience to feel a sequence of emotions that are not just disparate but contradictory – sorrow and laughter, engulfment and anxiety – toward identical objects. By those strategies, the meanings of events remain open to retrospective revision, new interpretation, yielding ambidexterity of response as an affective structure. *Cambises* records a sixteenth-century shift in drama, both by heightening emotional effect and by theatricalizing meaning as diachronic – and if changeable over time, perhaps inherently unstable, historical.

As the seat of desires and affections, the heart is *Cambises*'s most conspicuous image, establishing the primary, emotional level on which characters – and, vicariously, spectators – respond.[10] Cambises's "harts intent" is to subdue the Egyptians: "So shall I win honors delight" (18, 19).[11] War offers an honorable "delight," while drink poses a dangerous one (33–34). The play characterizes the king by his exuberance: "to see you heer, my hart it dooth delight" (488) and "O Lording deer and brother mine, I joy your state to see" (654; see also 671). Cambises expresses a like thrill even after murdering his brother: "Since he is dead this hart of mine, in corps I feel it joy" (874); and coercing the Lady into marriage evokes further exhilaration: "Come on my Lords with gladsome harts, let us rejoyce with glee" (935). Cambises can also treat his enemies to a savage irony of liking: "Untrustful traitor and corrupt Judge, how likest thou this complaint?," he says to Sisamnes (391; see also 407). Cambises strikes at his victims by obliterating their joys: "I knowe thou haste a blisful babe, wherin thou doost delight" (509), he exults, planning to murder Praxaspes's son.

The king's irrepressible pleasure makes for kinesthetic appeal, with auditors fascinated by "the scope and energy of his being."[12] Cambises, nonetheless, showcases the flaws of self-indulgence that humanists catalogued in tyrants: bestiality, effeminacy, and theatricality.[13] Yet, despite his degeneracy, the king's enthusiasm and energy invite a recuperative spectatorial pleasure – such as "king Cambises' vein" gives to Falstaff and his tavern spectators – one that operates too pervasively to be discounted as incidental to the play's ethical sentiments. That pleasure may unveil an incipient appeal to fantasy and wish fulfillment of the sort later realized in *Tamburlaine*. Delight so obviates morality that critics find it politically subversive as well as psychologically provocative. It suggests a movement away from the spectatorial poetics imagined by Elyot and Bavande, in which the audience responds to the stage representation of evil from within its own strongly held ethical perspective. But is delight's tension with morality merely latent in *Cambises*, or does it structure response?

We can begin to answer by noting that *Cambises* institutes a pattern of auditorial anticipation and surprise. The corrupt Sisamnes's beheading is highly theatricalized, and not only by means of its visual effects. If *Appius and Virginia* draws out the death of its heroine, Preston goes farther with Sisamnes's execution, delaying it enough that it acquires the rudiments of suspense. Three times (415, 420, 439) Cambises proclaims that Sisamnes will be publicly executed, but events intervene.[14] The king calls for the executioner and then for Sisamnes's son, Otian, who arrives and speaks, and then for the executioner again. Although Cambises declares his verdict, Otian's plea for mercy forestalls action. The king then orders Execution to "Dispatch with swoord this Judges life" and adds, shockingly, "draw thou his cursed skin, strait over bothe his eares" (437–38). But the father and son take leave for so long that Cambises loses patience: "Dispatch even now thou man of death, no longer seeme to stay" (457). Expectation and delay create enough suspense that the moral lesson of justice recedes as the paramount audience response. The Sisamnes episode invites varying reactions from spectators, and sympathy may even shift toward the condemned judge as the execution approaches: "the victim, stripped of the power that made him fearsome before, is newly perceived as one who suffers, while the righteous avenger begins to accrue some of the distancing qualities previously associated with his antagonist."[15] That shift in sympathy is abetted by the filtering of the execution through the eyes of Sisamnes's loving son.[16] Yet the violence is a virtuosic theatrical spectacle that would now divert audience response from sympathy itself. The famous stage direction "*Flea him with a false skin*" (s.d. at 464) aims for a *coup de théâtre* of spectacle. Its hyperrealism is all the more striking for following a stage direction to pantomime: "*Smite him in the neck with a swoord to signify his death*" (s.d.

at 460) – the miming occasioning a flow of realistic stage blood (461). Pathos or Grand Guignol? The dialogue and visuals make both effects available, propinquitous, as if audience response could so oscillate between them that they become coextensive.

The audience may not turn completely against Cambises until the killing of Praxaspes's son, an episode that mirrors the father's previous slaying. The second killing's "proximity and similarity" to the first "blur the distinction between them, making Cambises in retrospect seem responsible for parallel atrocities,"[17] so that the play achieves a powerfully theatrical – not logical – effect. We might call that effect retrospective revision. Yet for the second time spectators will also be diverted by the visual *coup de théâtre*, here Cambises's slaying of the boy with an arrow and the evisceration of his heart as proof of marksmanship.[18] The spectacle enforces contrary responses. In the Sisamnes–Praxaspes sequence – the central and longest scene of the play – audience reactions will move from moral outrage to sympathy for prospective suffering to morally disengaging absorption in spectacle: *Cambises* orchestrates Senecan multiplicity of response and, finally, mutually canceling attitudes toward the same event.

If Cambises's cruelty can obliterate our sense of his earlier justness, furthermore, present and past can interpenetrate moments later in the Mother's lament. Here the counterpoint of memory and stage spectacle theatrically overpowers the fourteener's conventionalism. Raising her son's bloody body from the ground, wrapping it in her white apron, the Mother memorializes him in imagery that juxtaposes former vitality with present death: "O blisful babe, O joy of womb" (579). She remembers the travail and delight of childbirth, the nurturing, the play: "And daunced thee upon my knee" (592). The passage culminates verbally and visually as she kisses her child's now-lifeless lips, "silk soft and pleasant white" (597), the poignance of his death amplified by the contrast between the kinesthetically felt past and the child's slack corpse.

As the harrowing infanticide and the Mother's pathos might hint, *Cambises* offers the most highly theatricalized violence in Tudor drama to 1561; indeed, *Cambises* "may well be the first English play to use violence rhetorically."[19] As Charney observes, nonetheless, Renaissance drama demonstrates a theatrical, even aesthetic fascination with stage violence that exceeds any moral consideration.[20] Some of *Cambises*'s taste for violence may derive from political memory. Cambises's war against the Egyptians and his execution of Sisamnes, for example, might recall Henry VIII's French war and his execution of Sir Richard Empson and Edmund Dudley at the beginning of his reign.[21] Ambidexter likens Cambises to Bishop Bonner (1141), the infamous persecutor of Protestants under Mary, called "Bloody Bonner" and notorious for his cruelty and rage. In the Marian burnings between 1555 and 1558, one hundred and thirteen men and women (almost one third the total) were executed in Bonner's diocese of London.[22] Mary's deadly politics may inform Ambidexter's threat to have Hob and Lob "martered" (792). How do the powerless respond to a violence that in a half decade left its image seared into the English consciousness? *Cambises*'s transformation of political butchery into an aesthetic event may illustrate English society's need to assert distance from, even power over what in *Realpolitik* remained outside its control. The play's theatrical experience may occupy common ground with its political message to endure a tyrant; theatrical subversion and political containment emerge strangely as two faces of the same coin.

Ambidexter generates anxiety in the audience about its absorption in spectacle. After the Sisamnes-Praxaspes episode and the Mother's lament, the Vice takes the stage and addresses the audience: "In deed as ye say I have been absent a long space. / But is not my cosin Cutpurse, with you in the mene time?" (602–03). That thrust may shock playgoers into awareness of their engulfment by the play and thus their vulnerability to pickpockets. Ambidexter's mention of Cutpurse cultivates anxiety about the very pleasures that spectators have just experienced. The pleasures *of* the theatre are dangers *in* the theatre, which tension Ambidexter weaves back into the play itself. Later, in the middle of exciting the audience about Cambises's and the Queen's impending banquet, Ambidexter suddenly shifts focus, prompting momentary confusion and surprise: "is it not best: / That I be so bolde as to bid a gest? / He is as honest a man as ever spurd Cow: / My cosin Cutpurse I meane" (998–1001). Ambidexter then addresses Cutpurse directly in the audience, perhaps "spotting" an actual spectator (1002–09). By contrast, Haphazard, the Vice in R. B.'s *Appius and Virginia*, invites Cutpurse to go with him to execution almost as an afterthought; in Pickeryng's *Horestes*, as the

Vyce exits the play, he likewise casts a backward glance at Cut-purse among the spectators. While both Haphazard and *Horestes*'s Vyce are duplicitous, they do not attempt to shock playgoers as does Ambidexter, who can deliver a *frisson*, a shudder in the theatre of spectatorship akin to the earlier shudder in the theatre of horror.

Ambidexter renders feelings unstable and meaning diachronic. His soliloquy over Smirdis's pathetic and lurid murder divides into two halves, the first evoking tears (732–42), the second, laughter (743–53). "O the passion of God, yunder is a hevy Court" (732), the Vice begins, escalating in the next eight lines: "*Weep*" (s.d. at 739); "O my hart, how my pulses doo beat" (740). How ought the actor to play that speech, ironically or sincerely? To represent ambidexterity fully, the actor might well imitate authentic sorrow, especially since the stage direction and the monologue demand symptoms of grief. Enacting sorrow would then make Ambidexter's collapse into laughter all the more shocking, an effect consonant with others in the play. Theatre works partly by infection: spectators laugh or laugh harder because others are laughing; thus the stage-acting of sorrow or hilarity invites spectatorial reciprocity. One dramaturgical goal of Ambidexter's speech, then, is to make the audience feel grief succeeded by the shock of amusement toward the same object – retrospective revision – and by means of that apposition to threaten the validity of both emotions. To some degree, of course, such Vice business is standard: *Horestes*'s Vyce speaks contemptuously about Clytemnestra, condemned to death by her son; but when Horestes suddenly sighs in anguish at what he has commanded, the Vyce likewise launches his own weeping and wailing. More than other Vices, however, Ambidexter cultivates the audience's participation in his histrionics.

Now enters another dialectic, in the form of the country neighbors Hob and Lob. According to *Cambises*'s acting scheme, the performers who play Hob and Lob also play Crueltie and Murder respectively, who slay Smerdis moments before they re-appear as the harmless bumpkins. Crueltie and Murder make a homey pair when they enter earlier "*with bloody hands*" to execute Smirdis: "My coequall partner *Murder*, come away. / From me, long thou maist not stay" (710–11), opens Crueltie. They sound a bit like clowns as they drift verbally for a moment before getting to work. Crueltie's opening line finds a later echo from his double, Hob: "Gods

hat Naibor come away, its time to market to go" (754). Likewise,
Crueltie and Murder's exit, dragging their victim's carcass, is
closely followed by Hob and Lob's entrance, discussing slaughtered
farm animals: says Hob, "Chave twoo Goslings . . . and a Calves
hed: / A zennight zince to morrow it hath been dead" (760–63).
They proceed to shake their own heads over the king's cruelty:
"Zome zay he deale cruelly, his Brother he did kil," offers Lob
(772; see also 777). The murderers become the moralists – and
imminently the victims. At first joining Hob and Lob in denouncing Cambises, Ambidexter suddenly threatens to have them mar-
tyred for speaking treason against the king. The threat occasions
a comic, quivering retreat by the two: "O gentleman ye shall have
two Pearepyes and tel not of me" (794), offers Hob. Because the
audience knows that nothing will happen to Hob and Lob by virtue
of their burlesque ontology, members can enjoy seeing "Crueltie"
and "Murder" tremble in their buskins. Preston also makes sure
that Ambidexter receives a swingeing from Marian May-Be-Good
(acted by the boy who played Otian), a business convenient for
spectatorial venting of residual animosity toward him. With its
doubling of parts, comic exaggeration, and ethical redress, the
scene encourages spectators to guffaw – with nervousness or
relief – at circumstances that moments before excited pathos.

　　Such auditorial ambidexterity constitutes a pattern in *Cambises*.
Critics suggest that Ambidexter may reflect back to playgoers
their own deviousness, but we might say that Ambidexter, and the
dramaturgy, seek rather to fashion the audience. Spectators learn
to experience sudden and shocking emotions and moral responses
but to privilege none of them, because meaning turns contradictory over time. With its delays, surprises, juxtapositions, and
reversals, Preston's dramaturgy of chronology keeps meaning open
and contingent, darkly mirroring England's religious and political
changes in the 1550s and 1560s. *Cambises* registers the complexity
and difficulty in finding a useful perspective toward violent social
change.

2

The first English neoclassical tragedy, *Gorboduc*, like *Cambises*,
experiments with anticipation, retrospection, and open possibility.
Written by Thomas Sackville and Thomas Norton for Twelfth

Night of the 1561–62 Christmas revels of the Inner Temple,[23] *Gorboduc* came to court on January 18. In the 1560s the Inns of Court nurtured "a compact, self-conscious, renaissance movement" of young Protestant humanists conspicuous for a burst of translations.[24] They sought to distinguish themselves from the preceding generation of scholars and leaders and identified instead with the young queen and the Protestant leadership at court, particularly Lord Robert Dudley.[25] "Minerva's men" contributed translations of the classics and of Continental writing to the new politics, some instructing England in the modern arts of war, others emphasizing the obedience the populace owes to the prince – important issues in Elizabeth's infant reign.[26] Translated works promoted, as well, the humanist idea of an "organic" state that grows, prospers, or declines.[27] John Brende expatiates upon the perils of such a state: "In historyes it is appara[n]t how dau[n]gerous it is to begyn alteracions in a co[m]men wealth, how enuy & hatredes oft risyng upo[n] smal causes, haue ben the destruction of great kyngdomes."[28] Minor disturbances can have gigantic consequences that jeopardize the state's delicate balance, and here Minerva's men reveal a political circumspection compatible with Elizabeth's instincts. *Gorboduc* will virtually embody their critique.

That a play would arise alongside the new interest in historiography is not accidental. While humanism was promoting the study of history and the recognition of historical difference,[29] drama was beginning at mid-century to draw plot and inspiration from the chronicle histories. Earlier, historical study had been strongly commended by Elyot who, in *The Gouernour*, describes reading Julius Caesar and Sallust as a dramatic experience.[30] In 1574, Thomas Blundeville published *The true order and Methode of wryting and reading Hystories*, the "first separately printed treatise in English on the art of history"[31] – actually a translation of two Italian works – as a contribution to the Inns of Court humanist movement. Sackville and Norton surely knew Blundeville, with whom they shared political attitudes. Blundeville's *Of Councils and Counselors* (1570),[32] for example, agrees strikingly with the perspective on royal advisors in *Gorboduc*. Blundeville dedicates *Of Councils* to Robert Dudley, earl of Leicester, and suggests that in the attributes of counsellorship the earl may see himself "as it were in a glasse."[33] Blundeville had a long relationship with

Leicester, a prominent member of the Inner Temple, and he was also connected with court scholars who embraced the new Italian views of historiography.[34] According to Blundeville, Leicester was an avid reader of histories, and in *Of Councils*, Blundeville names as a counsellor's fourth most important quality "To be a good Hystoriographer."[35] Blundeville's pioneering *The true order and Methode* was "the direct outgrowth of the enthusiasm for the study of history on the part of an important group at court – men of affairs, who were certain of the real value of historical learning."[36] Dudley patronized that group. He also served as the constable-marshall and a leading participant in the Inner Temple revels of 1561 for which *Gorboduc* was written and staged.

Gorboduc's presumed advice about succession has attracted attention, but dramaturgically the play investigates something broader, the problem of historical agency, as we shall see. Concerning the writing of history, Blundeville stresses the importance of human actions and urges the historian to discuss the background, education, reasoning, and affections of the doer. He also emphasizes attention to the conditions and context in which events occur. Overall, Blundeville describes historical action as having a dramatic structure: the story of a city or country will divide into "beginning, augmentacion, state, declynacion, and end."[37] Those stages recall the five stages of dramatic action that humanists derived from Terence: beginning, protasis, epitasis, climax, and dénouement. Likewise, Blundeville recommends narrating a complex event in a manner that in drama corresponds to a succession of scenes within an act.[38] The organic state parallels the organic play.

But for Blundeville, writing history is not the same as reading it. For one, the history writer explores human agency, but the reader learns "to acknowledge the prouidence of God, wherby all things are gouerned and directed."[39] Unlike the writer, moreover, the reader may proceed according to three different "methods": in "obseruing the meanes to attayne the ende," the reader may move (1) forward from the beginning to the end, or (2) backward from the end to the beginning, or (3) in stages of "general kinds" of means.[40] These methods produce different impressions.[41] When tracing a war from beginning to end, for example, one might start with the provisioning of money and armor, the levying of soldiers, and the like, on to the final battle. In the second method, "you

begin at the victorie, and co[n]sider the next causes thereof, as to
haue fought with more valiauntnesse, or wyth greater force, or
with more aduauntage eyther of place, time, or occasion," and
move back to the beginning.[42] But an account of how well the army
was provisioned will not necessarily yield the same impression as
an account of how valiantly the soldiers fought. When one reads
history, the sequence of details influences the meaning. *Gorboduc*'s
sophisticated grasp of effects available from narrative chronology
coincides with Blundeville's sense of the difference between writing and reading history and his three reading strategies. While
Gorboduc does favor certain political actions, it also advocates more
subtly a cautious perspective sensitive to multiple ways of seeing.
That virtue finds embodiment in a type, the advisor-
historiographer. One individual well poised to offer himself to Elizabeth as such a counsellor (among other things) was that royal
intimate and Inner Templar extraordinaire, Lord Robert Dudley.[43]

For *Gorboduc*'s first audiences, its neoclassic "austerities"
amounted to a dramatic "novelty," a startling and "glamour[ous]"
challenge to theatrical convention – and, according to Tillyard,
only when we imagine "a certain awe" created in its spectators
can we explain the play's impact.[44] A recently discovered first hand
account by a courtier who attended the premier performance confirms that impression.[45] The play's innovative dumb shows strike
the courtier, who contends that the second pantomime favors Elizabeth's marriage to Dudley rather than to the king of Sweden and
adds that "Many things were handled of marriage," as if the dumb
shows crystallized *Gorboduc*'s meaning.[46] The courtier's account
illuminates a problem in the history of the play's reception. In the
twentieth century, literary critics often adhere to the tenet that
the best interpretation is that which explains best the whole of a
narrative. A sixteenth-century viewer, however, might single out
the political implication of one aspect of a play as definitive, without excessive concern for its relationship to every other part. In
the 1560s an interpretive tension registers between the part and
the whole,[47] as drama begins to take on an "organic" form akin to
that of the state. *Gorboduc* has tempted modern critics to apply
analytical protocols resembling those used by the courtier. Most
interpreters stress *Gorboduc*'s presumed political advice about succession, weighing disproportionately the royal counsellors'
speeches in the last scene (although no consensus has formed

about what their advice may be).[48] The weakness of partial interpretations is that each can claim as much viability as the next. *Gorboduc* makes itself vulnerable to such "episodic" readings because it seems overdetermined with causes: tryanny, unnatural affection, ambition, jealousy, misunderstanding, the will of the gods – the play offers a tightly woven action, but an excess of human and cosmic agents. Considered episodically, *Gorboduc* falls into segments: each act is virtually self-contained (as "The Argument of The Tragedie"[49] demonstrates), and its characters develop separate tragic mistakes, so that any act could be read as the explanation of the whole. The play further undermines certainty with reversals and retrospective revisions, as in the case of Ferrex and Porrex. On the other hand, the action acquires, and characters announce, a certain fatalism driving the whole, and the play reiterates images, such as the responsive heart, and themes, such as the gods' curse on the descendants of Troy.[50] Dramaturgically, *Gorboduc* trades on the tension between local contingency and overarching inevitability.

Of interest for our purposes are temporal impressions, prospective hints, and retrospective revisions used to establish and then overthrow interpretations. As a blueprint for spectatorial response, *Gorboduc* invites its audience to note connections, compare characters and events, and ponder causal relationships. The play sets up emotions of anticipation and foreboding, intellectual pleasures of discernment, and surprises from retrospective recognition: those feelings constitute a major affective dimension, but the play also shares *Cambises*'s destabilizing of certainty and presages *Damon and Pithias*'s elaborate suspense. *Gorboduc*, as we shall see, complicates its spectatorial experience with ambivalences and ambiguities, creating an open-endedness in which "smal causes" can have unpredictable results. Dramaturgy invades agency, which comes to reflect not so much the chronology of deeds as the chronology of report; as with Blundeville, the order for revealing history shapes the meaning of history.[51]

Gorboduc begins from the point of view of Videna, the queen.[52] Sleepless with anger, Videna fears that Gorboduc "will endeuour to procure assent / Of all his counsell" that day to his "fonde devise" of dividing the kingdom (1.i.49–50). Videna tags the king with a "froward will" (14) and a mind "firmly fixed" against objection (46), because, presumably, he spites her love for their

older son, Ferrex (22–29). She fears, too, that sycophantic counsellors will give in "To please the present fancie of the prince"
(60). By opening with Videna, the scene would explain Gorboduc's
behavior prejudicially and in advance; it asserts jealousy, not
reason, as the king's motive and declares his obduracy. The scene
also isolates Videna. She will play no part in the ensuing decision,
which sets the tragedy in motion, yet her protective love for Ferrex
and her wrath against Porrex – whom she regards as "enuious"
(33) and disdainful – will lead her to murder her younger son.
The scene has one more twist. Ferrex resists Videna's appraisals:
"Iust hath my father bene to euery wight. / His first vniustice he
will not extend / To me" (41–43). The episode thus anticipates
Gorboduc ambivalently, with passionate opposition, yet also a hint
of demurring generosity.

Despite Videna's answer-in-advance, the question lingers over
the play: why does Gorboduc divide his kingdom and bestow the
halves upon Ferrex and Porrex? The counsellors differ about his
plan: Arostus favors both parts; Philander, the first but not the
second; Eubulus neither. They debate – at some length – serious
Elizabethan issues: nature versus nurture; love for "kinde" versus
personal ambition; precedence by birth versus precedence by
merit; learning by authority versus learning by model or experience. Each argument can claim some credibility, and no one position clearly defeats the others. If the dissenter Eubulus "wins" in
the spectator's mind, it may be less because of his irrefragable
logic and more because Videna has scoured the king's plan first
and because Eubulus speaks last. Dramaturgy as much as reason
selects the most convincing argument; the sequencing of events
offers a determinism that ratiocination cannot.

But why does Gorboduc reject Eubulus's logic? Contrary to Videna's accusation of willfulness, Gorboduc earnestly solicits advice
(i.ii.29), and positively, too, he declares as one of his purposes that
"The kingdome yet may with vnbroken course, / Haue certayne
prince" (8–9). The critic Franco Moretti, nonetheless, enlarges
Videna's position into a theory of tyranny. He identifies Gorboduc's decision as a seminal moment of conflict between will (the
"tyrant" king) and reason (the counsellors) that will characterize
English tragedy and eventuate in civil war.[53] Gorboduc's response
to his counsellors appears almost breezy: after listening
silently for 260 lines he dismisses all reservations in a half-dozen

pentameters, that abruptness seeming to confirm Videna's caricature. But Gorboduc does answer, if briskly, Philander and Eubulus's negative arguments – and in a way that law students at the
Inns of Court might recognize. The last two advisers have couched
their arguments in universal principles. Philander fears what
broils might erupt if the young sons are given their head but
insists that he does not single out Ferrex and Porrex ("[w]hom I
esteeme" [216]) so much as acknowledge "certeine rules, /
Whiche kinde hath graft within the mind of man" (218–19),
whose violation "doth corrupt the state / Of myndes and thinges,
euen in the best of all" (221–22). Eubulus also speaks in hypo-
theticals and categoricals: "perhappes" (284) Ferrex shall think
himself wronged; "Perhappes" (290) Porrex will become
ambitious; "flatterie" will "assaile / The tendre mindes of yet
vnskillfull youth" (291–92). Gorboduc rejects Philander and Eubulus's essentialist arguments by claiming that the facts do not fit
the principles:

> But sithe I see no cause to draw my minde,
> To feare the nature of my louing sonnes,
> Or to misdeme that enuie or disdaine,
> Can there worke hate, where nature planteth loue,
> In one selfe purpose do I still abide.   (337–42)

My sons are not as you describe, Gorboduc insists not unreason-
ably. While each speaker's argument builds on universal principles, those values inevitably conflict with each other. Love for
kindred is strong, but is ambition or envy stronger? *Gorboduc* recapitulates a Renaissance philosophical problem, one that dogged
Tudor legal practice: the problem of multiple and sometimes
incompatible absolutes. Thus the appeal to maxims turns out,
ironically, to be open-ended. The king's rejection of conflicting
categoricals in favor of a self-flattering empiricism rebounds as a
sudden, unexpected resolution to the debate – a theatrical surprise. Dramatically, then, as well as rhetorically, doubt leaks into
the moment like light under a door. Gorboduc's answer remains
cryptic, its philosophical dimensions difficult to absorb, and he now
seems dismissive in a way that belies his initial receptiveness. For
spectators, the opening act juxtaposes expectation and surprise,
producing a tension built on the chronological arrangement of
events and the variations in stage time allotted to them.

Sackville and Norton's dramaturgy of chronology colors the struggle between Gorboduc's sons, Ferrex and Porrex. In the second act, each impression we have of the two is overthrown by subsequent information, in a repeated rhythm of provisional clarity followed by retrospective revision – the technique employed so successfully in *Cambises*. We begin at Ferrex's court, where the elder brother and his counsellors "meruaile much" (II.i.1) over Gorboduc's decision, the previous act's doubt hanging in the air. Views of Porrex are contradictory: Ferrex caricatures Porrex's "pride, his rage, / The mindefull malice of his grudging harte" (61–62), terms that recapitulate Videna's denunciation of her younger son, while Dordan, a good angel, claims in contrast that he never saw in Porrex fraternal malice or "vnyelding pride" (72). In these disagreements, however, antagonism edges out good will. The debate creates the dramaturgical frame, the field of possibility, that will help define the yet-unseen Porrex, just as Videna and Ferrex defined the absent Gorboduc.[54] Ferrex rejects Herman's advice to attack Porrex; nonetheless, since he fears his "yonger brothers rage" (185), Ferrex decides to arm himself defensively "in secrete" (190). Thus Ferrex apparently chooses the middle course of probity and caution – but as the scene closes, Dordan predicts civil strife and rushes off to urge the king to intervene.

Views of the brothers alternate in the ensuing scenes. At his own castle, Porrex ponders his elder sibling's intentions: "And doth he so prepare, / Against his brother as his mortall foe?" (II.ii.1–2). The news that Ferrex prepares for war gives an impression rather different from that left in the previous scene, and Tyndar, a bad angel, eggs Porrex on by claiming that Ferrex's courtiers traduce Porrex and exclaim against "so great a wrong" (13) done to their lord. The report rewrites the events just witnessed by the audience. Braving his brother, Porrex resolves to "inuade" Ferrex's "realme, / And seeke the traitour prince within his court" (54–55). The scene ends with the adviser Philander, like Dordan earlier, hastening off to the king "Ere this mischiefe come to the likely end" (74). Is Porrex a prideful hothead, as Videna and Ferrex have painted him? Or is he prudent in the face of danger? The present circumstances and the previous caricatures may favor the former view, but only temporarily. Subsequent action challenges auditorial impressions. Dordan's letter to Gorboduc claims that Ferrex (not Porrex), "misledde" by the fraud of "yong vntempred wittes, / Assembleth force" against his brother and, full of the "furyous panges of hys enflamed head," prepares "to wreke the great pretended wrong" of his disinheritance "With ciuyll sword vpon his brothers life" (III.i.32–39). Dordan describes an impetuous firebrand rather than a cautious elder brother: Ferrex here sounds like Porrex. Next, the king learns that Porrex has "with soden force invaded" (159) Ferrex's kingdom, has slain Ferrex, and has possessed his realm. That message locates aggression unambiguously in young Porrex. There's more. Porrex now appears before his father, describes his previous efforts to win his brother's love, and accuses Ferrex of having once tried to poison him: thus, explains Porrex, he resolved "To shed his bloud and seeke my safetie so" (IV.ii.129).

Will the real Ferrex and Porrex please stand up? The troubles here are not a matter of artless bungling by Sackville and Norton. Rather, the pendulum-swings of information and assessment suggest orchestration, each new shading or revelation a challenge to established belief. Porrex's poisoning story is a dramaturgical tactic – information revealed late in the game that revises interpretation of a whole chain of events. Sackville and Norton experiment with the spectatorial effects of details, impressions, and evidence arrayed contrapuntally, a dramaturgy by chronology. It would appear impossible and finally inappropriate to extract the "true" promptings of Ferrex and Porrex – just as Gorboduc's initial "reason" resists scrutiny. The two brothers' "characters" ultimately seem called forth, invented, by the circumstances that embroil them. Sackville and Norton invite the audience first to infer motives, then progressively and retrospectively to revise those motives, until the process defeats any conclusions – an effect that makes local interpretations attractive. The dramaturgy may be the message.

While the play's first half stresses action – swift, compressed, elliptically reported – the second half, particularly Act IV, stresses reaction. The fourth act focuses on moments of suspended time in which a character experiences a kind of transcendence or fixation.[55] Videna's lament for the murdered Ferrex (IV.i.1–81) provides one such occasion. She refers progressively to "these handes" (5), "this brest" (6; see also 19), "this palace here" (7), "these hugie frames" (9), "this most hard and cruell soile" (11). Such deictic references, particularly to hands and breast, invite actorly gesture and movement that draw the audience toward the local and immediate. That kinesthetic imagery facilitates Videna's transformation. In a long address, she imagines Porrex's blood-lust, his "murderous minde" (37), and his bestiality; consum-mately, she "refuse[s]" (65) a maternal bond with him: "Never, O wretch, this wombe conceiued thee" (67). Videna's apostrophe to Porrex rises to an incantatory and feverish pitch. In Seneca's *Medea* the heroine's passionate rage produces after the infanticide an eerie calm, a sense of having passed through to another exper-iental realm. Likewise, Videna not only alienates Porrex as her son, she also transcends her hesitations, achieves the detachment that makes the murder possible. The queen intrudes powerfully on *Gorboduc*. Baffled, marginalized, she recovers the stage in a way that gives human will a rapturous and mysterious agency. The kingdom's political "system" has no place for Videna, her con-cerns, or her anger – just as Corinth had no place for Medea. But if politically marginal, she becomes dramatically central, pos-sessing a voice and ghostly presence that expose the flaws of the political system.

Marcella's lament for Porrex and narrative of his death (IV.ii.166–266) constitute a different kind of suspended moment. Videna soliloquized alone, but Marcella's rehearsal is punctuated by responses from the men around her: Gorboduc repeatedly interjects and finally hurtles offstage with Eubulus; Arostus reacts with horror as she unfolds Videna's revenge. In contrast to the responses of the king and his advisors, Marcella appears spell-bound by what she has witnessed. The nurse's fixation represents the last ripple of the stone dropped in the water by Videna's hor-rific possession. Marcella's opening dialogue recalls the queen: "Oh where is ruth? Or where is pitie now? / Whether is gentle hart and mercy fled" (166–67) when a mother can murder her own child? The question "where is pitie now?" will become almost palpable when Marcella describes Porrex calling out to his mother for help (204–13). Echoing Videna's deictic phrases, Marcella refers to the queen's "owne hand" (183; see also 188, 213) and "stony brestes" (168; see also 172, 182), the image of hardened maternal breasts redounding especially through the episode – "O Queene of adamant, O marble brest" (233) – so that Marcella's language evokes and completes Videna's metamorphosis.

As Porrex's "ruthefull stedfast eye" (220) had fixed upon

Marcella's face, her mental gaze now fixes upon him: "O what a
looke, / . . . which to my death / Will neuer part fro me" (219–
22). Sight, or rather the memory of sight, channels the audience's
imagination: "these eyes behelde . . . the driery sight" (184–85).
What Marcella sees most is the transition to death: "That with
these eyes of him a perelesse prince, / Sonne to a king, and in the
flower of youth, / Euen with a twinke a senselesse stock I saw"
(200–02). Marcella's mind's eye traverses again and again that
transformation from "flower of youth" to "senselesse stock," as
each of four speeches culminates in the shock of Porrex's sudden
lifelessness (187–90, 199–202, 203–26, 248–56). The repetition,
a kind of "stop-time" disrupting the play's chronological linearity,
makes for powerful dramaturgy. Marcella's fixation even achieves
a psychological resonance, for beneath the horrified gaze pools the
shadow of something personal:

> Ah noble prince, how oft haue I behelde
> Thee mounted on thy fierce and traumpling stede,
> Shining in armour bright before the tilt,
> And with they mistresse sleue tied on thy helme,
> And charge they staffe to please thy ladies eye,
> That bowed the head peece of they frendly foe?   (248–53)

That picture offers the final reinvention of Porrex, here nostal-
gically as the heroic knight of chivalric romance. To infer that
Marcella was in love with Porrex seems presumptuous – Lamb's
suggestion notwithstanding[56] – but his image deeply stirs her
emotions and imagination. "[To] please thy lady's eye" conjures
forth the fantasy world that has been replaced by the horrific. As
a last surprise, Marcella's affection for Porrex relumes her shock
at Videna's cruelty – the soft breast against the stony. Marcella
acquires dramatic life; perhaps for that reason, she brings Porrex
remarkably alive, too, remembering his chivalry and poignant
death. In that, she recalls the Mother in *Cambises*, who, clutching
the body of her dead son, evokes his extinguished vitality. The
Renaissance stage learns to resound with what is absent, lost.[57]
Videna's metamorphosis and Marcella's fixation create a discrete
sense of time working in *Gorboduc*, as their soliloquies claim an
immediacy made resonant with the future and the past.

Act v initiates a pattern of displacement that will become familiar in Elizabethan tragedy. In contrast to the expanded time of
Marcella's story, the act leapfrogs over events and introduces new

characters with a different, more national perspective. It opens with an assembly of the nobles, who resolve to join forces to suppress the popular rebellion and reestablish authority in the fractured kingdom. But when they leave the stage, Fergus, duke of Albany, lingers.[58] Like the two slain princes, Fergus is a proud, ambitious opportunist, and he sees through the present chaos a way to the throne. "Shall I," Fergus asks himself, "Refuse to venture life to winne a crowne?" (v.i.136–41). In the next scene the other nobles, returning from victory over the rebels, discover that Fergus and his army await them in the field. Again, the sequencing of events – the registering of success undercut by the surprise of new broils already known to the audience – maintains an effective dramaturgical rhythm.

In the last act England assumes the character of maiden or mother in a way that brings the play's past alive in the kingdom's future. The earlier forlorn maiden and unnatural mother both haunt the language. For Fergus, England is a damsel in distress: "*Brittayne* land now desert left alone / . . . Offers her selfe vnto that noble hart / That will or dare pursue to beare her crowne" (132–35). The other nobles imagine a more maternal England. Eubulus wonders that "from thy wombe should spring / . . . those, that will needs destroy / And ruyne thee and eke themselves" (v.ii.20–22), a sentiment that recalls Videna, as if her unnatural motherhood had produced its mirrored image magnified across the land. More simply, Mandud calls England the "common mother" who "Cries vnto vs to helpe our selues and her" (98–102). Arostus combines the images of England as mother and as vulnerable maiden: "For Brittaine land the mother of ye all" (135), he says, is now threatened by "climbing pride" (131), "lust" (133, 141), and "proude attemptes" (137). Even with the new field of action, the newly compressed events, the new characters, and the new stakes among them, Sackville and Norton keep the past adumbrated in the present.

Just as the play insists upon alternate impressions of human nature and events, the ending of *Gorboduc* offers two visions of the future. In the first, Arostus foresees victory for the united dukes but pleads with the nobles to surrender their individual aspirations to the "common counsell" (157). The more fatalistic Eubulus declaims the second vision: he imagines England destroyed by ambition, pride, "rising mindes" (193), a scenario that occasions a thinly veiled appeal to the Elizabethan Parliament to settle the succession question. Of the two closing visions, Eubulus holds the darker view of human nature, his fears are alarmingly credible, and he speaks last, the truth-position. We have now circled back to *Gorboduc*'s opening question: are human pride, greed, and aspiration so great that men will destroy kind and kindred to satisfy them? While the past is prologue, the play's multiple responses to the same circumstance admit a certain open-endedness. Can we control our destiny? The play affords the audience – the Inns audience composed of Parliamentarians and counsellors to the queen – another chance, a *present* chance, to decide that consummate question. By reiterating the historical past in the actual present, the presumably removed *Gorboduc* bridges the distance between the world and the play.[59]

What in *Gorboduc* might have appealed to Elizabeth? One might argue that the play encourages inaction on the queen's part as much as it encourages disposition by Parliament. In the 1560s, of course, Elizabeth was troubled by two claimants to succession: Catherine Grey, the Protestant, and Mary of Scotland, the Catholic. For Elizabeth to declare one of them her heir in 1561 would have been to make attractive and powerful a woman who was either partially or completely outside Elizabeth's own control. For Gorboduc, after all, the best course of action would have been no action – no dividing the kingdom, no designating successors. The problem of a throne without an established heir was, for England, a prospective one; the threats from Catherine and Mary were, for Elizabeth, immediate. *Gorboduc*'s ending shows the dangers of no succession, while its beginning shows the perils of overzealous succession. Overzealousness, in fact, results in no successor: better to pursue a politics of caution and counsel.

While *Cambises* employs the platea-centered Vice figure of morality drama, and *Gorboduc* the psychological realism and locus-based narrative complexity of classical drama, the two share dramaturgical common ground. Both achieve emotional and psychological impact by managing stage chronology – juxtaposition, retrospective revision, expectation, surprise, and expansions and contractions of time. That characteristic squares with the new humanist interest in historiography. *Cambises* teaches the audience to laugh at circumstances that have just caused it to weep, so as to unhinge the fixed meanings of events; *Gorboduc* sets up impressions of characters which it then undermines with new information, doubt. Both plays assert that meaning can be provisional; both deny their audience stable perspectives; and both stake their value on a capacity to arouse emotional and psychological responses as much as to enshrine eternal wisdom. Broadly speaking, each play reflects a new sense of historical contingency.

3

Richard Edwards's *Damon and Pithias* (1564) mediates the popular and learned traditions; in doing so, it marks a definitive step in Tudor dramaturgy by offering our best early instance of a play structured according to a principle of suspense. That dramaturgical interest defines a change. Medieval drama employs a narrative of salvation, early Tudor interludes often a structure of debate; both take only occasional advantage of suspense, and neither make it a governing pattern. While a fourteenth-century saint's play such as the Digby *Mary Magdalene* covers a huge sweep of time, it tends to realize each stage event fully in the moment; the play proceeds leaving nothing behind. But by the advent of the University Wits, suspense has become a dramatic feature, as Lyly's tantalizing plots suggest. That infusion of uncertainty marks a shift along the theatrical continuum, from the allegorical and intellectual toward the psychological and emotional. While the Expositor of the Chester mystery cycle, for example, discourages the audience from responding emotionally, *Cambises*, *Gorboduc*, and climactically *Damon and Pithias* now elicit emotional engagement as one of drama's preeminent effects.

Even before he wrote *Damon and Pithias*, Edwards was celebrated by Barnaby Googe as a playwright excelling Plautus and Terence.[60] Not only Googe but other Elizabethans – Turberville, Twine, Puttenham, Webbe, and Meres – sang Edwards's praises as dramatist and poet.[61] The young Edwards achieved distinction in the 1540s at Oxford, where he was imbued with the new humanist learning; he later moved to Elizabeth's court, becoming its chief literary ornament and a model humanist playwright. *Damon and Pithias*, performed first for the court during Christmas 1564, was probably the Edwards play produced on 2 February 1565 at Lincoln's Inn, where Edwards had gained a prestigious honorary fellowship the previous year.[62] In 1568 the play was revived at Merton College,

Oxford, perhaps in memory of Edwards's triumphant presentation of *Palamon and Arcite* there before Elizabeth in 1566, the year of his death.[63] Popular, *Damon and Pithias* appeared in print by at least 1571 and again in 1582.

Several themes and motifs link *Damon and Pithias* with *Cambises* and *Gorboduc*: tyranny and counsellorship, as well as trial, threatened execution, and violence.[64] In particular, *Damon and Pithias* attempts to resolve the dilemmas of tyranny posed in the earlier plays by effecting King Dionisius's change of heart before the aestheticized image of friendship. As many commentators have noted, tyranny presents Elizabethan drama with a thorny problem: the dilemma of displaying the horrors of oppression yet refusing the populace the right to rebel against it. To that conundrum, Edwards responds by giving the prospective victims the role of humanist reformers. Structurally, furthermore, *Damon and Pithias* represents a melding of *Cambises* and *Gorboduc*. According to Leicester Bradner, the play blends for the first time the popular antics and low comedy of *Cambises* and the morality dramas with the formal humanist rigor of *Gorboduc* so as to create a compact, complex, and successful narrative.[65] The interest of *Damon and Pithias* in chronology and suspense, furthermore, confirms the common ground shared by the popular and the humanistic.

In his Prologue to *Damon and Pithias*, Edwards forswears his previous manner of comical "toying Playes" (Pro.6),[66] offering instead a theory of *"decorum"* (Pro.26) for presenting characters: "So correspondent to their kinde their speeches ought to bee" (Pro.22). The story of Damon and Pithias will record an historical event (Pro.32) as well as a "rare ensample of Frendship true" (Pro.31). But Edwards warns his courtly audience against allegorical reading: "Wee talke of *Dionisius* Courte, wee meane no Court but that, / . . . Loe this I speake for our defence, lest of others wee should be shent" (Pro.40–43). In Edwards's humanist theory of representation and affect, characters will be historically true but fitting to type so that his heroes can embody a real example of an abstract virtue – an aesthetic that recalls Elyot's *The Gouernour*. Viewing the play as topical allegory about a known court would subvert the spectatorial response Edwards intends. The Prologue ends with the nervous (and likely vain) hope that effects will not exceed intentions, as the speaker asks the audience to "take thinges as they be ment" and attend with "upright Judgement" and "heedeful eare and Eye" (Pro.44–45). That Edwards should be so seismically attuned to spectators makes sense, for the play demonstrates how audience engagement can function virtually to co-create action.

Damon and Pithias organizes itself around a pivotal, mid-point event: Pithias's appeal to the tyrant, King Dionisius, to procure a two-months stay of execution for his wrongly condemned friend, Damon. Dionisius grants the stay on condition that Pithias's own life will stand as surety for his friend's. That episode (712–858) constitutes a quasijudicial proceeding, marks Dionisius's first appearance, and occupies the drama's climactic middle. For the remainder of the play, suspense builds about whether Damon will or will not return. While the major suspense-movement develops in the play's second half, the first half nonetheless conditions the audience by creating expectation and doubt through local intrigues and stage violence.

As *Damon and Pithias* opens, Aristippus – a bankrupt humanist intellectual who has turned his knowledge and wit to amusing Dionisius for personal gain – forges a back-scratching alliance with the sycophant Carisophus, who curries favor by denouncing "traitors" and "spies" to the paranoid king. Aristippus's career brings to mind Edwards himself. An accomplished academician whose duties as Master of the Chapel Children included entertaining the queen, Edwards may have feared that he and other humanist courtiers "might be tempted to bend their values rather than sacrifice their positions."[67] Exemplifying such a compromised courtier, Aristippus allies himself with the unlearned parasite Carisophus to forward each other's court interests. The two thus present the play's model of false friendship: self-serving, convenient, conspiratorial, materialistic, and treacherous. Although their dialogue employs the language of alliance, Aristippus subsequently laughs the pact to scorn: "I promist frendship . . . but I meant it not" (124). Based on "commodity" (325, 550, 1431, 1445) rather than on "vertue" (see 318–29), this "friendship" will necessarily fail when the "commodity" of either partner is jeopardized. Edwards's attack on the commodification of friendship reflects humanist uneasiness with the threat to traditional and patrician values posed by a rising market mentality.[68] False friendship brings with it doubt, suspicion, uncertainty – and

spectatorial suspense. Carisophus fears his new friend: "he flat-
treth so finely, that I feare mee, / He wyll licke all the fatte from
my lippes, and so outwery mee" (176–77). Nervous about Aristippus's loyalty, Carisophus snuffles about to find new "traitors" to
denounce so that he may surpass his rival in the tyrant's graces.
The pact of false friendship only intensifies the rivalry. Who will
strike first? In their subsequent soliloquies (98–138 and 159–79),
Aristippus and Carisophus register distrust of each other, their
speeches implying that the rivalry will build to a moment of climax
and exposure.

   The false allies have already begun their mutual suspicions
when the two true friends arrive in Syracuse. Damon and Pithias
enter from a raging sea voyage, followed by their servant, Stephano, who accents both humor and unease. Staggering under the
luggage, he enters in slapstick fashion, but also curses the
country's courtesy: "a Pockes take these Maryner knaves, / Not
one would healpe mee to carry this stuffe" (151–52). As the
drama progresses, Stephano will voice anxiety about the "close
secret wise" (251) of the countrymen and the tyranny of the king,
whose harshness Stephano witnesses in a man condemned to die
for a bad dream (289–97). After the brief arrival scene, Carisophus re-enters, still ranging for victims to "catche" and "accuse"
(165, 166). Foreboding hangs in the air, and the juxtaposition of
exits and entrances promises collision. When the agitated Stephano tells his masters of the executed citizen, he frets: "Oh that
we had never set foote on this land" (280; see also 305). Pithias
shares Stephano's apprehensions (298–300), but Damon turns to
philosophical reflections on tyranny and friendship, an irresistible
subject into which Pithias quickly wades (306–15). As Damon and
Pithias wax rhapsodic about losing their identities in each other,
Stephano brings the conversation comically down to earth,
exclaiming, "That could I never doo, to forget my selfe, full well
I know, / Wheresoever I go, that I am PAUPER STEPHANO" (338–
39), and balancing Damon and Pithias's philosophizing with his
own plebeian, immediate, materialist perspective. Foreboding
returns as Stephano warns Damon: "But I pray you sir, for all your
Phylosophie, / See that in this Courte you walke very wisely," for
"many eyes are bent" on the newcomers; there are "spies" abroad,
and "you can not be too circumspect" (339–43). Damon assures
Stephano that they will observe the city only in the manner of

philosophers (344–51). But, as the dialogue has hinted, it is exactly the philosophical mode that will prevent Damon from recognizing the threat to his safety.

Damon's naive philosophizing prompts him to speak loosely of Syracuse within hearing of the hidden Carisophus: "The Seate is good, and yet not stronge, and that is great pitie" (413). Although Carisophus cannot draw Damon into concurring about the king's cruelty (as Ambidexter draws Hob and Lob), Damon does acknowledge his canvassing of the city as a curious traveller (436–37). With that, Carisophus concludes, "He is a spie" (449) and rushes off for Snap the Tipstaffe to arrest Damon.[69] Soon after, Aristippus re-enters from the court with money earned by delighting Dionisius with "sondrie sports and tauntes" (488). With his coup, however, Carisophus has bested his rival by reversing the king's mood: "beinge very mery before, / He sodenly fell in a dump" (518–19). Dionisius's renewed rage and paranoia have put Carisophus back in the driver's seat and Aristippus on the frosty side of the king's favor. Edwards means this reversal as a surprise to auditorial expectations: the learned, witty, humanist Aristippus – presumably more sympathetic than his rival – out-maneuvered by the crude toady Carisophus, who gloats as the shaken humanist exits to look upon Damon.

This first-half rhythm of entrances and exits merits attention. The viewpoint of the court largely dominates *Cambises* and *Gorboduc*, but in *Damon and Pithias* the king does not appear until the play's mid-point, although he is the recurrent subject of conversation. The dramaturgy thus suggests that the play's action proceeds as a response to what is happening somewhere else, the audience experiencing desires and opinions about, but removal from, the absent locus. Edwards enhances the suspense this condition generates by shuffling characters, alone or in changing pairs, across the stage: first Aristippus, joined by Carisophus; then Damon and Pithias, joined by Stephano; then Carisophus alone; then Wyll and Jacke, servants of the two courtiers; then Stephano alone; then Aristippus and Wyll; then Damon, Pithias, and Stephano; then Carisophus; then Damon and Stephano – all in only the first 400 lines. This restless movement of characters repeats a dramaturgical strategy typical of the moralities, from Skelton's *Magnificence* through later plays such as *Respublica*. In *Magnificence*, the rapid displacement of conspirators by one another gives the impression "that something mysterious is going on behind the scenes."[70] Likewise in *Damon and Pithias*, fitful activity amid talk of the absent court creates tension and desire.

The second half of *Damon and Pithias* presents its other and more highly wrought movement of suspense. First, Damon is condemned to death: can he be saved from immediate execution? Pithias offers himself as a pledge for Damon's return to face execution, but that expedient assures that one of the friends must necessarily die to save the other. Will Damon return? Which of the friends will perish? What can save either or both from Dionisius's tyranny? Those questions reveal the virtue of *Damon and Pithias*, for, as we shall see, Edwards uses Tudor theatre's mania for variety to engineer the *frisson* of suspense: gallimaufry will meet narrative coherence. The substitution scene sets up the dilemma; then, with the protagonists – Damon, Pithias, and Dionisius – offstage, Edwards uses a cornucopia of characters, dramatic tones, and perspectives to create events that seem to be diversions but that actually sound the drumbeat for the day of reckoning. In this half of the play, Edwards applies on a grander scale his early spectatorial strategies of tension, surprise, and displacement. Through them emerges the possibility of narrative resolution.

Damon's sudden arrest ratchets up the pathos and emotional tension. Pithias and Stephano enter (s.d. at 559) reeling with the news of Damon's condemnation. In Senecan fashion, Stephano calls on the gods for redress, "hote consumyng fire" upon the malefactors (568), and dashes off in hope of securing Aristippus's help. Pithias, left onstage alone, bewails the dire circumstances, even singing a lamentation: "O, what a death is this to heare, / DAMON my friende must die" (594–95). Stephano returns with news that Damon is to be executed immediately; Aristippus follows, now chastened, wiser, but reluctant to intercede for Damon; instead, he sends Pithias to Eubulus. That summary of stage action before Dionisius's entrance shows Edwards at great pains to tighten the emotional vise: expressions of woe, hopes suddenly raised and disappointed, urgent entrances and exits, disaster accelerating. King Dionisius appears at last (s.d. at 711), emblematically, with Eubulus on one side, pleading for mercy, and the executioner Gronno on the other side, preparing to strike off Damon's head. Dionisius's stichomythic debate with Eubulus on the relative merits of severity and mercy confirms his paranoid victimizing of Damon: "Better he die, then I to be tormented with feare," concludes the king (784). But suddenly, on a whim that he quickly regrets, Dionisius grants Damon's request to order his affairs back home in Greece before his execution, if a "pledge" (813) for Damon can be found. Pithias rushes into the breach. Disconcerted, Dionisius seeks to void the reprieve, but Eubulus convinces him that a king must honor his word. At every opportunity in these episodes, the tension between despair and hope heightens.

With Damon now departed and Pithias languishing in prison, Edwards turns his heroes' absence into a virtue. Carisophus, the boy servants, Aristippus, and Grimme the Collier reclaim the stage in a comic interlude, but they do so in ways that allude to and enhance the suspense of the friends' dilemma. Throughout their own quarrels and practical jokes, these characters keep raising the question of whether Damon will return to save Pithias. Edwards incorporates every mid-century tragicomic value rehearsed by Nicholas Grimald in his dedicatory epistle to *Christus Redivivus* (1543): "great things . . . interwoven with the small, joyous with sad, obscure with manifest, incredible with probable. Moreover, just as the first act yields to tragic sorrow . . . so the fifth and last adapts itself to delight and joy; likewise, in order that variety may be opposed to satiety, in all the other intermediate acts sad and cheerful incidents are inserted in turn."[71] Edwards improves on that humanist prescription by deploying variety in a way that reinforces narrative tension and suspense.

Dionisius himself raises with Pithias the question of Damon's return: "Whether he die by the way, or lie sicke in bed, / If he retourne not then, thou shalt either hange or lose thy head" (852–53; see also 875–76). Later, in the middle of the diversion provided by Stephano's beating of Carisophus, Aristippus echoes the question, observing that "Damon is now at libertie, / For whos return Pithias his friend lieth in prison, alas in great jeopardy: / To morow is the day, which day by noone if Damon return not . . ." (1031–33). The subject then weaves through the plebeian comic business, as Grimme speaks of Damon: "And he is gone, and should be here to morow to die, / Or els his fellow which is in prison, his rowme shall supplie: / . . . I think Damon be to wise to returne agayne" (1190–93). Carisophus next reiterates this urgent doubt about Damon: "Pithias . . . / Which to morrow shall die, but for that false knave Damon: / He hath left his friend in the briers and now is gone" (1380–82). Eubulus laments further: "The day is come when he in Damons place, / Must lose his life, the time is fully spent" (1462–63), and the Muses join him in "dolefull tunes" (1479). Edwards keeps pathos alive, in counterpoint to comedy.

The moment of execution approaching, attention reverts repeatedly to the closeness of time, how the clock verges upon the noon hour of execution. If the two months of Damon's stay have whizzed past on stage, the last few minutes before the execution occupy a dramatic eternity. Edwards exercises those expansions of dramatic time dear to modern filmmakers, when the fifteen seconds before the bomb explodes stretch into five minutes of reel time. The play capitalizes on a dramaturgy first seen in *Cambises*, where Sisamnes's execution is repeatedly ordered and delayed. "[T]he time is fully spent" (1463), Eubulus says. "It pricketh fast upon noone" (1531), proclaims Dionisius in his entrance speech, after which he proceeds to harry Pithias: "You know what time a day it is, make you ready" (1542). More time elapses as Pithias delivers a thirty-line valediction. Just as Gronno forces his victim to kneel for the beheading, *"Here entreth DAMON running and stayes the sword"* (s.d. at 1582).

With that, Edwards shows himself the conscious master of an almost melodramatic suspense.[72] Although Terence and Plautus were models, Renaissance commentators perceived in their plays something more like surprise than suspense. Grimald speaks of how the last act in a tragicomedy "adapts itself to delight and joy," and he praises Plautus's *Captivi* because it "passes moreover from a sad beginning to a happy ending."[73] But Edwards's efforts at time-protraction and last-minute recuperation exceed mere surprise and "happy ending." When Damon comes rushing in, shouting, "Stay, stay, stay" and "myne appoynted time is not yet fully past" (1583–84), Pithias, eager to die for his friend, claims that Damon "came not at his just tyme" (1603). The two break into a brief and hilarious disagreement about what the time actually is (an issue never settled). *Damon and Pithias* offers a virtual primer for suspense as an affective device: deferred expectation – reiterated, pathetic, uncertain – balanced by comic release.

But Edwards's dramaturgical skill shows itself more subtly than in Damon's return. Through onstage violence, allusions to

execution, and shaving as metaphor, *Damon and Pithias* also generates psychological suspense (and comic anxiety) about the ending.
A physical combativeness enters the play after Damon leaves that
exacerbates the tension of the impending execution. The parasite
Carisophus has gone to Damon's lodging to snarf up his pos-
sessions as spoils, but Stephano discovers and beats him (at 924).
In that action, the real malefactor instead of the innocent victim
finally suffers physical punishment. The beating gratifies the audience's desire for moral and emotional redress at the same time
that it heightens tension by making violence suddenly realistic –
as the blood seen on Carisophus's head proclaims (1003). After
Stephano beats him, Carisophus keeps alive the play's muscular
edginess by passing along Stephano's blows to his own servant,
Jacke (983). Moments later Jacke and Wyll fall to fisticuffs (s.d.
at 1075) that express the unresolved competition between their
masters as well as the "tragidie" that Carisophus has caused: "the
devell take him, he doth much hurt" (1067). As in *Cambises*, the
action seems capable at any moment of breaking into violence.

Even the long comic interlude with Grimme the Collier invokes
the idea of violent death. First the collier refers to a public
execution: "One preached of late not farre hence, in no Pulpet,
but in Waayne carte" (1144); he then mentions young "roysters"
who have been "cut off be times, or they have gone halfe their
journey" (1155). His reminiscences bring to his mind Damon,
"condemned to die" (1175). Grimme also describes himself as so
intoxicated that he could not speak plainly even if he were "to be
hanged by and by" (1184); and after Jacke and Wyll have stolen
his debentures, the collier seeks Officer Snap, crying "an halter
beswenge them" (1368). The apparent diversion of the Grimme
episode develops another powerful, serio-comic motif connected
with the main narrative: shaving. Aristippus has earlier told the
audience that Dionisius, fearful of assassination, makes his
daughters shave him by singeing his beard with "hote burning
Nutshales" (1045; see also 1042–46). Aristippus describes the
tyrant's anxiety about barbering: "Not with Knife or Rasour, for
all edge tooles he feares" (1044). The anecdote has the force of
revelation. Dionisius, friendless, suspicious, pathologically afraid
of execution, of *beheading*, wrests control over his terror by projecting it onto others, that is, by having anyone he suspects
beheaded. Edwards experiments with the kind of complex

psychological parody that Shakespeare will master. Grimme's shaving by the boy-servants enacts what the king refuses. The boys succeed, furthermore, in deceiving and robbing the collier, a comic gesture that confirms the fact of vulnerability. The episode contains the physical roughness that amused Renaissance audiences, as Jacke scours Grimme's face painfully (1282) with fetid water "vengeaunce sower" (1293). Using the "chopping knyfe" as a razor, Jacke shaves Grimme aggressively enough to inflict pain, possibly bleeding (1306–07). Grimme's role as a buffoonish surrogate king produces comic release; at the same time, the episode aggravates spectatorial anxiety by enacting a mock throat cutting. Ambiguity multiplies the suspense.

In the climactic scene, the plot almost reaches an impass: who will be executed? Edwards solves the dilemma in a classically humanist stroke by effecting a wondrous personal transformation in the tyrannical king. As critics have noted, the execution place resembles a stage and the ending, a play-within-a-play: Attempting to replace Pithias, for example, Damon cries, "Geve place to me, this rowme is myne, on this stage must I play" (1589).[74] Now ready to die, Damon avails himself of the condemned man's right and, like an orator, addresses to Dionisius a lengthy argument on friendship: "O you earthly kinges, / Your sure defence and strongest garde, standes chifely in faithfull friends" (1643–44). Just as Dionisius had marveled at Pithias's "straunge" willingness to die for his companion (1574), he is now struck dumb with wonder at the pair's heroic and sublime friendship: "Eubulus, my spirites are sodenly appauled, my limes waxe weake, / This straunge friendship amaseth me so, that I can scarse speake" (1651–52). The whole court reverberates with wonder: "O unspeakable frindship" (1655), echoes Eubulus; "My hand with soden feare quivereth" (1660), exclaims Gronno, as he grips the axe. Dionisius completes the theatrical, even kinesthetic effect: "Stay Gronno: my flesh trembleth . . . / O noble friendship, I must yeld, at thy force I wonder: / My hart, this rare frindship hath pearst to the roote, / And quenched all my fury, this sight hath brought this aboute" (1662–67). The gods, Dionisius concludes, have made the two friends "play this Tragidie" for his "behove" (1670). Dionisius then revokes the death sentence, renounces tyranny, and pledges himself to Damon and Pithias as their "thirde friend" (1683).

Critics have linked that climactic scene with Renaissance theories of tragic experience, particularly the myth of the tyrant king brought to tears by an enactment that recalls his murders.[75] But what moves Dionisius is *not* his cruelty's mirrored reflection; rather, what moves him is the image of a Platonic ideal made manifest in *response* to his cruelty. Dionisius must recognize himself as the tyrant in Damon's speech, but the operative principle of his transformation is not shame or remorse but inspiration. Edwards's great fountainhead for that theory of affect is Elyot's *The Gouernour*. Elyot believes that the embodiment of abstract virtues in fictional characters can move readers to wonder, a response of heightened emotion and contemplation. His recurring image for the metamorphic power of literature is the "courage" or heart of the student "inflamed" with desire to emulate the virtues that heroes portray. For Elyot the inflamed spirit achieves an almost sensory investment, evoked with words such as "sweet" and "delectable" as well as "delight" and "pleasure."

As spectator to the highly theatricalized "tragidie" played before him, Dionisius stands, symbolically and empathically, for the spectators of *Damon and Pithias* itself. To some extent Edwards seeks to alter his audience as Damon and Pithias have transformed Dionisius. The dramaturgical treatment of Dionisius deserves credit, for while Dionisius is offstage between the play's middle and final episodes, other characters hint that he has been moved by the friendship of Damon and Pithias; they hint, that is, of his capacity for change. Yet the ending's very theatricality communicates a certain unbelievability. Here suspense becomes crucial to narrative success. Because suspense builds the spectator's emotional and intellectual investment, it contributes to transformational wonder; indeed, it makes wonder not simply a matter of surprise or "happy ending" but the fulfillment of narrative movement and spectatorial desire. First, as we have seen, Edwards's relentless provocation of uncertainty about the heroes' fate seeks to arouse spectatorial interest and desire. Second, the play's escalating physical confrontations, its edginess, and its reiteration of the beheading theme amplify the climax. Suspense works to increase the audience's psychic investment in the play's outcome, to feed its desire for a resolution commensurate with the psychic energy it has called forth. Narrative and aesthetic strategies intersect, for the strength of the audience's desire for resolution might be said to make emotionally plausible an ending that scants probability. Suspense, that is, privileges wonder.

Implicitly, *Damon and Pithias* would urge on its Elizabethan audience a politics of friendship. In Dionisius's court friendship leads to an inclusive metamorphosis. The king proclaims his "changed conditions: / Tirranie, flatterie, oppression, loe, hear I cast away, / Justice, truth, love, frindship shall be my joy" (1692–94). Stephano is freed; Damon and Pithias receive, in the manner of the moralities, "new apparell fitte" (1706); Gronno acquires their old garments; Eubulus beats Carisophus from court and rejoices in friendship as a virtue essential to house, land, and kingdom. The modern audience might find a facile and sentimental optimism in all that. Indeed, the ending of *Damon and Pithias* demonstrates the poignance of humanist solutions to institutional or systemic problems. Renaissance humanism proposes change on the level of the individual – through education, through literature – as the means to creating a better society. Such an approach labors at a disadvantage before a problem, such as tyranny, that expresses the very structure of institutions. The humanist answer is to invent a drama, an art, that would marshall emotional and intellectual resources to transform its spectators on a scale rivaling the institutional. In this regard, *Damon and Pithias* brings to a culmination the paradigmatic concern for the individual heart that rings through *Cambises, Gorboduc, Gismond of Salerne,* and other 1560s plays. For all those characters who have displayed overly impassioned or cruelly hardened hearts, for all those efforts literally to grip the heart – the heart of Praxaspes's son or of Guishard – *Damon and Pithias* distills the answer: a change of heart, like that of Dionisius, whose center has been "pearst to the roote." Striking here is the way in which 1560s politics and dramaturgy converge inextricably, for the solution that 1560s culture offers to the real problem of tyranny is a theatrical one, the witnessing heart awed and changed before the ideal of virtue.

But Edwards omits one character from the ending's transformation and celebration: Aristippus. That university-trained humanist philosopher-turned-courtier helps to redeem the play's conclusion from the charge of fatuousness. Aristippus evokes the missing or unreconciled figure sometimes conspicuous in the endings of Shakespearean comedies. He may also give to *Damon and Pithias* a certain Elizabethan realism. As commentators have

noted, Aristippus's language intersects curiously with the authorial voice. Some have conjectured that Edwards had earlier
offended the queen or perhaps the court's women with a too-
irreverent satire; now, the Prologue claims, "his Pen that shall
amende" (Pro.12). Likewise, Aristippus learns that the women of
Dionisius's court complain about him because he constantly makes
"sporte" of them (262; see also 263–65). With the vow, "I wyll
change my coppy" (269), Aristippus promises a reform of his
entertainments suspiciously similar to the reform Edwards claims
for his plays ("A soden change is wrought" [Pro.6]). But Aristippus wavers in his commitment, reverting again to a "pleasant
toye" (472) and "sondrie sports and tauntes" (488) to amuse the
king, then recoiling when Dionisius's change of humor puts him
out of favor again: "I perceyve it is no safe playing with Lyons"
(654). Does Aristippus learn and grow? In his last appearance, he
repudiates Carisophus and verifies true friendship based on honesty and virtue. He criticizes his own behavior, elevating his moral
standing. Yet he has earlier declined to intervene for Damon and
has been dismissed by Grimme as "a suttel Vox, he wyll not tread
on thornes for none" (1198). By the end, Aristippus may have
come to recognize the tenuousness of his court position; he may
even have gained some moral backbone; but he disappears from
the play an ambiguous and still-compromised character. To the
extent that Aristippus stands for the humanist at court, or even
represents Edwards himself, the play acknowledges the modest
and incremental nature of personal growth and the difficulty of
avoiding moral compromise. Aristippus, then, casts a shadow on
the dream of personal transformation.

The humanist courtier returns us to a sense of both the responsible human agent and the countervailing doubt and open-
endedness that haunt 1560s drama. That tension reflects the
infusion of humanist historical awareness into allegorical and
mythic narrative. One expression of that historical interest is the
dramaturgy of stage chronology that we have seen in *Cambises*,
Gorboduc, and *Damon and Pithias*, articulated variously in strategies
of anticipation, surprise, retrospective revision, expansions and
contractions of stage time, and suspense. That dramaturgy identifies an increased attentiveness in 1560s theatre to moving the
audience with strong emotional and psychological effects: fear,
exhilaration, pity, doubt, anxiety, and wonder. While the

historically oriented plays of the era reflect drama's religious and public crises, they also demonstrate the intertwining of the objective and the subjective, the realistic and the aesthetic, as narrative meaning and credibility become contingent on dramaturgy's affective power.

Humanism and the dramatizing of women

Medieval morality plays such as *Mankind* (*c.* 1470) or Medwall's *Nature* (*c.* 1495) present women as temptations to sin or as embodiments of virtue, but in sixteenth-century drama representations of women change from virgin and whore stereotypes to complex and engaging figures. How could that change happen? While Tudor popular theatre contains a full quota of bawds, shrews, scolds, and angelic virgins, its demonized or idealized women, a line of different, critically underappreciated female characters appears in humanist drama. Spanning the More circle interludes, the 1560s woman-centered plays, and the 1570s romances, these humanist theatrical works grant women personal and political influence, show them harmoniously combining male and female traits, and confer stage authority upon them. Stereotypical views of women permeate most sixteenth-century plays, but humanist dramaturgy nurtures female protagonists whose compelling stage presence – expressing griefs, doubts, private desires, and secret identities – contributes to the achievement in Renaissance theatre of individualized women characters.[1]

Most critical discussions of women characters in "Renaissance Drama" limit themselves to Shakespeare and his contemporaries,[2] dismissing earlier Tudor drama as patriarchal and repressive of women and postulating an Elizabethan misogyny whose "diverse legal, moral, popular, and medical discourses ... link women's agency to transgression."[3] Those views contain considerable justice. The popular morality and saints plays, for example, typically divide women into the opposing categories of whore and virgin. Although those popular categories balloon in sixteenth-century drama – women become, on the one hand, gossipy, irrational, shrewish, and weak or, on the other, obedient, patient, silent, and chaste – the basic opposition remains intact. Accordingly, as Linda

Woodbridge argues, the terms of the formal controversy about women in popular polemical literature circulate through 1560s plays containing prominent female characters – for instance, Patient Griselda and the biblical figures Susanna and Mary Magdalene.[4] Shakespeare's *The Taming of the Shrew* thus emerges archetypically, concludes Lynda Boose, from a "world where women defined as 'shrews' and 'scolds' became, during the late sixteenth century, an obsessive sign of monstrous disorder."[5] In that critical narrative, the preceding era's "obsession with taming unruly women"[6] becomes the cultural condition that Shakespeare's contemporaries embrace or repudiate. I would complicate that narrative by suggesting that Tudor theatrical representations of women were not monolithic, that an array of humanist heroines through the century actually privileged the multifaceted female figures of Elizabethan and Jacobean drama.

Tudor humanists introduced attitudes toward women sharply opposed to popular misogyny, argues Pamela Benson.[7] Benson identifies "profeminist" defenses in which women possess the same "cardinal virtues" as do men or possess "specifically female virtues."[8] I shall refer to Benson's argument, but we should also acknowledge (as does Benson) the complexities, limitations, and differences among humanist approaches to women. While humanist writers such as More, Vives, Ascham, and Mulcaster advocated and participated in women's education, challenging doubts about distaff mental capacity, Erasmus showed little interest in female learning, and other humanists, such as Thomas Salter, actively opposed it.[9] The humanist record is thus one of partial advances and a "messy mix" of opinions about women.[10] However narrow or elitist it may appear in hindsight, humanist "profeminism" gains potency when applied to drama. Humanist intellectuals sometimes justified, for example, educating women who might serve as royal consorts; that rationale is dramatized in *Godly Queene Hester* (c. 1527), whose low-born but liberally educated heroine wins marriage to a king by her eloquence and good sense, qualities she later employs to save her people from persecution. This new humanist woman inspires a fantasy life that cuts across class boundaries, as spectators are invited to engage with a learned, articulate, and politically skillful female advancing by merit. The defense of women thus achieves a stimulating embodiment on stage.

Few English humanists did more to revise views of women than

Sir Thomas More, who established a home school for his son and daughters and other dependent children. More's educational system "gave his female students spiritual and ethical autonomy," "a capacity for moral judgment," and "the power of wise speech" – all meant to free them from the "bondage to male authority" characterizing "conventional marriage."[11] For More, the private, domestic realm of women offers an access to spirituality that elevates it above the corrupt realm of politics.[12] More's humanist vision differs from popular stereotypes by affirming female moral sense, judgment, and autonomy, despite his guarded view of women in public life. Although Juan Luis Vives's writings about female education take a conservative, even restrictive line, they implicitly admit "woman's capacity for self-control."[13] Sir Thomas Elyot, in his *Defence of Good Women* (1540), broadly argues for women's equality, contending that "one system of virtues exists for both sexes, that women participate in virtue equally with men, and that, as a consequence, educated women are as capable of governing nations and living moral lives as educated men."[14] According to Benson, the mid-century discussion of women takes two directions: a misogynistic line, pursued in popular literature, that either attacks or defends women according to "a docile, chaste, conventional ideal"; and the humanist line, expressed in marriage manuals, translations, and defenses of Elizabeth's rule, that confirms women's "equality of body, soul, reason, and will."[15] Sixteenth-century rhetorical works entertaining woman's ethical ability, political power, and social role, then, reflect a humanist viewpoint; in addition, they argue by humanistically inflected strategies of paradox and classical exempla – devices seldom used in the popular tracts.[16]

Although the ideal of women as chaste, silent, and obedient saturates much sixteenth-century drama, the more expansive, humanist vision also blooms.[17] That latter vision may not dominate Tudor theatre, but it recurs sufficiently to challenge any generalization that early plays only reproduce a social agreement consigning women to demonized or idealized categories. In the era of Erasmus, Vives, More, and Colet, Henry Medwall's interlude *Fulgens and Lucres* (*c.* 1490) presents a woman with both a subjective voice and the power to decide her future. *Godly Queen Hester* makes women important to political life, since Hester possesses not only a secret identity but a sense of justice that unites the kingdom against the threat of violent repression. By aligning women with political justice, *Hester* anticipates the later interests of *Respublica* (1553). John Redford's *Wit and Science* (*c.* 1530–47), as we have seen, grants its leading female character an agency insulated from partriarchal control.[18] Even a schoolboy farce such as *Roister Doister* (*c.* 1552) promotes a serious, sympathetic, and realistic female, Dame Custance. Those plays suggest the theatrical authority available to women characters and explored subsequently by heroine-centered plays such as *Mary Magdalene* (*c.* 1558) and *Patient Grissell* (*c.* 1559). Many of the era's dramatic works define a female theatrical presence and domain of values that the male world must acknowledge. Because of the humanist interest in spectatorial wonder, female models here acquire theatrical magnetism. Perhaps Tudor drama's least-discussed representations of women occur in the stage romances of the 1570s and early 1580s, which, along with the moralities, dominated both plebeian and aristocratic tastes before public theatres emerged. Only three romances survive: *Common Conditions* (1576), *Clyomon and Clamydes* (*c.* 1576), and *The Rare Triumphs of Love and Fortune* (1582), although the era's drama lingers in the later *Mucedorus* (*c.* 1590), Peele's *The Old Wive's Tale* (1590), and Beaumont and Fletcher's *The Knight of the Burning Pestle* (*c.* 1607). Stage romances present female protagonists with voice, initiative, and volition, such as Neronis in *Clyomon and Clamydes* and Fidelia in *The Rare Triumphs of Love and Fortune*. In combining both male and female traits, Neronis and Fidelia mediate gender conventions. Here the romance tradition shows its adaptability to humanism's stage representations of women, just as humanist thematics permeate literary romances such as Sidney's *Arcadia*. The popular morality tradition denies, rather than predicts, the complex female characters of Lyly, Greene, and Shakespeare; those characters gather strength from the heroines of sixteenth-century humanist drama.[19]

1

Starting with *Fulgens and Lucres*, a group of stage heroines from the first half-century reiterate specific virtues: intelligence, independence of mind, wit, compassion, and a sense of mutuality that compensates for male blindness – the same qualities that the humanist Sir Thomas Elyot defends in women. Henry Medwall's

Fulgens and Lucres, notes Alan Nelson, is the first surviving English play with a secular theme, a developed secondary plot, and a female protagonist.[20] In Medwall's source, Buonaccorso's humanist treatise *De Vera Nobilitate* (trans. 1481), the choice of Lucres's groom is left to the Roman Senate, but in Medwall's play the father, Fulgens, allows his daughter the decision, as she rejects the sybaritic aristocrat Publius Cornelius and accepts the poor but virtuous civil servant Gayus Flaminius (who echoes Henry VII's "new men").[21] Medwall's Lucres springs from his, not Buonaccorso's, imagination,[22] and she is notable for her rational judgment.[23] According to Fulgens, not only does Lucres possess "beaute and clere understanding" (1.263), but also "She is so discrete and sad in all demeanyng, / And therto full of honest and verteous counsell / Of here owne mynd, that wonder is to tell" (1.267–69). Because of those qualities, Lucres will have "fre choyse and . . . lyberte" in selecting her husband (1.428).[24] The dialogue between father and daughter reveals their affectionately negotiated relationship. After Fulgens grants Lucres the power of choice, she accepts it but asks her father if he would have her marry his candidate, Cornelius; Lucres's deference evokes only her father's further assurances of satisfaction with whatever choice she will make. Lucres's speeches contain no self-serving, manipulative, or hypocritical hints; her deference returns authority to her because of its sincerity.[25]

Critics have celebrated Lucres's rational authority and command of audience sympathy.[26] In Part I she is given control of her interview with Gayus, and in Part II she displays such discernment that "we accept her unreservedly as the arbiter of Medwall's debate."[27] Catherine Belsey goes further, arguing that Lucres becomes "the author of meaning" and that the play allows the "remarkable possibility" that a " 'woman's mind' " guarantees the definition – a central humanistic concern – of true nobility.[28] In addition, Lucres undertakes an adventure beyond rational disquisition or dissections of nobility. Although she has probed her father's preference for Cornelius and offered her obedience, her subsequent dialogue reveals her own desire to choose Gayus and to win her father's favor for him: she promises Gayus, "For if he like you as well as I, / Your mynde in this behalf shalbe sone easid / If my seyd fader can be content and pleysid" (1.558–60). Hints arrive likewise of her low estimation of Cornelius. In Part II,

Cornelius narrates to B how Lucres, in her garden, once asked him to startle away a nearby cuckoo bird (II.181–88). B leaps to the inference from popular lore: "He that throwyth stone or stycke / At suche a byrde, he is lycke / To synge that byrdes songe" (193–95). In her request, that is, Lucres had likened Cornelius to a cuckoo or cuckold. The anecdote pictures Lucres slyly amusing herself by fashioning signs of Cornelius's foolishness – a foolishness he confirms by twice missing the point. The play contains other signs of Lucres's attitude toward Cornelius: she warns him, for example, against brawling (II.371–74), and although her injunction includes both suitors, she directs it toward Cornelius only; later Lucres reproves Cornelius for violating her edict (II.536–38). At the great debate, she sends Cornelius and Gayus away so that she can hear "the commune voyce of the countrey" regarding the two, but she then proceeds simply to announce her decision without consultation. While in its plot *Fulgens and Lucres* advances toward the difficult weighing of the rival lovers' merits, in the play's theatrical signals Lucres has already made her choice.

Because the audience is made to sympathize with Lucres and to appreciate her preference, her selection of Gayus satisfies emotionally.[29] In her first interview with Gayus, Lucres promises to answer his proposal "Evyn as sone as I godely may" (I.552) once she can "assay" her "faders mynde" (I.556) – since she is determined to have her father "content and pleysid" (560).[30] Lucres's problem is to arrive at a choice acceptable to her father that also expresses her heart's desire. Her negotiation of that dilemma constitutes a theatrical subtext. The play emphasizes Lucres's prudence, her cautious misgivings, and her elusiveness, as "she escapes from interview after interview."[31] Circumspectly, Lucres reconfirms the two suitors' agreement that she judge their final debate and follow only her "owne fantasie" (II.429) – evidence that she harbors her own wishes. Yet never does Lucres proceed hypocritically, manipulate cynically, or submit deceptively. Rather, her skillful aligning of desire, good sense, and parental approval gives *Fulgens and Lucres* much of its theatrical delight – something different from the pleasures of debating *in utramque partem*. To the extent that Lucres's project influences the action and spectatorial experience, to the extent that she arbitrates the claims of fathers and suitors, of logic and heart's desire, she gains subjective agency and voice. In some moments, such as when she signifies Cornelius as a cuckoo, Lucres even seems self-consciously at play while still entertaining the suitors in earnest. If Lucres possesses a sense of game, her representation may share something with those change-able-taffeta characters A and B, sometimes spectators, sometimes actors, who blur the boundaries between "earnest" and "play." As Lucres's emotional partiality creates tension with her role as dispassionate adjudicator, moreover, it confirms the audience in a sympathetic theatrical knowledge beyond the strictly rational. The discomfort between those two perspectives, evident in *Fulgens and Lucres*, will color sixteenth-century drama through Lyly, Greene, and Shakespeare.

It is tempting to dismiss *Fulgens and Lucres*'s theatricalized "pro-feminism" as anomolous, but other More circle plays echo it. A and B in *Fulgens and Lucres* may provide a model for Mery Report in John Heywood's *The Play of the Wether* (c. 1528);[32] likewise, *Wether*'s Gentylwoman and female Launder seem to draw from *Fulgens and Lucres*, for the Gentylwoman bears reminders of Cornelius's aristo-cratic idleness and abuses while the female Launder takes on the voice exposing them. In the Launder, Heywood creates a woman of righteous – and comic – indignation. Like Gayus, she embodies the virtues of work and duty, and she links them to a sense of female integrity: "It is not thy beauty that I dysdeyne / But thyne ydyll lyfe that thou hast rehersed, / Whych any good womans hert wolde have perced" (913–15).[33] Heywood invests the Launder with a past (904–911) and awards her some of the play's best entrance and exit speeches. When Mery Report inveigles the Gentylwoman with "I never desyred to kys you before" (867), the Launder recap-tures theatrical attention with a speech whose every line requires a different nuance: "Why, have ye alway kyst her behynde? / In fayth good inough yf yt be your mynde. / And yf your appetyte serve you so to do, / Byr lady, I wolde ye had kyst myne ars to" (868–71). No character gets the better of Mery Report as does she. While the Launder's earthiness may distinguish her from Lucres, her theatrical presence likens her.

Like Lucres, Lady Science in John Redford's *Wit and Science* judges her suitor's merits. Father Reason must take seriously Lady Science's doubts about Wit and must negotiate their resolution: as the earlier play valorizes Lucres, *Wit and Science* credits Science's reservations about marriage and distinguishes her, in Belsey's words about Lucres, as the play's "author of meaning." *Wit and*

Science also hints at Lucres's and Science's similarity of intentions, as Science, pretending to know less than she does (about Wit dressed as Ingnoraunce), is allowed to work her own purposes. Dalilah of *Nice Wanton* (*c.* 1547–53) also possesses an unusual stage energy.[34] When she and her brother fall under Master Iniquity's influence, Dalilah intrudes so much into the dialogue that both men strike her. Dalilah registers not as unruly, however, but as sharper of wit than her male counterparts. After the play's interval, she dominates the stage as she describes and enacts the affecting spectacle of her fall. Misogynistic themes cannot explain Dalilah's affective power. Though no Lucres, she nonetheless demonstrates, with Lady Science, the authority potentially available to a female character in early sixteenth-century theatre.

Dame Custance of *Roister Doister* (*c.* 1553) constitutes a "realistic" character also negotiating betrothal's troubled waters.[35] Nicholas Udall's school comedy contains, in effect, two plays: the first, a Terentian or Plautine farce in which a parasite, MeryGreeke, ridicules a preposterous *miles gloriosus*, Ralph; the second, a comedy of social realism, in which a virtuous, sensible widow of means suffers beleaguerment by a pernicious suitor and must marshall forces to salvage her threatened reputation.[36] In that second play, Udall sympathizes remarkably with widows, who faced serious social difficulties in Tudor England – a sensitivity all the more striking if, as Linda Woodbridge argues, widows constitute Renaissance literature's most satirized females.[37] Sympathy bends toward Dame Custance, as incident after incident confirms her discretion, good sense, and innocence in contrast with the willingness of males – even her betrothed, Gawain Goodluck, and his factor, Sim Suresby – to leap to unwarranted and mean-spirited conclusions. Since in this second play Custance's perspective dominates, the overly suspicious males acquire an air of priggishness. Against male hierarchism, concludes Bevington, Custance asserts "feminine values of concord, domesticity, and forebearance."[38] As Lucres manages her courtship with initiative and caution, so Custance manages her household. Against the farcical Plautine tone, Custance acquires a theatrical seriousness and reality matching the complexities of her social situation. She confirms that Lucres's voice, agency, and authority are not exceptional to humanist dramaturgy of women.

Godly Queene Hester concerns a heroine, discreet like Lucres, projected into the realm of politics. According to Greg, *Godly Queene Hester* was likely written between 1527 and 1530, although it was not published until 1561.[39] Thus the play derives from the More era but participates in the 1560s dialogue about women shared with *Mary Magdalene, Patient Grissell, Susanna*, and *Appius and Virginia*.[40] Following the biblical story of Esther, *Godly Queene Hester* relates how Hester marries the Babylonian king Assuerus and subsequently persuades him to save the Jewish people from destruction by the villainous counselor Aman, after which Hester reveals her identity as a Jew and the king installs her uncle as chancellor in Aman's place.[41] The play pivots on the theme of justice. In humanist fashion, *Godly Queene Hester* begins with a discussion of what virtue most befits a king, with justice the consensus choice. King Assuerus then turns to choosing a chancellor and a wife. Aman wins the chancellorship because his "learnyng and reason pleaseth vs [i.e., the king] well" (106). Likewise, Hester will become the king's bride because of her wisdom and her facility in "learninge and litterature" (258). In selecting Hester, Assuerus tests her by demanding that she orate on the virtues of a queen, as in a humanist student exercise. Hester's "bolde" (272) declamation accepts the king's authority but argues that sometimes he might seek his queen's counsel or she might govern in his absence, so that a queen must have the wisdom and virtues of a king. Hester's oration so awes Assuerus that he responds with an offer of marriage and political position: "Then I doute not, but the wysdome of vs two / Knytte both to gether in parfytte charyte / All thynges in thys realme shall cumpas" (296–99) with truth, justice, law, and equity. Hester takes advantage of Assuerus's goodwill to speak forcefully about the need to distribute wealth to the poor: striking here is how much, within a patriarchal framework, a woman can claim political standing. Hester's trenchant sentiments are matched by her humanist rhetorical skill and commanding stage presence, as she becomes the central spectacle. *Godly Queene Hester* allows us, in Belsey's words, "to conceive of a woman as a unified, rational being, the virtuous author of her own eloquence."[42]

Besides possessing a Belseyan voice, Hester stands for God's "hospitalitie" (311), a term whose meaning includes attendance to the hunger and poverty of the poor: "Let God alwaye therfore haue hys parte / And the poore fedde by hospitalitie" (318–19).

Later, as Aman's persecutions begin, the Jews turn to Hester for succor. In response she prepares a great banquet for Assuerus, a "pewer" and "exauisite" (888) feast aglow with Hester's "mirth eke and manners so pleasuante to attaste" (890). The king pronounces himself so pleased that he offers to surrender to Hester half the kingdom and more, "with louinge intente" (899). Again Hester holds center stage as she reveals her Jewish birth, accuses Aman of seeking to destroy her people, and rebuts his lies. Hester represents "hospitalitie": her earlier speech to the king about feeding the poor establishes that association; her banquet provides an object lesson in "hospitalitie" and the mutuality, concord, and good counsel that can result; and she celebrates the "hospitalitie" of the Jewish people as she unveils her lineage. Hester possesses a political gravity reciprocal with her theatrical presence and voice. Her principle of "hospitalitie" – mercy and care for the poor – complements in a revelatory way the political principle of justice discussed ingenuously by the king and his counsellors in the opening scene. When Hester reveals her identity, she simultaneously reveals political justice's missing counterpart, whose absence has facilitated Aman's intended persecutions, for Aman, proud and greedy, lacks compassion for the powerless. The patriarchal system of justice is incomplete, tending toward persecution, without the balancing matriarchal principle of "hospitalitie." Hester, then, emerges as essential to the political system: her humanist eloquence gives her the power of voice, and her vision of "hospitalitie" commands authority because it can create mutuality and social transformation.

Defending women's concern for justice, Sir Thomas Elyot's contemporaneous *The Defence of Good Women* (1540)[43] reads like a humanist philosophical gloss on *Godly Queene Hester*. Women deserve complementary and coequal status with men, argues Elyot, because both have virtues that "seme to be contrary one to an other, and yet in conclusion they agree to one purpose."[44] Elyot defends what Hester illustrates: a woman's capacity to govern. Positing that women possess reason as much as do men, the character Candidus concludes, "Than haue wome[n] also Discrecio[n], Election, and Prudence, which do make that wisedome, which pertyneth to gouernaunce" (47). Candidus defends women's "eloquence" (48) and their "lernynge and wysedome" (49), the attributes extoled in Hester, while Queen Zenobia adds that a woman must be prepared to give "wise counsaile" (57) to her husband, the queenly virtue that Hester enshrines.[45] Zenobia celebrates the usefulness of her own learning, noting that education enabled her to content her husband and that, later, "such circumspection, good lerning minystred vnto me, that in . . . pastymes, I retained alway suche grauitie" (57) as protected her reputation. That last comment recognizes widowhood's social dangers, such as those Custance faces in *Roister Doister*.[46] The "hospitalitie" Hester practices on Assuerus bears kinship to the "delite" (58), "grauitie," and "wise cousaile" that Zenobia brought to her marriage. Thus, in attending personally to her kingdom's plights and its administration of justice, Zenobia does what Assuerus fails to do, and what Hester corrects: "watchfully administer in his own name."[47] Capturing Elyot's humanist vision of coequal, even superior womanhood, *Godly Queene Hester* expatiates on the intelligence of women and the female principle of mutuality, values that radiate from *Fulgens and Lucres*.

The compassion for the poor and oppressed, displayed by Hester and Zenobia, reappears in *Respublica*, in which the eponymous heroine (created to celebrate Queen Mary) sighs sympathetically for the character People.[48] Lois Potter's argument that the comedy is partly "classical" acknowledges its humanist coloration, which its treatment of female virtue supports.[49] Respublica insists on talking personally to People and listens feelingly to his sufferings (III.iii).[50] Although the play's Vices constitute the most interesting personages, and although the play operates as an anti-Reformation tract, Respublica's own story has the texture of a woman's morality play. A benevolent female (the commonwealth) is duped by self-aggrandizing Vice-figures posing as virtuous ministers. Respublica's sympathy for the people, however, makes her suspect her Vice-ministers: "people dothe dailie and hourelye to me resorte, / Chalenging my promise of relief and comforte. / I reporte to hym, as my rewlers doe to mee, / people still affirmeth that they devourers bee" (IV.i.971–73). Respublica seeks redress for People but depends upon her ministers, whom she wishes to trust. God answers Respublica's prayers and near-despair by sending the heavenly Compassion, who reveals to Respublica the Vices's deceptions, after which the "fowre sisters" (V.iii.1387) – Compassion, Veritas, Justice, and Peace – set about reordering the kingdom and deposing the pretenders. In this female morality play, the heroine never surrenders herself to depravity as male morality heroes do; rather, Respublica's only failing is her willingness to trust. *Respublica* enacts the female political virtues hinted by Lucres and exemplified in Hester and Zenobia: sympathy and mutuality, virtues that complement masculine strengths and lend the kingdom balance. The similarities among these many plays challenge any dismissal of a single play as anomalous, while together they undermine any assessment of early sixteenth-century drama as uniformly misogynistic. Evident, rather, are humanist heroines with voice and eloquence, theatrical presence, and political virtues that rival, even exceed, those of men.

2

The late 1550s and particularly the 1560s witnessed an effusion of plays concerned with women and featuring females as central characters: *Mary Magdalene, Patient Grissell, Appius and Virginia* (*c.* 1564), *Susanna* (*c.* 1569), as well as the Inns of Court plays *Jocasta* (1566) and *Gismond of Salerne* (*c.* 1566). Even plays of other thematic interests showcase compelling women: the Mother and Wife in *Cambises* (1561) and Videna and Marcela in *Goborduc* (1562), for example. According to Woodbridge, many of the heroines – Grissell, Susanna, Hester – appear as examples in the contemporaneous pamphlet controversies about women, and the plays about them "use their title figures as the formal defense had used them – as exemplars of virtuous womanhood; four of the plays further the sense of controversy by staging characters who play the role of detractors of women . . . This is the point at which the formal controversy most clearly intersects with Tudor drama."[51] Woodbridge notes that "After lying dormant through the 1550s, the formal controversy was resurrected in the 1560s."[52] Given her assessment that the decade's defenses of women proceed along condescending, patriarchal lines,[53] stage figures such as Mary Magdalene, Patient Grissell, and *Cambises*'s Mother might appear as victimized and pathetical sufferers whose idealization exposes the misogynistic titillations of playwrights and audiences. Yet Wager's *Mary Magdalene* and Phillip's *Patient Grissell*, as two examples, confer on women a theatrical power that transcends, even transgresses their narrative functions. Indeed, *Patient Grissell* identifies a woman's sphere regulated by beneficent female values necessary to the kingdom's health.

Lewis Wager's *The Life and Repentaunce of Mary Magdalene* (*c.* 1558; pub. 1566) manifests a hybrid character: popularist, Protestant, and humanist.[54] Performed by a professional touring group of five actors, the play evinces humanist dramaturgical values and educational interests.[55] The Prologue – "the first known English Protestant defense of the stage"[56] – cites Valerius Maximus and Horace, quotes Latin, mentions performances "at the vniuersitie" (26), twice calls on academic scholars as authorities, and affects "good iudgment" (14), learned virtue, and political obedience[57] – gestures that evoke humanism. Maintaining its educational interests, the play later notes that aristocratic adolescents whose parents have died need guidance and training,[58] and Infidelitie, Mary's would-be teacher, will don an academic cap and gown to disguise himself as "Prudence, / Or else Counsell, full of wisedome and science" (553–54). Unlike the panoramic, biographical, travel adventure of the Digby *Mary Magdalene* (*c.* 1490), Wager's narrative follows a morality-play structure, with Mary succumbing to degeneracy at the Vices' hands and then rising to repentance and salvation through the intervention of God's Lawe, Jesus Christ, and various allegorical virtues.

Embodying the sense of vivid spectacle and emotional effect emerging in 1560s drama, Wager's Mary projects an engaging and magnetic stage presence, her moral force expressing itself visually and sensually, even in her silence.[59] To emphasize Mary's repentant silence would seem to argue that *Mary Magdalene* evokes the patriarchal ideal of the chaste, silent, and obedient woman, but such an assertion would miss the theatrical point, for Mary's moral authority exceeds the authority of speech; it derives instead from the iconic and sensate, even kinesthetic appeal of her spectacle. Such an authority does not conform neatly to patriarchal categories, and it signals the subversive command that a silent woman can convey on stage. If that is so, then *Mary Magdalene* implicitly defends stage-playing in the very terms – excitation of the senses and emotions – that detractors used to discredit it.

Mary Magdalene's early dialogue between the heroine and the Vices sparkles with details of personal demeanor and dress: "Let your garmentes be sprinkled with rose water. / Vse your ciuet, pommander, muske, which be to sell, / That the odor of you a

myle of, a man may smell" (770–71). The play's close attention
to Mary's appearance – her eyes, her hair, her complexion – takes
from humanist Petrarchan love poetry the cataloguing of the idealized object's physical attributes. Wager stages that Petrarchan
anatomizing. In the play's first half, Mary emerges as the epitome
of female vanity, easily flattered by the Vices' attention to her
beauty and sexual allure. The play so focuses on the minutiae of
Mary's presence that she becomes the object of looking and
response. Mary first enters *"triflying with her garmentes"* (s.d. at 142)
and drawing attention to the fit of her clothes: "Haue you eyer
sene an ouerbody thus sytte?"; "Thinke you in the waste I am so
great?" (147, 154). She immediately invites scrutiny as a spectacle – one of vanity. When Mary re-enters, the Vices direct the
audience's gaze toward her: *"Infidelitie* . . . behold, yonder com-
meth Marie . . . *Pride of Life* It is a pretie wenche . . . *Cupiditie* . . .
She seemeth to be a proude little elfe . . . *Carnal Concupiscence.* I
pray you behold how she trimmeth her geare?" (501–7). The Vices
proceed to instruct Mary in sexually alluring dress, behavior, and
poses: how to roll her eyes fetchingly (which she practices on
stage); how to pile her hair, dye it golden, and "crispe" (632) it
to fall in curls around her eyes; how to bejewel her hair; how to
cover up her pock marks with cosmetics; how to paint her complexion; how to wear clothes that exaggerate and expose her
bosom; and how to deploy her "nether garments" (696).[60] Mary
stands onstage as an eroticized spectacle being worked over by
the counsellor Vices, who climactically describe how men react to
women who wear revealing bodices

> Purposely men to allure vnto their loue,
> For it is a thyng that doth the heart greatly moue.
> At such sights of women I haue known men in dede
> That with talking and beholding their noses will blede.
>
> (680–83)

Before this picture of erotic women and rapt men, Mary becomes
correspondingly agitated: "Your wordes do not onely prouoke my
desire, / But in pleasure they set my heart on fyre" (686–87).
Mary pants over the image of a cosmetized feminine beauty that
arouses others, herself excited with heat ("fyre"), moved
("provoke[d]") with sexual stimulation by her own spectacular
power. Small wonder that this play, as the Prologue acknowledges,
inspired disapproval![61]

Mary Magdalene emphasizes erotic spectacle in other ways, including some close whispering in Mary's ear and an unusual amount of stage kissing; likewise, the Vices' counsel about Mary's appearance might be embroidered with pointing, staring, and physical contact. The play also aims to induce smirking and lewd laughter as audience responses to the sexual double-entendres: at Mary's first appearance, for example, Infidelitie jokes leeringly about the "piece . . . in the mydst of your garment" (171), and he later invites Mary to play on a musical instrument particularly his own: "Truely you have not sene a more goodlie pipe, / It is so bigge that your hand can it not gripe" (843–44). We are asked repeatedly to gaze at Mary, to scrutinize her as an elaborate sexual object, to respond viscerally and kinetically to the arousing sight, and to listen for a subtext of sexual titillation.

Next, Wager's *Mary Magdalene* converts the signs of iniquity into the signs of repentance, so that spectacle will become dramatic action. Thus the play exposes the female body's affective and semiotic power, making the feminine central to issues of sin and redemption, and repudiating the marginalization of women implied in "chaste, silent, and obedient." What the play's first half eroticizes, the second half turns to soteriological effect: the wonder of sexual spectacle becomes the agent of religious transformation. Mary's change begins with the entrance of The Lawe (at 1108), which launches the second half of the play. In Mary's epiphany, eyes and hair figure prominently, along with a sense of the physical body. Lawe, who has proclaimed himself a "glasse" (1121) where people can see what duty they owe to God, strikes Mary with visible bewonderment: "And in dede will you be gasying on him styll?," Infidelitie asks her (1159; see also 1157). "Gasyng on hym still": Mary experiences her conversion by means of the gaze: "O frend Prudence, doe you see yonder glasse? / I will tell what therin I doe see" (1161–62). Lawe explains this process of visual imagination: "I am euermore before the conscience sight, / Shewyng before hym his condemnation" (1193–94), as if he were a Renaissance prospective glass. Mary appears in that vision as "horrible, lothsome, and stinkyng" (1202), and she responds in the spirit of future-sight: "I see that I am but a damned deuill in hell" (1206) and "O this knowledge of synne is so in my syght" (1241).[62] With the impact of immediate material reality, the ugliness of her iniquity strikes Mary.[63]

The power of spectacle now switches from transgression to transformation. What in *Mary Magdalene*'s first half were the sensual terms for sin reinvest the second half as the sensual terms for salvation. According to Repentaunce, the eyes must turn from "carnall delectations" (1442) to "wepyng and teares" (1443); the ears and tongue must turn from "blasphemyng" (1446) to God's word; and likewise all the body's "members" (1457): salvation becomes a sensual experience.[64] Finally re-entering, Mary comes *"sadly apparelled"* (s.d. at 1764), and her first speech emphasizes the spectacle of sin and salvation: "The more I see myne owne synne and iniquitie, / The more knowledge therof, the more greuance" (1766–67). Mary repeats the thesis of salvation as transformation of the spectacle of the body:

> But like as the parts of my body in tymes past,
> I haue made seruants to all kynd of iniquitie,
> The same iniquitie away for euer I do cast,
> And will make my body seruant to the veritie.
>
> (1789–92)

Accordingly, she invokes the instruments of seduction – hair and eyes – as the implements of repentance: her eyes, once employed in "wanton lookes" (1797), will here "shed out teares and water" (1801) to wash the Lord's feet; and her alluring hair, now "vile and vnworthie" (1794), will wipe them. Thus Mary prepares for the dominant spectacular event, toward which the action has been leading: *"Let Marie creepe vnder the table, abyding there a certayne space behynd, and doe as it is specified in the Gospell"* (s.d. at 1828). Mary, who has just delivered a speech of sixty-odd lines, falls virtually silent here, while the other characters describe her movements as onlookers and commentators before this spectacle of humility compelling their attention, revulsion, and admiration. Even when Christ tells a parable, attention returns irresistibly to Mary, weeping and drying his feet with her hair: "See you this woman?" (1869).

Mary's womanliness, I would argue, is central to this play's effect. Wager structures the drama as spectacular action, a strategy that makes him unusual, perhaps original, among mid-century playwrights. His transforming of the signs of iniquity into the signs of salvation, moreover, takes as its site a woman's body, especially her eyes and hair. Those terms suggest, first, how plastic the body's significations are and, second, how powerfully a woman's body can register theatrically. It is surely no accident that, for his visceral theatre, Wager makes a play not about a medieval male subject, such as Saint Paul, but about Mary Magdalene. The female body seems chosen as more commanding and affecting than the male's: even Mary finds the image of her allure sexually arousing. In this play the most compelling spectacle must be gendered female. If *Mary Magdalene* seems misogynistic because it offers alternatively demonized or idealized visions of woman, Mary comes away, nonetheless, as not exactly contained or marginalized. She has magnetic power; she is the cynosure of all eyes; and, for the all-important issues of sin and salvation, she emerges as rivetingly central. Vitality spills beyond misogynistic categories. In the irony of theatre, Mary's extremities give her an authentic, realistic, and affective emotional life, a stage possibility that in the 1560s seems unique to female representation.

Although John Phillip's *The Play of Patient Grissell* (*c.* 1558–61) contains the pro and con voices of the popular women's controversy, its heroine's sufferings make the play appear perversely cruel toward women. The story is familiar. The Marquis Gautier plucks Grissell from poverty to make her his wife (a privileging of virtue over wealth that reiterates the humanist values of *Fulgens and Lucres*). Prompted by the antifemale Vice, Politicke Perswasion, Gautier undertakes a decades-long testing of Grissell, in which he pretends infanticide of her two children – and makes her low social birth indirectly responsible. In these acts Gautier and Politicke Perswasion study clinically Grissell's reactions to see whether the latest blow will stagger her. The humiliations culminate when Gautier announces that he will cast Grissell aside and take a wife younger and of better social station than is Grissell. Gautier sends Grissell back in poverty to her village, while – the bathetic nadir – she gushes with gratitude because he allows her a ragged smock rather than booting her out naked. Gautier then adds insult to injury by bringing Grissell back to court to supervise the wedding festivities. Ultimately Gautier reveals that his pretended bride is really Grissell's daughter, a revelation that effects the family's reknitting and Grissell's restoration. Throughout, the play celebrates Grissell's sense of duty, unquestioning obedience to patriarchal authority, and constant good will in the face of blow after blow.

Turning the story into theatre imposes dramaturgical choices
that complicate, even undermine, its weirdly misogynist thematics. How do you dramatize silence, chastity, and obedience?
How do you make passive resignation interesting on stage for
2121 lines? If on the Jacobean stage the heroism of endurance (as
opposed to the heroism of action) becomes a tragic virtue, as Mary
Beth Rose argues,[65] its dramaturgical coordinates emerge a half-
century before in the voice, authority, political import, and theatrical magnetism of *Patient Grissell*'s women. The play establishes
Grissell's own voice early by introducing her separately from Gautier, and, upon her mother's death, showcasing Grissell's grief.
Grissell takes the stage alone for a mourning soliloquy that
appeals directly to the audience for empathy:

> Thou now art motherlesse become, the graue hir lodge doth rest,
> Whose deth to mourne wt sobbing shrieks, & sighs, y^u now art prest
> Was neuer child had greater losse, nor cause of carking care,
> Help me to weep all such (ah las) that carefull Children are.
>
> (483–86)[66]

Grissell then asks the nine muses to "Strayne forth your noates
of wailfull woes, weepe you & mourne with mee: / That Gods and
men, my inward grief, apparant now may see" (491–92) and proceeds to sing her song of mourning. Just as *Cambises* affords the
Mother a moving speech, her dead son in her arms, or as *Gorboduc*
confers on Marcella a theatrical stop-time in which she laments
Porrex,[67] so, too, *Patient Grissell* displays its heroine's "inward
grief" as noble and affecting spectacle. Since expressing grief at
Gautier's actions would compromise Grissell's patient obedience,
Phillip accentuates early what he must later hide: voice, subjectivity, authenticity. Grissell, then, will carry forward a kind of
inner life known residually to the audience, even as she suppresses
it. Traces of that inner life surface variously, such as when she
praises Gautier's prospective bride but warns him not to push her
too far: "Take heed thou pricke her not, with the Needles of dis-
dayne: / As thou hast done the other, for shee hath bin brought
up dayntelie, / And peraduenture, can not take the matter so paci-
entlie" (1934–36). By conjuring forth Grissell's submerged subjectivity – something characteristic of humanism but not of the
popular tradition – Phillip offers his audience an engaging female
protagonist.

Phillip also creates drama through the responses of the people around Patient Grissell, emphasizing how her detractors and persecutors react to her with wonder. When Gautier wrenches her first child from her for slaughter, Grissell cries out affectingly: "Helpe spoused Dames help Grissill now, hir fate w^t teares to plore / Gushe forth your Brinie streames let tricklinge teares abound" (1202–04). Following that appeal, however, she quickly resolves to hide her pain with patience: "Albeit such dirfull hap haue chauncst, graunt pacience to my paine / That I may seme this cross of thine, with ioye for to sustaine" (1207–08). Gautier wonders at her "wiflie troth" (1211), and Politicke Perswasion signals his awe to the spectators by comparing her favorably to them: "Bodie a God what woman here cold take the matter so pacient / . . . Yet she semeth with this fact to be well content" (1213–15).[68] We are to study Grissell for her absence of grief, as if her very inscrutability evidenced a humanist interiority. Reacting to Grissell's humble acceptance of his intention to divorce her, the marquis staggers with revulsion at his ineffectual persecutions: "Oh hart now reaue and rend, nowe breake thou cleane in sonder / The heauens aboue & lumiuing stars, at this atte[m]pt may wonder / All liuinge wights that heare thys fact will me reward with shame" (1568–71). As he proceeds to rehearse Grissell's virtues, she silently stands by, like Patience on a monument. Gautier's cruelty has so collapsed that Politicke Perswasion must buck him up: "my Lord plucke up your hart, / . . . Are you not ashamed to blubber and weepe" (1580–82). Grissell strikes her oppressors with wonder until finally Gautier begins to feel grief and sympathy on her behalf. Grissell not only commands attention, she infuses other characters and audience members with her displaced feelings, evoking from them the demonstration of her interiority – a theatricality particular to humanist dramaturgy. Again, stage silence can be commanding.

Using displacement in an even more sophisticated and subversive way, Phillip creates a world of women who speak for Grissell and who come to represent values alternative to those of the male world and without which the kingdom is politically unstable. Here *Patient Grissell* recalls More's humanist celebration of women's domestic realm and *Godly Queene Hester*'s portrait of female "hospitalitie" as a social principle. When Diligence seizes Grissell's infant daughter, she is accompanied by the Nurse, who expresses outrage, resistance, and pity that the dramatist cannot show in his heroine. The Nurse takes Grissell's place, continuing to resist after Grissell consents: "Alas my Lorde be mercifull, commit not such offence"; "Thou shalt not kyll, let this procept of the be right-lye waid" (1114, 1122). With Grissell bearing silent witness, the next sixty lines of dialogue pit male aggression against female sympathy. The Nurse decries the unnaturalness of the father's intended infanticide and climactically offers, as a solution to Gautier's problems, to take the child with her into exile: "For I will fead and nourishe hir, and take hir as mine owne / . . . Thus doing thou shalt stop the mouthes, y^t would the babe deuoure" (1170–73). The Nurse's pleading associates women, first, with a realm of mercy and unselfish nurture and, second, with a solution to an apparent dilemma. Gautier must lose either child or kingdom, so he says, to which the Nurse proposes a third alternative that would save Gautier from the Scylla and Charybdis of the play's male imagination.

Those effects are not accidental, because the Countess of Pango (Gautier's sister) and her Maid stand for the same values represented by the Nurse. *Patient Grissell* again employs strategic displacement: for the silent heroine the playwright substitutes other women who can fully express female values. The Countess enters mourning for her long-deceased husband – an action that links her to the early Grissell – while her Maid attempts to console her. Through these characters, Phillip establishes women as the vessels of deep, sympathetic, and constant emotion: "My heauie minde you comfort much, but nature shoes her kynd" (1251). Gautier pays tribute to this other realm when he orders Diligence to take his baby daughter "To the Countise of *Pango* my sister, without let or staye, / Who will nourish it and giue it sustentacion: / And bring hir vp in Godlye and honest conuersacion" (1027–29) – an almost Morean sense of female education.[69] The Countess accepts the baby willingly as her own sorrow's balm: "My hart reuyues and skipes for ioye, to see thy pretye face" (1274). After Diligence departs, the Countess and the Maid exude delight: "behould hir seemly face, / Hir smillinge cheare doth comfort me, God pour on hir his grace" (1285–86). Following the birth of Grissell's second child, the Nurse carries it onstage with motherly affection: "And I poore *Nurs*, am not a littell glade, / To dandle this sweet soule my hart is faine" (1374–75). When Diligence enters, the Nurse attempts physically to protect the baby from him (1417–20) and, after he grapples the child away, to stop Diligence with words and tears bespeaking the female perspective: "Thy raige and furye vouch thou, with pittie to season: / . . . knowe it is better to please God, then anie mortall man" (1427–33). When Diligence answers with the male dilemma – "But if I kill it not I myselfe shall dye" (1435) – the Nurse replies with the female third way: "I will nourish it I and bring it vp as mine owne, / And that it liueth to my Lorde neede not be knowne" (1442–43). After Diligence exits with the child, the Nurse pours out a soliloquy of rage against the "cruell father" (1448) and laments for "poore Grissill" (1468). While Gautier shows his manliness by choking back sympathy, the women ring with sympathy, invent solutions, and take humane action.[70]

For overcoming the dramaturgical problem of a silent and docile heroine, Phillip's last strategy is a catharsis that, in one gesture, tests, restores, and celebrates Grissell. His rabbit-in-the-hat is the young woman, toward whom Gautier pretends betrothal, but whom, at the penultimate moment, he reveals to Grissell as her lost, first-born child: the daughter and son "were not slayne, but Nourished tenderlye, / With my sister, the Countis of *Pango* verelye" (1949–50). Gautier's revelation reintegrates his family and stills the populace's murmuring about his cruelty to Grissell. With the significance special to a 1560s play, the kingdom will now have heirs, so that the personal solutions of *Patient Grissell* become also the political solutions: to align and perpetuate the kingdom, Gautier must publicly acknowledge the suppressed world of female nurture and alternative solutions, the values embodied in the Countess, her Maid, and the Nurse, who have served as silent Grissell's displaced voice.

Patient Grissell lacks the bold humanist coloration of some early plays, although it does invoke humanist classical allusions and political themes ("the plea for stable succession, the prince's insistence on personal choice") found in Boccaccio, Petrarch, and Chaucer,[71] and it turns on the difference between virtue and social status that so occupied humanists. The play celebrates not female learning or reason, however, as does *Fulgens and Lucres*, but rather a self-disciplined Calvinist devotion. *Patient Grissell* seems dedicated at first to idealizing its heroine's thorough repression, yet the play recuperates dramaturgically what it surrenders

thematically.[72] Dramaturgical possibilities advanced by humanism
work against the grain of popular misogyny. The humanist vision
of women as capable of eloquence and action and as defining a
realm of feeling and behavior that render male action incomplete – a vision advanced by More and Elyot – makes possible
dramatic solutions to the theatrical problem of silence and obedience that restore women's displaced voice, agency, and passion.

  Patient Grissell shares the humanism evident in *Mary
Magdalene, Godly Queene Hester, Wit and Science*, and *Fulgens and
Lucres*. Phillip's and Wager's plays make their heroines spectacles,
cynosures of rapt attention and scrutiny – an effect that occurs
with female protagonists of such other 1560s plays as *Susanna* and
Appius and Virginia. Women in these dramas become theatricalized
objects of knowledge. They possess secrets; their natures are enigmatical, their identities sometimes hidden. Roman drama, such
as Terence's *Andria*, had already introduced humanists to women
whose secret identities provide solutions to dramatic problems.
Humanist drama's search for knowledge, as modeled in *Wit and
Science*, appreciates visual deceptions and encourages close observation, humanist motifs as early as *The Foure PP*. In subsequent
plays featuring female leads, that search for knowledge centers on
the scrutiny – visual and moral – of women. The connection makes
sense in terms of humanist poetics. Because they are virtuous,
Hester, Mary Magdalene, and Grissell have the power to transform their onlookers, to awe them, to strike them with reformative
wonder. These female protagonists serve the moral purposes that
Elyot extolled in literature generally, its capacity to inflame the
heart through images of virtues,[73] so that heroines in their powerful theatricality make a keen instrument for humanist moral purposes. The humanist commitment to affective poetics advances
the new 1560s spectacle of women as magnetic, transformative
objects of knowledge.

3

Some of Renaissance drama's least-discussed heroines appear in
the extant romances of the 1570s and early 1580s: *Common Conditions* (S.R. 1576), *Clyomon and Clamydes* (*c.* 1576), and *The Rare
Triumphs of Love and Fortune* (1582). Although only these three
romances survive from the decade when theatre changed from

itinerant to fixed-venue, the form held pride of place as a theatrical genre: of the approximately sixty-five plays performed at court between 1570 and 1585, almost half may have been romances.[74] Stephen Gosson's *Playes Confuted in Fiue Actions* accuses playwrights of pilfering plots from old romances, and Sir Philip Sidney and George Whetstone both scoff at the incredulity of such dramas. The significance of 1570s romances is verified by the echoes and parodies in later stage versions, for example, *Mucedorus*, *The Old Wive's Tale*, *Orlando Furioso* and *The Knight of the Burning Pestle* – and by their influence on the heroines of Lyly, Greene, and Shakespeare, such as Margaret of *Friar Bacon and Friar Bungay* and Imogen of *Cymbeline*. The 1570s romances appealed broadly across all classes of Elizabethan spectators, and they confirm a humanist-informed strain of sixteenth-century female characters.

According to some scholars, the romances constitute part of the popular theatrical tradition deriving from the morality plays. *Common Conditions*, for example, advances by episodes rather than by the structured action and five-act format associated with humanist plays, such as *Gorboduc*.[75] *Common Conditions* and *Clyomon and Clamydes* also contain a transmogrified Vice-figure who both supports and subverts the romance protagonists. Despite Bevington's view that these texts repeat the morality formula of progressive narration, suppression of acting roles, and thematic alternation in scenes, the stage romances have affinities beyond the morality tradition and cannot be summarized as reincarnated moral interludes. The romance's tripartite saga of separation, wandering, and reunion has its own generic history, going back to Greek versions and recalled in Roman comedies such as *The Brothers*, independent of morality narrative. Indeed, a process of stasis, disruption (with separations, estrangements, misunderstandings, plots, complications), and reintegration follows a comedic pattern closely discussed in humanist poetics and shared with much drama, moralities included. Romance drama must be understood as produced from several influences: long-standing chivalric romance narratives, popular moralities, classical models, and humanism. The three romances considered here reflect these influences differently. *Common Conditions* uses the chivalric narrative for crowd-pleasing complications and surprises. *Clyomon and Clamydes* and *Love and Fortune*, more sophisticated, make romantic conventions serve thematic and dramaturgical interests associated with humanism.[76] The stage romances's wide appeal places humanist-influenced drama in the mainstream of commercial public theatre more than a decade before the University Wits flowered.

The link between humanism and romance was forged early in the century: *Wit and Science* in the 1530s, was, as we have seen, an early effort to appropriate the romance form, along with that of the morality, for humanist purposes. In *Wit and Science*, humanism eroticizes the student's thirst for knowledge as romantic desire, whose goal is the beautiful but doubting Lady Science. Romance brings emotion, glamour, and adventure to humanist pedagogical ends; it offers an engaging fantasy about scholastic learning, which might otherwise seem remote and abstract. Romance holds attractions for many sixteenth-century humanist translators and writers, such as Sir John Harington, Sir Philip Sidney, and Edmund Spenser; the genre accommodates humanist values unusually well. Both *Common Conditions* and *Love and Fortune*, for example, concern themselves with bad counsellors to the prince, a central issue for humanist plays such as *Gorboduc* and *Damon and Pithias*. While romance tends to reinforce aristocratic values, *Clyomon and Clamydes* and *Love and Fortune* promote the humanist program of social and political ascendency through merit, a theme of *Fulgens and Lucres* and *Godly Queene Hester*. Love offers an even more pervasive humanist interest and one with no counterpart in the moralities. Romantic love, in the spirit of Petrarch, allows for Platonic idealism to merge with the celebration of physicality, the experience of wonder, and the perseverance of longing. Romantic love is a driving force in *Common Conditions*, *Clyomon and Clamydes*, and *Love and Fortune*. That last play suggests another recurrent romance theme: fortune and its relationship to love. Action in each of the surviving romances develops from faithful love beset by chance, circumstance, and vicissitude. The double heroes of *Clyomon and Clamydes* bewail fortune,[77] and the Vice figures in all three romances act as agents of upheaval. Fortune and love often activate dramatic structure, for these plays begin with lovers (or family members) separated by circumstances and end with their reunion. Gosson wondered disparagingly what a romance's typically silly plot could teach – "what learne you by that?"[78] – but the genre's implicit credo is that true love can survive malign fortune, as *Love and Fortune* makes manifest.[79] With humanism that theme has much to do, but with the morality tradition, little. Even if humanism may not own exclusive rights to the themes of good counsel, merit, and conflict between love and fortune, those issues strongly animate it.

In humanist fashion, the 1570s romance stage is dotted with mythological figures, such as Providence in *Clyomon and Clamydes* and a dozen-odd Roman gods in *Love and Fortune*.[80] In the latter play the mythological gods Love and Fortune operate as orchestrators of the action and as spectators. In the last act these wrangling audience-figures leave their seats and move into the human drama itself, in a manner that recalls A and B's traversing of *Fulgens and Lucrece*'s borders and the gods' intervening like spectators in John Lyly's humanist plays. (Here humanist drama offers its counterpart to the morality play's liminal Vice, who also crosses the boundary between characters and spectators.) The transformation of characters from spectators to actors also hints at humanist drama's interest in the changeable nature of identity and role. The motif of transformed identity, often figured in disguise, recurs in the romances. In *Common Conditions*, Sedmond, the brother shamed by his cowardice in combat, regains his knightly stature and dignity by assuming the identity of Nomides and deceiving his sister, Clarisia, just as her disguise deceives him. In *Clyomon and Clamydes* the Vice, the evil enchanter, the two heroes, and the principal heroine, Neronis, all go incognito. Sidney's *Arcadia* offers perhaps the meta-example of romantic disguise and its humanist thematic possibilities, for there the motif becomes a central element of the action, creating confusions about gender and personal identity. Romance disguise demonstrates the maleability of selfhood, aligning its dramaturgy, like the motifs of love and fortune, with humanist concerns rather than those of morality drama.

Humanist dramaturgy manifests itself in another way in the romances. While the three extant plays vary stylistically, *Clyomon and Clamydes* deserves note for its elevated manner, its rhetorical abundance, and its construction of scenes as "rhetorical rather than dramatic units,"[81] features associating the play with humanism's rhetorical interests. In *Love and Fortune*, the two goddesses, Venus and Fortune, argue over their relative hegemony: are human affairs ruled by love or chance? The two put the matter to a test, with each goddess alternately dominating segments of the human drama, so that at the end of each act, one goddess gloats and the other promises retaliation. Thus at a structural level *Love and Fortune* argues *in utramque partem* proceeding as would an academic disputation in which each goddess has her say, until Jupiter must finally adjudicate the controversy. The protagonists' ups and downs in *Common Conditions* and *Clyomon and Clamydes* reflect the dialectic that *Love and Fortune* embodies in the two quarrelling divinities. That roller-coaster movement bears little kinship with the morality tradition. Moralities certainly showcase opposing values, but their conflicts occur at the level of cosmic good and evil, and they work dramatically as psychomachia, the struggle for the protagonist's consciousness and soul. Stage romance involves no psychomachia; rather, its protagonists attempt to win their way by steadfastness to love in a vicissitudinous world. A romance such as *Love and Fortune* identifies a humanist-influenced commercial drama whose nearest relation is not the late moralities but Lyly's imminent romantic comedy.

Rather than see 1570s romance drama as expressing the morality tradition, we might consider it as exemplifying a line of humanist-influenced dramas that extends from *Fulgens and Lucres* to *Friar Bacon and Friar Bungay*. Women in the three surviving romances might be understood as instances-in-miniature of that tradition (differing from some of their humanist predecessors, however, in that romance characters tend to be more "general and representative"[82]). In *Clyomon and Clamydes*, Neronis, daughter to the Queen of the Strange Marshes, makes one of the romances' most appealing and roundly etched characters. According to Littleton, Neronis's representation as "independent, aggressive, almost audacious" – a "'new woman',," – cannot be explained by the French prose source, *Perceforest*:[83] Like Lucres, Neronis is an original creation. She and Clyomon fall in love but are separated, and one plotline of the play pursues their reunion. From her entrance onward, Neronis maintains a distinct point of view. She proposes a walk abroad to a group of lords and ladies, and when the men promise not to gainsay her, Neronis wittily replies, "Yes yes, men they love intreatie much, before they will be wonne" (746). That line reverses the expected relationship between men and women, for Neronis casts herself as suitor and men as delayers. Thus, when she and Clyomon fall in love, Neronis proclaims her affection before he admits his. The play accords Neronis a playfully assertive, gender-role-reversed position and voice. When

she acknowledges her love to herself, she wonders whether or not
to assume a masculine forwardness and speak: "Because shamefastnesse and womanhood, bids us not seek to men. / Ah carefull
Dame loe thus I stand, as twere one in a trance, / And lacketh
boldnesse for to speake, which should my words advance" (1021–
23). With more dramaturgical deftness than commentators have
expected from 1570s romances, Neronis's divided sensibility
anticipates her later assumption of a masculine identity through
her page's disguise.

Neronis solves her dilemma – can a female be bold? – by posing
an allegorical problem to Clyomon: if an owner's ship is torn away
from its anchor, tossed in a storm and wrecked, and if the wreck-
age is recovered and rebuilt by another party, to whom does the
new ship belong, the first or the second party? In the ensuing
conversation, Clyomon recognizes himself as the ship and Neronis
as the new owner, with now-vested property interests. Since Clyomon is indebted to Neronis for saving his life, the allegory turns
a chivalric obligation into a property right – her right. In an
emerging market economy, that vesting of property rights in
Neronis signals a powerful and independent position. The metaphor receives another twist when Thrasellus, King of Norway,
abducts Neronis by posing as a merchant and luring her onto his
vessel. She escapes, and Thrasellus condemns Neronis for her
"womens subtiltie" and "deceit" (1346, 1355) in defeating his
attempt to make her his own property. His treachery, of course,
repudiates his misogyny, and the playwright drives home that
point by having Clyomon upbraid Thrasellus as the traitor who
"stolest" Neronis (1370).[84] *Clyomon and Clamydes* thus rejects
women's commodification and the misogyny behind it, and awards
Neronis an independent quasi-commercial status usually reserved
for men. The fantasy-world of romance here makes possible a
voice and standing for women that reverses typical social relations.

If 1570s romance drama can give its heroines a voice and a
place from which to speak, stage women with active, initiatory
power cannot be far behind. Neronis saves Clyomon's life, as Clamydes claims Julianna does for him.[85] She escapes from Thrasellus
by her own devices, then assumes a male disguise, and finds
employment first as a shepherd's assistant and later as a page.
When she believes mistakenly that Clyomon is dead, she solilo-
quizes heroically and raises her sword warriorlike to slay herself,

forcing Providence to *"Descend"* (s.d. at 1549) comically from the
heavens to stay her hand in the nick of time. *Clyomon and Clamydes*
portrays Neronis as skillful in her man's part, while sometimes
investing her male role-playing with humor. Despairing of finding
Clyomon, Neronis still has enough initiative to ask employment
as page from a passing knight. When she discovers that the knight
is Clyomon, she not only undertakes a page's labor but also
devises, with Clyomon's mother, a means to test the knight and
reveal her identity.[86] *Clyomon and Clamydes* has its passive women –
Julianna must be saved from a flying serpent, and the Queene's
right to rule the Strange Marshes must be defended by a champion – but Neronis wends her separate way through the play,
refusing to be commodified, making her male identity serve her
female interests.

Character after character assumes a disguise in *Clyomon and Clamydes*, but only Neronis's disguise raises the questions about
gender and identity explored later by Lyly and Shakespeare. Clyomon and Clamydes's disguises are parallel versions of themselves
that help the two heroes prove their honor by their deeds rather
than their noble names. Brian sans Foy, the evil enchanter,
assumes a mask (as Clamydes) the opposite of himself: bravery
for cowardice. But Neronis's disguise as a boy symbolizes an aspect
of herself, her boldness and initiative, that courtly women's
apparell tends to repress. In the 1590s the emergence of "the
disguised woman as equal or friend" to her male counterpart illustrates for many critics the last stage in the master narrative of
women in Renaissance drama, who advance from oppression to
defiance to independence.[87] But Neronis, almost two decades
before Shakespeare's cross-dressed heroines, calls the tidiness of
that narrative into doubt. On the other hand, the gender issues
surrounding Neronis resolve themselves with far less difficulty
than do those of Shakespeare's Viola or Imogen, who also assume
pages' disguises. Neronis as page must endure the swooning of all
the country lasses and the jealousy of all the country swains, but
such awkwardness lacks the comic tension of Viola's duel or her
wooing by Olivia, or Imogen's vulnerability in the forest and
during the war. Nonetheless, as with the characters in Sidney's
Arcadia, disguise allows Neronis to explore and fulfill a "masculine" aspect of her character otherwise partially suppressed. She
demonstrates, as well, the female secret identity, occurring in earl-

ier humanist drama, whose public admission facilitates the play's resolution. The willingness to invest a woman with qualities outside the misogynistic or conventional, a willingness specific to *Clyomon and Clamydes* rather than its source, confirms the play's proximity to humanism. In 1581 Richard Mulcaster argued in *Positions* that women have abilities and intellectual capacities equivalent to those of men:[88] *Clyomon and Clamydes* evidences a parallel, contemporaneous view.

Neronis's assertiveness even loses its masculine aura, as she engages in something remarkable, a female testing of male constancy that inverts the Griselda formula. Neronis discovers that the stranger she serves is Clyomon, who, ignorant of her true identity, sends her ahead of him to announce his homecoming. Neronis immediately invents a device in which she will enlist Clyomon's mother, the Queene. Preceding Clyomon to Denmark, she subsequently disappears in conference with the Queene before Clyomon enters. To his father, Clyomon laments his failure to locate the missing Neronis and compares her favorably to famous women – some of whom double as *querelle de femmes* exempla, such as Susanna, Saba, and Martha (see 1981–97). After the comic testing of Julianna's constancy to Clamydes, the Queene re-enters with a lady "unknowne" (2152), presumably veiled, whom she urges Clyomon to take for a bride, since he has not found Neronis. Clyomon refuses the Queene's entreaties; he refuses even to look on the unknown lady. Finally, Neronis exposes her identity by revealing not her face but her deeds as page: "Of truth Sir Knight, my selfe am he: / I brought your message to the King . . . / I gave you drinke in Forrest sure . . . / I found you once upon the shore full sicke . . . / And I it was that all this while have waighted like a Page on thee" (2192–97). Her masculine service as a page comes in gestures of female healing, as if Neronis overcomes, or unites, gender conventions. The episode tests Clyomon's honor toward Neronis by tempting him with another woman in the face of his futile search for Neronis, and as the disquisition unfolds, Neronis herself replaces the Queene as the chief urger. While Grissell proved her worthiness to Gautier by constancy, here the male must prove a similar worthiness to the female, who now devises and executes the test. Artfully, the testing of Clyomon reveals Neronis's prior constancy and, in effect, prior testing through her service. Neronis commands Gautier's position, and the unveiling of

her secret identity completes the trial of love. *Clyomon and Clamydes*
reverses the misogynistic format of *Patient Grissell*.

Love and Fortune also ends with a beseiged woman in the driver's
seat, for there the king's daughter, Fidelia, gains the power to
negotiate a solution to its marital and political problems through
her body's magical healing properties. Fidelia wishes to marry
Hermione, whom her brother Armenio opposes because Hermione
is below the princess's station. After Hermione is banished from
court, Fidelia attempts to rendezvous with him but is captured by
Armenio; as they return to court, Armenio is struck dumb. Bomelio, Hermione's disguised father, living as a hermit-conjurer-sham
physician, tells the king that Armenio can be cured only by having
his tongue washed with the blood of his greatest enemy, who turns
out to be Fidelia (at odds with him over her marriage). Later,
after madness seizes Bomelio, the gods intervene and reveal that
Bomelio's only cure is to have his face sprinkled with Fidelia's
blood. Fidelia's healing blood – for both Armenio and Bomelio –
must be taken from (or under) her breast. For her part, Fidelia
possesses wit and intelligence, as her opening stychomythic
exchange with Hermione demonstrates (285–306). In rhymed
couplets, Fidelia answers tit-for-tat Hermione's attempts to
smooth over love's rough spots: "*Hermione.* Can that be feruent
loue wherin suspition leads the minde? / *Fidelia.* Most ferue[n]t
loue wher so much loue doth make [the] fancy blind" (297–98).
Armenio, eavesdropping, calls Fidelia "all to bolde" (311), a comment that links Fidelia to Neronis and repeats the female assertiveness of 1570s romantic drama. Fidelia subsequently intervenes
when Armenio accosts Hermione (325ff.) and insists to him, in
the spirit of Lucres, that she will marry Hermione for his good
parts and "vnstained" mind (335), despite his birth. Subsequently
Fidelia steals away from the court's comforts to be with Hermione
and to share his "good or ill" (796) and offers her own life as
"sacrifice" (1722) to save Hermione from her father's wrath.

Fidelia uses the magical healing powers of her female body to
bargain with her father for consent to marry her "chosen loue"
(1724), the condition for giving her blood to Armenio. The king
agrees (helpfully, Hermione has also been revealed as of noble
birth). As she undergoes an onstage bloodletting, Fidelia proclaims her deed a sacrifice for Hermione: "And for they sake, *Hermione*, my deare, / See what I doo, although it touch me neere. /

Now take thy fill, and for his madnesse proue" (1793–95). The blood here constitutes the "deerest blood," taken from the "tenderest part" (1182), "from de hart" (1218). The spectacle of wounding awes the onlookers: "O sweet and fearefull sight, the signe of loue!" (1796), exclaims Hermione. The stage image may recall the wound in the side of the crucified Christ, prominent in medieval and Renaissance paintings, the spilled blood of which also figures as healing's balm and love's sign. Alternatively, it might function as a substitute for milk, evoking and surrounding with mysticism the female power of nurture.[89] So viewed, Fidelia's act could signify merely patriarchal idealizing – but the gesture seems more complicated than that because the female body is not treated here as threatening or as weak and eroticized.[90] Fidelia seems courageously to wound herself: "See what I doo, although it touch me neere," and neither stage directions nor dialogue indicate that any other character performs the deed.[91] Fidelia's masculine qualities take resonance, furthermore, from her intervention in Act II to save Hermione, her attempt just moments before to offer herself as sacrifice for him, and her characterization of the present ordeal as "for thy sake." Even more, Fidelia's self-wounding constitutes a form of violent reciprocity and expiation for Hermione's wounding of Armenio in their second-act fight, when Phizanties had called attention to Armenio's spilled blood (374). Fidelia's spectacular gesture, then, is a masculine act of heroic, martial, self-inflicted pain, just as it is also a female act of nurturing and healing. Fidelia uses the power of her body as leverage to secure her "chosen loue" at the same time that she heals the royal family and a noble father. Since Armenio is heir to the kingdom, Fidelia's bargaining power is inescapably political. Finally, Fidelia gives back to men the gifts of speech (to Armenio) and reason (to Bomelio), so that the nurturing female body becomes associated with those central humanist values that popular misogyny often denies (reason) or represses (speech) in women. In her negotiating skill and her uniting of male and female, Fidelia recalls not only Neronis but also earlier characters such as Lady Science, Hester, and Grissell, even as her wit and intelligence take us back to Medwall's Lucres, and her willingness to sacrifice herself looks forward to Greene's Margaret. Neronis and Fidelia demonstrate how romance offers a dramatic vehicle for the humanist vision of empowered women. As culminating examples in a line of capable females who overcome the limitations of gender categories, Neronis and Fidelia confirm how sixteenth-century drama could move from the misogyny and gender conventions of the popular morality tradition to the more open views of women in Shakespeare and other later playwrights: that transformation was made possible by the intervening humanist dramaturgy of women.

6

The confusions of Gallathea:
John Lyly as popular dramatist

The dramaturgy of women that we have been considering brings us to the plays of John Lyly, who invests romance with a new, sophisticated dynamism. We have learned to think of Lyly as the archetype of the failed "humanist as courtier."[1] In that melancholy conception, the humanist endeavors to put his high ideals and intellectual skills to work for the court, only to discover that it values him solely as an entertainer. We can consider Lyly, however, from another, less familiar angle, that of the humanist as "popular playwright" who adds to the emotional power of public theatre. To do so calls into question once more the prevailing paradigm of sixteenth-century drama: that humanist plays differ from popular ones in that the former are intellectual, arid, and aristocratic while the latter are visceral, imaginatively arousing, and plebeian, and that consequently playwrights such as Lyly failed with the public because they wrote a static "drama of ideas." Reappraisal of that reigning paradigm of Tudor drama involves recognizing a virtue in humanist plays exactly where they presumably fall short of popular ones, in the aspect of theatricality.

Toward that end, I offer two arguments about Lyly's drama, using the "court comedy" Gallathea (c. 1584) as my leading example.[2] First, although Lyly's plays have been treated by modern critics as static and intellectual dramas of ideas, Gallathea generates emotional and visceral delight from, not exactly ideas, but a pleasurable "confusion" that displays theatrical values one expects from popular plays. Here Lyly demonstrates humanist drama's contribution to public theatre: an engaging tension between intellect and emotion, a juxtaposition of didacticism with life's uncertainties. Second, Gallathea shares conventions, strategies, and goals with popular drama. Its structure, mythological machinery, and language recall, while pushing beyond, the stage romances, in particular, of the previous decade. These two aspects converge, in that *Gallathea*'s kinesthetic and emotional confusions work to fashion the kind of desire for theatre helpful in attracting repeat spectators to the permanent playhouses.

At Elizabeth's court two types of drama came to prevail by the 1580s: humanist classical stories, often enacted by school-boy companies, emphasizing courtly themes of love, chastity, friendship, valor, and magnanimity; and chivalric romances, typically performed by professional men's companies, showcasing adventure, love, enchantment, intrigue, exotic characters, and spectacle. These qualities might overlap, as in *The Rare Triumphs of Love and Fortune* (1582), a romance performed by Derby's Men and before the court, in which classical gods oversee an exotic story of human love. By the 1580s, then, the repertoire of the popular stage had come to make up an element of court drama; Lyly is credited with further merging classical and popular playmaking.[3] Hunter praises Lyly's "complex and sophisticated plays," "genuine literary contribution," and "dainty artifice,"[4] literary and intellectual qualities that Lyly presumably contributes to popular drama from his humanist training. But behind such commendation lurks an implicit detraction. Instead of emphasizing the theatrical appeal of Lyly's plays, Hunter suggests that popular drama acquired humanist sophistication; he links public and elite drama by allowing the former to assume "literary" qualities, while leaving kinesthetic excitement the exclusive property of the amphitheatre. Thus, paradoxically, modern criticism brings the popular and humanist lines together in Lyly only by stressing a literariness and refinement that estrange him from theatrical values.

How can we distinguish a theatricality in Lyly's works comparable to that of popular drama? Literary court plays typically possess three characteristics, according to Saccio: mythology as their matter, plotlessness as their dramatic technique, and allegory as their mode of meaning.[5] These qualities are related, for the stasis of plot common in court drama – that is, its persistent focus on a central situation – allows for meanings to accrete slowly into allegory, a possibility unavailable to popular theatre, which must engross its spectators through change: movement, liveliness, suspense.[6] We have, then, a point of contrast: the more dynamic the play, the more it resembles the pattern of popular drama. Accord-

ingly, Lyly's humanist *Gallathea* will gravitate toward popular theatre to the degree that it transgresses the stasis of the drama of
ideas; the play will do so, I shall argue, by means of a dynamism
manifested in the tension and vitality of its "confusions." Lyly's
works may lack the excited passions and fervent eroticism that
provoked Stephen Gosson to attack the amphitheatres, but the
plays are still charged with emotion and erotic energy. *Gallathea*
emphasizes the physical and visceral, eroticizing bodily behavior
and expression; it makes sexual attraction into something performed. Indeed, Lyly's plays in general contain a critically under-
appreciated sense of human physicality. Lylyan spectacle also parallels popular drama's capacity for wish-fulfilling engulfment, a
quality at odds with the image of intellectual and courtly allegor-
ism attributed to Lyly.[7] The dynamism of popular drama leads to
a cognate interest: the playhouses had a stake in creating desire,
most importantly the desire for theatre itself. Desire for theatre
develops partly from the cultivating of appealing themes, conventions, and fashions; audience desire can then be answered by
further works that fit those templates.[8] In that regard, Lyly
appears to be one of the first Elizabethan writers of what might
be called a "serial" drama. In *Gallathea* he undertakes to engage
his audience with the play's mystifications as a theatre-piece, so
that spectators might depart satisfied but longing still for the pleasures that only drama can provide.

1

To a degree unprecedented in Tudor theatre, John Lyly makes
drama an object of pleasurable psychological agitation or "confusion." Critics, however, have seldom seen Lyly that way.
Reviewing the seminal discussions of Lyly's drama by Knight,
Hunter, and Saccio, Robert J. Meyer writes, "Most recent critics
of Lyly's dramatic work agree that his plots are essentially undramatic, characterized by a static, emblematic quality which contra-
dicts our modern notions of what drama should be."[9] Other critics
agree. Mary Beth Rose, for example, calls Lyly's consciousness
"inherently undramatic."[10] Joel Altman likewise argues that Lyly
"prefers to hypothesize his *quaestiones* by means of loosely connected deliberations and disputations which are developed through
a variety of exemplary proofs," concluding that Lyly's drama "is

concerned primarily to stimulate the intellect."[11] Yet at the heart of the Lylyan aesthetic, I would argue, dwells a reluctance to conceptualize. Action in Lyly's plays may proceed by definitional questions ("What is love?"), but those questions are rarely answered definitionally. Instead, Lyly's stage figures receive a confused heightening of their physical and emotional awareness. A visceral level of meaning works in collaboration with the fantasies, dreams, and wish fulfillments that haunt Lyly's plays and that recall popular values in drama. Lyly's works trail in their wake a sense of both ideas and their limitations – confusion. *Gallathea*'s ideas, for example, do not square with its theatrical pleasures, so that experience exceeds intellectual description, leaving spectators to depart wondering. Lyly's plays pursue the cultivation of emotion that Gosson abhorred in playhouse drama, the emotion whose "construction," Steven Mullaney argues, characterizes early modern theatre.[12]

In Lyly's drama ideas falter variously. Sometimes Lyly parodies formal reasoning itself, as in the syllogism wars of the "pages" in *Sapho and Phao* and *Midas*. In *Gallathea* straightforward propositions have a way of turning enigmatical. The eponymous heroine states her play's best-known "idea": "Destenie may be deferred, not preuented" (1.i.69–70).[13] Varied and repeated, that maxim seems to govern this and other Lyly plays: "But destinie is seldome foreseene, neuer preuented," claims Timoclea at the outset of *Campaspe* (1.i.36–37); "they that contend with the gods doe but confound themselues," asserts Niobe in *Loues Metamorphosis* (1.i.36–37). In *Gallathea* Neptune, the force of destiny, has for many years demanded the sacrifice of the city's most beautiful virgin. But that destiny is prevented in a literal sense, because no virgin suffers sacrifice – although one will undergo a change of sex (which neither regards as sacrificial). Lyly overthrows destiny – and even before doing so he renders it inoperable. The impending sacrifice to Neptune prompts Tyterus to disguise his beautiful daughter, Gallathea, and send her into the woods. But just two scenes later, Lyly gives us a second virgin, Phillida, as beautiful as the first, likewise disguised by her father. Lyly humorously denies the condition necessary to fulfill destiny: one and only one most-beautiful virgin. Lyly's multiplication of most-beautiful, sacrificial virgins throws destiny into chaos – and it's still the first act. *Gallathea* proffers "ideas" that its action leaves playfully confused.

As Lyly's play-world defies its own maxims it reveals the kind of theatricality one expects in popular drama. In *Campaspe* or *Sapho and Phao*, the pages resolve their syllogism battles with singing, so that theatrical performance displaces logic and ideas. Indeed, Lyly often employs singing in this way, along with other skills. In *Campaspe*, for example, Act V, scene i, sets out three virtuosic displays – dancing, tumbling, and singing – in quick succession. Lyly's theatre returns repeatedly to a concrete interest in the body, in the physical, kinetic, and emotional dimensions of experience. Characters know the confusions of love because, like the nymphs in *Gallathea*, they feel them as shocks of sensation beyond their ken or control. Fantastical, Ovidian transformations of the body drive Lyly's plays: a girl becomes a boy; a king acquires a golden touch and ass's ears; a lover goes to sleep as a youth and awakes an old man; three nymphs turn into, respectively, a rock, a rose, and a bird, and then back again to nymphs – all changes that must be realized onstage through properties and costumes. In Lyly's drama, intellectualism yields to sensation and spectacle. Juxtapositions and shifts of tone, verbal style, texture, and point of view also define Lyly's theatrical rhythm. While Lyly's drama is termed "static," such plays as *Gallathea* and *The Woman in the Moone* depend upon dynamic contrasts and changes of focus. Consider the multiple perspectives in *The Woman in the Moone*. With squabbling gods who manipulate each act, with Pandora or Gunophilus betraying knowledge to the audience that is withheld from the characters, or even with action swirling around the sleeping Pandora, *Woman*'s skillful management of "several layers of discrepant awareness" gives evidence of its "stageworth[iness]."[14] Theatrically, *Woman* employs audience asides, staged playacting, deceptions, near-frantic entrances and exits, and considerable physical comedy. A different planet dominates each of the acts, which reveal corresponding aspects of Pandora, and her fluctuations provoke in turn the comic confusions of the Utopian shepherds. While the play's world may be small in circumference, it churns with a sense of world-in-process.[15]

Lyly's plays also achieve emotional energy from their teasing symmetries. Characters and actions parallel but then diverge; language and ideas become ironical as they are reiterated: these plays have mirrors in their corners. No English playwright before Lyly writes with such an engaging sense of internal correspondences and contrasts – a dramaturgy akin to Lyly's prose style.[16] Resemblances circulate among the plays, as well, hinting at Lyly's larger interest in a lively, self-referential theatrical world. Lyly repeats elements from comedy to comedy, creating a kind of "serial" drama. The plays involve recurrent motifs, such as the limits of reason, the bodily orientation of plebeian characters, fidelity and fickleness, longing and wish fulfillment. Mythological figures resurface again and again – Venus, Cynthia, Diana and her nymphs, Cupid – and Lyly's dénouements frequently usher forth a *deus ex machina*. One has the vague sense of encountering different versions of the same drama. Such mirroring and repetition reveal not a theatre of static intellectualizing but a theatre building its own collective *mise en scène*, its own physical and emotional environment, a theatre perpetuating a desire for its familiar satisfactions.

2

Gallathea displays Lyly's skill at structural and intellectual confusion. The traditional critical approach sees *Gallathea* as varying an "idea" from episode to episode, like a wave of energy that passes through concentric circles. But *Gallathea* strays from that metaphor. As it progresses to new character groups and story lines, it allows the relationship among them to become ironic, even opaque. Each of its four plot-lines organizes a portion of the play: (1) Gallathea and Phillida have five scenes in Acts I and II; (2) the apprentices cluster from the end of Act I through Act III; (3) the gods and nymphs dominate Act III; (4) the subplot of the citizens and Haebe develops in Act IV and early Act V. Thus the initial stalemate between Gallathea and Phillida recedes as the more dynamic stories of the rustics, the immortals, and Haebe move into the foreground. Where Gallathea and Phillida are comically awkward, the apprentices turn buffoonish, and Haebe's subplot accelerates into hilarious satire. Finally all the plot-lines weave together in the last scene (v.iii). Act by act, one center of narrative interest displaces another, and tone, energy, and comedic quality differ correspondingly – a dramaturgical rhythm characteristic of other Lyly plays such as *Campaspe* and *Endimion*. This pattern offers an analogy to the popular morality plays' "progressive" action identified by Bevington, in which scenes alternate between the forces of good and evil, and vice characters successively supplant each other with new points of view.[17]

Gallathea may compare to popular theatre, but it diverges from the drama of ideas, where each plot-line rearticulates the same question or statement. We can test that model against the Raffe scenes, which highlight the problem of making sense. The pages, or apprentices – the rustic sons of a miller – wander through the woods, each in search of a master and a vocation. Although largely neglected by criticism the apprentices' scenes command approximately the same number of lines as those featuring the deities and more lines than the other stories prior to the finale, facts that suggest their importance.[18] But the business of these scenes squares awkwardly with *Gallathea*'s other strands of action. Lyly tempts the audience to think that the rustics connect allegorically with the rest of the play: their adventures refer, after all, to Neptune's roiling sea, presumption to godlike knowledge and power, and elusiveness of language. Into the apprentices' second scene, for example, spill diverse strands of the play – gods, fairies, devils, enchanted woods, and deceptive appearances. First Raffe enters describing disembodied noises and spirits (II.iii.3–5) – whereupon fairies suddenly cross the stage *"dauncing and playing"* (s.d. at 5), and Peter, the Alchemist's unhappy apprentice, arrives covered in soot like a demon and muttering about the "beating of spirits" (10). With the Alchemist, furthermore, a theme of metamorphosis emerges that will color each plot-line and the dénouement. The boys also introduce the idea of "multiplication" (29), suggestive of allegorizing. At the play's end the apprentices make comically explicit their ability to "duble" and "treble" melodic lines (v.iii.193) – and, figuratively, story lines – "[b]aselie" and "[m]eanely" (189, 191), a virtual metaphor for the concentric-circles theory of Lylyan structure.

But if such images and ideas multiply from story line to story line in *Gallathea*, what do the apprentice scenes mean? What ideas do they confirm? Critics generally consider the transforming power of love to be one of *Gallathea*'s main ideas, but the apprentice scenes have nothing to say about love. On the other hand, the vanity of godlike aspirations emerges as a theme via Raffe's masters, for the Alchemist and Astronomer are as presumptuous as their pseudosciences are feckless. Yet it is the efficaciousness of god-like aspirations, rather than their vanity, that marks

Gallathea–Phillida story line, as the fathers, Tyterus and Mele-
beus, succeed in circumventing the god's original will. Can destiny
be altered? Yes, despite Gallathea's opening maxim, though not
always in the way one wishes. The fathers' success seems to nullify
the ridiculing of such aspirations in the Raffe scenes, which appear
more moralistic – erringly so – than the main action. The story
line pursues not didactic clarity but, rather, confusion.

The theme of transformation pervades the play, and it achieves
extravagant confirmation when love acquires the power to resolve
the Gallathea–Phillida problem physiologically. By contrast, Raffe
emerges at the play's end metamorphosed hardly at all. Instead,
the apprentice scenes affirm the human *enthusiasm* for transformation and the pleasure in anticipating it, regardless of its improbability. Despite the vanity of god-like presumptions that Raffe witnesses, his encounters delight more than disillusion him – and
presumably the audience. Raffe's enthusiasms soar repeatedly,
even when confusions of language riddle his conversation. His
business is to meet prospective masters and to tender his service
ecstatically. In such a spirit, Raffe exits with the Alchemist: "I
must blesse my selfe, and maruell at you"; "I followe, I runne, I
flye" (II.iii.126, 128). When disenchanted with the Alchemist,
Raffe yet billows before the Astronomer's promise of metamorphosis: "Then I shall be translated from this mortality . . . O fortune! I feele my very braines moralized, and as it were a certaine
contempt of earthly actions is crept into my minde, by an etheriall
contemplation. Come, let vs in" (III.iii.80–85). Raffe exits his
scenes "enamored" of his masters' arts (II.iii.74), just as the masters are impassioned by mysteries, even if they wear rags or fall
into ponds as a result. Later, when Raffe meets his brother Robin,
he cannot refrain from boasting of the Astronomer and Alchemist,
the latter of whom could "of a little fasting spittle, make a hose &
doublet of cloth of siluer" (V.i.29–30). Unmasked as charlatans,
the masters persist as comic sources of inspiration.

The rustics take joy in imagining. As we have noted, Raffe,
accepting service with the Astronomer, revels in the prospect of
"etheriall contemplation." He has expressed that same joy
moments earlier: "Happie am I, for now shall I reach thoughts"
(III.iii.64). When the fortune-teller prognosticates that Robin
"should liue to see [his] father hangd, and both [his] brothers
beg," Robin optimistically misinterprets: "So I conclude the Mill

shall be mine, and I liue by imagination still" (v.i.34–36). At Peter's news of Dick, Raffe is eager to leave: "I pray thee bring vs to him quickly, for I am great bellied with conceite till I see him" (74–75). Expectation delights and buoys the rustics. An irrepressible expectation drives their scenes, and the apprentices accept the poverty of reality with a humor that impersonalizes and disarms it. Their delight does not constitute an "idea" as do the play's aphorisms – for example, the warnings that destiny cannot be prevented nor the gods deceived. The apprentices' optimism in fact *defies* their disillusionments. At the page's inability to learn, the Mariner rejoins, "Hast thou no memorie?" (i.iv.62): the apprentices represent an enthusiasm that obviates both memory and learning. Their scenes illuminate not wise counsel, not epigrams for living, but rather an experience, a delight, antecedent to – perhaps independent of – wisdom. That enthusiasm defines their central place in the play. With the rustics a wide swath of *Gallathea* refuses to fit the concept of a drama of ideas. The apprentice scenes link circumstantially to other plot-lines, but those links never explain the action of the scenes, their length, or their frequency. The rustics are inherently confused – they are confusion-as-being – and their interludes display a pleasure inaccessible to abstract intellectualizing.

The theatrical pleasure of the pages extends to their festive physicality and comic foreshadowing. The page's humor evokes bodily experience (as if to suggest a humanistic sense of the carnivalesque). "Multiplication," for example, is first associated with singing and alchemy (e.g., ii.iii.29, 39 and iii.iii.29, 71) but takes on sexual connotations when Raffe reports of the Alchemist: "I sawe a prettie wench come to his shoppe, where with puffing, blowing, and sweating, he so plyed her, that hee multiplyed her" (v.i.18–20). Other concerns of the apprentices revolve around food and warmth. Similarly in *Campaspe*, the dialogue of the philosophers' pages is dominated by food, hunger, and meager provisions, as opposed to the preoccupations of the masters: "giue me pleasure that goes in at the mouth, not the eare; I had rather fill my guttes then my braines" (i.ii.52–54), says Manes, Diogenes's servant. The antic wit, wordplay, and unpredictable energy of *Campaspe*'s pages not only convey delight but also infuse a sense of possibility into other story lines, such as the romance between Campaspe and Apelles. In *Gallathea*, the pages register an experience more expansive – more "multiple" – than that of most other character groups. Their transcendent enthusiasms and physical pleasures constitute a theatricalized answer to intellectual pretension. The apprentices' first scene may also provide a form of dramatic prediction for the spectators. The boys enter the play having washed ashore after a shipwreck that has apparently claimed the life of their master. If the bubbling sea recalls the roaring waters associated with Agar that threaten the virgins – the subject of the scene preceding – then the safe landing of the pages may function proleptically for the maidens: despite dangers, the principals will weather their peregrinations comically intact (or mostly so). Such business shows the apprentice scenes operating at the margins of the narrative to establish not a parodic "counter truth" so much as the enlarged frame of reference of the theatrical itself. Those scenes may bring to mind what Weimann describes in popular drama as a *platea*-based authority of the performers and performance as distinct from a *locus*-based authority of the representation.[19] The pages' enthusiasm – irrepressible, overflowing, infectious – evokes just such a theatrical provenance and pleasure.

The page scenes stand for the recognition of *Gallathea*'s own theatricality. The apprentices infuse *Gallathea* with a stage vitality comparable to that of the clowns and vices of popular comedy. Weimann and others have taught us to associate a visceral theatrical pleasure and self-consciousness with the popular moralities, yet Lyly's pages do not derive from that tradition. Although their theatrical virtues may parallel qualities found in popular drama, they arise out of the humanist enterprise. The pages' antecedents are students: initially, the often witty, glib students of school texts, such as the *Colloquies* of Erasmus and *Dialogues* of Vives; later, the comic figures of student-acted plays such as *Wit and Science* and *Roister Doister*.[20] Related to the main action – but carnivalesquely so – the apprentice-action upsets the metaphor for the play's structure as concentric rings through which a central thematic statement ripples; instead, that action carries its own wayward sense of expectation, pleasure, and exuberance. Just as the apprentices are ontologically confused, their scenes manifest a structural confusion linked to *Gallathea*'s theatrical dynamism.

The Gallathea–Phillida love plot also creates theatrical pleasures that exceed the drama of ideas. According to Robert Y. Turner, Lyly's "experiments with dialogue . . . put on stage probably for the first time conversations not about love but conversations that dramatize love."[21] In that dramatization of love, what attracts the maidens to each other? "Confusion" in two senses, one physiological, the other psychological. Both forms of confusion generate a pleasurable agitation uncharacteristic of intellectual drama. First, Lyly makes the two virgins' physical embarrassment attractive. Wandering in the woods, apparelled unhappily as men, the maidens behave toward each other as flustered, tongue-tied, and blushing: "confused" – and thus desirable in a manner associated with male desire. Gallathea and Phillida's first scene together requires bodily expressiveness as much as declaiming. Gallathea enters blushing with self-consciousness: "Blush Gallathea that must frame thy affection fitte for thy habite . . . Thy tender yeeres cannot dissemble this deceipt, nor thy sexe beare it" (II.i.1–4). Similarly, Phillida draws attention to her own gait as "vntoward" and her appearance as "vnfit" and "vnseemely" (13–14). Gallathea's observation of her counterpart, "I perceiue that boyes are in as great disliking of themselues as maides" (16–17), indicates that Phillida's movements betray awkwardness and embarrassment. Likewise, Gallathea's worry that she will curtsy when she means to bow (23–24) invites a display of her own physical confusion. Both Phillida and Gallathea fear that they will blush or actually do blush (25, 28). So caught up are the two in struggling to present themselves as men and in simultaneously noting their own ungainliness before the gaze of the other that they fall in love without exchanging a word. Overall, Lyly makes beauty not a cool Petrarchan inventory – grey eyes, red lips, fair skin – but a performance, a flustered, blushing, physical confusion. That change has implications for the staging of attractiveness in popular drama.[22]

To call the Gallathea–Phillida scenes "static," then, belies their theatrical liveliness. The maidens' asides, furthermore, stress their awareness of watching and being watched – a condition inherently theatrical – and implicate the spectators in the self-consciousness of the characters, so that the audience's position amplifies the maidens' embarrassment. According to Anne Lancashire, *Gallathea*'s characters are not humans but "fixed representations of different moral points of view."[23] While that argument contains some truth, it inevitably misses a theatrical richness in the characters that has little to do with "moral points of view" and much to do with emotions and feelings. In addition, Gallathea and Phillida's sense of their own "presentations" briefly confers upon them a status that approaches subjectivity. In *The Woman in the Moone* Pandora experiences moments of subjective awareness when she witnesses herself suddenly altering emotionally but feels powerless to control the change. Similarly, as Gallathea and Phillida sense an alienation from their own identities they suggest an inchoate subjectivity. A character's consciousness of her fractured self has the paradoxical effect of implying her potential wholeness. That effect registers something beyond an amusing irony here, because the new dramaturgical status of Gallathea and Phillida as, for the time, more "subjects" than they were before tints them with emotional credibility.

Beyond physical embarrassment and blushing, confusion has a second sense that also carries theatrical implications. Although each maiden is confused about the facts of the other's sex, both prefer that confusion over clarification. By having Gallathea and Phillida each address the audience in soliloquy after their first scene, Lyly emphasizes their ambivalence. Gallathea will hardly acknowledge what she almost says: "It may be Gallathea, – foolish Gallathea, what may be? nothing" (II.iv.11–12). Likewise, Phillida can hardly believe her own transformation: "Art thou no sooner in the habite of a boy, but thou must be enamored of a boy?" (II.v.3–4). The male costumes may have released in the maidens a transgressive, carnival energy. But Phillida founders, too: "I will, – I dare not; thou must, – I cannot. Then pine in thine owne peeuishnes. I will not: I wil . . . Well, what I will doe, my selfe knowes not" (7–8). Neither character dares to recognize what she obviously intends. As confusion becomes the condition – and the camouflage – for transgressive erotic fantasy, it achieves the status of psychological pleasure. To link confusion with transgressive fantasies is to draw closer on the horizon than we might have expected to popular plays such as *Tamburlaine*, in which the hero's capture of Zenocrate instances the larger fantasy of violating social boundaries.

Gallathea and Phillida lengthen confusion into the pleasure of delay. Their longest exchange ends with the pair's removal off-stage to continue their sexual fencing and paradox-making: "Come let vs into the Groue, and make much one of another, that cannot tel what to think one of another" (III.ii.58–59). But, of course, they have already inferred each other's gender, as their various asides admit: "Aye me, he is as I am, for his speeches be as mine are" (41–42). Gallathea and Phillida avoid confirming, would deny, what they also find manifest. That denial allows the two virgins to appear in the next scene (IV.iv) now openly in love; their willing confusion has created the interval for commitment to solidify. The Gallathea-Phillida scenes thus possess a dynamic narrative trajectory. For the two girl-boys, pleasure and titillation arise from unknowing, postulating, guessing, hypothesizing – that is, deferring certainty. The characters' admissions to the audience of their willed uncertainty, moreover, make their deferrals into a spectatorial pleasure (just as the apprentices' urgency predicates a pleasure of anticipation). Mental confusion and bodily confusion can both please – and in *Gallathea* they are related: the "drama of ideas" cannot account for such rich and agitating theatricality. Indeed, both Raffe's enthusiasm and the maidens' confusions stand in an oppositional relationship to knowledge.

Just as deferral contributes to the pleasures of Lylyan theatrical confusion, so too does disruption of the formulaic. The "rejection of Haebe" scene (v.ii), as it parodies theatrical convention, might mark an unusual moment in the development of Elizabethan comedy. The episode receives surprisingly little critical comment, and neither Hunter nor Saccio treats it as comedic.[24] In the fourth act (scenes i and iii), Lyly heightens expectation and suspense about the prospective virgin sacrifice, anticipated earlier in Act I, scenes ii and iii. According to convention, all virgins are fair, and in *Gallathea* the most beautiful virgin must be sacrificed to Neptune's wrath to save the city (the sacrifice suggests, of course, a barely sublimated sexual ravishment). Brought in ceremonially and bound to the golden tree, the virgin Haebe delivers a farewell speech that takes up two thirds of the scene. Her speech proceeds through the stages of leave taking: from her opening misery at the injustice of her fate, through analogies for the unnaturalness of savaging youth and beauty, toward a growing fatalism, on to tender valedictory evocations of maidenhood and the court and farewell apostrophes to goddess and parents, rising to a repudiation of the world's vanity, and achieving finally a readiness to be cruelly devoured: "Come *Agar* thou vnsatiable Monster of Maidens blood, & deuourer of beauties bowels, glut thy selfe till thou surfet, & let my life end thine" (48–50). An authentic sense of the stages of despair, loss, and hard-won reconciliation informs her speech.

But Haebe's situation also veers toward the ridiculous, for her tragic farewell ends in hilarious anticlimax. Even as Haebe cries out, "Come death . . . Come *Agar* . . . Tear these tender joints . . ." (46–51), these last sentences must be punctuated theatrically with expectant but empty pauses, as her dialogue finally indicates: "Why abatest thou thy wonted swiftnesse?" (52–53). She cries out her readiness one last time, "Come *Agar* thou horrible monster, & farewell world thou viler Monster" (54–55), which can only be followed by another pregnant pause. Finally in surprise or consternation, Augur must intervene: "The Monster is not come" (56). After the suspenseful build-up through the scenes, after Haebe's operatic leave taking, after the expectant pauses for the moment of ravishment – *nothing happens!* Lyly achieves here a comedy that Monty Python might envy, for he obliterates the most sacred of romantic conventions: Haebe is not beautiful enough to be sacrificed. Augur drives the point home, "[T]ake in this Virgine, whose want of beauty hath saued her owne life" (58), while another townsman apologizes comically, "We could not finde any fairer" (60). Haebe exits feeling both fortunate to be alive and regretful at not being sacrificed: she thus rings another variation on Lylyan confusion. The townspeople leave muttering that "it had beene best for vs thou hadst beene most beautifull" (69–70), a hilarious opposing of homeliness to communal good. Although the scene draws attention to Haebe's physical appearance, her plainness is hardly tragic, since it saves her life. Rather, her embarrassment becomes delightfully humorous. The play has already made blushing confusion a source of spectatorial pleasure, and the climax of Haebe's scene provides ample occasion for a blushing reminiscent of *Gallathea* and *Phillida*. Lyly's presumably abstract drama makes comedy here, first, through its dramaturgy of anticipation, suspense, and surprise and, second, through the actor's physical ungainliness and facial perturbations.

The larger targets, of course, are the literary and theatrical conventions of virgin sacrifice. Illustrative of such conventions, George Buchanan's humanist Latin drama *Jepthes* (*c.* 1543) eroticizes and idealizes the sacrifice of Jeptha's virgin daughter, Iphis.[25] *Jepthes* takes its inspiration from the humanist fascination with Euripides' *Iphigenia* – since classicism and Christian humanism converge on the theme of sacrifice – translated by Eramus into Latin in 1506 and reprinted numerous times in the sixteenth century.[26] In Seneca's *Troades*, as well, a beauty like that of Iphis irradiates Polyxena as she is sacrificed to the ghost of Achilles.[27] The parody of eroticized virgin death, however, does not depend on literary allusions, for threats to virgins were part of the popular stage tradition immediately preceding Lyly. In the romance *Common Conditions* (S.R. 1576) for example, Clarisia is tied to a tree and threatened with rape, and in *Clyomon and Clamydes* (*c.* 1576), Juliana lives under peril from a flying serpent who devours virgins. That play even treats a threatened virgin death parodically, when Neronis offers suicide at the discovery of a grave that she believes to be her lover's and Providence must descend from the heavens as a comic *deus ex machina* to stay her hand (Neronis has not bothered to read the notice on the grave marker). Later Neronis barely escapes ravishment by the king of Norway. Precedents such as Iphis's pathetic sacrifice and the sometimes comic near-misses of the embattled virgins in *Clyomon and Clamydes* may have intersected in Lyly's imagination to produce his parody of the motif. Few playwrights previous to Lyly had been capable of creating such a funny, comically triumphant climax by using the bodily immediacy of theatre to identify and lampoon its more literary conventions. That *coup de théâtre* reveals an underappreciated virtue of humanist drama.

Lyly's sense of humor is often discussed in terms of his prologue to *Sapho and Phao*: "Our inte[n]t was at this time to moue inward delight, not outward lightnesse, and to breede . . . soft smiling, not loude laughing: knowing it to the wise to be a great pleasure to heare counsell mixed with witte, as to the foolish to haue sporte mingled with rudenesse" (7–11). Although critics accept "soft smiling" as Lyly's comedic aim, an image that fits the paradigm of Lyly as a court dramatist, the prologue to *Sapho and Phao* attempts to excuse the apparently lukewarm public reception of *Campaspe*; it cannot and should not be taken as exhaustively descriptive of Lyly's comedic effects throughout the rest of his playwriting career. On the contrary, *Gallathea* shows Lyly developing a comic dynamism, from the blushing confusions of the maidens, to the absurd confusions of the apprentices, to the hilarious baffling of conventions for virgin sacrifice – "soft smiling" yielding to a broader "loude laughing."

Gallathea's final scene brings the characters and the audience not so much to a resolution of ideas as to a climax of desire. At the play's close, of course, the two maidens head offstage where Venus will transform one of them, so far undesignated, into a man to complete their love. Many of Lyly's other characters undergo psychological and physical metamorphosis. Venus makes Sapho incapable of loving Phao; Endimion falls asleep young and awakens old; Midas grows ass's ears; nymphs are changed into objects and animals. At the end of *The Woman in the Moone*, Gunophilus suffers an onstage transformation: "Vanish into a Haythorne as thou standst" (v.i.273), commands Nature. Lyly's figures seem so malleable and permeable that they hardly qualify as self-contained "characters" in the modern sense. Yet in *Gallathea*, as we have noted, confusion lends Gallathea and Phillida a flickering self-consciousness, observable in Lyly's other plays. That hint of the maidens' subjectivity makes the ensuing transformation theatrically charged beyond its ideas. Fantastical wish fulfillment saturates Lyly's plays: a touch of gold (*Midas*); different parents or children (*Mother Bombie*); the love object of your dreams (*The Woman in the Moone*). Characters receive what they fantasize – for better or, often, worse. The emergent subjectivity of Lyly's stage figures may ignite for the spectators the fantastical dream of real human transformation – the dream in which Lyly approaches Marlowe's popular appeal.

Gallathea's ending excites a pleasurable psychological confusion as it plays an abstract, intellectualized response against a more local, concrete, and visceral one – a conflict that Shakespeare employs in *Twelfth Night* and elsewhere. One of the two virgins will be transformed into a boy. Should we ask which one? The more formal and conceptual perspective answers, "No." The metamorphosis ought not to be completed onstage nor the choice revealed because the maidens resemble each other enough to make the selection irrelevant, so the argument goes. Revealing the choice would compromise the resemblances on which the drama depends and would violate the play's wish-fulfilling narcissism. Leaving the two as maidens, one might add, affirms chaste love between virgins as morally equivalent to heterosexual love, an effect perhaps flattering to the Queen. Venus reiterates, furthermore, the pleasure of deferral, of confusion, when she says of the prospective sex change that "neither of them shall know whose lot it shal be til

they come to the Church-dore" (v.iii.170–71). Here Lyly recalls
the suspense of Ovid's Iphis and Ianthes, where one of the woman's bodies becomes muscular and her pace invigorated as she
proceeds to the wedding. The two virgins will marry exactly as
they have wooed; to ask the question "Who?" sweeps aside the
tone and titillation of the story.

But another line of theatrical business encourages us to wonder
about who changes sex. According to some, the play *does* hint tan-
talizingly at its choice, in that Gallathea's concern for honor (I.i)
and Phillida's for clothing (I.iii) predict which virgin will become
a man and which will remain a woman.[28] It is in her male disguise,
furthermore, that Gallathea first greets the audience; Phillida
enters in her maiden's weeds – stage images that may function
proleptically. Furthermore, "Phillida is played by a boy with a
voice still soprano, whereas Gallathea is a superannuated choris-
ter, with a broken voice (or one breaking)," argues Gair, citing
Phillida's lines: "I feare me he is as I am, a mayden . . . Tush, it
cannot be, his voice shewes the contrarie" (III.ii.30–33).[29] The
ending continues to raise the question of who will be transformed
and encourages its auditors to wonder and guess. Venus even
promises the spectacle of metamorphosis: "Then shall it be seene,
that I can turne one of them to be a man, and that I will"
(v.iii.139–40). Her mention of Iphis and Ianthes foregrounds a
story where the choice of woman for the sexual change does
matter. Next, the fathers intervene. Their interlude delays the
outcome and creates suspense precisely over the question of which
virgin shall be transformed. Neither father wants his daughter
metamorphosed into a male, and Tyterus, Gallathea's father,
specifies his objection: "for by that meanes my young sonne shall
lose his inheritance" (1152–53). In terms of primogeniture, transforming Gallathea would be hilariously disruptive; the choice
makes a difference. The final teasing comes in Gallathea's epi-
logue, which she (or he) delivers in the manner of a man, referring
to "You Ladies" and "your Sexe" and adjuring them to "Yeelde
Ladies" (1, 4, 5).

Should we speculate about which maiden Venus will change?
The play's local hints answer, "Yes," while a more detached logic
says, "No." *Gallathea* in its culminating moments tempts its spectators to identify the object of transformation and, more reflec-
tively, to doubt whether they should be wondering about "Who?"

at all. The friction between immediate emotional effects and cumulative contemplative effects gives *Gallathea* an afterlife, a stimulus to rumination after the spectator departs the event. The play creates a desire on behalf of the characters, a desire for resolution, that in reason it must not satisfy. That tension is not "static" but dynamic. Confusion, as it makes up the experience of Gallathea and Phillida's love, becomes likewise the experience of *Gallathea*'s theatre. Just as each maiden wishes – and wishes not – to know whether her opposite is the same as she, so the play invites the spectators to wish – and wish not – to know what will finally emerge under those disguises. Gallathea and Phillida in their seek-avoidance wooing become models for the audience, which is invited at the dénouement to assume their eroticized fibrilations of confusion and desire.

3

The apprentice's enthusiasm, the maidens' *pas de deux*, the parody of virgin sacrifice, and the dénouement's confusions all demonstrate Lyly's persistent and rich attention to dynamic theatrical effects, to emotional and visceral experience, and to a progressive structure, high-spiritedness, and spectatorial engagement comparable to virtues praised in popular morality drama. The qualities that, to Bevington and Weimann, authorize the morality tradition as the pathway to the great public drama of Shakespeare and his contemporaries touch also Lyly's humanist comedies. I would like to draw Lyly even closer to the strategies and conventions of the public drama that preceded him. By focusing on these connections I do not mean to undermine Lyly's significance as a court playwright; rather, I hope to lower further the critical barrier between popular theatricality and the dramaturgy of the court and academy. First, Lyly's plays are linked variously to public performance. Second, the seemingly elitist qualities of his works – their mythological personages and formal dialogues – attempt to make theatrical capital on the contemporaneous but now largely lost stage romances, exemplified by *Clyomon and Clamydes* and *The Rare Triumphs of Love and Fortune*, plays which appealed to both popular and elite audiences. Third, Lyly's theatre influenced subsequent playhouse dramaturgy.

Scholars postulate that Lyly wrote to achieve preferment at

court rather than popular success, yet the road to court performance led for Lyly through public drama, and his playhouse career survived the ruin of his court ambitions. As we have noted, Lyly has recently been placed by Pincombe in the tradition not of court entertainment but of "commerical juvenile drama." Lyly's adventure in 1583 as a principal in the Blackfriars Theatre locates him in public playmaking prior to his debut at court.[30] The Blackfriars productions arose through a consortium that included Lyly as playwright, the earl of Oxford as patron, and a combination of child performers.[31] By amalgamating boy acting troupes from the Chapel Royal and St. Paul's, the promoters aimed at a commercial coup.[32] Lyly took over as a leaseholder at Blackfriars and also as a resident, and from his experience there, he "evidently became something of an impresario."[33] Only concerted effort by Lyly in that domain explains Gabriel Harvey's attack on him as "'the Vicemaster of Paul's and the Foolmaster of the Theatre'."[34] By 1584, Lyly must have gained some notoriety as a popular playwright – at least for topical satire – since a letter of that year warns its recipient to keep his private highjinks away from Lyly's knowledge lest the playwright "'put it in print or make the boys in Paul's play it upon a stage'."[35] Thinly veiled topical drama appealed widely, and Lyly had a knack for it, as plays such as *Midas*, with its anti-Spanish motif, or Lyly's apparent anti-Martin efforts suggest.[36] Gabriel Harvey confirms Lyly's "publique reputation" as a dramatist when he warns others to beware of Lyly "'for feare less he be mooved, or some One of his Apes hired, to make a Playe of you; and then is your credit quite un-done for ever and ever: Such is the publique reputation of their plays'."[37] Lyly's return to playwriting in the late 1580s or early 1590s affirms his playhouse ambitions. *Mother Bombie* aims at popular farce, for example, and *The Woman in the Moone* seems written for adult actors in a public theatre.[38] A revival of *Loues Metamorphosis* in the mid-1590s may even account for a publication boomlet of Lyly's plays.[39] Such evidence suggests that, to a noticeable extent, Lyly wrote for, and was recognized as writing for, popular consumption.

Second, Lyly's comedies adapt one of the then-dominant dramatic genres, the romances of the 1570s and early 1580s.[40] Today only three Elizabethan romances survive – *Clyomon and Clamydes* (*c.* 1576), *Common Conditions* (S.R. 1576) and *The Rare Triumphs of Love*

and Fortune (*c.* 1584) – but the form was extravagantly successful
on the stage. It has been estimated that of the sixty-five plays
performed at court between 1570 and 1585, a third to one half of
them were romances.[41] On the popular side, Gosson, in *Playes Confuted in Fiue Actions*, railed against romances performed at the playhouses, and George Whetstone, Philip Sidney, and Lyly "all
poured scorn on the medleys of romantic fantasy staged with card-
board monsters and knockabout clowns."[42] Such attacks acknowledge both the appetite for stage romances and, among some
observers, an emerging desire for something better.[43] Lyly sought
to provide it by employing romantic conventions, sometimes parodically, in his complex, humanist dramaturgy. *Gallathea*
resembles the romances in specific ways: its virgin-threatening
monster, its shipwreck, its episodic narrative of multiple charac-
ter-groups, its wanderings in a fairylandish wood, its clowns and
pastoral figures, its contrasts of high and low personae, and its
gods who intervene directly in the action.[44] Other of Lyly's plays,
such as *Endimion*, add knights and enchanters to this formulaic
brew. Both *Gallathea* and the romances also traffic heavily in disguise, particularly of gender, such as Neronis's disguise as a page
in *Clyomon and Clamydes*, which resembles the cross-dressing of Gallathea and Phillida. In both the stage romances and the Lylyan
plays, personal identity turns unstable: not only does gender
become muddled but *Clyomon and Clamydes* and *Gallathea* deploy
characters in matched pairs that create doubleness and confusion.
Finally, both the romances and Lyly's drama make romantic love
a central theme, and each treats it not only seriously but also
comically.

Viewing Lyly as an adapter of romance helps to clarify features
of his drama that might otherwise be taken as evidence against
popular interest: for example, his liberal use of mythological
characters. Subsequent public drama develops away from such
figures, but in the playhouse romances contemporaneous with
Lyly's, mythological and mythologized characters appear regularly.[45] Alexander the Great, for one, figures in both *Campaspe* and
Clyomon and Clamydes, and in the latter play Providence also
descends as a *deus ex machina* in a comic episode about love. The
dramaturgical use of the gods in *The Rare Triumphs of Love and
Fortune* bears a striking resemblance to Lyly's strategies in *Gallathea* and *The Woman in the Moone*; one might even conjecture that

Lyly actually drew from either *Love and Fortune* or very similar plays. The action in *Love and Fortune* originates from a contention between Venus and Fortune about their relative power. Each goddess proceeds to demonstrate her mastery as they alternately control the successes and tribulations of two earthly lovers, Hermione and Fidelia. In the end Mercury must intervene to forge peace between the goddesses and bring the lovers to safety. The feud between Venus and Fortune anticipates that between Venus and Diana in *Gallathea*, just as Mercury's intervention in the earlier play anticipates Neptune's in the later one. Likewise *Love and Fortune*'s deployment of goddesses as puppetmasters for alternate acts of the play presages Lyly's use of individual gods to direct each act of *The Woman in the Moone*. There the action begins in Utopia, where shepherds petition Nature to create a female companion for them. The planetary gods take umbrage at Nature's compliance and decide that they will control Pandora's behavior. Thus, each act features successive gods – Saturn, Jupiter, Mars, Phoebus, Venus, Mercury, and finally Luna – governing Pandora. In both *Love and Fortune* and *The Woman in the Moone* the god in question remains onstage throughout the act as a spectator and silent manager. The resemblances among *The Rare Triumphs of Love and Fortune*, *Gallathea*, and *The Woman in the Moone* register strikingly, and it seems probable that Lyly is giving his own twist to conventions common in playhouse romances.[46]

Lyly's proximity to the stage romances throws light on another feature of his dramaturgy that might seem to diverge from the popular: the application of euphuistic language to the theatre. Staging euphuistic language, with its symmetrical clauses, artful parallels, antithesis, rhymes, and alliterations, was Lyly's biggest dramaturgical adventure. Perhaps he sought to make his mark by infusing public drama with a more sophisticated and suggestive style. Euphuism, of course, derives from the language of academic humanists, but the artificial rhetoric of the romances may have suggested to Lyly the plausibility of transferring his version of literary language to the stage.[47] The experiment seems to have fared poorly, and Lyly's later plays dilute the earlier balanced and complex dialogue, a change noticeable in *Midas* and even more evident in *Mother Bombie*, *Loues Metamorphosis*, and *The Woman in the Moone*, and one that implies Lyly's sensitivity to reception in the public theatre.

Yet Lyly's euphuistic dialogue is not so far removed from the language of the popular stage as one might think. Lyly often employs pairs of lovers or other characters in debate about the paradoxes of love, frequently in a stichomythic rhythm of alternating lines:

ERISTUS   No, sweet *Caelia*, in loue there is varietie.
CAELIA   Indeed men varie in their loue.
ERISTUS   They varie their loue, yet change it not.
CAELIA   Loue and change are at variance; therefore if they varie, they must change.
ERISTUS   Men change the manner of their loue, not the humor . . .

(*Midas*, II.i.7–12)

Such verbal duels by witty lover-adversaries punctuate virtually every Lyly play. The same pattern marks the opening dialogue of the lovers Hermione and Fidelia in *The Rare Triumphs of Love and Fortune*:

FIDELIA   But sure is it that ielousie proceedes of feruent loue.
HERMIONE   Can that be feruent loue wherin suspition leads the minde?
FIDELIA   Most ferue[n]t loue wher so much loue doth make [the] fancy blind.
HERMIONE   But faithfull loue can neuer be wherin suspect doth dwell.
FIDELIA   The faithfull louers doo suspect because they loue so well.

(II.296–300)[48]

Here occurs the same witty, rapid-fire exchange, each lover gathering up the words of the other as they debate the paradox that love can doubt. Lyly, of course, employs such stichomythia more distinctively and pervasively than do the romances, but the earlier plays may have encouraged his attempt.

Even more telling similarities occur between *Clyomon and Clamydes* and *Gallathea*. Neronis, the heroine of the former play, enters alone and declares her love for Clyomon, whom she has just met. She talks to herself in alternating lines of assertion and hesitation, with her divided male-female will recalling Gallathea and Phillida in their male disguises:

Ah wofull Dame, thou knowest not thou, of what degree he is,
Of noble bloud his gesters showe, I am assured of this.
Why belike he is some runnagate that will not show his name,
Ah why should I this allegate, he is of noble fame.
Why dost thou not expresse thy love, to him *Neronis* then?
Because shamefastnesse and womanhood, bids us not seek to men.

(xi.1016–21)[49]

Neronis's inability to speak openly what her heart admits privately bears a generic relationship to Gallathea's and Phillida's own "shamefastnesse" in acknowledging their loves. Neronis feels bound by female modesty and conventions of womanhood; at the same time, she longs to declare herself and take command of the situation in a traditionally masculine way. Some scenes later, Neronis assumes a male disguise and comes to serve Clyomon as squire (a masquerade that goes on much longer than necessary). While in disguise, Neronis begins to take on male characteristics, just as do the maidens in *Gallathea*, and even becomes the object of sexual attraction among the village women and of correlative jealous animosity from the village swains. In her speech and accompanying action, Neronis plays out the same titillating confusions that Lyly develops in *Gallathea*.

In other ways the language of *Clyomon and Clamydes* and the other romances sets the stage for Lyly's euphuism. *Clyomon*, for example, is capable of extended comparison between a lover and the elements of the natural world (such as the tree, vine, and spay of xi.992–1010), just as Lyly pauses for elaborate comparisons of the paradoxes of the natural world to those of love (such as the cotton tree of *Gallathea*, III.i.17–22). The fourteeners of the romances widely employ alliteration, internal rhyme, and end rhyme: "As to the wearie wandring wights, whom waltring waves environ, / No greater joy of joyes may be, then when from out the Ocean . . . " (*Clyomon and Clamydes*, i.1–2). Might Lyly have hoped to captivate the musically attuned ears of his public auditors with a richer relation of musicality and meaning: "then might you see shippes sayle where sheepe feede, ankers cast where ploughes goe, fishermen throw theyr nets, where husbandmen sowe theyr Corne" (*Gallathea*, I.i.28–30)? The fourteeners posit an audience alive to poetical effects: extended conceits, parallel and contrast, balanced clauses, antitheses, alliteration, rhyme and off-rhyme – effects that euphuism embraces. Littleton calls attention to *Clyomon and Clamydes*'s formal and stylized speeches and to the abundance of rhetorical devices (rhetorical question, exclamation, apostrophe, interjection, repetition, anaphora),[50] devices that populate Lyly's drama. Thus the language of the romances makes plausible Lyly's experiment with euphuism on the public stage.

Lyly also fits his rhetorical language to the theatre's physical resources of properties and acting. When the nymph Telusa enters, for example, wondering, "Can *Cupids* brands quench *Vetas* flames, and his feeble shafts headed with feathers, pearce deeper the[n] *Dianaes* arrowes headed with steele?" and calling upon herself to "Breake thy bowe *Telusa*" (III.i.10–13), the soliloquy affords the actor precise occasion to brandish the arrows and bow that Telusa would carry as a follower of Diana. Similarly, *Gallathea*'s references to trees, buds, leaves, and roots provide opportunities to invoke the forest *mise en scène*. In the story line of the gods and nymphs (like that of the maidens), the play's considerable mention of sighs, sobs, glances, wild looks, wanton eyes, sadness, blushing, and paleness invite continuous physical gestures, expressions, and reactions from the actors (even if a performer might not be able literally to blush or turn pale). Such opportunities lend a particular theatrical energy to a speech such as Diana's reprimand of her lovelorn nymphs: "Nowe Ladies, dooth not that make your cheekes blushe, that makes mine eares glowe? or can you remember that without sobs, which *Diana* can not thinke on without sighes?" (III.iv.16–18). Later, an aspect of the narrative is enacted physically as the nymphs force Cupid to untie the love knots with which he has bound his victims (IV.ii.21–62). Here and elsewhere Lyly attempts to give language material realization. We have noted the theatrical rhythm and crescendo of Haebe's valediction; similar rhythms can be found in many other set speeches, such as Telusa's or Ramia's laments about love (III.i.1–27, 66–72), wherein Lyly would infuse the long speeches of the romances with a theatrical potential not realized in the earlier drama. Further evidence of Lyly's sensitivity toward language in the theatre appears in Raffe and the apprentices' running parody of professional jargon and linguistic confusion; indeed, the play as a whole affects a slightly amused detachment toward its characters' linguistic enthusiasms and excesses. Euphuism may have failed as a stage language, but not because Lyly was unaware of the need to give it theatrical energy. Rather, Lyly's efforts to make complex, paradoxical language theatrically engaging through the resources of acting and staging might be said to complement his use of confusion to generate tension in the drama of ideas. The differences between Lyly's plays and successful popular ones are sometimes more of degree than kind.

If Lyly's domain is the court, why did his plays exert such an influence on subsequent popular drama? Scholars have regularly acknowledged Lyly's dramaturgical contributions: the new and sophisticated use of disguise, the expanded use of properties and scenery, the prominence of women, the careful dramatic construction, for example. Later public playwrights knew Lyly's work. Greene alludes to *Campaspe*, and euphuism is well enough known on the popular stage for him to parody it in *Friar Bacon and Friar Bungay*; Shakespeare returns to Lyly throughout his career; and Jonson has been seen as Lyly's "spiritual heir."[51] Lyly's works may have lacked – fatally – the bombast, shocking spectacle, and cruel tyrants that catapulted such plays as *The Spanish Tragedy* to glory. Yet Lyly gave cross-dressing its theatrical prominence and virtually invented romantic comedy, both major contributions to playhouse drama. Shakespeare frequently invokes Lylyan theatrical strategies. The gods feuding in the woods of *Gallathea* look forward to those of *A Midsummer Night's Dream*; the Petrarchan sonnetese of *Gallathea*'s Cupid and nymphs receives later exploration in *Romeo and Juliet*; the device used in *Gallathea* of four nymphs entering successively to confess their love-infection to the audience, each eavesdropping on the next, Shakespeare employs famously in *Love's Labour's Lost*; the love duets of Gallathea and Phillida provide the model for the dialogue of Viola and Olivia; the *deus ex machina* endings of several Lyly plays seem to have influenced the ending of *As You Like It*; and even the statuesque image that comes alive in *Loues Metamorphosis* anticipates the wondrous statue of Hermione in *The Winter's Tale*. Insisting upon Lyly as exclusively a court dramatist renders these contributions to public drama incidental or even accidental – an awkward logic.

4

Throughout the foregoing discussion, I have emphasized the parallels between Lyly's stage works and popular theatre. I would like to conclude on a more conjectural note by speculating how a dramaturgy such as Lyly's might have advanced the interests of the playhouses conceived – to refocus the terms somewhat – as commercial enterprises. Situating Lyly's interests close to the public theatre, as we have done, implies his link to the commercial. In the case of *Gallathea*, its confusions – its juxtapositions of ideas with experience – bespeak a longing for resolution and a pleasurable deferral that have the potential to engage audiences ongoingly with theatre itself, that is, to encourage their continuing patronage. *Gallathea* ultimately separates desire from the precise nature of its object. Gallathea and Phillida desire each other no matter who the other exactly is or will be, and in the last scene Venus and Cupid even celebrate love and desire as independent forces under the command of the gods. Raffe's enthusiasm for metamorphosis survives his experiences with its practitioners and putative forms. One of *Gallathea*'s most fascinating qualities is the way in which desire – as both represented in and evoked by the theatrical performance – acquires a life of its own, slightly removed from any immediate object, capable of transforming physiology and reality. Lyly honors desire in a way that hints at the marketplace, with its qualities of wish fulfillment and commodification and with its symbolic monetary economy that allows for an infinite number of goods to be made equivalent. As it displays the effortless substitution of one object of desire for another and revels in the experience of desire as something detached from a single or precise target, *Gallathea* may offer a symbol of the self-perpetuating commercial theatre, its interchangeable pleasures inviting repeated spectatorship without surfeit.

If a Lyly play can create a desire or longing in spectators for what seems just to elude one's grasp, if Lyly can repeat that longing through what I earlier called a "serial drama" of special pleasures and variations, then we have, perhaps, the formal conditions for theatre as a market commodity. Both within a single play and among these "serial plays," Lyly's achievement is to convince the audience to embrace objects as if they were different when they are essentially alike. A market economy can create desire by creating artificial distinctions, and Lyly's theatre may provide an early exemplum. The stock repetitions and variations that characterize playhouse drama of the late 1580s and 1590s seem to validate that model, as Knutson's study suggests. Such a formulation, of course, makes sense of Lyly's drama as equally a humanist résumé presented to the queen and a commodity for the market. Lyly's aestheticism and his proto-commercialism take on a certain simultaneity in this description, and it would be false, I think, to make Lyly's specific aesthetic a function of the marketplace. No market analysis could predict the exact nature of Lyly's plays, and aesthetic desire itself seems only one of many possibilities congruent with market dynamics. Beyond the potential commercial value of confusion and desire, Lyly's works instance an ongoing trend away from drama as a cautionary vehicle and toward drama as a perpetuator of a certain kind of experience. Lyly makes drama not just a transmitter of understanding but the object itself of interest, scrutiny, doubt, and feeling; such a change can only help draw spectators to theatre. That shift in the nature of theatrical experience may be Lyly's greatest legacy to later writers of commercial comedy. Shakespeare, too, appreciates subtle dissonances between the local and the formal – illustrated by the confusions and deferrals in *Twelfth Night* – and he may have found in Lyly the ambivalent theatrical energy by which his own plays can sometimes haunt the consciousnesses of their spectators.

Lyly can be placed in proximity to the popular stage without denying his desire for success at court. Such a view helps to overcome the formulaic distinction between the aristocratic and the plebeian, and the humanist and the popular, by suggesting how humanist theatricality could infiltrate the arena of material culture. Recent critical work on the reciprocity between playacting and nascent capitalism has moved in a different direction. Finding in Renaissance drama an exploration of the problems of a burgeoning market economy, Jean-Christophe Agnew asserts that "The theatre of late medieval and early modern England . . . was a theatre in and of the marketplace."[52] But how do we account for an academically inspired drama that uses humanist "confusions" or characters from school dialogues to create a theatricality that compares to, and finally influences, that "of the marketplace"? If a dramaturgy such as Lyly's contributes to the strategies for economic success at the playhouses, then Agnew's claim requires revision. Moving Lyly back from the margins of dramatic history and toward popular Elizabethan theatre, moreover, hints at the larger possibility of integrating Renaissance intellectual values with the appreciation of the theatre's material life.

7

Bearing witness to Tamburlaine, Part 1

In Christopher Marlowe's *Tamburlaine, Part 1*, the hero succeeds by overcoming increasingly powerful opponents who refuse to grasp his inevitability and provenance. What resistance does the play overcome as a means to success in performance? Marlowe's piece apparently had the effect of conquest. According to Richard Levin, Elizabethan playgoers responded with wonder, conveyed in such language as "gapers," "gazing," "rauishes," "dead stroke," and "strike . . . dead with admiration."[1] Gaping, admiration, and ravishment occur elsewhere in descriptions of Renaissance drama, but they adhere to *Tamburlaine* insistently. Because not every Elizabethan stage warrior will strike spectators dead with admiration, the responses to *Tamburlaine* bespeak a certain transference, as if what Tamburlaine does to his opponents, the play does analogously to the audience. Part of the drama's originality lies there: *Tamburlaine* induces and then defeats audience resistance, as if Marlowe wills on his spectators the paradox of the vanquished Soldan: "And I am pleasde with this my overthrow" (1.i.482).[2]

Criticism continues to turn on the question of whether Tamburlaine is repellent or admirable – or both.[3] Wishing to discredit *Tamburlaine*'s "hero ideology," political critics see the play as exposing the protagonist's imperialistic strategies and pronounce auditorial disaffection an appropriate response.[4] By contrast, theatrical criticism tends to treat the spectators' engulfment by Tamburlaine as normative – as Levin's historical evidence suggests.[5] Engulfment can blur into approval, however, as the ideological critics fear, who are left insisting that "Though [Tamburlaine's] claims to divine sanction work on his onstage audiences, they should not work on us."[6] Both positions may make sense if we consider that *Tamburlaine* attempts to evoke the audience's admiration for its hero by deploying obstacles to credibility and moral acceptance which the play then surmounts. To that end, *Tamburlaine* adapts from humanist dramaturgy the technique of "bearing witness." Marlowe introduces witness figures such as Theridamas to make Tamburlaine's gigantism believable; later he deploys Zenocrate to reduce moral resistance. Disbelief and disapproval become the predicates of *Tamburlaine's* success. Because Tamburlaine craves admiration, the overtly imperialistic relationship between victor and vanquished takes on the unexpected undertones of dependence and reciprocity.

Witnessing in Marlowe hints at an historical change in how Elizabethan playgoers responded. With *Tamburlaine* a transition noticeable in 1560s drama accelerates. In 1559, a commentator such as William Bavande could argue, like Erasmus, that audience members should bring their ethical judgments to a play.[7] But in *Tamburlaine* an action becomes defensible if it wins the acceptance of those audience surrogates whom spectators trust; a sympathetic witness figure allows spectators to bracket their own ethics. That newly empowered witnessing in *Tamburlaine* derives from academic humanist drama. We have come to appreciate the influence of popular morality plays on *Tamburlaine's* episodic construction and on its protagonist's representation.[8] Marlowe's adaptation of the choric function, however, reveals the humanist imprint at the heart of his theatre.

The famous prologue to *Tamburlaine, Part 1* imagines the playgoer as a follower inside the Tamburlainean camp: *"Weele leade you to the stately tent of War: / Where you shall heare the Scythian* Tamburlaine" (Pro.3–4). Not accidentally, Tamburlaine will make his first entrance *"leading Zenocrate"* (s.d. at I.ii.0), who will move through the play as a prime audience figure. Just as the Prologue commands the hero's spectators to *"View but his picture in this tragicke glasse"* (Pro.7), Tambulaine at the end directs his onstage assemblage toward another mirror image as he observes the strewn bodies of Bajazeth, Zabina, and Arabia and calls them "Al sights of power to grace my victory: / And such are objects fit for *Tamburlaine. / Wherein as in a mirrour may be seene, / His honor, that consists in sheading blood"* (v.i.474–77). His victims' corpses reflect something immaterial, his honor. The equation summarizes what Marlowe attempts: to compel his spectators to substitute in their vision the imagined for the actual. Marlowe's symbolic "sights of power" arrive with all the *energia* of metaphor,[9] and often with the aesthetic appeal of "grace" and "fit[ness]." *Tamburlaine* may effect a "violent reduction of meaning to the terms of sight," as one critic puts it,[10] but "sight" in *Tamburlaine* involves a paradoxical ability to see exactly what is not there.

At work in *Tamburlaine* is a new conception of theatrical representation. Marlowe appears at a cultural moment when response has been loosened from the audience's prior ethical values. In its new imaginative freedom the audience can participate in the act of representation itself, which becomes, in turn, an excitingly tenuous agreement between playwright and playgoer, so that a character stands no longer for something natural or ideal but for a temporarily shared desire. Without the audience's engulfment, Tamburlaine can appear absurd, as Elizabethan responses reveal, but with it Tamburlaine becomes admirable. At stake here is more than an actor's capacity to be lifelike or convincing, for the spectator's belief is the necessary condition of heroic representation. Tudor dramaturgy has reached a watershed, in that representation in *Tamburlaine* tests the creative limits of spectatorial engagement. In his use of resistance and engulfment, Marlowe paves the way for Shakespearean tragedy, not because Shakespeare's heroes imitate Marlovian ones but because Shakespeare achieves a rhythm of engagement and detachment reminiscent of Marlowe's dramaturgy.[11]

1

In that paradigm of spectatorship, *Tamburlaine* negotiates a disturbing position between the humanist defense of literature and the antitheatricalists' attack. Marlowe confirms the humanist process of poetic response but repudiates its ethical grounding; conversely, he rejects parts of the antitheatrical model of response but confirms the antitheatricalists' moral fears. Sir Thomas Elyot and Sir Philip Sidney share a neo-Platonic conception of literary response: fictional representations of idealized heroes will so enflame the heart of the readers (or spectators) that they will be moved to emulate the models set before them. Elyot emphasizes the appeal of literature's "eloquence and lernyng." He commends Homer for praising noble princes, "where with the reders shall be so all inflamed, that they most feruently shall desire and coueite, by the imitation of their vertues, to acquire semblable glorie."[12]

Sidney moves away from Elyot's verbal wisdom and toward what Forrest Robinson calls "visual epistemology," in which sight produces knowledge.[13] For Sidney, poetry, with its "feigning notable images," can "strike, pierce," and "possess the sight of the soul" and thus move it in delight toward "virtuous action."[14] Although both writers acknowledge the power of idealized virtue to attract the reader magnetically, Sidney's difference from Elyot suggests that visual experience gains importance as the sixteenth century advances.

Marlowe's poetics of spectacle share part of that humanist ground, but with departures. For Marlowe, "perswasions . . . patheticall " (1.ii.211) – the kind that Tamburlaine works on Theridamas, as we shall see – can reinvest what is immediately visible. Here the rhetorical does not so much contradict the visual as transmogrify it, with effects like those that "speaking pictures" have for Sidney. At play is the kind of imagination that Fulke Greville describes in his "A Treatie of Humane Learning." Because "our affections cast / False shapes, and formes," imagination has the capacity to make the "pictures" of "Sense" "still too foule, or faire": "Hence our desires, fears, hopes, loue, hate, and sorrow, / In fancy make us heare, feele, see impressions, / Such as out of our sense they doe not borrow."[15] The pathetical can warp sight. The danger sensed by Greville that affection, acting on imagination, can distort impressions of the senses Marlowe celebrates as something like the wonder or admiration valued by humanists. Pathetical persuasions can move the auditor to action – as Theridamas is moved to allegiance or, in a different way, Agydas to suicide – but ethics have little bearing. In Marlowe, speaking pictures lead to individual action not by means of a neo-Platonic delight in the beautiful and the good but rather by means of their amoral "stronge enchantments." The enchantments of the pathetical subdue and overwhelm. That process reflects J. S. Cunningham's description of the "psychology of emotion" in *Tamburlaine*, whereby "a sight or other stimulus directly generates intense feeling, and that feeling then imposes itself, peremptorily, as a pervasive *state* of feeling."[16] Cunningham's description parallels Goldman's identification of a Marlovian action of "abandon": heroes "abandon themselves to what has ravished them."[17] That action of protagonistic "abandon" mirrors the yielding of witnesses. Elyot and Sidney imagine attraction, Marlowe compulsion.

If theatre is powerful, as Sidney argued, it may harbor dangers feared by the antitheatricalist Stephen Gosson, who goes beyond the humanists in acknowledging drama's power to infect by sights and sounds. "[H]ow wary ought we to be," he contends, "that no corruption of idols, enter by the passage of our eyes & ears into the sole" because "that which entreth into vs by the eyes and eares, muste be digested by the spirite."[18] Gosson sees a danger in the audience's tendency to become overexcited: "the meaner sorte tottre, they are caried away with euery rumor, and so easily corrupted, that in the Theatres they generally take vp a wonderful laughter, and shoult altogether with one voyce."[19] Response generates its own excess: "many times wee laught so extreemely, that striuing to bridle our selues, wee cannot."[20] Gosson returns to that fear in suggesting that "vice is learned with beholding, se[n]se is tickled, desire pricked, & those impressions of mind are secretly co[n]ueyed ouer to the gazers, which the plaiers do cou[n]terfeit on the stage" (192–93). Gosson fears an auditorial overidentification and overengagement that will drive spectators to wild, immoral behavior. If so, drama's effects exceed its intentions. Humanist academic defenders of the stage, such as John Case in *Sphaera Civitatis* (1588) and Alberico Gentili in *De actoribus et spectatoribus fabularum non notandis disputatio* (1599), argue that acting is merely representation, that even orators imitate, and that audiences always know feigned from true. But such arguments miss Gosson's sense of volatile emotional synergy in group response. Marlowe follows a different line still. *Tamburlaine*'s theatrical poetics of domination would seem, on the one hand, to rule out Gosson's agitated spectators, for Tamburlaine renders his witnesses spellbound, immobilized with admiration. On the other hand, Marlowe's theatre is amoral, and its sense of surrender accords with Gosson's fears about drama's penetration of the eyes, ears, and soul. Marlowe imagines a dominated audience, different from Gosson's unleashed spectators, but Marlowe's roughly humanist model produces a "state of feeling" impermeable to moral considerations and thus dangerous. Marlowe stops short of Gosson's underdistancing but confirms his fears; conversely, he applies humanist wonder to ends that obviate humanist values.

These considerations impinge on another humanist controversy, the problem of representation itself. As we have noted, academic defenders of the stage – Case, Gentili, also Gager – argue that spectators understand themselves to be watching mere acting, that, for example, the actor in women's garb is still manifestly a male. Antitheatricalists fear that the imitation can "contaminate" both performer and observer. *Tamburlaine* brings the question of representation to the boiling point. Part of the play's power derives, as we shall see, from the physical likeness of Edward Alleyn to the Tamburlaine envisioned. Audiences will depend on the impressiveness of Alleyn's physique and bearing to make him credible, even as they recognize the highly rhetorical and artificial terms applied to him. *Tamburlaine* thus both employs and transcends the humanist's representational view of drama. In such spectacle, one senses finally a frustration with the limits of what can be affirmed or known, and in that respect the play looks forward to *Doctor Faustus*. *Tamburlaine* fastens on the physical world, but what the play wants to reveal swells beyond the limits of the empirical. Marlowe's humanist interest in material fact cannot satisfy his humanist sense of wonder: the desire for experience that humanism releases exceeds the world's objective capacity to fulfill it. Here Marlowe sets a marker, for he is the first Tudor playwright to acknowledge and resist the circumscription of the knowable. He begins to suggest the boundaries of a certain kind of humanist inquiry whose limits Greene will explore in *Friar Bacon and Friar Bungay*.

Marlowe solves the problem of representation by turning it into a problem of perspective, of the observer's visual angle and emotional susceptibility. To do so, Marlowe refashions the chorus that humanist drama inherited from Senecan theatre and internalizes it into the plot. Academic playwrights such as Thomas Legge practice manipulations of point of view. Marlowe follows their experiments by transforming the choric figure from a moral commentator who forestalls audience identification with the protagonists into a witness whose presence facilitates their hyperbolic representation. Marlowe's development of such witnesses may have encouraged Shakespeare's sophisticated use of similar figures – Horatio and Octavius, for example.[21] In Senecan tragedy the chorus distinguishes itself from the protagonists by enunciating its plebeian social condition, extolling the virtues of simple living, and recoiling at the heroes' horrific fates. Seneca's chorus helps to isolate the tragic figures – Medea, Hercules, Thyestes – in a removed world of mythic boldness, transgression, and suffering. The classical chorus is a bystander, reflecting a disinterested viewpoint, who bespeaks a moral vision.[22] Tudor drama, however, employs the choric function unsystematically. In academic drama Nicholas Grimald's *Christus Redivivus* (pub. 1543) and his *Archipropheta* (pub. 1548) use the chorus in the classical spirit, as do Thomas Watson's *Absalom* (*c.* 1536–44) and George Christopherson's *Jephthah* (*c.* 1544).[23] The later neo-Latin playwright William Gager also employs the chorus in the familiar manner in *Meleager* (1582) and elsewhere. Thomas Legge's *Richardus Tertius* (1579), however, departs by seldom using the commoner as choric voice, preferring instead to disperse the function among characters active in the narrative. The Inns of Court tragedy *Gorboduc* (1562) manages the chorus function three times over: it begins each act with a dumb show that signifies the meaning of the ensuing action; it follows each act with a chorus that summarizes, comments, and predicts; and it deploys characters who recoil at recent events or prophesy future ones.[24] In contrast to Senecan choruses, *Richardus Tertius*'s witnesses lack detachment, and *Gorboduc*'s multiply responses confusingly. Those late experiments in academic and courtly plays fracture the chorus's consistency and its distance from the plot; instead the chorus often raises doubts about the meaning of events and their emotional value.

Marlowe and Shakespeare experiment further with choric secondary characters as mediating "witnesses" who make something real: because the scholarly Horatio witnesses it *Hamlet*'s ghost assumes more reality than if only the Watch saw it. Likewise, at the end of *Antony and Cleopatra*, the pedestrian empiricist Octavius validates Cleopatra's self-monumentalizing in a way that no other character could. If a similar witnessing distinguishes *Tamburlaine*, then the play marks a juncture in sixteenth-century theatre. Heretofore, drama had little need to verify its characters or actions: the problem of the authenticity of the ghosts in *Hamlet* or *Macbeth* did not exist in drama early in the century or in the recent works of Peele or Lyly. Within a few years of *Tamburlaine*, however, Kyd's *The Spanish Tragedy* explores delusional states of madness onstage: what before our eyes is real? The letter that drops from Belimperia in the middle of Hieronimo's solicitation of the heavens raises, almost comically, the problem of authentication. As it highlights bearing witness, *Tamburlaine* admits the possibility that a character might possess an inauthentic, perhaps merely subjective status. Behind *Tamburlaine*'s need to affirm its spectacle lurks the fear that an experience without public verification may not exist. Words have a way of becoming things in *Tamburlaine*, as Harry Levin notes;[25] likewise, the play validates subjective beliefs that sound a little mad. Culturally, *Tamburlaine* suggests the humanist interest in personal experience brought to a new level of anxiety by Protestant subjectivism.[26]

2

Tamburlaine, Part 1 brims with spectatorship. At the beginning of every act and often elsewhere, characters wonder who Tamburlaine is and what he signifies. The first act sets the problem's opposed terms as Mycetes refers to Tamburlaine as "a Foxe in midst of harvest time" (I.i.31), and Meander announces Tamburlaine's hope "To make himselfe the Monarch of the East" (43). Will Tamburlaine prove fox or monarch? Likewise, as late as Act IV, the Soldan of Egypt dismisses Tamburlaine as the "rogue of *Volga*" (IV.i.4) with a "troope of theeves and vagabondes" (6), while the Messenger cautions that if the Soldan had seen "The frowning lookes of fiery *Tamburlaine* / . . . It might amaze your royall majesty" (13–16). Here and throughout, characters – Mycetes, Cosroe, Bajazeth, the Governor, the Soldan – establish a field of conflicting possibilities for Tamburlaine. The play thus enunciates a problem of spectacle: how can the barbarian thief be theatrically credible as the monarchical scourge of God? Tamburlaine plays for kingship as a jest and a game; he enslaves his enemies and then pleasures in their insults about his legitimacy; he has beautiful virgins butchered and then talks of love; he slaughters the innocent and revels in dead bodies as emblems of his honor. Tamburlaine does not resolve but rather insists upon his contradictions.

For Tamburlaine to succeed, a flesh-and-blood actor on the stage must be translated imaginatively into something Herculean; buskin-stomping and tear-a-cat bombast must be received as heroical grandeur. Marlowe proceeds as aggressively as possible, calling attention to the actor's body and insisting that it is more than what the audience actually sees. Secondary characters talk repeatedly about Tamburlaine's looks: "Of stature tall, and straightly fashioned, / Like his desire, lift upwards and divine," says

Menaphon (II.i.7–8), who then declares Tamburlaine's shoulders to be broad enough to bear *"Old Atlas* burthen," his head "A pearle more worth, than all the world" (11–12), his amber hair wrapped in curls "as fierce *Achilles* was, / On which the breath of heaven delights to play" (24–25).[27] Descriptions treat Tamburlaine's features as emblems: "The man that in the forhead of his fortune, / Beares figures of renowne and myracle" (3–4); the "fiery cyrcles" (15) of his eyes that "beare encompassed / A heaven of heavenly bodies in their Spheares" (15–16); "his lofty brows" that "in foldes, do figure death" (21). As the play develops, Tamburlaine becomes ever less the mere physical presence before us and more an emblem, but one whose meaning – heaven or hell? – remains unstable.

Who is Tamburlaine? On one level, Tamburlaine is Edward Alleyn – only more so. Edward Alleyn was an actor of remarkable physical stature and bearing, so that he leant the role a striking and outsized presence.[28] The play's celebrations of Tamburlaine's imposing appearance and voice suggest that Marlowe wrote the part to take advantage of a specific actor's exceptional physique and manner. That strategy is rare in drama until this time. It diverges from the assumptions about acting implicit in the doubling lists commonly published with sixteenth-century popular drama, which seldom presuppose actors with specific physical traits (age requirements and acrobatic skills notwithstanding), and it deviates from the medieval tradition of allegorical representation, in which it would make no sense to ask if an actor looks the part of Mankind or in which a series of different actors might play Christ on the same day. Alleyn, that is, fulfills an unusual demand for verisimilitude. His voice, physique, and manner provide the basis in *reality* for the celebrations of Tamburlaine in the *drama*, so as to make inherent in the play the issue of authenticity. At the same time, the descriptions of Tamburlaine by Theridamas and others consistently edge beyond the literal figure before them. Could the frowns of Alleyn-as-Tamburlaine "menace heaven" or "figure death"? Were his shoulders as broad as those of Old Atlas? Were his eyes "fiery cyrcles" encompassing "heavenly bodies"? Was his head a "pearl"? Literally speaking, no.[29] Given the wide gap between Alleyn's stature and that of the average Elizabethan, the slippage between reality and metaphor might seem small. Yet the spectacle so central to Tamburlaine remains rhetorically transmogrified, not literal, a matter of seeing what the language would impel the audience to believe. Humanist interests encouraged historical representation on the stage, and Marlowe seizes on a new proximity of the realistic and the emblematic to assert their uncanny identity.

Marlowe makes hyperbole realistic through deft management of point of view, a technique that he may have learned at Cambridge from humanist academic drama, which sometimes employs the witness function to confer suspenseful realism on melodramatic spectacle. In 1579, Cambridge saw the first performance of one of the most celebrated sixteenth-century tyrant tragedies, Thomas Legge's tripartite Latin drama, *Richardus Tertius*. The production was apparently revived for the earl of Essex in 1582, when Marlowe was in residence at Cambridge.[30] *Richardus Tertius* might have been seen by Marlowe, and whether or not he saw it, such a famous Cambridge play could hardly have remained unknown to him. The first part of Legge's trilogy reaches its theatrical high point when Richard, duke of Gloucester denounces Hastings before the council (I:V.v), a striking scene that apparently influenced Shakespeare's *Richard III*. The representational problem is to make Richard's absurd, self-theatricalizing behavior credible, even terrifying – the kind of problem that occupies *Tamburlaine*. Legge's denunciation scene is a dramaturgical *tour de force*, as point of view helps to create an unnerving spectacle. Earlier, the would-be usurper Richard has been fretful and psychologically torn ("Hope and fear distract my mind" [I:V.iii.1488][31]) about his course of action, but he has conceived a daring gambit to stifle support for the still-living nephews by striking down their naive defender, Lord Hastings: "I'll attack him publicly... and the Council will be so astonished that it will not detect my trickery" (1544–46). With that hope in place, Legge manipulates viewpoint in the denunciation scene to transform Richard into, first, a dominating spectacle and, then, something fearsome, beyond the expectations of the audience. The hyperbolic spectacle acquires realism as it is mediated through key witness figures. Before Richard joins the waiting council, his crony Buckingham inveigles the lords to see him burdened and to sympathize with his distress (I:V.v.1615–17); Buckingham then heralds the duke as the cynosure of all eyes (1617–18). The scene is Gloucester's great moment, for he must rise to the occasion theatrically, ignore the

insecurities that he admitted earlier, and boldly act the play-within-the-play that is his scheme against Hastings. Richard walks in yawning grandly, apologizes for his tiredness, speaks jovially: he dominates attention with his physical presence and personality, confirming Buckingham. Then, just as quickly, he leaves on obscure business. In his absence the center of attention is held by the unsuspecting Hastings, who then directs all eyes back to Richard, suddenly returned in much-altered mood. The audience now sees Richard through Hastings's eyes: "But see here ... Fuming, he shakes his head and frowns. With a sharp tooth he ferociously gnaws his lip" (1657–60). Evident here is the kind of move favored in *Tamburlaine*: the victim has been made into the witness.

Now the dialogue bounces quickly between Richard and Hastings, with perspectives again counterpointed in a way suggestive for Marlowe. Finally Richard accelerates the action as he accuses the queen of sorcery; denounces Hastings's lover, Mistress Shore; and tops off his charges with spectacular, madcap raging: "My frame staggers with disease, my eyes deny me sleep, my sluggish digestion refuses food, my pulse grows weak, this bloodless arm of mine has grown withered and refuses to work" (1676–79). The lines call for bombast, posturing, and stagey acting of the type famously indulged in *Tamburlaine*. During the exchange, the other councillors stand "amazed" (1668) – like Tamburlaine's frequent auditors – presumably arrayed as spectators around Richard and his uncomprehending victim. Now Hastings trembles with sudden asides of dread as he realizes the threat to his paramour. When he attempts to intervene for her, Richard climactically turns the accusation of treachery against him. Richard creates confusion by pounding the council table, and, amid shouts of "Betrayal! Betrayal!" (1688), one of his soldiers wounds Lord Stanley. With the councillors confounded by bloodshed and chaos, Richard arrests Hastings.

In this scene, Legge establishes toward Richard an outside perspective, mediated initially by one of his supporters and secondly by his victim. Viewed externally, Richard is perceived with a kind of awe: first he appears disarming, then unpredictable, then something passionate, unleashed, and terrifying. He becomes the source of both disruption and restored order. As unwitting chorus figure and victim, Hastings registers convincingly the personal nightmare of the duke's rule: "Ah, my heart palpitates with chill dread" (1680); "Who could adequately mourn my misfortune?" (1701) – a response that will typify *Tamburlaine*. The victimized audience-surrogate responds with an energy that makes Richard's hyperbolic antics theatrically compelling, real. As additional suspense, Richard must carry off an act of trickery, despite his earlier inner doubts, whose success depends upon a brazen theatricalizing of the self. While much of the atmosphere of *Richardus Tertius* reflects Seneca, the uncertainty over how and whether Richard will rise to the occasion carries the scene beyond the Senecan model. Because the audience knows of his self-doubts, Gloucester's swelling monstrousness – including his sudden, diversionary shedding of Stanley's blood – aims to strike the audience with the shock of discovery. Spectators – who had thought themselves privy to the situation's ironies – now, like Hastings, bear their own affirming witness to this newly terrifying Richard.

While Tamburlaine's "wooing" of Theridamas does not imitate Richard's denunciation of Hastings specifically, it shows the same heady brew of suspense, spectacle, self-theatricalizing, witnessing, and surprise. Between the soldier's announcement to Tamburlaine that a thousand Persian horsemen are massing against them and Theridamas's entrance, forty-odd lines elapse. During that interval, suspense builds: Zenocrate and the captured lords hope for rescue; Tamburlaine acknowledges his troops' limitations against the thousand horsemen; his captains advise battle, but Tamburlaine surprises them by calling for a parley and has his treasures and "golden wedges" (1.ii.139) laid out so that "their reflexions may amaze the Perseans" (140). The Scythians are outmanned, at odds over the best course, with only an inchoate strategy. In this air of crisis, Tamburlaine asserts himself as theatricalized spectacle, stepping forward alone to "bide the danger of the brunt" (151).

As Tamburlaine and Theridamas encounter each other, the point of view shuttles between them, with each establishing the other as a visual object. The exchange stresses actorly face-making and spectatorship (Hastings has also "read" Gloucester's body language in *Richardus Tertius*). Theridamas begins, surprised by what he sees:

THERIDAMAS   His looks do menace heaven and dare the Gods,
His fierie eies are fixt upon the earth,
As if he now devis'd some Stratageme:
Or meant to pierce *Avernus* darksome vaults ...

TAMBURLAINE   Noble and milde this Persean seemes to be,
If outward habit judge the inward man.
THERIDAMAS   His deep affections make him passionate.
TAMBURLAINE   With what majesty he rears his looks.   (157–65)

The dialogue focuses the audience's gaze alternately on each figure as the other studies him: eyes, head movements, facial reactions, all interpreted for heroic signification. The alternating celebrations allow the two warriors' physical presence to dominate the moment, that presence given validity by the separate-but-mirrored monologues. As with the asides in *Richardus Tertius*, the language here demands that the audience look closely, follow the guiding chorus figures, and take in the interpretive reflections. Tamburlaine will proceed, of course, with a self-dramatizing speech of consummate hubris, parallel in its own way to Richard's self-presentation, whose purpose is to overwhelm his auditor. At play between Tamburlaine and Theridamas is a process of spectacle and witnessing, as if the pair stood inside a charmed circle rimmed by their onlookers and the Scythian treasures. Marlowe works comparably to Legge in *Richardus Tertius*: he employs risk and surprise; leaves the audience with uncertain knowledge (what is Tamburlaine's plan?); captures spectatorial attention with the performers' physicality, even their overacting; creates the effect of an inner play encircled by amazed observers; allows the hero-tyrant to manipulate the scene; keeps viewpoint dynamic; and invests the audience in the victim's perspective.

Marlowe takes the next step beyond *Richardus Tertius*, however, by imagining a play that might embrace, not condemn, its tyrant-protagonist and by extending the possibilities of witnessing to accomplish that task. Of Theridamas's first speech surveying Tamburlaine, Eugene Waith observes, "The description is perfect, though to use it when the character described stands before the audience is to risk a ludicrous incongruity. Marlowe depends on unhesitating acceptance of the verbal picture."[32] Waith calculates the risk tellingly – but what dramaturgical mechanism creates "unhesitating acceptance"? How does Marlowe incriminate the audience? The answer is in a curious doubling and reciprocity. When Theridamas first looks on Tamburlaine, he is surprised by what he sees: *"Tamburlaine? / A Scythian Shepheard, so imbellished / With Natures pride, and richest furniture?"* (154–56). Theridamas repeats the contradiction about Tamburlaine that saturates the play: shepherd or lord? Rather than avoiding it, Tamburlaine's long seduction speech to Theridamas embraces the contradiction: "*Jove* sometime masked in a Shepheards weed, / And by those steps that he hath scal'd the heavens, / May we become immortall like the Gods" (199–201). Tamburlaine, moreover, casts Theridamas in the same terms in which Theridamas has imagined him: "Art thou but Captaine of a thousand horse, / That by Characters graven in thy browes, / And by thy martiall face and stout aspect, / Deserv'st to have the leading of an hoste?" (168–71). Tamburlaine's description of Theridamas mirrors the play's descriptions of Tamburlaine, who "in the forhead of his fortune, / Beares figures of renowne and myracles" and whose "lofty browes in foldes, do figure death" (II.i.21). It is to the consanguinity between the two that Tamburlaine appeals: "Joine with me now in this my meane estate, / . . . Then shalt thou be Competitor with me, / And sit with *Tamburlaine* in all his majestie" (202–09). Conversely, Theridamas's first impressions of Tamburlaine ("imbellished / With Natures pride, and richest furniture") resemble the hero's description of the Persians, "exceeding brave and rich" (127), with golden helmets and massy chains. Underlying the seductiveness of the scene is an uncanny, half-articulated identification of the two "competitors." That identification creates conviction through the discrepancy between the self's imaginative potential and its actual circumstances. The appeal to spectators can cut across class barriers with its intoxicating promise, for Tamburlaine says implicitly to Theridamas, "As you can see greatness in me, I can see it in you," so that to reject the other is to reject the self.

As in *Richardus Tertius*, the audience believes itself to possess an omniscient awareness, since it is privy to the multiple perspectives of the alternating commentators. Because each viewpoint is partial, the audience alone seems to be receiving the whole objectively. But each single perspective leads to the same intoxicating, self-aggrandizing, and self-incriminating fantasy of the observer: I will believe in your greatness if you believe in mine. Highly charged, enclosed in a magic circle of onstage spectators and glittering golden wedges, the spectacle seems irresistible, yet to enter into it with seeming objectivity is actually to forfeit detachment. Marlowe brings into play the kind of dramatic effect that Shakespeare will make familiar, with audience figures inside the drama, such as Friar Lawrence or Kent, who seem at first impartial guides, but whose relieability is eroded when they become incriminated in the action. While Legge produces the surprise of Richard's monstrousness, Marlowe creates his own subtext of reciprocity between the two soldiers and between the audience and the play, an unspoken contract to treat the heroic hyperbole as if it were manifestly real. For Marlowe spectatorship becomes ultimately something conspiratorial.

In a play relentlessly concerned with rhetoric and spectacle, the dramaturgy is in some sense identical to the action. Under Marlowe's tutelage, characters and playgoers intersect – conspire – to reinvent the visible world with language. The primal, childhood magic of that conspiracy differs finally from Shakespearean effect. Repeatedly, Shakespeare creates self-conscious fictions within a drama, such that the difference between the inner play and the framing play becomes analogous to the difference between make-believe and reality. Thus "The Murder of Gonzago" makes *Hamlet* more real than it was before. Numerous moments in *Tamburlaine* also have the quality of staged events, such as the wooing of Theridamas that we have been discussing. But the difference between "The Wooing of Theridamas" and *Tamburlaine* is not the difference between make-believe and reality; the former does not make the latter more real by contrast. Rather, the success of the first constitutes the success of the second; to the extent that Tamburlaine woos Theridamas convincingly, *Tamburlaine* so woos the audience. Tamburlaine's "acting" before his adversary only replicates and reinforces Alleyn's acting before his potential "competitors" across the stage threshhold. The effect is of a ceaseless, exhilarating, high-stakes gambling operation, because those successive inner dramas put *Tamburlaine* itself constantly at risk.

3

So far, we have been describing spectatorship in *Tamburlaine* as a conspiratorial act in which the auditor becomes incriminated in the illusion. But spectatorship gains realism through its other dimension, an oddly clinical detachment, that will recall both the 1570s stage romances and William Gager's Latin academic play *Meleager*. In this second aspect of viewpoint, Theridamas records his own spectatorial engulfment. Tamburlaine's "perswasions . . .

patheticall" have begun to move Theridamas; Usumcasane entices further, imagining how enemy hosts will "stand amaz'd at us" (221) and will confess, "Theise are the men that all the world admires" (223). Like a third party, Theridamas watches himself surrender to these blandishments: "What stronge enchantments tice my yeelding soule?" (224). When Tamburlaine demolishes the last question of loyalty, Theridamas collapses: "Won with thy words, and conquered with thy looks, / I yeeld my selfe, my men and horse to thee" (228–29). The earlier involuntary "yeelding" Theridamas here climactically embraces, speaking as a witness not only to Tamburlaine but also to his own susceptibility to the Tamburlainean magic. He has become, in a sense, Usumcasane's outside observer, full of amazement. The scene allows Theridamas to surrender without making him morally liable, since he is conscious of the process (and thus responding as best he can) yet unable to stop it (and thus not responsible for the results). Theridamas presents to the audience the spectatorial prototype for admiring Tamburlaine in defiance of ethical reservations.

That prototype – the disembodied witnessing of one's own psychological or physical processes – has its antecedents in the humanistically inflected stage romances of the 1570s and the Latin university drama of the late 1570s and 1580s.[33] In the romance *Clyomon and Clamydes* (*c.* 1576), the knight Clyomon, wounded in battle, surveys his injuries and addresses his absent beloved in apostrophe: "Lo here all gorde in bloud thy faithfull Knight doth lye, / For thee, ah faithfull dame, thy Knight for lack of help shall dye. / For thee, ah here thy *Clyomon*, his mortall stroke hath tane" (1385–87).[34] Clyomon's use of the third person to decribe his painful condition identifies a detachment familiar from stage romances. We might be tempted to see in such moments an amateurish dramaturgy, but William Gager's humanist Latin drama, and subsequently *Tamburlaine*, put that sense of detachment to impressive theatrical use. Gager's tragedy *Meleager*, first performed at Oxford University in 1582, depicts how Meleager's mother, Althaea, acting in revenge, brings about her son's death by burning a log that, in effect, contains his life. Gager sets up the stage as two independent but related loci, a visual metaphor: with Althaea tending the (real) bonfire on one side of the stage, Meleager enters on the other side, suddenly wracked with a consuming internal heat. He describes his anguish in an almost clinically detached language, blending both engagement and detachment:

The flame is ravaging my limbs, with my liver scorched, the fibers of my lungs are burning, while the liver itself is distended and swollen, and a creeping mist licks at my parched blood . . . As the vapor overflows the cavern of Aetna, thus it rages. Alas, what Scorpio, abandoning heaven's tract, or parching Crab is burning my vitals? . . . I die, but pierced by no sword. $(1374-90)^{35}$

Gager's combination of intimate detail with distanced allusion works well here, especially because the audience, watching Meleager's suffering on one half of the stage and the puppeteerlike tending of the burning brand by Althaea on the other half, completes the action by imaginatively connecting cause and effect. Marlowe understands such split-screen, double-consciousness effects, as Theridamas's yielding demonstrates.

That simultaneous engagement and detachment, evident in the Theridamas episode, appears at other moments in *Tamburlaine*. Cosroe's death, for example, is anatomized and poeticized but little felt.

My bloodlesse body waxeth chill and colde,
And with my blood my life slides through my wound,
My soule begins to take her flight to hell:
And sommons all my sences to depart.   (II.vii.42–45)

Like Meleager, Cosroe speaks graphically but in regularized iambic pentameters and objective voice. If anything, Cosroe's tropes are as interesting as his traumas: "now dooth gastly death / With greedy tallents gripe my bleeding hart, / And like a Harpyr tires on my life" (48–50). The image of the Harpy removes attention from Cosroe, since it points at Tamburlaine perhaps now reaching down to snatch the crown from Cosroe's head. Visually, Cosroe's writhing on the ground while Tamburlaine gossips with his men about "The sweet fruition of an earthly crowne" (29) creates a version of Gager's split-screen. Tamburlaine's cruelties are fully acknowledged yet auditorially distanced, a feat of perspective like Gager's engagement and detachment. The juxtaposition of distanced self-awareness inside a play fascinated by physical and psychological realism enhances the strange, dissociated quality of *Tamburlaine*'s speeches. Spectators witness the effects of Tamburlaine's "tyrannies" (41) from the victim's point of view but remain detached. Cosroe watches himself die at Tamburlaine's hand, just as Theridamas watches himself "yeelding." Thus Marlowe transforms the artificiality of romance and academic drama into the last act of spectatorial seduction, in that succumbing to Tamburlaine is something impersonal.

The yielding of Theridamas fulfills a humanist fantasy about the power of rhetoric. At the beginning of his *Art of Rhetoric* (1560), Thomas Wilson recalls that "When Pyrrhus, king of the Epirotes, made battle against the Romans, and could neither by force of arms nor yet by any policy win certain strongholds, he used commonly to send one Cineas . . . to persuade with the captains and people that were in them that they should yield up the said hold or towns without fight or resistance."[36] The Ciceronian idea of overcoming a city "with a word" fascinates Wilson because it mythologizes the humanist dream of eloquence: "what greater delight do we know than to see a whole multitude with the only talk of a man ravished and drawn which way him liketh best to have them?"[37] Wilson's anecdote, with its key verb "yield," resembles the wooing of Theridamas. The idea that eloquence can make men yield involuntarily persists in Wilson's treatise: "such is the power of eloquence and reason, that most men are forced even to yield in that which most standeth against their will."[38] By way of example, Wilson cites Hercules – a pattern for Tamburlaine[39] – whose wit, eloquence, and experience were such that "no man was able to withstand his reason."[40] The dream of compelling men "with a word" to "yield . . . against their will" lies at the heart of Wilson's fantasy of rhetoric. Applied to *Tamburlaine*, Wilson's view demonstrates the conservatism of the hero's verbal prowess, as he merely makes concrete a humanist ideal. These associations help to anchor the Elizabethan credibility of Theridamas's involuntary yielding.[41] Central to Marlowe's dramaturgy is a subtextual action of "bearing witness," in which an audience figure affirms Tamburlaine's heroic stature from a position of apparent detachment, but in which that affirmation is achieved through the figure's incrimination in the illusion yet exculpation from moral responsibility for its implications.

Marlowe converts hyperbole into reality by skillful management of viewpoint in Agydas's suicide scene (III.ii) – where Tamburlaine need not even speak. Its subject is bearing witness to Tamburlaine; its subtextual action is interpreting him; and its meaning is that not to admire Tamburlaine is to die. As with the denunciation scene of Legge's *Richardus Tertius*, the episode emphasizes the victim's perspective. It begins with Agydas asking Zenocrate what her "unquiet fits" (III.ii.2) mean. In answer, Zenocrate admits to a "passion . . . / Which dies my lookes so livelesse as they are" and which might render her "the ghastly counterfeit of death" (13–17). "[D]ies," "livelesse," "death": to lose Tamburlaine's favor – Zenocrate's concern – is to lose life. Ironically, Agydas will discover for himself the death that Zenocrate needlessly fears, and his revelation will come at the moment of Zenocrate's recuperation, when Tamburlaine frowns back "wrathfully" upon him but leads her away *"lovingly"* (s.d. at 65). Before this, precisely when Zenocrate confesses to Agydas her desire to "live and die with *Tamburlaine*" (24), the king himself enters, an unseen spectator, almost conjured by her words. While Agydas denounces Tamburlaine as "vile and barbarous" (26), Zenocrate defends him in mythological terms (47–55), finally admitting that her tears arise from fear that she has lost his love. Agydas's scrutiny of Zenocrate plus her elusiveness give her theatrical authority; that authority testifies to Tamburlaine's mythic stature, and he arrives to witness her conversation like an answering deity. In the uncanny reciprocity of this play, dialogue materializes Tamburlaine, although his presence in another sense already dominates their lives.

In the Agydas scene, Tamburlaine turns emblematic as he controls the action silently. When Tamburlaine leads Zenocrate away, Agydas, still representing the audience's viewpoint, remains onstage alone – "Surpriz'd with feare" (68), "agast" (69), "astonied" (69) – to divine the meaning of Tamburlaine's looks. His long speech reiterates one idea: "Upon his browes was pourtraid ugly death" (72). Employing the language of portraiture, such as shining eyes and pale cheeks, the speech represents Tamburlaine as a figure with symbolic power. It also emphasizes Agydas's terror by means of an epic simile of a storm-tossed sailor revealed as himself. When Techelles enters with a knife, no explanation is needed from Agydas: "I prophecied before and now I proove, / The killing frownes of jealousie and love" (90–91). Agydas takes the proffered knife, and, in an act of aesthetic interpretation, stabs himself.

Looks can kill. In many ways the episode recalls Legge's manipulation of viewpoint. Using multiple perspectives and building to a climactic reversal of fortunes followed by a kind of dénouement, the scene itself is structured like a play. Tamburlaine's silence inverts Gloucester's rant, and the witnessing victim's emotional recognition makes the protagonist's hyperbolic representation theatrically credible. The scene repeats the conflicted terms of Tamburlaine's existence – barbarian or mythic being – but it avoids any potential "ludicrousness" by locating the hyperbolizing in the shocked reactions of the victims, as does Legge's scene. When Agydas grasps the emblematic meaning of Tamburlaine's frowns, he recognizes for himself a kind of Calvinist hell (as will Faustus later), the present horror of his predestinate death. In addition to conquest, Tamburlaine seeks the admiration, demonstrated by Zenocrate, due a godlike personage. To characters and spectators both, the scene urges Tamburlaine's exaggerated believability; Tamburlaine exists largely in Agydas's interpretation. Here Marlowe works beyond the willing suspension of disbelief; rather, he alters the sense of reality by managing its witnessing.

4

But *Tamburlaine* also sets up moral obstacles to the audience's engulfment. The play juxtaposes awe and approbation so clashingly that admiring Tamburlaine will entail accepting a corpse-littered stage as a site of honor. For that effect Zenocrate makes the key audience figure, expressing complicated responses and metaphorically gendering the audience as female. Tamburlaine's military progress has its spectatorial correlative in the capturing of Zenocrate, the overcoming of her fears and reservations, and the crowning of her as queen of Persia. Zenocrate's concerns dot almost every phase of the action: she resists Tamburlaine's seductive rhetoric when he first captures her ("wretched *Zenocrate*" [I.ii.259]); later, finding herself in love, she worries about Tamburlaine's flagging attentions to her; she participates in the baiting of Bajazeth and Zabina but puzzles over Tamburlaine's amusement; she pleads for the lives of her father and her countryman before Tamburlaine's implacability. In the last scene, Zenocrate articulates the play's moral objections to Tamburlaine's atrocities against the virgins and his humiliations of Bajazeth and Zabina. The play continuously tests her spectatorship, as it does that of Theridamas. *Tamburlaine, Part 1* cannot end until the first and last witness, Zenocrate, is won, confirmed, and installed as partner.

The last act – arguably the most complexly orchestrated scene in Tudor drama to date – returns again and again to Zenocrate. Tamburlaine grapples with the implications that she holds for him, and she grapples with his implications for her: those ruminations constitute the subtextual action. Thus Zenocrate resides at the center of the play's famously difficult crux: how can Tamburlaine's mind move so unaffectedly from his slaughter of the pathetic and innocent virgins to his reflections on Zenocrate's beauty and his love for her? The moment verges on grotesque self-parody, one that easily explains the moral resistance from many critics to Tamburlaine's magnetism.

Zenocrate's response to Tamburlaine – in effect, her spectatorship of him – moves him in a strong, subliminal way that is complexly linked to his slaughter of the virgins. The last scene reveals Tamburlaine's vulnerability to Zenocrate; in exposing his need for her affirmation, it defines a tenuousness in his identity. In essence, Tamburlaine can sing his hymn to Zenocrate and to beauty's power only after he has proved his mastery of them through atrocity. Marlowe has a way of inserting strange doubles into his plays: here the virgins double for Zenocrate. Both Zenocrate and the virgins are war's captives and victims. They are outsiders, and they function largely as witnesses to the play's actions. Both come to Tamburlaine in supplication, the virgins for Damascus, Zenocrate for Damascus and her father (the last two acts repeat Zenocrate's anguish enough that the motif helps to structure the play's resolution). Both ask for "pitie." As the seige of Damascus begins, Zenocrate pleads, "Yet would you have some pitie for my sake" (IV.ii.123); the virgins, too, repeat "pitie" like a mantra (V.i.80, 81, 83, 99, 119). The maidens and Zenocrate are linked by tears, as well: the virgins will supplicate "with teares" (25), and Zenocrate strikes the same figure in Tamburlaine's mind: "That in thy passion for thy countries love, / . . . With haire discheweld wip'st thy watery cheeks" (137–39; see also 142, 143, 145). Tamburlaine rejects the pleas of Zenocrate and the virgins on the same grounds, his binding oath: "Not for the world *Zenocrate*, if I have sworn" (IV.ii.125); and "Virgins, in vaine ye labour to prevent / That which mine honor sweares shall be perform'd" (V.i.106–07). In her supplication, the First Virgin imagines a lord and wife who once embraced in "loving joy" (84) but do so "now with teares of ruth and blood" (85) in expectation that their lives

and love will be cut short by Tamburlaine. That image finds fulfillment in Bajazeth and Zabina, suddenly poignant in their love,
who become objects of Zenocrate's sympathy. Tamburlaine
slaughters the virgins, but they will haunt the play's ending when
he ceremoniously returns to Zenocrate the title that these women
share.

If the virgins function as doubles for Zenocrate, then the juxtaposition of gruesome slaughter and delicate romanticism allows
Tamburlaine both to deny and to admit his vulnerability to her.
The virgins take Zenocrate's place; they do not symbolize her so
much as stand in for her. Tamburlaine, that is, displaces his resistance to Zenocrate's beauty by killing the virgins. His own lines
after sending them to their deaths give the hint: "I will not spare
these proud Egyptians, / Nor change my Martiall observations, /
. . . for the love of *Venus*, would she leave / The angrie God of
Armes, and lie with me" (121–25). Slaughtering the virgins – and
thus proving his implacability, his fidelity to his self-fashioned persona, and his resistance to "the love of Venus" – allows Tamburlaine subsequently to yield to Zenocrate's wish. He fears, as his
soliloquy admits, that love-thoughts are "effeminate and faint"
(177). Thus Tamburlaine's brutality compensates for his effeminate "sufferings" (160) on behalf of beauty. The play's dynamic
of involuntary and voluntary response, notable with Theridamas,
reformulates in Tamburlaine himself, as his subliminal displacement legitimizes his volitional acceptance.

Linking the virgins with Zenocrate has several advantages. It
makes sense of the sudden transition in Tamburlaine's thought;
it suggests how, even as Tamburlaine dooms the virgins, another
part of his mind also revolves around Zenocrate, "Whose sorrowes
lay more seige unto my soule, / Than all my army to *Damascus*
walles" (155–56). (As evidence that Zenocrate has infected his
consciousness, Tamburlaine repeats the metaphor of siege and
soul that she has used to him.) The slaughter and the rhapsodizing
seem to emanate from a single "state of feeling." That explanation confirms the close relationship sensed by critics between
the external and the internal in Tamburlaine's psyche. The link
also helps to explain Tamburlaine's otherwise ungrounded claim
in his soliloquy that he has both experienced and mastered love:
"I thus conceiving and subduing both: / That which hath stoopt
the tempest of the Gods" (183–84). The action that constitutes

domination from one perspective reveals itself from another as displaced, even involuntary, compensation, a process very close to the heart of *Tamburlaine* and its reciprocities of spectacle and spectatorship.

Tamburlaine also moves Zenocrate. Marlowe's witness figure embraces what has terrorized her. Zenocrate will perceive Tamburlaine's atrocities with fear and pity, a witnessing that reverberates among the play's women. "What do mine eies behold, my husband dead?" (305), exclaims Zabina, re-entering after Bajazeth has brained himself. Zenocrate follows next, lamenting the slaughter of the Damascans and "the Sun-bright troope / Of heavenly vyrgins" (324–25) whose beauty caused even the slayer's steeds to hesitate. Zenocrate grasps intuitively and makes overt the link between the virgins and herself: "Ah *Tamburlaine*, wert thou the cause of this / That tearm'st *Zenocrate* thy dearest love?" (335–36). The virgins' lives, she adds, "were dearer to *Zenocrate* / Than her owne life" (337–38). From there her sight turns to "another bloody spectacle" (339), Bajazeth and Zabina, for whom she calls upon the earth to "wet thy cheeks for their untimely deathes: / Shake with their waight in signe of feare and griefe" (348–49). Zenocrate apostrophizes to Tamburlaine three times to "Behold the Turk and his great Emperesse" (354, 357, 362); she fears that fortune will turn against Tamburlaine for his ruthlessness, concluding, "And pardon me that was not moov'd with ruthe, / To see them live so long in misery" (369–70). The moral case against Tamburlaine is made in the form of pity for his victims.

At work is a process somewhat opposed to what the modern Western sensibility would endorse. We might infer that terror is somehow the condition for Zenocrate's surrender to Tamburlaine, for she accepts his marriage proposal without reservation in the corpse-strewn finale, "Els should I much forget my self, my lord" (500). The problem of resistance and admiration takes its last twist, for Zenocrate's horror at Tamburlaine's atrocities and her pity for his victims inspire her to deepened concern and love for him. One need not be condescending here. The spirit at play resembles the message of Deuteronomy, with its God of anger and annihilation toward his enemies and apostates, and its God of mercy and care toward his loving and obedient followers: "For the lord thy God is a consuming fire, *and* a ielous God" (4:24); "For the Lord thy God is a merciful God" (4:31).[42] The pattern of fear aroused in a woman and relieved by a powerful male recalls Stephen Greenblatt's generalization about the spectatorial poetics of Elizabethan drama: "one of the defining characteristics of the dramaturgy of Marlowe and Shakespeare, as opposed to that of their medieval predecessors, is the startling increase in the level of represented and aroused anxiety... Marlowe's *Faustus*... seems like a startling departure from everything that has preceded it precisely because the dramatist has heightened and individuated anxiety to an unprecedented degree and because he has contrived to implicate his audience as individuals in that anxiety."[43] Greenblatt identifies a pattern of heightened anxiety and sudden release as one of the fundamental strategies of Elizabethan drama. While *Tamburlaine* lacks the shock of relief, it does display a pattern of heightened anxiety followed by a freeing embrace of authority. *Tamburlaine* terrorizes the spectators, first, through the virgins, who are witnesses like Zenocrate and factors for her, and, second, through Zenocrate herself, who observes and understands the danger of resistance. From a modern perspective, we might wish that she would grasp the full implications of what it means to be Tamburlaine before she chooses him; such awareness would fit a Western sense of individual responsibility. But in the dynamics of the play, Zenocrate's love for Tamburlaine and her terror of him stand close together – as do Tamburlaine's complex feelings for her. They emerge as perhaps more a continuous "state of feeling" than we expect. In *Tamburlaine*, Marlowe approaches drama in a perversely Aristotelean way, since he wants to evoke a vicarious sense of fear in the audience and then salve it with the embrace of the persecutor. Thus it matters that Zenocrate's response affects Tamburlaine, for it suggests that he, too, is susceptible and seeks a like embrace.

The power flowing between Tamburlaine and his witnesses turns out to be more reciprocal than is apparent. In that context it is useful to consider the gendering of the audience, in the figure of Zenocrate, as metaphorically female. "Women must be flatered," says Tamburlaine, "[b]ut this is she with whom I am in love" (I.ii.107–08): the attitude is condescending yet dependent. In the course of the play, its women – Zenocrate, the virgins, even Zabina – show pity and sympathy for the sufferings of others. And it is to those women that the men turn for succor and support, as

the Governor turns to the virgins and Bajazeth to Zabina. Zenocrate's pity and comeliness move Tamburlaine irresistibly. Exactly
because the play accords women a dimension – however conventional – of feeling and expressive beauty beyond the capacities of
men, they can make demands on the warriors. To create the play's
audience figures as women, then, is to recognize that pity has
some claim to accommodation. Confirming that reciprocity, *Tamburlaine* installs the resolution of the stage romances: the displaced
suitor is granted a bathetic death; the Soldan is saved, happy in
his overthrow; and the unsullied daughter is given in marriage to
the hero. So many female audience figures make such an ending
necessary, because it must address the kinds of concerns they
raise, with the result that in *Tamburlaine*, perhaps more than in
any of its predecessors, the nature of spectatorship delimits the
dénouement.

The last act – a singularly complex scene, as we have noted –
reveals how profoundly spectatorship structures the play. The
scene's strands all intertwine – the Damascans, Bajazeth and
Zabina, Zenocrate, Arabia, the Soldan – and in each context,
characters compete to control the action by dominating the spectacle. Through it all, Zenocrate emerges as the key witness. The
virgins offer Tamburlaine a crown to hide his angry brows, plying
him with an image of himself that is noble and flattering. Their
opposition occurs as a competing vision. But rather than bear witness to their spectacle, Tamburlaine makes the virgins witnesses
to his own: "shew them death" (120). Tamburlainean spectacle
obliterates Bajazeth's and Zabina's wished-for scenario, as well, so
that the husband and wife must poignantly bear witness to the
man they hate. As Tamburlaine exits for battle, Bajazeth curses
him in images: "roaring Cannons sever all thy joints, / Making
thee mount as high as Eagles soare" (223–24). But Zabina and
Bajazeth are forced finally to admit they "have no hope to end our
extasies" (238). As their own vision collapses, the two must face
the alternative, horrific image of their future: "A hell, as hoplesse
and as full of feare, / As are the blasted banks of *Erebus*" (243–
44). Despair comes as phantasmagoria. Pictorial imagery conveys
the prospect of personal disintegration as simultaneously deeply
felt yet weirdly remote: "Then let the stony dart of sencelesse
colde, / Pierce through the center of my withered heart" (302–
03), exclaims Bajazeth, about to brain himself. Re-entering,

Zabina cries, "What do mine eies behold, my husband dead?" (305). The idea of "beholding" recurs in Act V as a point of emphasis, for the term designates an affecting and meaningful sight. The word captures the spectatorial perspective, and its repetition measures how much the scene is about exploring and orchestrating audience response. Bajazeth dies almost literally from Tamburlaine's defeat of his imagination: "His Skul al rivin in twain, his braines dasht out" (306). Likewise, visions of Tamburlaine madden Zabina until she, too, "braines her selfe" (s.d. at 318).

Zenocrate enters to this ruin of images. As onetime opponent of Bajazeth and Zabina, Zenocrate in her sympathy and sorrow commands authority. Her tears for "this great Turk and his hapless Emperesse" (368) valorize theatrically the battle of spectacles. All conflict registers on her. No sooner has Zenocrate faced one sympathetic dilemma than another assaults her: "Whom should I wish the fatall victory, / . . . My father and my first betrothed love, / Must fight against my life and present love" (385–89). After Zenocrate asks the "powers devine" (400) to save "faire *Arabia*" (402), he enters from the battle fatally wounded. In the strange psychology of *Tamburlaine*, Arabia experiences himself as someone else's spectacle: "Lye down *Arabia*, wounded to the death, / And let *Zenocrates* faire eies beholde / That . . . Even so for her thou diest in these armes: / Leaving thy blood for witnesse of thy love" (407–11). The previous wars of spectacle now give way to a struggle of beholding, as Zenocrate responds, "Behold *Zenocrate*, the cursed object . . . Behold her wounded in conceit for thee, / As much as thy faire body is for me" (413–16). Her lines encapsulate the play's epistemology, because being "wounded in conceit" not only constitutes an equivalent to being wounded in "faire body" but also makes itself miraculously visible: "Behold." Arabia yokes those fantastical and real spectacles: "Then shal I die with full contented heart, / Having beheld devine *Zenocrate*" (417–18). The extravagant language of Arabia's speech may have been partly influenced by the stage romances of a decade earlier, with their sugared, chivalric devotions of knight and lady. Marlowe establishes between Zenocrate and Arabia a closed circuit, where each is the other's spectacle, each the other's beholder. That circuit is self-sufficient and paradigmatic, recalling the audience's complicity in Tamburlaine's wooing of Theridamas. Zenocrate the spectator achieves her apotheosis here. When Arabia says that he is "making now a vertue of thy sight, / To drive all sorrow from my fainting soule" (428–29), he means to be taken literally. The "sight" he witnesses is the spectacle of Zenocrate beholding him. Arabia can die in bliss because he experiences himself as completely externalized, objectified in the witnessing of Zenocrate (the Lacanian "mirror stage" with a vengeance!). Her reciprocal spectacle of bearing witness authenticates – even justifies – his death: "my heart with comfort dies, / Since thy desired hand shall close mine eies" (431–32). Through a series of potentially endless displacements, the palpable melts into the ethereal: I see in you that you see in me that . . . Marlowe would have the audience accept Arabia's hyperbolic, romanticized, and finally absurd joy, as the circuit of spectacle and beholding demonstrates its power to create what is not there. That exchange represents in miniature *Tamburlaine*'s larger processes, which will culminate in the final vision of Tamburlaine triumphant, but one that turns, as well, to the authenticating witness of Zenocrate. She is his resisting and idealized audience figure now made spectacle, confirmed in credibility, taken finally and completely inside the illusion.

Characters who perform the witness function provide an onstage model, as well as the specific guidance, for audience response. Their relationship to the audience is imitative. With Marlowe we can see the commercial theatre's need to imagine the audience into a play, to devise rather than assume its engagement. Why, apart from contemporary religious and psychological considerations, does Marlowe turn secondary characters to inventing for spectators a certain experience of reality and a desire for it? He does so because he requires a dramaturgy for mastering a potentially restless, diverse audience with no uniform identity or theory of theatre, and for creating an ongoing desire for theatrical experience, so that the audience returns again and again for the fulfilling fantasy that only theatre gives. It sounds like the dramaturgy of capitalism. For that dramaturgy Marlowe exploits the choric function and the humanists' innovations in perspective, just as he makes incursions on humanist theories of theatre. *Tamburlaine*'s very action invokes and recalls the terms of its theatrical existence, and its dramaturgy engages auditorial fantasies in such a way that theatre becomes the consummate means of satisfaction. Indeed, *Tamburlaine* illuminates an important step in establishing

Elizabethan drama as a special domain, in that it is capable, as Judith Weil says of its hero, "of sublimating an ethical conflict into an aesthetic programme."[44] Marlowe's audience figures serve, finally, to activate desire, to engage spectators with its elusive object, and to valorize theatre itself as the house of pleasure and the way of knowing.

8

Robert Green's Friar Bacon and Friar Bungay:
the commonwealth of the present moment

Although Robert Greene is often derided as a theatrical hack and pastiche-maker, his *Friar Bacon and Friar Bungay* (*c.* 1589) demonstrates how commercial drama in the late 1580s could exploit humanist techniques of imitation, allusion, and analogy to attract repeat playgoers to an emergent fixed-venue theatre.[1] Based on a prose romance, Greene's play recalls, imitates, and parodies contemporary plays, including those of Lyly and Marlowe; the earlier moralities and stage romances; his own previous dramas; and other literary and historical sources. The play's own characters and events mirror each other, too, so that actions resonate with multiple meanings; conversely, the heroine, Margaret, is developed in contrast to the literary metaphors and allusions that first define her. Such techniques help to cultivate a new public audience unified by a shared theatrical culture, so that commercial theatre now profits from humanist method. By affirming a knowledge accessible comparatively and theatrically, furthermore, *Friar Bacon and Friar Bungay* suggests the limits of academic knowledge – and thus offers a critique of the humanist dream of learning. In Greene's play, the troubled relationship between experience and knowledge that pulses through sixteenth-century drama achieves poignant culmination.

In the late 1580s, conditions at the playhouses were dynamic.[2] The advent of permanent venues meant that producers needed to attract repeat customers. Competition with other entertainments, such as bearbaiting, demanded that drama provide immediate stimulation and variety. In this fluid period the repertory acting system became temporarily unstable, as several adult companies "reshuffled membership."[3] "Gallimaufrey" romances such as *Clyomon and Clamydes* were yielding place to Kyd's and Marlowe's innovations, although at northern playhouses, audiences of apprentices, citizens, and educated gentry still found popular dramatic forms appealing. But tastes were changing. Demand for new plays soared, while its direction remained uncertain, and particular theatres and companies were not yet identified with certain kinds of drama. In these circumstances Greene and his fellow playwrights defined a paradigmatic playwriting strategy by seeking to capitalize on theatrical successes such as *Tamburlaine* while still endeavoring to satisfy the public's appetite for the new. These paradoxical goals encouraged plays that imitate others or employ familiar formulas or character-types but do so with a difference, an original twist, an unexpected angle.[4] Such plays exist in a dialogic relationship to their predecessors and create pleasure through spectatorial cognizance of that relationship. But this dialogic drama evidences more than a presumably inevitable "copycat" commercialism, since the market sustained many approaches. The dramaturgy of the previous decade, for example, generated economically successful plays, such as the romances, that employ generic formulas and conventions but exhibit none of the rich allusiveness of later theatre. What the new drama expressed, rather, is the intersection of playhouse conditions with humanist intellectual influences.

While the stylistic techniques of imitation, allusion, and analogy are not exclusive to Renaissance humanists, these devices are certainly representative because they capture humanist values and interests. Imitation – the imitation of Ciceronian prose or Terentian comedy – was a cornerstone of humanist discursive practice.[5] Humanist treatises argue by means of metaphor, comparison, analogy, and allusion – strategies central to humanist rhetoric. On the abstract level, such methods reiterate the humanist notion of Platonic similitude, namely, that variety radiates from oneness. These rhetorical techniques also reflect the desire to reimagine the Christian present by linking it to classical history and myth. Humanist "cross-referencing" accelerated with the development of the printing press, which changed scholarly commentary from glossing and elaborating to comparing, contrasting, and citing, as Elizabeth Eisenstein demonstrates.[6] In the case of humanist humor, Erasmus's *The Praise of Folly* shows how imitation can easily turn into satire and parody; indeed, imitation, allusion, and comparison often reveal, paradoxically, the discreteness of the present. William Gager's neo-Latin *Meleager* (1582), written at Oxford not long before Greene composed *Friar Bacon and Friar Bungay*, offers an example from drama. Dana Sutton observes that "the poetry of *Meleager* is something like a mosaic partially assembled out of bits and pieces of Seneca and other classical writers"; the playwright's challenge is to display "originality while working within the system," thus allowing his audience to enjoy the appositeness and individuality of the work, and even its playful cleverness.[7] By his use of imitation, allusion, and parody, Greene focuses that tradition on popular theatre.

Humanist method brings with it pedagogical concerns. Learning, of course, had long been an ingredient of sixteenth-century drama, whether one considers the school plays or the morality tradition. But in the 1580s Greene undertakes a critique of humanist learning that lends his drama form. Academic interests permeate *Friar Bacon and Friar Bungay*. Like Lyly's *Campaspe*, it displays "the Humanistic theme of the relationship between governance and learning," intermingling English peers with Oxford scholars.[8] Dons and sizars stand beside princes and swains, as disputations and scientific ventures create the central spectacles. The play alludes to contemporary academic life: Friar Bacon's interests recall those of Elizabethan polymaths such as John Dee, and the German Vandermast represents a satiric treatment of Giordano Bruno, who disputed at Oxford in 1583.[9] Yet toward formal learning the play's attitude wavers. Although some characters do succeed as learners – Lacie and notably Edward[10] – their transformations endorse experiential rather than abstract knowledge. Bacon's scholarship leads to tragedy, causing him to retreat from his humanist goal of mastery. Margaret makes a self-defining choice in rejecting a life of religious contemplation – despite her full appreciation of its claims – for Lacie's "inchanting face" (xiii.1984).[11] Introduced in literary terms and likened to a "booke" (ii.269), Margaret nonetheless reaches a decision by intuitive rather than formal means. In these ways *Friar Bacon and Friar Bungay* expresses disenchantment with the transformative power of knowledge. The wistful, even melancholy strain in the play's second half derives, in part, from the dimming of learning's magic.

We can trace these ideas in three regards. First, *Friar Bacon and Friar Bungay* combines theatrical conventions and techniques of humanist allusion to create a spectatorially engaging theatrical

"world." Second, although Margaret seems initially associated
with literary stereotypes, her climactic decision affirms a domain
of truth beyond academic knowing. Third, internal parallels and
contrasts among characters and storylines give the play an enigmatic sense of both celebration and sadness. Thus *Friar Bacon and
Friar Bungay* valorizes techniques of humanist dramaturgy even as
it embraces a chastened view of humanist learning.

1

Greene's is an inclusive and self-referential symbolic world.
Through the shorthand of stage conventions, *Friar Bacon and Friar
Bungay* activates a theatrical consciousness in its spectators, who
will derive pleasure from their connoisseurship of drama's protocols and references. Expertise in literary conventions could be
expected from Greene, given his humanist training, and that
facility now contributes to the development of fixed-venue theatre.
The first scene of *Friar Bacon and Friar Bungay* establishes the play's
domain. "*Enter, Edward the first malcontented*" reads the opening
stage direction, upon which Lacie's speech instantly capitalizes:
"Why lookes my lord like to a troubled skie, / When heauens
bright shine, is shadowed with a fogge?" (i.5–6). This stage direction is comprehensible only if it refers to conventional theatrical
behavior: Edward's frowning, to which Lacie calls attention.[12] We
are now, Greene insists, in the world of the theatre, where appearances have knowable meanings and where gesture and language
reinforce each other. But Edward also wears a Kendall green costume (146) that denotes hunting, an occupation of pleasure, not
discontent.[13] Upon that visually mysterious prince, Lacie focuses
the gaze of the characters and the audience. Likewise, the echoing
speeches by Warren, Ermsbie, and Raphe, which proceed in the
order of their entrances, suggest blocking that makes Edward the
central figure, with friends hierarchically arrayed about him. The
syntax of the theatre, then, creates the scene's focal point, problem, and environment. As Lacie now describes the hunt at "merry
Fresingfield" (10), the play establishes tonal contrasts, for his language – "frolicke" (8,14), "lustily" (11), "iolly mates" (11), "fat
venison" (12) – runs counter to Edward's "melancholie dumpe"
(15). Edward has fallen "into his passions" (23) because of Margaret, "the bonny damsell ... That seemd so stately in her stammell

red" (20–21). The opening language conjures forth a festive arcadia of utopian countrymen crossed by aristocratic lust.

With this matrix of signs, Greene orchestrates a specifically theatrical mode of response. The costumes, colors, and "disguises" of the first scene virtually motivate the play's action. In the course of events, Edward must change from his melancholy dump and his Kendall green to the agreeable behavior and sumptuous dress of a prince.[14] But he will do so only after temporarily abdicating his royal identity, in the form of his clothes, to his fool, Raphe. Margaret will migrate from her homely stammel red to a nun's habit (xiii) to the "richly" tailored "wedding robes" (1993, 1966) commissioned by Lacie. Lacie must himself pass from the "gray" (iii.423) disguise of his *"countrie apparell"* (s.d. 355–56) through the spurs and boots of his rough "testing" of Margaret to his own wedding garb. Thus the first scene launches a fertile drama of spectacle, as characters move away from confused or false visual significations toward self-knowledge and fulfillment. Overall, the play employs a new Elizabethan repertoire of spectacular devices and effects, including the prospective glass, Hercules and the Hesperidian golden tree conjured from below, the Brazen Head that talks, and the arm that appears in lightning to smash it with a hammer. Greene used the Brazen Head – perhaps even the same property – in *Alphonsvs, King of Arragon*; likewise the conjured tree would become a theatrical commonplace, if it was not one already; and some of Greene's stagings, such as the charming of swords (v.566–84), recur both in his own plays and elsewhere.[15] *Friar Bacon and Friar Bungay* even contrasts the burlesque, morality-Vice acting styles of Raphe and Miles to the newer, more naturalistic styles of characters such as Edward and Margaret.[16] Greene contributes to, and borrows from, a growing, shared inventory of properties, images, and gestures in 1580s theatre. One triumph of the new theatre is the mutually reinforcing synergy between commercial tactics and humanist method.

Into his theatrical grammar Greene integrates literary conventions and allusions as points of interpretive departure.[17] Edward's likening of himself to the rapist Tarquin (i.90), for example, offers a familiar Renaissance allusion that exposes his cruel intentions toward Margaret. That self-revelation, furthermore, brings to a deflating conclusion a passage in which Edward rhapsodizes over Margaret in Petrarchese:

I tell the Lacie, that her sparkling eyes,
Doe lighten forth sweet Loues alluring fire:
And in her tresses she doth fold the lookes
Of such as gaze vpon her golden haire,
Her bashfull white mixt with the mornings red,
Luna doth boast vpon her louely cheekes,
. . .
Her teeth are shelues of pretious *Margarites*,
Richly enclosed with ruddie curroll cleues.
. . .
But whiter than the milke her christall skin.

(55–60, 63–64, 84)

Edward celebrates qualities in Margaret similar to those admired by Thomas Watson's narrator in *Hekatompathia* (1582), one of the first Elizabethan love-sonnet sequences and a well-known "reference-book of Petrarchan themes."[18] Watson's speaker describes his disdainful lady in imagery nearly identical to Edward's: "Her yellowe lockes exceede the beaten goulde; / Her sparkeling eies in heau'n a place deserue" (Sonnet VII, 2–3); "On either cheeke a *Rose* and *Lillie* lies" (9); "Her lips more red than any *Corall* stone" (11); and "Her brest transparent is, like *Christall* rocke" (13).[19] It cannot be claimed that Greene is alluding to *Hekatompathia* specifically, but he is certainly referring to the fashion for sonnets.[20] Edward's literariness also trades on Raphe's bawdy metaphor of women as "bookes" (51).[21] Greene uses humanist reading to underwrite theatrical reality: Edward's literary language typecasts and subtly parodies him; it reinforces a sense of the pictorial and its powers of enchantment ("And in her tresses she doth fold the lookes"); and it establishes a Petrarchan view of Margaret, against which she can emerge contrapuntally.

If, as Gurr argues, the 1580s saw the creation of a new theatrical repertoire for the playhouses, then one feature of that repertoire was its collective reflexivity, in the forms of imitation, allusion, analogy, mimicry, and parody. The public playhouses developed, as we have suggested, a set of imitable, "stock" conventions expanded beyond those of the mysteries, late moralities, and interludes – gestures, sounds, colors, character poses, acting styles – that emphasize the theatre as an embodied fantasy. Mere imitation seems insufficient here: to be interesting, a drama must also transform its predecessor or engage it dialogically. Theatrical reflexivity, furthermore, invents and cultivates a particular kind

of spectator: the knowledgeable, theatrically alert, repeat playgoer
who would be the key to the commercial success of the permanent
playhouses. To write a play that not only alludes to another play
but also parodies or otherwise appropriates it is to tap a theatrical
pleasure based on previous playhouse experience. Because
Thomas Watson's *Hekatompathia* represents imitative poetry in
transition from the neo-Latin tradition to the vernacular, it provides a useful analogy. Watson's sonnets explore popular romantic
love while employing academic humanist trappings. The poems
are preceded by introductory paragraphs citing classical models,
authors, and mythological figures and are followed by footnotes
cross-referencing Latin sources and precedent works. The poems
themselves proclaim their imitativeness (and include translations
of Petrarch into Latin and English). That feature facilitates some
of Watson's better poetic effects, such as when his lovelorn narrator invokes classical models to identify his love-sickness by
means of contrast:

> And what though *Pryam* spent his vitall breath
> For *Thisbes* sake? or *Haemon* choase to die
> To follow his *Antigone* by death?
> In harder case and worser plight am I,
> > Which loue as they, but liue in dying still,
> > And faine would die, but can not haue my will.
> > > (Sonnet XXX)

Here is a subjectivity constructed by imitation and, simultaneously, by an evocation of suffering beyond the imitable. The
classical models' insufficiency proves the lover's authenticity.

The reassurance of likeness, the pleasurable enigma of contrast,
and the amusement of parody suffuse Greene's dramaturgy. *Friar
Bacon and Friar Bungay*'s references to the verbal styles of other
plays and writers are so direct that they seem intended to be perceived and enjoyed. Stylistic imitation can define a character, as
Petrarchese does with Edward. Likewise, Lacie appears to disadvantage later by couching his test of Margaret's constancy in a
letter notable for its Lylyan euphuism: "The bloomes of the
Almond tree grow in a night, and vanish in a morne, the flies
Haemere (faire Peggie) take life with the Sun, and die with the dew,
fancie that slippeth in with a gase, goeth out with a winke, and
too timely loues, haue euer the shortest length" (ix.1516–20).
The languid, highly wrought euphuistic style gives Lacie's decep-

tion an air of self-satisfaction and condescension. As another example, Friar Bacon's sizar, Miles, speaks frequently in what Weld calls "macronic Skeltonics": "*Saluete omnes reges*, that gouern your Greges, in Saxonie and Spaine, in England and in Almaine: for all this frolicke rable must I couer thee table, with trenchers, salt and cloth, and then looke for your broth" (viii.1326–29).[22] That speech comes on a comic entrance and seems addressed partly to the audience ("this frolicke rable"), elements that call attention to the parody. Miles possesses qualities reminiscent of the Vice figures in *Magnificence*, but he also ridicules their style: he is both of and not of what he mocks. Where Marlowe in a prologue had distinguished his mighty line from the "jygging vaines of riming mother wits,"[23] Greene pursues the same theatrical cause but brings the "jygging vaines" inside the play as an object of humor, so that his audience can have the joke as their own.

Friar Bacon and Friar Bungay has been most often associated with Marlowe's *Doctor Faustus* because of its overreaching scholar-magician. I would stress, however, a less obvious connection: to *Tamburlaine*. Greene had already imitated *Tamburlaine* in *Alphonsvs* and *Orlando Furioso* (which also owes a debt to *The Spanish Tragedy*). King Henrie's opening lines – "Great men of Europe, monarchs of the West, / Ringd with the wals of old *Oceanus*, / Whose loftie surges like the battelments, / That compast high built Babell in with towers" (iv.446–49) – recall, if indirectly, the poeticizing of geography and place names in *Parts 1* and *2* of *Tamburlaine*. More obviously, the verbal style in which Tamburlaine woos Zenocrate finds its echo in Edward's wooing of Margaret:

> In Frigats bottomd with rich Sethin planks,
> Topt with the loftie firs of Libanon,
> Stemd and incast with burnisht Iuorie
> And ouerlaid with plates of Persian wealth,
> Like Thetis shalt thou wanton on the waues
> And draw the Dolphins to thy louely eyes,
> To daunce lauoltas in the purple streames,
> Sirens with harpes and siluer psalteries,
> Shall waight with musicke at they frigots stem,
> And entertaine faire Margret with their laies.
>
> (vii.999–1008)

Behind those lines floats *Tamburlaine*'s expansive poetic vision: "A

hundreth Tartars shall attend on thee ... " (*Tam.* 1, 1.ii.93); its
evocation of riches: "Medean silke" (95), "precious juelles" (96);
its alliteration and assonance: "And scale the ysie mountaines
lofty tops" (100); and particularly its line-ending nouns that
climax a unit meaning: "With milke-white Hartes upon an Ivorie
sled" (98). But there is a difference. Unlike Zenocrate, who will
reject her betrothed for Tamburlaine, Margaret resists Edward's
rhetoric: "The dulcet tunes of frolicke Mercurie, / Not all the
wealth heauens treasurie affoords, / Should make me leaue lord
Lacie or his loue" (1017–19). The Tamburlaine-Zenocrate model
thus provides a scale for measuring Edward's attempt on Margaret's virtue and her answering fidelity. Edward aspires to the
theatrical imperiousness and exoticism of Tamburlaine, but his
seduction collapses before Margaret's constancy. By subjecting
heroic theatre to such parody, *Friar Bacon and Friar Bungay* gains a
persuasive realism.

In Vandermast's disputation with Bacon, Greene makes further
mock-heroic use of *Tamburlaine*, particularly the awed gaze that
Tamburlaine inspires. He has Bacon arrive just at the climactic
moment to disrupt Vandermast's demand of Henrie, "Crowne me
with lawrell" (viii.1232) for defeating Bungay. Taken aback by
this new figure inquiring into Bungay's bafflement, Vandermast
asks, "What art thou that questions thus" (1238). Bacon responds
mock-heroically, "Men call me Bacon" (1239). Vandermast tops
off the exchange: "Lordly thou lookest, as if that thou wert
learnd, / Thy countenance, as if science held her seate / Betweene
the circled arches of thy browes" (1240–42). The lines, the stagey
gazing, and the ritualized exchange recall the dazzled responses
to Tamburlaine: "His looks do menace heaven and dare the Gods"
(I.ii.157); "Whose fiery cyrcles beare encompassed / A heaven of
heavenly bodies in their Spheares" (II.i.15–16). *Tamburlaine* sets
the vogue for such rhapsodizing of a character as spectacle.[24] The
mock-heroic manner of *Friar Bacon and Friar Bungay* lends an outsized scale to the encounter between the scholar-magicians, while
Greene's insertion of friars and pedagogues within the epic-
combat forms creates humor by its parodic juxtaposition of comic
and heroic.

Two of *Friar Bacon and Friar Bungay*'s allusions to other styles
and plays deserve mention: those to Senecan revenge drama, such
as Kyd's *The Spanish Tragedy*, and to Lyly's *Campaspe*. When Marga-

ret receives the euphuistic letter from Lacie renouncing her love, she responds in a rival Elizabethan stage convention:

> Fond Atae doomer of bad boading fates,
> That wrappes proud Fortune in thy snaky locks,
> Didst thou inchaunt my byrth-day with such stars,
> As lightned mischeefe from their infancie,
> If heauens had vowd, if stars had made decree,
> To shew on me their froward influence,
> If Lacie had but lovd, heauens hell and all,
> Could not haue wrongd the patience of my minde.
>
> (ix.1531–38)

The classical Senecan imagery; the invocations of hellish Atae, opposing heavens, and decreeing stars as the source of her fate; the two "if" clauses; and the cumulative "heauens hell and all," which gathers up the influences enumerated: all these bespeak an epic stage rhetoric deriving from Seneca, emerging effulgently in 1560s Inns of Court plays such as *Gorboduc* and *Jocasta*, and achieving the status of sensationalist convention in the soliloquies of Kyd's Hieronimo. While in Renaissance rhetorical theory the apostrophe constitutes an emotionally affecting figure, Clemen calls its effect here "ridiculous."[25] But Greene is pursuing a dramaturgical strategy: he deploys two sharply contrasting, almost oppositional rhetorical styles familiar onstage, Kyd's and Lyly's, and sets the artificiality of each against that of the other. Margaret is as hyperbolically tragical as Lacie is hyperbolically languid. Thus Greene achieves a kind of theatrical *tour de force*, for seldom before has a playwright had the skill or opportunity to score a thematic point through allusion to verbal stage styles. The moment carries double voltage, because what must register foremost on the spectator is Margaret's sincerity, with the humor from rhetorical appreciation lurking in the background. Margaret's realism results not from roundedness in her character but rather from rhetorical layering. The technique recalls *Hekatompathia*'s evocation of classical lovers to distinguish its narrator's unique passion.

Edward's pursuit of Margaret owes a further debt to John Lyly's *Campaspe* (pub. 1584).[26] Edward's desire, his defeat by a rival, and his eventual magnanimity echo Alexander's tribulations with Campaspe. Greene also invokes Lyly's theme, that "love enfeebles the warrior-prince and jeopardizes his ability to govern."[27] The most obvious references to *Campaspe* come in Edward's confrontation with Lacie and Margaret, where Edward not only likens himself to Alexander ("Iniurious Lacie did I loue thee more / Than Alexander his Hephestion" [vii.970–71]) but the scene itself also imitates the parallel episode in *Campaspe* (v.iv), in which Alexander exposes but then forgives and unites Apelles and Campaspe.[28] While Greene calls on both Marlowe's Tamburlaine and Lyly's Alexander in delineating Edward, he qualifies those heroic allusions stylistically. The conflict proceeds in an exaggerated and theatrically self-conscious manner that suggests a joke shared with the audience. Greene treats the conflict between Alexander and Apelles to parody by converting Edward's threat to slay Lacie into the comic problem of too many willing victims. No sooner does Edward, poniard in hand, declare his intention to "quite" Lacie as a "traitor" (vii.981) than Margaret steps between them and declares herself responsible for having seduced Lacie with her looks and sighs (982–96). When Edward renews his determination to have Margaret, Lacie offers himself for stabbing, since he cannot live without her love (1027–29). But "Spare Lacie gentle Edward, let me die, / For so both you and he doe cease your loues" (1033–34), Margaret next interposes. As the dialogue accelerates, Margaret promises grandly to take her own life should Edward take Lacie's: "and fore the morning sun / Shall vaunt him thrice, ouer the loftie east, / Margret will meet her Lacie in the heauens" (1042–44). The battle, now between Lacie and Margaret as willing sacrifices, soars melodramatically – "*Lacie*: . . . Then Edward short my life. *Margaret*: Rid me . . . *Lacie*: Nay Edward . . ." (1049–1051) – until Margaret arrives at the obvious, now-comic solution: "in one toombe knit both our carkases" (1056). This over-the-top, take-me dialogue has visual reinforcement, for the two pleaders at some point fall to their knees (see 1068) and presumably crowd each other out crawling comically after Edward. Greene folds the heroic strains of Tamburlaine and Alexander inside the scene's strongest effect, the comedy of the sacrifice debate. That buffoonery, moreover, virtually mandates Edward's self-transformation, since, in the emotional economy of the stage, killing such eager victims offers no satisfaction. The contrast between heroic reference and present action fashions the comedy; humanist allusion provides form.

Greene adapts humanist "cross-referencing" to produce thematic and emotional effects and to ignite an intertextual dialogue. The imitative technique gives richness, humor, irony, and resonance to the characters and action onstage; it resembles Watson's humanist method made subtle. Rather than simply following a generic template, as do the writers of romance and morality drama in the 1570s and 1580s, Greene creates a humanist-inspired, dialogic relationship with the drama around him and thus conveys pleasure and motivation to the permanent playhouse's repeat spectators. When one adds Greene's references to other literary material (*The Famous History of Friar Bacon*, Holinshed's *Chronicles, The Ship of Fools*, Bale's history, the romance tale, the morality play[29]), to historical figures (Bacon, Henry III, Bruno, Tarlton), and to topical events (the Oxford disputations, the Armada's defeat), *Friar Bacon and Friar Bungay* suggests how playwrights in the 1580s attempt to establish drama as an Elizabethan "master discourse," a project to which the humanist method is perfectly suited.

Friar Bacon and Friar Bungay spawned successors, such as *Fair Em, The Miller's Daughter of Manchester* (*c.* 1590) and "sequel" *John of Bordeaux* (*c.* 1592).[30] Both plays borrow from Greene's first scene. *Fair Em* begins with William the Conqueror, surrounded by nobles, having suddenly left a ceremonial tilt in a "passion" (3) and "with frowns" (7) because he has just been love-smitten by the picture of Blanch painted on Lubeck's shield.[31] Likewise, in *John of Bordeaux*, Ferdinand, the emperor's son, encompassed by friends, enters the second scene in the "dumpes" (73) because of his unrequited desire for John's wife.[32] Each play engages in a thematic and dramaturgical dialogue with *Friar Bacon and Friar Bungay. Fair Em* emphasizes romantic love, *John of Bordeaux* magic. In *Fair Em* the heroine is not allowed a humble birth, as is Margaret, and its callow suitor receives the repudiation that Greene's play omits. In *Fair Em*, as well, Margaret's virtues are dispersed between two heroines, Em and Mariana, while Manvile and William the Conqueror share Edward's strengths and weaknesses. In *John of Bordeaux* the ignoble Ferdinand seeks Vandermast's magic to help him seduce John's wife; the stratagem's allusion to *Friar Bacon and Friar Bungay* may help the audience to predict its failure. These successors not only borrow Greene's theatrical shorthand but also exercise on *Friar Bacon and Friar Bungay* its own technique of thematic allusion.

2

Shakespearean drama has trained us to think of a character as developing psychologically, according to his or her experiences. That view has some validity for Margaret, since she demonstrates self-consciousness and gains insight. But Margaret also "develops" in dramaturgical ways inaccessible to a psychological model. She moves away from the literary and painterly images offered for her at the outset, and she changes in relation to the fantasy life of the play: at first the *object* of fantasy, she becomes finally its *vehicle*. Margaret begins the play as the idealized object of Edward's lust, but by the end, she has changed into a medium for the fantasy of upward mobility shared by audience members of the "middling sort."[33] Margaret fits Leinwand's model of middling-sort complexity, limited class-consciousness, and fluid upward-and-downward mobility. She offers the perfect appeal: a character of modest estate, made ambiguous by possessing personal attributes above her social rank, who faces calamity but then achieves a dizzying yet apt rise in status. Margaret thus maintains a dialogue with another audience-arousing figure, Tamburlaine, often discussed as an aggressive, even hostile, wish-fulfilling symbol for class competition. Margaret might be understood as an alternative paradigm for social advancement, one based on the values of flexibility, adaptability, and conciliation rather than class antagonism.[34]

We have already noted the Petrarchese by which Edward fantasizes Margaret and her affecting power. In conversation with Lacie, Edward calls further attention to the act of gazing upon Margaret: "Tell me Ned Lacie, didst thou marke the mayd, / How liuely in her country weedes she lookt" (i.41–42; see also 57ff.). Margaret is described, first, in painterly terms – "so stately in her stammell red" (21) and "liuely in her country weedes" – and, more pervasively, with the colors of portraiture: "golden haire" (58), "bashfull white mixt with the mornings red" (59), "ruddie curroll cleues" (64), "Lilly armes" (82), and "christall skin, / Checked with lines of Azur" (84–85). Edward makes the comparison explicit: "Her front is beauties table where she paints" (61; see also 86). To all that, Greene adds another quality, Margaret's brightness: "sparkling eyes" (55), "lighten" (56), "alluring fire" (56), "shine" (80), "ouer-shine" (140; see also v.686). Margaret launches her career in *Friar Bacon and Friar Bungay* as the consummate spectacle, the radiant object of connoisseurial gaze. Such objectification constitutes the backdrop for her development.

As Margaret is an object of Edward's wonder, she is also an object of study. We have noted Raphe's association of Margaret and women in general with "bookes," a link that promotes further wordplay on reading, "learning" (i.51), and "grammer" (53).[35] Thus, to "inchaine her love" (126), Edward will career off to the scholar-necromancer Bacon. The very next scene capitalizes dialogically on that association: Miles, carrying some volumes, enters on a Latin quibble about dwelling harmoniously with books,[36] and Bacon expostulates on the marvels he can perform by "Magicke bookes" (ii.227; see also 220). As we have noted, the scene pursues the book-woman pun with the baffling of Master Burden for his libidinous "stud[y]" of a certain "booke" (269) at Henley. Besides being the comic object of study and learning, women also take on another aspect of books: magic. In John Redford's *Wit and Science*, humanist learning could be represented innocently as a desirable woman, but by the 1580s the metaphor has collapsed into irony. In later plays, such as *Love's Labour's Lost*, academic knowledge is parodied for a presumed imperviousness to the emotional reality of love. Margaret stands early in that divide: she is imagined in literary terms and sought through learned sorcery, but her relationship to formal knowledge is ironically tinged.

Greene develops Margaret, in part, *against* the poeticized, pictorial, and passive image of her that dominates the first scene.[37] Margaret possesses agency. Her very first speech differentiates her from masculine concern with the price of produce, as she proclaims a feminine holiday playfulness (iii.361–73). While the scene retains her as an object of gaze – is she blushing with love or pale with anger? (410–13) – she declares her attraction to Lacie in an aside that much precedes his own protestation.[38] Attuned to patrician values, she notes Lacie's manners, debonair carriage, and handsome proportions. "But Peg disclose not that thou art in loue" (429), she cautions herself, "till time doth serue thy turne" (432). The scene begins to establish Margaret's initiative, and it also begins to align spectators with her by making them her confidants. Greene builds Margaret's agency further. The betrothal scene commences with Margaret declaring to Bungay her love for Lacie's personage, wit, and courtesy (v.665–71) and with Bungay offering his help in "entangl[ing]" (677) Lacie's love. Thus Margaret's intentions, declared before Lacie enters, orchestrate the scene. Greene has reversed conventional roles: if Edward appeared as the aggressive Tarquin in the first scene, Margaret takes the active role in pursuing honest love. Margaret asserts herself as she shakes Lacie out of his reverie (701–12); drives the dialogue with questions (702, 704, 710); cautions Lacie against overhaste in wooing her; jokes at Lacie's expense (she perceives his noble identity); and proclaims, "The keepers daughter tooke you prisoner, / Lord Lacie yeeld, Ile be your gailor once" (741–42). Having extracted Lacie's declarations of love, Margaret brings the wooing to its climax by asking, "What loue is there where wedding ends not loue?" (754; see also 756). The fair maid who cautioned earlier against haste is about to be wed on the spot.

A cynical view might treat Margaret as a manipulative, socially ambitious schemer, making good market on her beauty (despite her apparent indifference to the price of country goods). But the effect, I think, lies elsewhere. Margaret has good reason to distrust disguised courtiers: "Ah how these earles and noble men of birth, / Flatter and faine to forge poore womens ill" (749–50). Such a speech defines the comic pleasures of the scene, for Lacie has behaved questionably, and Margaret rightly accuses him, although the audience knows that his heart has made the approved decision. Margaret's forwardness is a just defense. Greene also gives Margaret a feminized deference to offset her assertiveness. As soon as Lacie says he will make Margaret his countess, she proclaims, "Handmaid vnto the earle so please himselfe / A wife in name, but seruant in obedience" (758–59; see also 662, 774). Margaret operates as a fantasy figure in this scene by evoking a male daydream of the dominant-submissive woman, a cross between the initiative-taking romance heroine, such as Neronis in *Clyomon and Clamydes*, and the obedient Patient Grissell. Edward's voyeurism and anger, moreover, only invite audience sympathy for Margaret, since male aggressions imperil her unbeknownst – she may be a "spectacle" to Edward, but the scene now discredits his objectifying gaze. Greene establishes a complex emotional economy, evidenced, first, in Margaret's self-assertions and self-negations and, second, in the varying detachment from and sympathy toward her, both neatly illustrating the coordinates of playwrighting in the 1580s. Objectors such as Stephen Gosson had worried about drama's eroticizing and emotional power, a version of which Margaret illustrates, but Greene's humanist romance manages its titillating fantasies with comedy and deft control of spectatorial distance.

By complicating the stereotypes that imbricate her – the romance heroine, Patient Grissell, Helen of Troy – Greene individualizes Margaret. Addressing Edward, she blames her own physical expressiveness for Lacie's fall: "I fed myne eye with gazing on his face, / And still bewicht lovd Lacie with my looks" (vii.987–88). Margaret here turns Lacie into the feminized object of "gazing" (Edward has just called Lacie "effeminate" [978]). If she infantilizes herself – arousing more male daydreams – her worshipful looking also has transformative agency. Thus Margaret fulfills the subservient role of Patient Grissell as she simultaneously undermines it. Likewise, allusions to Helen by the suitors, Lambert and Serlsby, function paradoxically. Lambert calls her "Suffolks faire Hellen" (ix.1425), and Margaret reinvokes the allusion herself when the suitors leave: "Shall I be Hellen in my forward fates, / As I am Hellen in my matchles hue / And set rich Suffolke with my face afire" (1483–85). Her question registers a consciousness of the classical reference and consequently its equivocalness – can she really resemble Helen if she does not wish to incite the countryside and if she looks for Paris (Lacie) to prevent such consequences? Margaret's stereotypes affirm only her complex difference; as with the narrator of Watson's sonnets, allusion individualizes her.

At the very moment that Margaret resolves to face out the suitor-problem by being "blith and of good cheere" (1493) as she awaits Lacie's return, the Post enters with the malignant letter. Margaret's response moves beyond the Patient Grissell pattern laid out for her, as she assumes less a passive patience than an active virtue:

> First for thou camst from Lacie whom I lovd,
> Ah giue me leaue to sigh at euery thought,
> Take thou my freind the hundred pound he sent,
> For Margrets resolution craues no dower,
> The world shalbe to her as vanitie,
> Wealth trash, loue hate, pleasure dispaire,
> For I will straight to stately Fremingham,
> And in the abby there be shorne a Nun
> And yeld my loues and libertie to God.   (1545–53)

Skillful in its shifting emotions, Margaret's speech successively evokes pathos, generosity, didactic wisdom, and hyperbolic action. Her saintly sentiments are as irreproachable as her renunciation is enthusiastic. Margaret appropriates the Grissell model with the same kind of comic, self-conscious energy that allows her to transcend all her stereotypes.

Margaret's next scene confers on her a power of choice extraordinary in Tudor drama and climaxes her development as an agent. She also takes the last step in her progress from idealized object to male wish-fulfillment figure to, finally, the character who stands closest to the audience. Apparently betrayed by Lacie, Margaret enters not in stammel red but *"in Nuns apparrell"* (s.d. xiii.1895). Her "base attire" (1927) is probably a habit made of coarse, colorless homespun and a wimple that covers her golden hair. Her physical change bespeaks her change of attitude and status, wrenching her father: "Margret be not so headstrong in these vows, / Oh burie not such beautie in a cell" (1897–98). The scene emphasizes humorously Margaret's visual alteration, as she preaches against "the shew of rich abilliments" (1929) and her father and friend stand aghast that she will be "shorn a Nunne" (1923). This conflict between worldliness and spirituality translates into a conflict over spectacle itself. Margaret's physical image demonstrates how completely the religious issue has been transformed in meaning by the power of theatrical representation. The insidiousness of the 1580s stage is that it can finally confirm only one answer to the choice between spectacle and drabness, and in that sense the Puritan assumptions about the theatre were more correct than erroneous.

When Lacie arrives, he fails to recognize Margaret. His companion Ermsbie, noting her father in conversation with a postulant, insinuates vulgarly, "The old lecher hath gotton holy mutton to him a Nunne my lord" (1941–42). Lacie seems to concur as he hails the keeper and inquires about Margaret – "How doth Peggie thy daughter and my loue" (1944) – whereupon Margaret's father must actually identify her to her breezy wooer: "See where she stands clad in her Nunnes attire, / Readie for to be shorne" (1946–47). Lacie appears incapable of recognizing his betrothed in any garb but her stammel red, a fact that may underscore the discontinuity of her habit but that speaks as tellingly about his limitations. Lacie presents a hurdle in the scene. Critics have noted his coarseness and impatience, which seem at odds with his manner in the wooing scenes (just as his crude testing of Margaret seems unmotivated).[39] He enters the scene symbolically *"booted and spurd"* (s.d. 1935), talking loosely to his friends ("Come on my wags" [1936]) and similarly to Margaret's father. He treats Margaret to a harsh jocularity ("Why how now Margret, what a male-content" [1950]), reinforces the representation of spiritual crisis as a matter of coiffure ("What shorne a Nun" [1963; also 1974]), breezily dismisses his trick ("Twas but to try sweete Peggies con-stancie" [1970]), and hurries her for an answer, as if checking his watch ("Peggie your answere must be short" [1982]). "[J]arring and intrusive," "loud," "unfeeling and arrogant," "offensive," and "flippant": such words pepper Crupi's commentary on Lacie. The fair maid of Fressingfield wants to marry this guy?[40]

By portraying Lacie as coarse, Greene offers Margaret a serious and real choice – God or Lord Lacie – and allows the issue to linger in doubt (xiii.1971–82). A now de-pedestalized candidate for marriage, Lacie seems to prove what Margaret has perceived, that "The world contains nought but alluring baites: / Pride, flatterie, and inconstant thoughts" (1915–16). Margaret risks making a bad choice, that is, wagering her happiness on a suitor as capable of insensitivity toward her as of kindness. The present revelations imply, as well, that Margaret may not be able to manage Lacie as easily in the future as she has in the past. Under those circumstances, yielding to Lacie's "inchanting face" (1984; no mention of "wit" or "courtesy" here) confers on Margaret's choice a certain poignancy and melodramatic heroism. Margaret may become at this moment the play's closest incarnation of an audience figure, for her decision entails the most inclusive, seri-ous, and comedic evocation – and questioning – of the magic of love. Margaret's choice thus hints at a profound moment of agency for a female character on the Tudor stage. Not since Medwall's *Fulgens and Lucres* (*c.* 1490) has one exercised such volition, and Margaret's greatest significance for the Elizabethan theatre may be that she is not only the most complex female character to date but also the most empowered.

"The flesh is frayle" (1983), says Margaret, apparently refer-ring to her own susceptibility. Does she also recognize how frail Lacie might be? What the play makes evident to the audience never registers in Margaret's dialogue; charges of coarseness and insensitivity never pass her lips. I would speculate that Margaret's choice offers an occasion in Elizabethan drama when an audience unconsciously invests a character with its knowledge. Audience members, that is, may impute to Margaret's decision their own understanding and formal desires. At work is a partial discrepant awareness: the scene makes Lacie's crudeness apprehendable by Margaret but more emphatically evident to the audience. Yet the audience also wants the comedic form to complete itself in the union of the two lovers. Weld emphasizes Margaret's self-consciousness, and Crupi hints that her acceptance of human frailty might include Lacie.[41] But Margaret, of course, remains silent about Lacie's callowness. There is something about this kind of restraint at the comedic dénouement that galvanizes spectators (Shakespeare employs the maneuver regularly). As critics and as auditors, we are tempted to fill in this silence with our desire for accommodation. We occupy Margaret's position sympathetically, using our discrepant awareness to imagine what Margaret cannot speak outright: thus spectators may grant her a knowing accept-ance. With that imaginative, empathic, audience-activating recon-ciliation, Greene makes Margaret a striking spectatorial figure, one who elicits an emotional investment from the playgoer.

The choosing scene also conjures up an especially dramatic spectacle in *Friar Bacon and Friar Bungay*. Under the spell of Lacie's "inchanting face," Margaret proclaims, "Off goes the habite of a maidens heart, / ... And all the shew of holy Nuns farewell" (xiii.1986–88). With those lines, she must suddenly pull off the drab habit that has covered her, revealing her gown of stammel red and her profuse golden hair. The gesture may be one last reference to *Tamburlaine*, to the scene in which Tamburlaine flings off his shepherd's weeds either to reveal armor underneath his coarse apparel or to don the glittering cuirass that Zenocrate car-ries for her betrothed (i.ii). To the extent that Margaret's flir-tation with turning nun proffers a Catholic solution to her crisis, her discarding of the nun's habit has the zing of dismissing Cath-olicism with a bold stage gesture. The disrobing also returns Mar-garet to her position as the central theatrical spectacle in the play, but with a difference. Earlier the idealized portrait of Edward's imagination, Margaret now actively reinhabits her spectacular beauty to affirm her love of Lacie; she thus relocates within her own agency the quality that has most objectified her.

Finally, Margaret evokes variously in the play, and climactically in her choosing scene, the play's motif of learning. Lacie fends off Edward's accusations of treacherous friendship by claiming: "Loue taught me that your honour did but iest" (vii.965), and Edward picks up the motif: "I have learnd at Oxford" (1020) that removing the cause will remove the effect. As Margaret prepares for the nunnery, she enumerates the lessons she has learned from the collapse of earthly love, and she wishes "all maides to learne of me, / To seeke heauens ioy before earths vanitie" (xiii.1921–22). Margaret's renunciation of her nun's habit, then, also rejects the didactic truism that worldly desires are vain. Here the play moves beyond the possibilities of "learning" as such. Margaret's choice is a "pure" choice, one without evidence that would direct it, a choice where sententious truth seems unconvincing and wisdom from experience insufficient. Humanist drama at the beginning of the century took inspiration from humanism's belief in the transforming power of knowledge. Even the enigmaticness of Heywood's Palmer, discussed earlier, opens a space for contextual and empirical insight.[42] Greene's theatre suggests the fading of that dream of learning. Humanist accommodation tends to mediate between formal and experiential knowledge, but Greene poses a dilemma, a choice that neither can resolve.

3

Besides its echoes of other plays, *Friar Bacon and Friar Bungay* structures its own internal comparisons and contrasts between characters, details, and events. We can list some of those doublings. The title itself signals its doubled friars: the one pledged to advance the love of Lacie and Margaret, the other agreeing to thwart it; the one defeated by Vandermast, the other triumphant; the two joining forces around the Brazen Head and the prospective glass. Characters come in twos: two noble wooers pursue Margaret, one for love, another for lust. That pair is further replicated in Lambert and Serlsby, the minor gentry lovers who mirror the nobles, and those last two are reflected in their two sons. Lambert and Serlsby, moreover, act out an alternative conclusion to the conflict between Edward and Lacie, a duel rather than a reconciliation. The play has two clowns, Raphe and Miles, and each bears the same relationship to his master: Raphe represents Edward's fall

into folly, just as Miles represents the human foolishness upon
which Bacon's superhuman project must finally founder.[43] The
parodic relationships between clowns and masters is also mirrored
in two different acting styles, the physical, buffoonish quipping of
Miles and Raphe versus the more rhetorical and oratorical style
of Edward and Bacon. *Friar Bacon and Friar Bungay* offers two
women, Elinor and Margaret – the fitting and unfitting mates for
Edward – who share not only the superlatives of physical beauty
but also the dubious analogy with Helen of Troy, and who converge
with their paired lords for the celebratory double wedding at the
play's end.

Doubling extends to small scenic details as well as large aspects
of action. Margaret receives two offers of money, for example, one
from Edward via his messenger Lacie, another from Lacie via the
Post; the first offer Margaret accepts with polite indifference, the
second she rejects with awakened dignity. *Friar Bacon and Friar
Bungay* also offers variations on the motif of portraiture. Margaret,
as we have noted, must develop *against* Edward's painterly idealization of her in the first scene. By contrast, Edward himself will
develop *into* the portrait that Elinor has of him.[44] In the marriage
negotiations Elinor has been sent "Edwards louely counterfeit"
(iv.467), his painted image. That "comly pourtrait of so braue a
man" (469), along with tales of his courageous deeds in battle,
has moved her, as if in complement, to undergo "perrils for his
sake" (475). Later, Edward forgives Lacie and Margaret by
recalling his own heroism and thus transforms himself to resemble
the image of the perfect prince that goes before him to Elinor.
Inciting his change is also Margaret's self-sacrificial heroism, by
which she paves the way for brave Elinor. On the level of action,
Friar Bacon and Friar Bungay offers doubled scenes, such as the two
"bafflement" scenes (ii and viii), and two prospective-glass
scenes – one comic, the other tragic. Greene also provides multiple
transformations of character: Edward and Lacie both alter, as do
Margaret and Bacon. Those latter two weather juxtaposed scenes
of parallel disillusionments, the one with magic, the other with
love – although Margaret will achieve a reconciliation unrealized
by Bacon. The play also has multiple demonic transportations: the
hostess from Henley, Vandermast by Hercules, Miles on a devil's
back. Characters, incidents, actions in *Friar Bacon and Friar Bungay*
occur in a matrix of imitative relationships. Such reiterations

create their own interpretive complexity and also establish the play's internal and external systems of meaning as parallel.

To take a specific example, Bacon's disillusionment has been compared to that of Margaret. Bacon's decision to "spend the remnant of my life / In pure deuotion praying to my God" (xii.1892–93) follows the failure of the Brazen Head and immediately precedes Margaret's entrance in nun's apparel (their respective renunciation speeches conclude with "vainly" [xii.1894] and "vainitie" [xiii.1922]). But Margaret's spectacular return to Lacie and the world has no counterpart in Bacon's fate, despite his apparent resumption of magic. Instead, the scene that follows Margaret's reconciliation features Miles, now an unemployed itinerant scholar who accepts transportation on the back of Bacon's devil in hopes that he might find a career as tapster in hell. Theatrically Miles's action oddly parallels that of Margaret. Both characters have been displaced, Miles comically from his employ with Bacon, Margaret seriously from her betrothal to Lacie; both are intercepted in their scenes, Miles by a devil, Margaret by Lacie; Lacie and his comrades exit their scene to eat and drink, while Miles goes off to become a tapster. The two scenes include a visual link: Lacie enters "*booted and spurd*" to carry Margaret off, and Miles dons spurs onstage (xiv.2068) – possibly the same stage props used by Lacie – so that he can ride off on the devil's back.[45]

But what does Miles's reiteration of Margaret mean? Margaret's reacceptance of Lacie seemed interpretively complete: she chooses the world, in both its fallibility and charm. Miles's "doubling" comes afterwards, retrospectively, as if to question a matter that seemed resolved. Does Greene hint that Margaret may be figuratively transported to hell by Lacie? The play's dynamics invite us to see scenes as analogous, to interpret, for example, Margaret's rejection of vanity in love as sanctioned by Bacon's prior rejection of vanity in magic. But analogies can import differences. The conflict between Lambert and Serlsby, for example, achieves a conclusion varying from, but potential in, the conflict between Edward and Lacie. Miles carried off willingly to a comic hell suggests a metaphoric future for Margaret imaginable but not inevitable in her marriage to Lacie. The point here is not that Margaret is really headed for something unpleasant but that Greene's system of imitation creates enigmatic potential meanings.[46] He achieves the dramaturgical equivalent of an afterlife, an imagined sequel – an effect consistent with the tendency of plays of the late 1580s and early 1590s to prompt theatrical sequels, even as *Friar Bacon and Friar Bungay* has the anonymous *John of Bordeaux*. Greene places Miles's scene after rather than before Margaret's. The order conveys a sense of closure – Margaret and Lacie reestablish their bliss – but then surprises the audience by hinting at a potential falseness in that ending, so that the effect is of a form neither quite closed nor quite open.

Such a discussion brings to mind *Friar Bacon and Friar Bungay*'s famous invention of the Margaret-Bacon "double plot," identified by William Empson, which dramatizes "a literary metaphor – 'the power of beauty is like the power of magic.' "[47] Charles Hieatt has, by contrast, seen four sequential plots centering individually on Edward, Bacon, Margaret, and Henrie.[48] We could as well divide the play into two halves, for by making a few minor changes, Greene could have ended *Friar Bacon and Friar Bungay* in the middle. With the reconciliation among Edward, Margaret, and Lacie (vii), the defeat of Vandermast, and the pairing of Elinor and Edward (viii), almost all the lines of action are wrapped up. Thus, in a sense, the present play contains its own sequel – another indication of how the internal structure of *Friar Bacon and Friar Bungay* mirrors the dynamic among 1580s plays. If the drama divides into two halves, the crucial difference between them is the wistful tone of failure, tragedy, and disappointment that enters the second part. Given that tone, the ending does more than knit up plot strands: it also reintegrates the community into hierarchical relationships of mutual bonding and support, providing the tonal resolution to the melancholy of the second half.

The play thus possesses two "spines" (to use theatrical terms): the spine of the first half is the idea that virtuous love will triumph; the spine of the second half, that virtuous intentions and valuable attributes can produce disastrous effects. Margaret recognizes this second theme in her affairs: "How Fortune tempers lucky happes with frowns, / . . . Loue is my blisse, and loue is now my bale" (ix.1480–82). Hieatt finds Margaret, along with Bacon and Edward, morally culpable: all three characters "are engaged in self-seeking enterprises . . . all three cause extreme danger to others."[49] But the play expends little energy on demonstrating that Bacon's and Margaret's pride and vanity cause disasters in any foreseeable way. While Bacon does blame himself for the deaths of the two sons and destroys his prospective glass, "magic's chief purpose in the play is to reveal the truth . . . What kills is literally truth."[50] Greene, I think, intends the disjunction: Bacon's and Margaret's powers have consequences, but those consequences exceed predictability. Just as *Friar Bacon and Friar Bungay* entertains the possibility of alternate endings to the same events, so does it reject any sense of determinate, chain-link causal necessity.

The tragic aspects of *Friar Bacon and Friar Bungay* can be metonymized in a motif introduced earlier: the insufficiency of learning. Learning turns out not to be simply the mastery of instrumentality and agency that Bacon believed. If Juan Luis Vives had begun the century convinced that empirical experimentation could be an act of piety,[51] Greene and Marlowe enter the 1590s sensing the limits of formal learning, of the humanist dream. As *Friar Bacon and Friar Bungay* demonstrates that causes can have unpredictable and scattershot effects, characters such as Bacon and Margaret recognize that they have more agency than they actually want. The humanist vision of individual empowerment has a nightmarish corollary. *Friar Bacon and Friar Bungay* articulates the darkest possibility of humanism, not the pessimism about human fallibility associated with Montaigne or even Shakespeare, but the more shocking hint that the capacity of individualism to spark disaster is greater than we ever realized. More positively, Greene's exploration of learning and knowledge uncovers, with Margaret, a domain of decision that is finally beyond information or knowledge or even rationalism, one that proceeds from intuition. In both respects the humanist dream of learning will have identified its limits concerning the deepest wellsprings or extremest consequences of individual action. The humanist exploration in drama, one might say, exhausts itself.

What *Friar Bacon and Friar Bungay* leaves us with is not so much knowledge as spectacle. Hieatt maintains that the Henrie plotline draws all the dangerous energies of the play back under the management of a benevolent hierarchical authority. As a theatrical experience, however, the ending of the play emphasizes something else, the beauties of the play world itself. Replete with sounds, vibrant colors, and symbolic movement, the last scene puts the theatrical pleasures of spectacle on full display: the elaborate ceremonial entrance, surely accompanied with appropriate music;

characters carrying symbolic swords, globes, rods, crowns, and scepters (s.d. xv.2074–77); Margaret attired in her glittering new court apparel; the other characters in ordered and sumptuous array; the decorous and celebratory speeches; and the exit to further banqueting.[52] Edward bends his knee to the great potentates (2081); Henrie cries tears of joy (2087); Elinor and Margaret "shine like to the cristall lampes of heauen" (2092); Margaret herself kneels to the assembled lords; and Bacon takes centerstage for a prophetic pastoral vision luxuriant with heliotropes, hyacinths, gilliflowers, bays, carnations, and "Dianas rose" (2141). Greene pulls out all the stops to create the fantastical sense of color, material beauty, and richness that theatre can excite. The fashioning of a visually inspiring community onstage affirms, furthermore, a sense of community in the audience. Weld argues that a performance of the ending should draw the audience into celebration and that Bacon's prophecy specifically celebrates the Elizabethan present.[53] If Henrie does unify the action, then the play achieves a particularly theatrical kind of communal synergy, in which the unresolved feelings from one storyline can be settled by the assuaged feelings of another. Even more, the doubled characters, doubled incidents, and doubled lines of action insist on a certain corporateness of experience. The play's final humanist image, then, might be the dream of community shared between play and audience, implicit in the theatrical dynamics from the beginning. While individualism is identified by Empson as one of the play's dangerous forces,[54] that individualism turns out to be subsumed within the community. The overall effect of Greene's dramaturgical imitations is to define an irreducible cultural commonality. If, on some level, Marlowe's *Doctor Faustus* is an attack on the very theatre that presents it, *Friar Bacon and Friar Bungay* constitutes that same theatre's defense. Despite Gosson's fear that emotionally arousing, erotically stimulating, theatricalized spectacle can have dangerous consequences, that same theatre affirms the spectacle of the world in a way constructed to draw audiences back again and again. To the public stage, Greene's humanist dramaturgy brings its "cross-referenced" and doubled world, its exploration of the possibilities of knowledge, and, finally, its most vivid treasure, the commonwealth of the present moment.

Afterword

Although this book is primarily about the drama of the sixteenth century, it is also about our contradictory perceptions of that drama in the twentieth century. Besides pondering the conflict between earlier humanist and later morality theories, present students of Tudor drama must face the problem of discussing literary history itself. While I have wanted to see sixteenth-century drama as exploring some characteristic dramaturgical problems throughout the era, I have also viewed drama, for certain purposes, as changing in the course of the century from one attitude to another. Thus, for example, while these chapters pursue recurring interests in enigma, doubt, and confusion, the discussion of female characters argues that a possibility in representation emerged by the end of the century that existed only inchoately at the beginning. I find myself wanting to claim that both perspectives – a certain repetition and a certain newness – are true. This paradox, I believe, can be defended logically – it may even be a way of making sense in the present intellectual climate – but it will really be plausible only as the chapters that advance it have been convincing.

At the outset of this project, I thought that I was simply writing about plays that seemed fascinating, but I now recognize that the "present intellectual climate" has affected the book far more than I first suspected. Somewhere along the line, challenging the thesis that the popular tradition was separate from, even superior to, the learned tradition came to possess a certain urgency. Teaching in a university adjacent to the capital of the United States makes it impossible to ignore the assault upon national funding for the arts and humanities, upon élite culture, and upon higher education in general and humanities professors in particular. Simultaneously, Western societies have witnessed an unprecedented celebration of "popular" contemporary culture, sometimes with a concomitant derogation of the intellectual realm. But all that is familiar territory. In my desire to claim that sixteenth-century popular morality drama and humanist academic drama may have virtues in common after all, I am probably expressing my desire to identify possibilities – new perspectives, solutions – that may have some indirect bearing on the present. So let me state the book's implicit advice: a *rapprochement* between popular and learned cultures would be a good thing, and it might commence with the recognition that they hold important values in common. Thinking about the presumably two traditions of Tudor drama, indeed, has led me to a renewed appreciation of the richness and adaptability of popular forms and likewise to an appreciation of humanism's vigorous, playful capacity to open the mind to the experience of life as we actually live it.

Notes

INTRODUCTION

1 In *The Defence of Poetry*, Sidney argues that poets "move" their readers to goodness through delight; related phrases such as "heart-ravishing knowledge" show Sidney's sense of poetry's active power (Sir Philip Sidney, *A Defence of Poetry*, ed. Jan Van Dorsten [Oxford: Oxford University Press, 1966], pp. 27, 21). Elyot likewise conceives of literature as "inflam[ing]" its readers to emulate models of virtue (Sir Thomas Elyot, *The Boke named The Gouernour*, ed. Henry Herbert Stephen Croft [London: Kegan Paul, Trench, and Co., 1883], vol. 1, p. 59).

2 William Gager, "To the Critic," *Ulysses Returned* in *William Gager: The Complete Works*, ed. and trans. Dana F. Sutton, vol. 2: *The Shrovetide Plays* (New York: Garland Press, 1994), p. 23.

3 Gager, *Ulysses Returned*, t.p.

4 See, for example, C. F. Tucker Brooke, *The Tudor Drama: A History of English National Drama to the Retirement of Shakespeare* (Boston: Houghton Mifflin, 1911); T. W. Baldwin, *William Shakspere's Small Latin & Lesse Greeke*, 2 vols. (Urbana: University of Illinois Press, 1944); T. W. Baldwin, *Shakspere's Five-Act Structure: Shakspere's Early Plays on the Background of Renaissance Theories of Five-Act Structure from 1470* (Urbana: University of Illinois Press, 1947); and Madeleine Doran, *Endeavors of Art: A Study of Form in Elizabethan Drama* (Madison: University of Wisconsin Press, 1954).

5 David M. Bevington, *From Mankind to Marlowe: Growth of Structure in the Popular Drama of Tudor England* (Cambridge, Mass.: Harvard University Press, 1962), p. 1.

6 Bevington, *From Mankind to Marlowe*, p. 3.

7 The small number of actors combines with the moralities' panoramic scale to produce characteristic features: scenes of godly forces alternating with scenes of the Vices; acting that emphasizes energy and adaptability; multiple features compressed into single characters; "progressive suppression" of certain characters and themes so as to make room for others; and repetition of details in a loosely knit,

coordinated, episodic drama of cumulative rather than climactic impact.

8 Robert Weimann, *Shakespeare and the Popular Tradition of the Theater: Studies in the Social Dimension of Dramatic Form and Function*, ed. Robert Schwartz (Baltimore: The Johns Hopkins University Press, 1978). The work was originally published in German in 1967.

9 See, for example, Alan C. Dessen, *Elizabethan Drama and the Viewer's Eye* (Chapel Hill: University of North Carolina Press, 1977).

10 Howard B. Norland, *Drama in Early Tudor Britain, 1485–1558* (Lincoln: University of Nebraska Press, 1995), p. xxiii.

11 Bevington, *From* Mankind *to Marlowe*, p. 6.

12 Norland, *Drama in Early Tudor Britain*, p. 37. Using REED evidence, John Wasson questions the importance of the moralities: "In East Anglia ... the most frequent performances were of miracles, then of single, non-cycle mysteries, then of Corpus Christi plays. I have not found a single reference to a performance of a morality play and thus am confirmed in my suspicion that despite all the recent books about them and their later influence, moralities were never part of the main stream of British drama" ("Records of Early English Drama: Where They Are and What They Tell Us" in *Records of Early English Drama: Proceedings of the First Colloquium*, ed. Joanna Dutka [Toronto: Records of Early English Drama, 1979], pp. 128–44, on p. 140). See also John Wasson, "The Morality Play: Ancestor of Elizabethan Drama?" in *The Drama of the Middle Ages: Comparative and Critical Essays*, ed. Clifford Davidson, C. J. Gianakaris, and John Stroupe (New York: AMS Press, 1982), pp. 316–27.

13 Norland, *Drama in Early Tudor Britain*, pp. 46–47.

14 Examining parish church records from 1520 to 1540, Wasson notes that "none of these 112 parishes presented a morality play so far as we can tell"; he also notes that "folk drama outnumbered religious drama by almost two to one, 59 plays to 31" (John Wasson, "The End of an Era: Parish Drama in England from 1520 to the Dissolution" in John C. Coldewey, "English Drama in the 1520s: Six Perspectives," *Research Opportunities in Renaissance Drama*, vol. 31, ed. David M. Bergeron [Lawrence: University of Kansas, 1992], p. 71). Wasson uses the term *folk drama* synonymously with mummers plays in his essay "The Morality Play: Ancestor of Elizabethan Drama?" For an overview of folk drama, see Norland, *Drama in Early Tudor Britain*, pp. 48–64. On "profane" drama's importance, see Richard Axton, *European Drama of the Early Middle Ages* (London: Hutchinson University Library, 1974).

15 Discussing John Bale's acting company on one of its peregrinations in the 1530s, Paul Whitfield White notes the variety of audiences for "popular" drama: "The records indicate a range of possible audiences, a popular one at Leicester and Shrewsbury, perhaps clerical

as well as popular at Shrewsbury if they played in the Abbey, and an academic audience at Oxford, although we know that even at the universities the townspeople were invited to attend (and spend their money)" (*Theatre and Reformation: Protestantism, Patronage, and Playing in Tudor England* [Cambridge: Cambridge University Press, 1993], p. 25).

16 On the unsatisfactoriness of the term *popular* for medieval drama, see Kathleen Ashley, "Contemporary Theories of Popular Culture and Medieval Performances" in *Mediaevalia*, Martin Stevens and Milla Riggio, eds., vol. 18 (Binghamton: Center for Medieval and Early Renaissance Studies, State University of New York at Binghamton, 1995), pp. 5–18.

17 See Bevington, *From* Mankind *to* Marlowe, pp. 26–47.

18 Richard Axton, *European Drama of the Early Middle Ages*, p. 201.

19 A virtue of Doran's *Endeavors of Art* is its supple sense of the way humanist and medieval values intertwine, as Renaissance thinkers often reformulate and develop medieval concerns.

20 See Joel B. Altman, *The Tudor Play of Mind: Rhetorical Inquiry and the Development of Elizabethan Drama* (Berkeley: University of California Press, 1978), pp. 229–320.

21 For a detailed discussion, see chapter 5.

22 See, for example, Bevington, *From* Mankind *to* Marlowe, p. 1.

23 *Ibid.*, p. 26.

24 See Weimann, *Shakespeare and the Popular Tradition*, pp. 100–12.

25 *Ibid.*, p. 106.

26 See Bevington, *From* Mankind *to* Marlowe, pp. 26–27. For reservations about efforts to distinguish between popular and élite drama for the Henrician period, see Greg Walker, *Plays of Persuasion: Drama and Politics at the Court of Henry VIII* (Cambridge: Cambridge University Press, 1991), pp. 24–28.

27 On the problem of constructing a history of sixteenth-century drama, see Robert S. Knapp, *Shakespeare—The Theater and the Book* (Princeton, N.J.: Princeton University Press, 1989), esp. pp. 3–44.

28 Jonathan Dollimore, *Radical Tragedy: Religion, Ideology and Power in the Drama of Shakespeare and his Contemporaries*, 2nd edn. (Durham, N. C.: Duke University Press, 1993), pp. xxvii–xxviii. For economy's sake, I allow Dollimore's critique to stand for cultural materialism. For other attacks on humanism, see Francis Barker, *The Tremulous Private Body: Essays on Subjection* (London: Methuen, 1984); and Alan Sinfield, *Faultlines: Cultural Materialism and the Politics of Dissident Reading* (Berkeley: University of California Press, 1992). For recent critiques of cultural materialism, see Brian Vickers, *Appropriating Shakespeare: Contemporary Critical Quarrels* (New Haven, Conn.: Yale University Press, 1993); Graham Bradshaw, *Misrepresentations: Shakespeare and the Materialists* (Ithaca, N.Y.: Cornell University Press, 1993); and Tom

McAlindon, "Cultural Materialism and the Ethics of Reading: or, the Radicalizing of Jacobean Tragedy," *The Modern Language Review*, 90 (October 1995): 830–46.

29 Dollimore, *Radical Tragedy*, pp. 160, 162.

30 *Ibid.*, p. 168. As "outside" estimates of essentialism, Dollimore offers More's "recognition of the extent to which social institutions form human nature" (p. 170), Bacon's view that "custom and education rather than nature . . . are the crucial determinants of human behaviour" (p. 171), and Montaigne's image of human nature as "in perpetual and restless motion" (p. 174). That More, Bacon, and Montaigne wrote "outside" the dominant culture is open to question. For a demonstration that Montaigne and Bacon, among others, accept basic attributes in human nature and thus do not fit the anti-essentialists' model, see McAlindon, "Cultural Materialism and the Ethics of Reading," esp. pp. 832–36.

31 Catherine Belsey, *The Subject of Tragedy: Identity and Difference in Renaissance Drama* (London: Routledge, 1985).

32 Belsey, *The Subject of Tragedy*, p. 17.

33 *Ibid.*, p. 8.

34 Norland, *Drama in Early Tudor Britain*, pp. 3–36.

35 That overidealizing becomes clear when Dollimore accuses "essentialist theories" of having "contributed powerfully" to racism (*Radical Tragedy*, p. 256). Dollimore's discussion ignores the contribution that essentialism has made to combating racism. Martin Luther King, Jr., for example, often publicly cited the vision of human equality in that most essentialist of social documents, the Declaration of Independence.

36 Charles Trinkaus, *The Scope of Renaissance Humanism* (Ann Arbor: University of Michigan Press, 1983), p. 430.

37 In *De ratione studii*, Erasmus writes: "In principle, knowledge as a whole seems to be of two kinds, of things and of words. Knowledge of words comes earlier, but that of things is the more important . . . For since things are learnt only by the sounds we attach to them, a person who is not skilled in the force of language is, of necessity, short-sighted, deluded, and unbalanced in his judgment of things as well" (*On the Method of Study*/De ratione studii ac legendi interpretandique auctores, Brian McGregor, trans. and annot., in *Literary and Educational Writings* 2: De copia, De ratione studii, ed. Craig R. Thompson, vol. 24 of *Collected Works of Erasmus* [Toronto: University of Toronto Press, 1978] , pp. 665–91, on p. 666).

38 For the classic study of Erasmian influence in England, see James Kelsey McConica, *English Humanists and Reformation Politics under Henry VIII and Edward VI* (Oxford: Clarendon Press, 1965).

39 Debora Kuller Shuger, *Habits of Thought in the English Renaissance: Religion, Politics, and the Dominant Culture* (Berkeley: University of California Press, 1990), p. 2.

40 Shuger, *Habits of Thought*, p. 11.
41 Richard Mulcaster, *Positions*, ed. Robert Herbert Quick (London: Longmans, 1888), pp. 170–71.
42 Dollimore, *Radical Tragedy*, p. xi.
43 Joel B. Altman, *The Tudor Play of Mind*. For an earlier discussion that allows for the theatrical effectiveness of the enclosed narrative associated with humanist drama, see Anne Righter, *Shakespeare and the Idea of the Play* (London: Chatto and Windus, 1962).
44 Bruce R. Smith argues, by contrast, that Tudor humanists understood classical Roman drama primarily in Horatian rhetorical terms; *Ancient Scripts and Modern Experience on the English Stage, 1500–1700* (Princeton, N.J.: Princeton University Press, 1988), esp. pp. 1–58.
45 Bevington, *Tudor Drama and Politics: A Critical Approach to Topical Meaning* (Cambridge, Mass.: Harvard University Press, 1968).
46 Greg Walker, *Plays of Persuasion*. See also Suzanne R. Westfall, *Patrons and Performance: Early Tudor Household Revels* (Oxford: Clarendon Press, 1990).
47 White, *Theatre and Reformation*.
48 Jean-Christophe Agnew, *Worlds Apart: The Market and the Theater in Anglo-American Thought, 1550–1750* (Cambridge: Cambridge University Press, 1986).
49 See Norland, *Drama in Early Tudor Britain*, p. xxvi; and Agnew, *Worlds Apart*, p. 11.
50 See, for example, Lisa Jardine, *Erasmus, Man of Letters: The Construction of Charisma in Print* (Princeton, N.J.: Princeton University Press, 1993); Richard Halpern, *The Poetics of Primitive Accumulation: English Renaissance Culture and the Genealogy of Capital* (Ithaca, N.Y.: Cornell University Press, 1991), esp. pp. 19–60; Anthony Grafton, *Defenders of the Text: The Traditions of Scholarship in an Age of Science, 1450–1800* (Cambridge, Mass.: Harvard University Press, 1991); and Mary Thomas Crane, *Framing Authority: Sayings, Self, and Society in Sixteenth-Century England* (Princeton, N.J.: Princeton University Press, 1993).
51 In that spirit, Jill Kraye stresses "the role of humanism as a broad intellectual and cultural movement" and "the complex interaction between the Latin-based and vernacular cultures of the Renaissance" (*The Cambridge Companion to Renaissance Humanism* [Cambridge: Cambridge University Press, 1996], p. xv).
52 Despite my suggestion that medieval drama can be considered as an instrument for religious understanding, I do not wish to propagate another binarial opposition, this one between pious medieval drama and worldly Renaissance fare. Criticism of medieval drama in the last two decades makes clear that religion sometimes furnished drama with a discourse useful for articulating a broad political and cultural critique; see, for example, Theresa Coletti, " 'Ther Be But Women': Gender Conflict and Gender Identity in the Middle English

Innocents Plays" in Martin Stevens and Milla Riggio, eds., *Mediaevalia*, vol. 18 (Binghamton: The Center for Medieval and Early Renaissance Studies, State University of New York at Binghamton, 1995), pp. 245–62.

53 On the disproportionate explosion of university drama, see Alan H. Nelson, "Contexts for Early English Drama: The Universities" in Marianne G. Briscoe and John C. Coldewey, eds., *Contexts for Early English Drama* (Bloomington: Indiana University Press, 1988), p. 141.

54 On Renaissance Tudor neo-Latin literature, see J. W. Binns, *Intellectual Culture in Elizabethan and Jacobean England: The Latin Writings of the Age* (Leeds: Francis Cairns, 1990). Norland's *Drama in Early Tudor Britain* takes up several neo-Latin plays, including Watson's *Absalom*, Christopherson's *Jephthah*, and Grimald's *Archipropheta*; and Rebecca W. Bushnell's *Tragedies of Tyrants: Political Thought and Theater in the English Renaissance* (Ithaca, N.Y.: Cornell University Press, 1990) discusses, among other plays, Buchanan's *Baptistes*. See also Frederick S. Boas, *University Drama in the Tudor Age* (1912; New York: Benjamin Blom, 1966). Latin-English editions of Legge, Gager, and Hawkesworth have recently appeared.

55 Quotations from Shakespeare follow *The Riverside Shakespeare*, ed. G. Blakemore Evans, with the assistance of J. J. M. Tobin, 2nd edn. (Boston: Houghton Mifflin, 1997).

56 Erasmus, *De ratione studii* in *Collected Works of Erasmus*, p. 683. Halpern, cited above, argues that humanist pedagogues sidestepped the moral problems of teaching pagan literature by turning attention to style. While Erasmus did consider language and style in his procedures for teaching an ancient text, he was also deeply concerned about the ethical impact of literature; see, for example, *The Education of a Christian Prince / Institutio principis christiani*, trans. and annot. Michael J. Heath, *Collected Works of Erasmus*, vol. 27: *Literary and Educational Writings 5: Panigyricus, Moria, Julius exclusus, Institutio principis christiani Querela pacis*, ed. A. H. T. Levi (Toronto: University of Toronto Press, 1986), pp. 250–53.

57 Erasmus, *Adages: I i 1 to I v 100*, trans. Margaret Mann Phillips, annot. R. A. B. Mynors, *Collected Works of Erasmus*, vol. 31 (Toronto: University of Toronto Press, 1982), p. 33. Erasmus speaks of a child being "instructed and fashioned with the deep wholsome preceptes of philosophy": *The Education of Children* (*De pueris instituendis*) in *A Treatise of Schemes and Tropes (1550) by Richard Sherry and his Translation of The Education of Children by Desiderius Erasmus: A Facsimile Reproduction*, intro. Herbert W. Hildebrandt (Gainsville, Fla.: Scholars' Facsimiles and Reprints, 1961), p. 101.

58 Halpern, *The Poetics of Primitive Accumulation*, p. 34.

59 William Munson notes a tension between doing and knowing in the medieval *Everyman*: "Knowing and Doing in *Everyman*," *The Chaucer*

Review, 19 (1985): 252–71. For Everyman knowing and doing finally merge; but for the characters of John Heywood's *The Foure PP*, who debate the surest way to heaven, knowing remains uncertain and doing tainted with vanity.

60 Mary Jane Barnett, "Erasmus and the Hermeneutics of Linguistic Praxis," *Renaissance Quarterly*, 49 (Autumn 1996): 542–72, on p. 547.

61 Roger Ascham, *Letters of Roger Ascham*, trans. Maurice Hatch and Alvin Vos (New York: Peter Lang, 1989), p. 162, letter to Johann Sturm, from Cambridge, 4 April 1550; see pp. 161–62.

62 Ascham, *Letters*, p. 162.

63 *Ibid.*, p. 162.

64 *Ibid.*, p. 269, letter to Johann Sturm, from London, late 1568.

65 *Ibid.*, p. 269.

66 *"Scripseram olim (studiose Lector) in Oeconomicae Aristotelis observationes paucas: sed tum, ut lector, aut spectator fabulae, non ut actor, scripst. Nunc verò, postquam viginti totos annos in Oceano versatus ad puppim navis privatae sederim, chartulas revisi, in quibus parum aut nihil omnino, quod scripserum, probavi: tantum senile iudicium à iuvenili no, quod scripserim, probavi:* tantum senile iudicium à invenili ingenio, tantum longa experientia ab arte & simplici cognitione differt" (John Case, "Epistola ad Lectorem," *Thesavrvs Oeconomiae* [London, 1597], n.p.). I am indebted to Robert Knapp for drawing this passage to my attention and to Robert Miola for helping me with the translation.

67 Roger Ascham, *English Works of Roger Ascham: Toxophilus, Report of the Affairs and State of Germany, The Schoolmaster* (Cambridge: Cambridge University Press, 1904), p. 214. Ascham's sentence derives from Erasmus: "You might also ponder the fact that philosophy can teach more within the compass of a single year than the most diverse range of experience stretched over a period of thirty years" (*De pueris instituendis*, in *Literary and Educational Writings 4: De pueris instituendis, De recta pronunciatione*, ed. S. K. Sowards, vol. 26 of *Collected Works of Erasmus* [Toronto: University of Toronto Press, 1985], p. 311).

68 Sidney, *A Defence of Poetry*, pp. 37–38.

69 Ascham, *Letters*, p. 162.

70 Erasmus, *The Education of Children*, trans. Sherry (1550), p. 110.

71 Marlowe also strikes the lugubrious tone: "think so still," says Mephistopheles to Faustus's pedantic theories about hell, "till experience change thy mind" (*Doctor Faustus*, A-text, II.i.131); quoted from David Bevington and Eric Rasmussen, eds., *Doctor Faustus: A- and B-texts (1604, 1616): Christopher Marlowe and His Collaborator and Revisers* (Manchester: Manchester University Press, 1992). Lyly, too, allows a certain cynicism toward the reformative powers of education when his eponymous hero in *Euphues: The Anatomy of Wit* (1578) replies to another character: "y bewray your own weaknes,

in thinking y^t nature may in any waies be altered by education" (*The Complete Works of John Lyly*, ed. R. Warwick Bond [Oxford: Clarendon Press, 1902], vol. 1, p. 191).

72 Arthur F. Kinney, *Humanist Poetics: Thought, Rhetoric, and Fiction in Sixteenth-Century England* (Amherst: University of Massachusetts Press, 1986), p. xi. Later, Kinney observes more starkly that "The tradition foundered because it rested its lessons on the educability of men who seemed, after a century of lessons, to be unteachable" (p. 17).

73 From a letter to John and Stanislaus Boner (pub. 1532), quoted in *English Humanism: Wyatt to Cowley*, ed. Joanna Martindale (London: Croom Helm, 1985), p. 60.

74 See, for example, Donald Kelley's comments on Nicholas of Cusa in *Renaissance Humanism* (Boston: Twayne, 1991), pp. 41–42. See also Charles H. Lohr's discussion of Nicholas of Cusa, "Metaphysics" in *The Cambridge History of Renaissance Philosophy* , ed. Charles B. Schmitt, Quentin Skinner, Eckhard Kessler, and Jill Kraye (Cambridge: Cambridge University Press, 1988), pp. 537–638, esp. pp. 548–57.

75 See, for example, Robert Weimann, "History and the Issue of Authority in Representation: The Elizabethan Theater and the Reformation," *New Literary History*, 17 (Spring 1986): 449–76, on p. 450. See also Robert Weimann, *Authority and Representation in Early Modern Discourse*, ed. David Hillman (Baltimore: The Johns Hopkins University Press, 1996), *passim*, and Agnew, *Worlds Apart, passim*. The term *crisis* in the phrase "crisis of authority" may overstate the situation.

76 Anthony Grafton and Lisa Jardine, *From Humanism to the Humanities: Education and the Liberal Arts in Fifteenth- and Sixteenth-Century Europe* (Cambridge, Mass.: Harvard University Press, 1986), p. xiv.

77 Weimann, *Authority and Representation*, p. 110.

78 Evelyn B. Tribble, *Margins and Marginality: The Printed Page in Early Modern England* (Charlottesville: University Press of Virginia, 1993), p. 2.

79 Cesare Vasoli, "The Renaissance Concept of Philosophy" in Schmitt et al., eds., *The Cambridge History of Renaissance Philosophy*, pp. 57–74, on p. 74. Although the sixteenth century saw the revival of a classical tradition of philosophical skepticism, I have not sought, for practical reasons, to bring that tradition to bear on the issues of this study. I would suggest, however, that such theatrical values as doubt and confusion, emphasized here, might be fruitfully considered in relation to skepticism. On Renaissance skepticism, see, among others, Richard H. Popkin, *The History of Skepticism from Erasmus to Spinoza* (Berkeley: University of California Press, 1979).

80 *Vives: On Education: A Translation of the* De tradendis disciplinis *of Juan Luis Vives*, ed. and trans. Foster Watson (1913; Totowa, N.J.: Rowman and Littlefield, 1977), p. 8.

81 Erasmus, *The Ciceronian: A Dialogue on the Ideal Latin Style* / Dialogus Ciceronianus, trans. and annot., Betty I. Knott in *Literary and Educational Writings 6; Ciceronianus; Notes; Indexes*, ed. A. H. T. Levi, *Collected Works of Erasmus*, vol. 28 (Toronto: University of Toronto Press, 1986), p. 402.

82 For an example of humanist interest in the physical body, here from the point of view of social decorum, see Erasmus's essay "On Good Manners for Boys / *De civilitate morum puerilium*," trans. and annot. Brian McGregor in *Literary and Educational Writings 3: De conscribendis epistolis; Formula; De civilitate*, ed. J. K. Sowards, *Collected Works of Erasmus*, vol. 25 (Toronto: University of Toronto Press, 1985), pp. 273–89.

83 See Michael Goldman, *The Actor's Freedom: Toward a Theory of Drama* (New York: Viking, 1975).

84 Robert S. Knapp, " 'It is not absurd, if a man should believe his wife better than himself': John Case on Marriage," forthcoming in *ELR*.

85 For an examination of Shakespeare along these lines, and particularly in terms of engagement and detachment, see Kent Cartwright, *Shakespearean Tragedy and Its Double: The Rhythms of Audience Response* (University Park: Pennsylvania State University Press, 1991).

86 Paul Whitfield White suggests such a distinction for Tudor dramatic texts. "Closed" texts are "designed to induce a pre-conceived range of responses in a clearly defined group of spectators"; "open" texts "assume considerably greater interpretive freedom in responding to the performance by spectators who do not necessarily resort to conventional reading strategies ... [W]hile a play script might be deemed suitably closed and sanctioned by political authorities, that same play in performance ... might turn out to be considerably more open, perhaps even subversive in its effects" ("Politics, Topical Meaning, and English Theater Audiences 1485–1575," *Research Opportunities in Rennaissance Drama*, vol. 32, ed. David M. Bergeron [Lawrence: University of Kansas, 1995], pp. 41–54, on p. 42).

87 For an illuminating recent examination of the difficult relationship between aesthetics and ideology, see *Aesthetics and Ideology*, ed. George Levine (New Brunswick, N. J.: Rutgers University Press, 1994).

THE HUMANISM OF ACTING: John Heywood's *The Foure PP*

1 In medieval drama generally, political, social, and cultural matters can be explored through religious discourse, as Theresa Coletti observes of the English Innocents plays; see " 'Ther Be But Women': Gender Conflict and Gender Identity in the Middle English Innocents Plays," in Martin Stevens and Milla Riggio, eds., *Mediaevalia*, vol. 18 (Binghamton, N.Y.: The Center for Medieval and Early Renaissance Studies, State University of New York at Binghamton, 1995), pp. 245–62; e.g. p. 247.

2 A. W. Reed assigns composition of *The Foure PP* to 1520–22; see *Early Tudor Drama: Medwall, the Rastells, Heywood, and the More Circle* (London: Methuen, 1926), pp. 142–44. Critics traditionally place Heywood's six extant plays between 1519 and 1528, often dividing the plays into two chronological groups, debate plays and farces; see Reed, pp. 118–47. An important recent edition, however, puts the plays' composition between 1525 and 1533 and rearranges the chronology; see Richard Axton and Peter Happé, eds., *The Plays of John Heywood* (Cambridge: D. S. Brewer, 1991). Axton and Happé set a late date for *The Foure PP* of 1531 (p. xiv) or 1528–30 (p. 45), based on what they consider the play's anti-Lutheran, pro-Catholic, and anti-Wolsey sentiments. I am reluctant to accept their argument because, for one reason, the play seems aimed at reform within the Catholic church, rather than at defending it from Lutheran attacks. I locate *The Foure PP* close to Erasmus in its ameliorative spirit.

The Foure PP's intersection of native and humanist theatre, of religious and marketplace values, and of court and country tastes makes it a good starting point for a discussion of Tudor drama. David M. Bevington acknowledges the play's complex relationship between the popular and the humanistic and suggests its appeal to both court and country; see *From* Mankind *to* Marlowe: *Growth of Structure in the Popular Drama of Tudor England* (Cambridge, Mass.: Harvard University Press, 1962), pp. 38–39. Who, then, was the audience for *The Foure PP*? Most critics envision an aristocratic spectatorship, possibly at court (where Heywood entertained in the 1520s) or at a wealthy household, such as that of Sir Thomas More, whose niece Heywood had married; see, for example, Susanne R. Westfall, *Patrons and Performance: Early Tudor Household Revels* (Oxford: Clarendon Press, 1990), pp. 117, 121. Greg Walker argues that Heywood likewise wrote *The Play of the Wether* for an evening performance in a dining hall, probably Henry's; see *Plays of Persuasion: Drama and Politics at the Court of Henry VIII* (Cambridge: Cambridge University Press, 1991), p. 134. But David Bevington contends that "The conflicts in *Four PP* are religious and domestic . . . for Heywood's audience in this earlier play is not courtly" (*Tudor Drama and Politics: A Critical Approach to Topical Meaning* [Cambridge, Mass.: Harvard University Press, 1968], p. 71). If so, *The Foure PP* might have been intended for public performance, on tour or even at the presumed playing house erected by John Rastell, Heywood's father-in-law, in Finsbury Fields in the mid 1520s; see Reed, *Early Tudor Drama*, pp. 230–33. The play, nonetheless, does seem to postulate an aristocratic or court audience. Apologizing for his "rudeness" of dress, for example, the Palmer enters into an already constituted and socially identifiable group ("Nowe God be here! Who kepeth this place? / Nowe by my fayth I crye you mercy!" [4, 1–2; quotations from Heywood's plays follow Axton and Happé, eds., *The Plays of John Heywood*]). Such behavior suggests the aristocratic milieu that Edward Burns discusses for Tudor interludes, where a pre-existing event (banquet, royal visit, celebration) makes possible a "dialectic" of identities between the spectators in their present social function and the characters; see *Character: Acting and Being and the Pre-Modern Stage* (New York: St. Martin's Press, 1990), pp. 53–54. *The Foure PP* acknowledges its nighttime setting (551); assumes an experienced relationship between character and audience; refers to London topography and the London book trade in Paul's Yard; and requires an audience composed substantially of women. Axton and Happé treat *The Foure PP* as intended for aristocratic viewers, but favor the More household over the court; see *The Plays of John Heywood*, p. 45.

3 Paul Whitfield White distinguishes between interpretively "closed" and "open" plays on the Tudor stage; see "Politics, Topical Meaning, and English Theater Audiences, 1485–1575," in David M. Bergeron, ed., *Research Opportunities in Renaissance Drama*, vol. 34 (Lawrence: University of Kansas, 1995), pp. 41–54.

4 See Westfall, *Patrons and Performance*, p. 198; and Walker, *Plays of Persuasion*, pp. 10–11. See also Alistair Fox, *Politics and Literature in the Reigns of Henry VII and Henry VIII* (Oxford: Basil Blackwell, 1989).

5 The apparent epistemological conflict between faith and sensory experience was an issue in Renaissance philosophy (as it had been for medieval thinkers); see Richard H. Popkin, "Theories of Knowledge" in *The Cambridge History of Renaissance Philosophy*, Charles B. Schmitt et al., eds. (Cambridge: Cambridge University Press, 1988), pp. 668–84. Renaissance pedagogues expressed a version of the authority–experience problem in preferring Aristotle over Plato for classroom use. Aristotle had the advantage of a systematic, accessible methodology, while Plato, although considered wiser and more inspirational, was too ambiguous, ironic, and unsystematic; see Jill Kraye, "Moral Philosophy" in *The Cambridge History of Renaissance Philosophy*, pp. 325–26. For a nontheological example, consider the rise in England of equity jurisprudence, where concerns for individual conscience challenged legal absolutes; see J. H. Baker, ed., *The Reports of John Spelman* (London: The Selden Society, 1978), vol. 2. Against the tendency of some critics to see Renaissance humanism as authoritarian and repressive, Rebecca W. Bushnell emphasizes humanism's "fluctuations between the extremes of liberation and control, variety and limits, play and discipline" that match "the heterogeneity of early modern society and practice" (*A Culture of Teaching: Early Modern Humanism in Theory and Practice* [Ithaca, N.Y.: Cornell University Press, 1996], p. 19).

6 See, for example, Charles G. Nauert, Jr., "Humanist Infiltration into the Academic World: Some Studies of Northern Universities," *Renaissance Quarterly* (Winter 1990): 804–08.

7 Erasmus, Praise of Folly *and "Letter to Martin Dorp 1515"*, trans. Betty Radice, intro. and notes by A. H. T. Levi (New York: Penguin, 1971), p. 160.

8 Erasmus, *Apophthegmes*, trans. Nicolas Udall (London: 1542), ff. 1–2ᵛ.

9 See S. K. Sowards, ed., *Collected Works of Erasmus*, vol. 25, *Literary and Educational Writings 3:* De conscribendis epistolis, Formula, De civilitate (Toronto: University of Toronto Press, 1985), pp. xxiv–xli.

10 Paul Oskar Kristeller, "Humanism" in *The Cambridge History of Renaissance Philosophy*, p. 126. The relation of humanism to individualism is a matter of debate. Against the notion that humanism promotes only a stable and authentic self, Mary Thomas Crane argues that, "Especially in its earlier stages (before 1550), English humanism fostered, alongside existing aristocratic individualism, concepts of a socially constituted subject, common ownership of texts and ideas, and a collective model of authorship" (*Framing Authority: Sayings, Self, and Society in Sixteenth-Century England* [Princeton, N.J.: Princeton University Press, 1993], p. 6).

11 On the educational theory of Erasmus, see S. K. Sowards, ed., *Literary and Educational Writings 3*, pp. ix–lix.

12 Pearl Hogrefe, *The Sir Thomas More Circle: A Program of Ideas and Their Impact on Secular Drama* (Urbana: University of Illinois Press, 1959), pp. 168–69.

13 Erasmus, *De pueris statim ad liberaliter instituendis libellus*, in *Desiderius Erasmus concerning the Aim and Method of Education*, ed. William Harrison Woodward, foreword by Craig R. Thompson (New York: Bureau of Publications, Teachers College, Columbia University, 1964), p. 214. For the complete text of *De pueris instituendis*, see Erasmus, *Literary and Educational Writings 4:* De pueris instituendis, De recta pronuntiatione, ed. S. K. Sowards, vol. 26 of *Collected Works of Erasmus* (Toronto: University of Toronto Press, 1985).

14 Erasmus, *De recta pronuntiatione*, in *Collected Works*, vol. 26, p. 400.

15 Walter M. Gordon, *Humanist Play and Belief: The Seriocomic Art of Desiderius Erasmus* (Toronto: University of Toronto Press, 1990), p. 145. Erasmus stresses play in *De pueris instituendis* (see esp. pp. 142–47), a work that helped to form the educational program of Colet's school at St. Paul's, to which John Heywood seems to have been connected; see Robert W. Bolwell, *The Life and Works of John Heywood* (New York: Columbia University Press, 1921), pp. 51–54.

16 Roger Ascham, *The Schoolmaster (1570)*, ed. Lawrence V. Ryan (Ithaca, N.Y.: published for The Folger Shakespeare Library by Cornell University Press, 1967), p. 6.

17 Juan Luis Vives, *Vives: On Education: A Translation of the* De tradendis disciplinis, trans. and intro. Foster Watson (Cambridge: Cambridge University Press, 1913), p. 214. Vives goes on to add a plea for tolerance: "So there is no reason why anyone should pride himself on his

knowledge, or should scorn others for thinking differently, or holding other views than his own" (p. 214).

18 Erasmus, *De pueris instituendis*, p. 191.

19 Giovanni Pico della Mirandola, *The Dignity of Man* in *Pico Della Mirandola On the Dignity of Man, On Being and the One, Heptaplus*, trans. Charles Glenn Wallis, et al., intro. Paul J. W. Miller (Indianapolis, Ind.: Bobbs-Merrill, 1965), p. 4. On humanist ambivalence about whether a child's nature is fixed or malleable, see Bushnell, *A Culture of Teaching*, pp. 73–116.

20 Levi, *Folly*, pp. 12–15.

21 Joel B. Altman, *The Tudor Play of Mind: Rhetorical Inquiry and the Development of Elizabethan Drama* [Berkeley: University of California Press, 1978], p. 59.

22 See Erasmus, "Letter to Martin Dorp 1515," pp. 215–19.

23 On the theatrical metaphor in Erasmus, see Gordon, *Humanist Play and Belief*, pp. 157–69. Vives also uses the metaphor of acting to depict man's potential to be like an animal or a god; see Juan Luis Vives, "A Fable about Man" (c. 1518), trans. Nancy Lenkeith, *The Renaissance Philosophy of Man*, ed. Ernst Cassirer, Paul Oskar Kristeller, and Herman Randall, Jr. (Chicago, Ill.: University of Chicago Press, 1948), pp. 387–93.

24 Erasmus, *The Praise of Folly*, pp. 56, 61.

25 William Roper, *The Life of Sir Thomas More, Knight* (written c. 1556), in William Roper and Nicholas Harpsfield, *Lives of Saint Thomas More*, ed. E. E. Reynolds (London: J. M. Dent and Sons, 1963), p. 3.

26 Nicholas Harpsfield, *The Life and Death of Sir Thomas More, Knight, Sometime Lord High Chancellor of England* (written c. 1557), in Roper and Harpsfield, *Lives of Saint Thomas More*, pp. 129–30.

27 Sir Thomas More, "A Dialogue Concerning Heresies" (1529), ed. Thomas M. Lawler, et al., vol. 6, pt. 1 of *The Complete Works of St. Thomas More* (New Haven, Conn.: Yale University Press, 1981), pp. 68–69.

28 For current views of humanism by historians, see Albert Rabil, Jr., ed. *Renaissance Humanism: Foundations, Forms and Legacy*, 3 vols. (University of Pennsylvania Press, 1988).

29 For some critics, the action of *The Foure PP* appears so discursive as to be almost formless; see, for example, Robert Carl Johnson, *John Heywood* (New York: Twayne, 1970), pp. 89–96. For a defense of the play's structure, see Alciun Blamires, "John Heywood and *The Four PP*," *Trivium* 14 (1979): 47–69. See also Axton and Happé, *The Plays of John Heywood*, pp. 18–19. T. W. Craik argues that a sense of spontaneity lies at the heart of interlude drama; see *The Tudor Interlude: Stage, Costume, and Acting* (London: Leicester University Press, 1958).

30 This comic reductiveness recalls Heywood's *The Play of the Wether*, where "the didactic and dramatic movement . . . is one of continual

reduction, both begun and measured by Merry Report" (Helen M. Whall, *To Instruct and Delight: Didactic Method in Five Tudor Dramas* [New York: Garland, 1988], p. 57; see esp. pp. 47–59).

31 On the invasion of traditional verities by marketplace values in Renassance drama, see Jean-Christophe Agnew, *Worlds Apart: The Market and the Theater in Anglo-American Thought, 1550–1750* (Cambridge: Cambridge University Press, 1986).

32 Johnson observes that Heywood in his nondramatic works "delights in poking fun at proverbial wisdom and at those who accept it in complete faith" (*John Heywood*, p. 50).

33 Heywood employs this shifting orientation as a structural principle elsewhere. Johnson notes, for example, that *The Play of the Wether* moves its focus from conflicts over the most preferable weather to conflicts of character; see *John Heywood*, p. 83.

34 Burns, *Character*, p. 53. Discussing *Youth*, Burns writes, "The climax of allegorical drama is thus a combat of definition . . . When we reach a position from which all the participants in the action can be put into a settled relation to each other and to us, the play ends . . . The biblical text serves as the final authoritative definition of the subject" (*Character*, pp. 50–52).

35 As Garrett P. J. Epp observes, "Clarity of doctrine is a cardinal virtue of the didactic playwright and must extend beyond the written text to the performance; there can be little room for variation and interpretation by the actors – or simple forgetfulness – in order that the doctrine of the play be delivered relatively unimpeded" ("Visible Words: The York Plays, Brecht, and Gestic Writing," *Comparative Drama* [Winter 1990–91]: 289–305, on p. 291). Epp's article identifies how medieval playwrights attempt to "direct or control the action onstage through dialogue" (p. 290). For a suggestive discussion of medieval dialogue orchestrating attention, see David Mills, " 'Look at Me When I'm Speaking to You': The 'Behold and See' Convention in Medieval Drama," *Medieval English Theatre* (July 1985): 4–12.

36 Meg Twycross, "The Theatricality of Medieval English Plays" in Richard Beadle, ed., *The Cambridge Companion to Medieval English Theatre* (Cambridge: Cambridge University Press, 1994), pp. 37–84, on p. 44. Diverging from the prevailing view, John R. Elliott, Jr. argues that certain humanized roles in medieval drama attempt to move audiences to weeping through realistic pathos and identification of actor with character; see "Medieval Acting" in *Contexts for Early English Drama*, ed. Marianne G. Briscoe and John C. Coldewey (Bloomington: Indiana University Press, 1989), pp. 238–51. Alexandra F. Johnston also finds an instance of emotional development for a character in the representation of Mary in the N-Town plays; see "Acting Mary: The Emotional Realism of the Mature Virgin in the N-Town Plays," in John A. Alford, ed., *From Page to Performance: Essays*

in Early English Drama (East Lansing: Michigan State University Press, 1995), pp. 85–98.

37 Twycross, "The Theatricality of Medieval English Plays," p. 54.

38 Functioning through ambivalence, the Vice, "stands for himself alone" and operates "as a champion of 'sporte' and game, between the fiction of the moral action and the audience's festive expectations" (Robert Weimann, *Shakespeare and the Popular Tradition of the Theater: Studies in the Social Dimension of Dramatic Form and Function*, ed. Robert Schwartz [Baltimore: Johns Hopkins University Press], pp. 151, 153). But the Pardoner and the Palmer are not Vice figures, and their ambiguity does not derive from the difference between *locus* and *platea*; rather, the play as a whole expresses the dilemma between the moral and the festive.

39 In a postmodern view of theater, Herbert Blau describes the paradox of the actor's inscrutable presence: "there is always somebody there thinking, or a piece of him ... it always returns to the actor ... The technology of the visual arts, which increases energy by directing it to a flat plane, is undermined in theater, which is forever seized upon by receding space ... the corporeality of the body is ... a merciless skeptic, insisting on perspective, and therefore the illusion of depth" (*Take Up the Bodies: Theater at the Vanishing Point* [Urbana: University of Illinois Press, 1982], pp. 13–14).

40 Quoted from *The Riverside Shakespeare*, ed. G. Blakemore Evans, with the assistance of J. J. M. Tobin, 2nd edn. (Boston: Houghton Mifflin, 1997).

41 David Bevington, *Tudor Drama and Politics*, pp. 71, 73.

42 Lois Potter, "The Plays and the Playwrights," in *The* Revels *History of Drama in English*, vol. 2: *1500–1576*, ed. Norman Sanders, Richard Southern, T. W. Craik, and Lois Potter (London: Methuen, 1980), pp. 171–72.

43 Scholars tend to agree that Heywood wrote *The Foure PP* for adult, professional or semi-professional actors, while a play such as *Wether* seems intended for choristers. *The Foure PP*'s limited number of parts, its distinctions among the roles, and its opportunities for subtle acting as well as broad and raucous comedy suggest why the play seems to have become a choice for touring professionals.

44 The Pedler hints at a character type that will emerge in the plays of Marlowe and particularly Shakespeare: the chorus figure who also participates, and becomes incriminated, in the action. On Marlowe's use of chorus figures, see chapter 7.

45 Why does Heywood make his arbiter and eventual spokesman a Pedler? The Palmer and Pardoner bear a dialectical relationship to each other, and the Potycary seems a parody of them. But the Pedler makes a less obvious vocational presence. As one possibility, previously unnoted, the Pedler may be an exemplar of Folly derived from

More's writing. In an early verse farce, "A mery jest how a sergeant would learne to playe the frere," More refers jokingly to the chaos ensuing "Whan a hatter / Wyll go smatter, / In philosophy, / Or a pedlar, / Waxe a medlar, / In theology" (*The English Works of Sir Thomas More*, vol. 1, ed. W. E. Campbell [London: Eyre and Spottiswoode, 1931], p. 327). Heywood's Pedler repeats that notion himself: "It behoveth no pedlers nor proctours / To take on them judgemente as doctours" (386–87). Since Heywood's Pedler eventually does delve into theological issues, he may suggest for the More circle a generic figure of Folly, with his "wisdom" always in doubt.

46 Axton and Happé pair the Palmer and Pedler as "sunny, optimistic, orthodox" and the Pardoner and Potycary as "cynical, aggressive, blasphemous, heretical" (*Plays*, p. 19; see pp. 12–13, 19–20).

47 Quotations from *The Croxton Play of the Sacrament* follow John C. Coldewey, ed., *Early English Drama: An Anthology* (New York: Garland Publishing, 1993).

48 Erasmus, "A Pilgrimage for Religion's Sake" (1526), *The Colloquies of Erasmus*, trans. Craig R. Thompson (Chicago, Ill.: University of Chicago Press, 1965), p. 294.

49 The smelly slippers bring to mind another Erasmian relic, the presumed shoes of St. Thomas à Beckett offered to Gratian to kiss; see "A Pilgrimage for Religion's Sake," p. 310.

50 For the pitchman speeches by both the Potycary and the Pardoner, the opening warning of Erasmus's Folly seems applicable, for she tells her spectators to hear her not with the ears "you use for preachers of sermons, but the ears you usually prick up for mountebanks, clowns, or fools" (*The Praise of Folly*, p. 64). Clarence Miller repeats Renaissance commentator Gerard Lister's claim that, by "mountebanks," "Erasmus had in mind Italian mountebanks, selling patent medicines or performing magic tricks in a public square" (Erasmus, *The Praise of Folly*, trans. Clarence H. Miller [New Haven, Conn.: Yale University Press, 1979], p. 10, n. 8). The enigmatic Folly identifies herself with the same kind of mountebanks that Heywood employs.

51 Frederick S. Boas, for example, describes the Pardoner's lie as "a masterpiece of grotesque narrative" (*An Introduction to Tudor Drama* [Oxford: Clarendon Press, 1933], p. 14); Johnson likewise calls it "a masterpiece of imaginative detail and selected satire" (*John Heywood*, p. 92).

52 For the humanist attack on the excesses of pilgrimage, see Erasmus, "Rash Vows," "A Pilgrimage for Religion's Sake," and "The Usefulness of the *Colloquies*," *The Colloquies of Erasmus*, pp. 4–7, 285–312, and 623–37. Erasmus harshly criticized those who neglected their responsibilities to families and others to pursue pilgrimages, whereby "the name of religion is used as a cover for superstition, faithlessness, foolishness, and recklessness" ("Usefulness," p. 626).

53 William Carew Hazlitt refers to Sir John Mandeville's *Voyages and*

Travailes (c. 1357), which claims that travellers might see Noah's ark far off on Mount Ararat but could not reach it for the snow; see W. Carew Hazlitt, ed., *A Select Collection of Old English Plays*, vol. 1 (London: Reeves and Turner, 1874), pp. 334–35, n. 5. Hazlitt's notes largely follow those in Isaac Reed, ed., *A Select Collection of Old Plays*, vol. 1 (London: Septimus Prowett, 1825); see *Mandeville's Travels*, ed. M. C. Seymour (Oxford: Clarendon Press, 1967), p. 109. "After the departyng fro Cornaa," the region of "Noes schippe," according to the Mandeville-narrative, "men entren into the lond of Iob" (p. 111). Heywood follows the same order.

54 Axton and Happé, *Plays*, p. 251, n. 4P50.

55 *Ibid.*, p. 249, n. 4P31; Hazlitt, *Collection*, p. 334, n. 1.

56 *Ibid.*, p. 335, n. 2, quoting from Lombarde's *Dictionarium* (1730).

57 *Ibid.*, p. 335, n. 2; and Erasmus's "A Pilgrimage for Religion's Sake"; see also Axton and Happé, *Plays*, p. 249, n. 4P35. In 1538, during the monasteries's dissolution, Hazlitt reports, the icon of Mary from Walsingham was carried to Chelsea and burned, along with that from Saint Saviour's (47) and others.

58 Erasmus, "A Pilgrimage for Religion's Sake," p. 287.

59 Hazlitt recalls *The Praise of Folly* (*Collection*, pp. 337–38, n. 4); Erasmus also glances sarcastically at St. Patrick's Purgatory in "A Pilgrimage for Religion's Sake," p. 311.

60 Hazlitt, *Collection*, pp. 337–38, n. 4; see also Axton and Happé, *Plays*, p. 250, n. 4P40.

61 See Hazlitt, *Collection*, p. 339, n. 2; see also Axton and Happé, *Plays*, p. 250, n. 4P41.

62 Erasmus pokes fun at the notion of healing powers derived from the waters at holy places; see "A Pilgrimage for Religion's Sake," p. 294. Much of "Pilgrimage" satirizes shrines associated with Mary and the religious houses that maintain a cultism for financial gain. Erasmus lampoons vessels (an inordinate number, claimed in various places) venerated as containing the Virgin's dried milk (pp. 295–99) and even approaches bawdy wit regarding "the secrets of the Virgin" (p. 301). Later Erasmus had to defend himself against accusations of having "droll'd upon" the Virgin in his colloquies ("The Usefulness of the *Colloquies*," pp. 634–35). Erasmus disparaged the practice of begging boons from saints "in the belief that this or that one would grant something or other more readily, or be able to perform it more readily, than would Christ himself" (p. 635).

63 A. G. Dickens, *The English Reformation*, 2nd edn. (University Park: Pennsylvania State University Press, 1989), pp. 20–21.

64 For an insightful study arguing that the Ps' assertions about women's sexual voraciousness, unruliness, and competitiveness really expose how these males "[project] their negative traits on to women" (p. 147), see Richard Finkelstein, "Formation of the Christian Self in

The Four P. P.," in *Early Drama to 1600,* ed. Albert H. Tricomi, ACTA vol. 13 (Binghamton: Center for Medieval and Early Renaissance Studies, State University of New York at Binghamton, 1987), pp. 47–69.

65 Q1 and Q2 read "maryed," Q3 "taried." Axton and Happé preserve the Q1 reading (p. 260, n. 4P998a-9), though most editors have followed Q3, which seems to make the clearer sense.

66 The word "consyens" waves a Reformation flag, for it hints at the validity of demurring from a proposition on subjective grounds. In Tudor equity law, behavior based on a litigant's "conscience" would be able to deflect the categorical application of a legal principle; see J. H. Baker, *Reports,* pp. 37–42.

67 Jill Levenson, "Comedy," in *The Cambridge Companion to English Renaissance Drama,* ed. A. R. Braunmuller and Michael Hattaway (Cambridge: Cambridge University Press, 1990), p. 266.

68 I would demur from Axton and Happé's assertion that the Pedler judges in favor of the Palmer "with reasoned analysis" (*Plays,* p. 20).

69 In *Mankind,* piousness and play, Lent and carnival, are juxtaposed, but in *The Foure PP* those two qualities converge; that difference suggests one of the paths taken in Renaissance drama. Overall, a spirit of play and game, with the audience invited to take part, pervades *The Foure PP* – and that spirit would seem appropriate to an afterdinner interlude. In understanding that sense of play, I am indebted to Stephen Urkowitz for sharing with me a videotape of his own production of *The Foure PP.* For a review of that production, see Milla C. Riggio, *"The Play Called the Four PP* by Thomas [sic] Heywood, City College of New York, Emmanuel Courtyard" in David H. Bergeron, ed., *Research Opportunities in Renaissance Drama,* vol. 32 (Lawrence: University of Kansas, 1993), pp. 164–65, on p. 165.

70 Johnson says of No lover nor loved that "In this one character, Heywood makes the important move from abstraction to individual" (*John Heywood,* p. 77).

71 Johnson, *John Heywood,* p. 106.

72 For further innovations on playing against a character's type, see the discussion of *Gammer Gurton's Needle* in chapter 4 below.

73 Whall, *To Instruct and Delight,* p. 56.

74 Citations of *The Four Elements* and *Calisto and Melebea* refer to *Three Rastell Plays: Four Elements, Calisto and Melebea, Gentleness and Nobility,* ed. Richard Axton (Cambridge: D. S. Brewer, 1979).

75 Alan H. Nelson, ed., *The Plays of Henry Medwall* (Cambridge: D. S. Brewer, 1980), p. 22.

76 Quotations from *Fulgens and Lucres* follow Nelson's edition.

77 On the interlude tradition of acting as, by the 1580s, "brilliant stereotyping" (p. 14), see Scott McMillin, "The Queen's Men and the London Theatre of 1583" in *The Elizabethan Theatre X,* ed. C. E. McGee (Port Credit, Canada: P. D. Meary, 1988), pp. 1–17.

78 Catherine Belsey, *The Subject of Tragedy: Identity and Difference in Renaissance Drama* (London: Methuen, 1985), p. ix.

WIT AND SCIENCE AND THE DRAMATURGY OF LEARNING

1 On early humanism and print, see Lisa Jardine, *Erasmus, Man of Letters: The Construction of Charisma in Print* (Princeton, N.J.: Princeton University Press, 1993) and David L. Carlson, *English Humanist Books: Writers and Patrons, Manuscript and Print, 1475–1525* (Toronto: University of Toronto Press, 1993). On the impact of print, see Elizabeth L. Eisenstein, *The Printing Press as an Agent of Change*, 2 vols. (Cambridge: Cambridge University Press, 1979).

2 See Charles H. Herford, *Studies in the Literary Relations of England and Germany* (Cambridge: Cambridge University Press, 1886), especially chs. 2 and 3, pp. 21–164; James L. McConaughy, *The School Drama, Including Palsgrave's Introduction to* Acolastus (New York: Teachers College, Columbia University, 1913); and T. Vail Motter, *The School Drama in England* (London: Longmans, Green and Co., 1929).

3 See Motter, *The School Drama in England*, p. 50.

4 Sir James Whitlock, quoted in E. K. Chambers, *The Elizabethan Stage*, 4 vols. (Oxford: Clarendon Press, 1923), vol. 2, p. 76.

5 I shall treat the plays named in this paragraph as examples of early "pedagogical drama," whose characteristic is a thematic interest in educational issues; many such plays were first performed by students in academic settings. See also McConaughy, *The School Drama*, p. 7; and Motter, *The School Drama in England*, "Preface."

6 Alan H. Nelson comments about Oxford and Cambridge that "By 1545 play-acting had become . . . an established part of college life . . . The motive expressed in the various statutes is essentially pedagogical: the performance of plays aided the scholars in learning and pronouncing Latin and Greek . . . The pedagogical intention alone, however, can scarcely account for the enormous burgeoning of dramatic performances by the colleges": "Contexts for Early English Drama: The Universities" in Marianne G. Briscoe and John C. Coldewey, eds., *Contexts for Early English Drama* (Bloomington: Indiana University Press, 1988), pp. 137–49, on p. 141. Motter finds the origin of university drama in school drama (*School Drama in England*, pp. 12–13) and adds that "The closer we come to the middle of the century, the more apparent is the fact that all over England child acting was the rule rather than the exception" (p. 14).

7 See Lois Potter, "The Plays and Playwrights" in Norman Sanders, Richard Southern, T. W. Craik, and Lois Potter, *The Revels History of Drama in English*, vol. 2: *1500–1576* (London: Methuen, 1980), pp.124–26. Quotations from *Wit and Science* follow the text in Peter Happé, ed., *Tudor Interludes* (Middlesex: Penguin, 1972).

8 Alan R. Young, *The English Prodigal Son Plays: A Theatrical Fashion of the Sixteenth and Seventeenth Centuries* (Salzburg: Institut für Anglistik und Amerikanistik, Universität Salzburg, 1979), p. 69.

9 See, for example, John W. Velz and Carl P. Daw, Jr., "Tradition and Originality in *Wyt and Science*," *Studies in Philology* (July 1968): 631–46; Werner Habicht, "The *Wit*-Interludes and the Form of Pre-Shakespearean 'Romantic Comedy' " in *Renaissance Drama*, vol. 8, ed. S. Schoenbaum (Evanston: Northwestern University Press, 1965), pp. 73–88; and Howard B. Norland, *Drama in Early Tudor Britain, 1485–1558* (Lincoln: University of Nebraska Press, 1995), pp. 161–74. On *Wit and Science*'s borrowings from Mummer's and folk plays, see Trevor Lennam, *Sebastian Westcott: The Children of Paul's and* The Marriage of Wit and Science (Toronto: University of Toronto Press, 1975), p. 92. Analogies between Henrician court theatricals and *Wit and Science* are discussed by R. A. Duffy, "*Wit and Science* and Early Tudor Pageantry: A Note on Influences," *Modern Philology*, vol. 76, no. 2 (November 1978): 184–89.

10 Edgar Schell, ch. 2, "*Scio Ergo Sumus*: The Marriage of Wit and Science" in *Strangers and Pilgrims: From* The Castle of Perseverance *to* King Lear (Chicago: University of Chicago Press, 1983), pp. 52–76, on p. 65.

11 On the prodigal-son play, see Lester E. Barber, ed. *Misogonus* (New York: Garland, 1979), pp. 50–59; Norland, *Drama in Early Tudor Britain*, pp. 149–60; and Young, *The English Prodigal Son Plays*.

12 Reavley Gair observes that *Wit and Science* presents the prodigal-son story "at its simplest and most explicit" (*The Children of Paul's: The Story of a Theatre Company, 1553–1608* [Cambridge: Cambridge University Press, 1982], p. 89; see pp. 89–90). Gair notes that Wyt reacts against Science in the manner of the prodigal, that his transformation reflects the prodigal-son motif, and that Reson forgives Wyt in a manner "directly analogous to the behaviour of the Prodigal's father in Luke 15" (p. 90).

13 Schell, *Strangers and Pilgrims*, pp. 72–73.

14 On how Protestant playwrights and schoolmasters used academic drama to promote the interests of an emerging Protestant state, see Paul Whitfield White, *Theatre and Reformation: Protestantism, Patronage, and Playing in Tudor England* (Cambridge: Cambridge University Press, 1993), pp. 100–29.

15 Rebecca W. Bushnell describes the contradictory nature of pedagogical authority in English humanist education, given the weak social standing of teachers and the opposition of aristocrats to education: *A Culture of Teaching: Early Modern Humanism in Theory and Practice* (Ithaca, N.Y. : Cornell University Press, 1996), pp. 21–72.

16 Erasmus, *A Declamation on the Subject of Early Liberal Education for Children / De pueris statim ac liberaliter instituendis declamatio*, Beert C. Ver-

straete, trans., in *Literary and Educational Writings 4:* De pueris instituendis, De recta pronuntiatione, ed. S. K. Sowards, vol. 26 of *Collected
Works of Erasmus* (Toronto: University of Toronto Press, 1985), pp.
295–346, on p. 299.

17 Erasmus, *De pueris instituendis*, p. 303. The Messenger in John Rastell's *The Nature of the Four Elements* acknowledges similar sentiments
about wealth and learning: "Yet amonge moste folke that man is
holdyn / Moste wise, whiche to be ryche studyeth only; / But he that
for a commyn welth bysyly / Studyeth and laboryth and lyvyth by
Goddys law, / Except he wax ryche, men count hym but a daw" (52–
56). All quotations of *The Four Elements* follow Richard Axton, ed.,
*Three Rastell Plays: Four Elements, Calisto and Melebea, Gentleness and
Nobility* (Cambridge: D. S. Brewer, 1979).

18 Erasmus, *De pueris instituendis*, p. 301.

19 Sir Thomas Elyot, *The Boke Named The Gouernour*, ed. Henry Herbert
Stephen Croft, vol. 1 of 2 (London: Kegan Paul, Trench, and Co.,
1883), p. 99, pp. 104–05.

20 *Tudor School-Boy Life: The Dialogues of Juan Luis Vives*, trans. Foster
Watson (London: Dent 1908), p. xxxiv.

21 Vives, *School Dialogues*, p. 69.

22 *Ibid.*, p. 236.

23 Roger Ascham, *The Scholemaster*, ed. Edward Arber (Westminster: A.
Constable and Co., 1895), p. 57.

24 *Misogonus*, ed. Lester E. Barber (New York: Garland, 1979), I.i.75;
subsequent quotations follow Barber's edition.

25 P. L. Carver, "Introduction," The Comedy of Acolastus, *Translated
from the Latin of Fullonius by John Palsgrave*, ed. P. L. Carver (London:
Early English Text Society, 1937), pp. xxiii–xxxiii. See also Bushnell,
A Culture of Teaching, p. 39.

26 Vives, *School Dialogues*, p. 173.

27 Palsgrave in a letter to Sir Thomas More, cited in Carver, "Introduction," p. xxxi.

28 Quotations from *Nice Wanton* follow the edition in *English Moral Interludes*, ed. Glynne Wickham (London: Dent, 1976).

29 Thomas Ingelend, *The Interlude of the Disobedient Child*, ed. James
Orchard Halliwell (London: The Percy Society, 1848), p. 13. Quotations from *The Disobedient Child* follow that edition.

30 David M. Bevington, *From Mankind to Marlowe: Growth and Structure
in the Popular Drama of Tudor England* (Cambridge, Mass.: Harvard
University Press, 1962), p. 22.

31 Citations of *Mankind* refer to the edition in *English Moral Interludes*,
ed. Wickham.

32 Citations of *Youth* refer to *Two Tudor Interludes: The Interlude of Youth,
Hick Scorner*, ed. Ian Lancashire (Manchester: Manchester University
Press, 1980).

33 Citations of *Lusty Juventus* follow the edition in *Four Tudor Interludes*, ed. J. A. B. Somerset (London: The Athlone Press, 1974).

34 Paula Neuss, ed. *Magnificence: John Skelton* (Manchester: Manchester University Press, 1980), p. 30.

35 Catherine Belsey, *The Subject of Tragedy: Identity and Difference in Renaissance Drama* (London: Methuen, 1985), p. 56.

36 Belsey, *The Subject of Tragedy*, p. 58.

37 On pedagogical drama's difficulty with proving the connection between knowledge and virtue, see Belsey, *The Subject of Tragedy*, pp. 67–70.

38 See Introduction above.

39 Doubling likely comes when "Reson sendyth Instruccion, Studye, and Dyligence and Confidens out" (s.d. at 1020) and presumably those four actors return eighty lines later as musicians: "Heere cumth in fowre wyth violes" (s.d. at 1104). The same actors would have probably also played Fame, Favour, Riches, and Worship earlier. On doubling possibilities, see T. W. Craik, *The Tudor Interlude: Stage, Costume, and Acting* (Leicester: Leicester University Press, 1958), pp. 47–48.

40 Anne Righter argues that "The identity of the audience with its part [i.e. that of Mankind] was the unquestioned, essential fact of mediaeval religious drama" (*Shakespeare and the Idea of the Play* [London: Chatto and Windus, 1962], p. 19; see pp. 13–86).

41 Rebecca Bushnell relates an anecdote about the schoolboy Prince Edward in 1544 that resembles Wyt's chivalric narrative. Richard Cox, the prince's tutor, "set up Edward's studies as a kind of military campaign or series of 'valiant conquests,' in which the young prince might emulate his father's recent capture of Boulogne ... His enemies were named 'the captains of ignorance' " (p. 56). Among the commandments made part of this narrative was one " 'to beware of strange and wanton women' " (p. 57), an injunction that recalls Wyt's lesson regarding Idlenes. Some aspect of these commandments Edward resisted with his own "Will," which Cox defeated in an ensuing " 'battle' " (p. 57), apparently by striking the prince (see Bushnell, *A Culture of Teaching*, pp. 56–58). Cox's pedagogical game and his struggle with "Will" bear considerable likeness to the adventures of Wyt.

42 Young, *The English Prodigal Son Plays*, p. 3.

43 Palsgrave, *Acolastus*, p. 145.

44 *Ibid.*

45 *Ibid.*

46 *Ibid.* pp. 145, 146. Palsgrave's *compassion* deserves notice in relation to the prodigal-son story. In the Geneva Bible (1560), Luke 15:20 reads, "So he arose and came to his father, and when he was yet a great way of, his father sawe him, and had compassion, and ran & fel on his necke, and kissed him." "Compassion" is pivotal in the responses of the father and the audience to the prodigal son.

47 Gair briefly notes Wyt's transformational stages: "From his self-disgust, he progresses to an awareness of how he has slandered others, . . . and he deeply regrets his folly" (*The Children of Paul's*, p. 90).

48 Stephen Hawes' *The Pastime of Pleasure* (c. 1505) offers a narrative verse romance source for *Wit and Science* in which a Vice-like character, False Report, receives a whipping rather than the protagonist. *Wit and Science* departs from the romance for the sake of its pedagogical argument and dramaturgical effect.

49 Bushnell, *A Culture of Teaching*, pp. 23–72.

50 The historical information about mirrors in this paragraph derives from Benjamin Goldberg, *The Mirror of Man* (Charlottesville: University Press of Virginia, 1985), esp. pp. 135–62.

51 Metaphorically, the clear, sharply etched mirror that we associate with the Renaissance began to replace the murky reflection glimpsed " 'through a glass, darkly' " associated with medievalism: Goldberg, *The Mirror of Man*, p. 135.

52 Goldberg, *The Mirror of Man*, p. 142.

53 Goldberg observes that "In the humanistic philosophy of the times, the mirror reflected clearly, and the clear mirror became the clear spirit, and the clear spirit then liberated man" (*The Mirror of Man*, p. 147). Pedagogical drama here asserts a sharpened vision, claimed against the dim reflection of the medieval self and the Pauline folding of identity into God.

54 Quotations from *Magnificence* follow the edition in *Four Morality Plays*, ed. Peter Happé (Middlesex: Penguin Books, 1979). On Magnificence's repentance, see Robert Potter, *The English Morality Play* (London: Routledge, 1975), pp. 74–77.

55 Elyot, *The Gouernour*, p. 71.

56 Quotations from Shakespeare refer to *The Riverside Shakespeare*, ed. G. Blakemore Evans, with the assitance of J. J. M. Tobin, 2nd edn. (Boston: Houghton Mifflin, 1997).

57 Debora Kuller Shuger, *Habits of Thought in the English Renaissance: Religion, Politics, and the Dominant Culture* (Berkeley: University of California Press, 1990). Differently, Jean-Christophe Agnew argues that early modern capitalism provoked a crisis of authority that can be seen in the Elizabethan sense of the "self" as "in no wise a firm and settled entity" but a "serial self . . . a self composed in, of, and for successive performances" (*Worlds Apart: The Market and the Theater in Anglo-American Thought, 1550–1750* [Cambridge: Cambridge University Press, 1986], p. 83; see esp. pp. 57–100).

58 The most famous statement of this principle is, of course, Pico della Mirandola's *Oration on the Dignity of Man*. See also Juan Luis Vives, "A Fable about Man." Both are collected in Ernst Cassirer, Paul Oskar Kristeller, and John Herman Randall, Jr., eds., *The Renaissance Philosophy of Man* (Chicago: University of Chicago Press, 1948).

59 See chapter 6 below.
60 Cicero, "Laelius: On Friendship" in *Cicero: On the Good Life*, trans. Michael Grant (Penguin, 1971), p. 189.
61 Francis Barker, *The Tremulous Private Body: Essays in Subjection* (London: Methuen, 1984).
62 See Kent Cartwright, *Shakespearean Tragedy and Its Double: The Rhythms of Audience Response* (University Park: Pennsylvania State University Press, 1991), pp. 89–138.
63 On *Friar Bacon and Friar Bungay* and its pattern of mirroring, see chapter 8 below.
64 Katharine Eisaman Maus, *Inwardness and Theater in the English Renaissance* (Chicago: University of Chicago Press, 1995), p. 171; see esp. pp. 171–77.
65 Maus, *Inwardness*, p. 171; Maus explores inwardness as an effect of Protestantism.
66 Reson's line here echoes his earlier use of "dowte" concerning Wyt and Science, "I dowte not my dowghter welbestowde" (28). "Dowte" and "dowghter" make a virtual pun.
67 See also 1047, 1082, 1084, 11088, and 1089.
68 *Wit and Science* here and elsewhere bears a striking resemblance to John Rastell's earlier *The Nature of the Four Elements*. See, for example, the opening speech of Rastell's Messenger. *The Four Elements* contains characters akin to those in Redford's play, including Experience and Ignorance, as well as Nature, Humanity, Studious Desire, and Sensual Appetite. It would seem likely that Redford knew Rastell's play. On resemblances between *Wit and Science* and *The Four Elements*, as well as between Redford's play and Medwall's *Nature*, see Trevor Lennam, *Sebastian Westcott*, pp. 93–95.
69 Belsey, *The Subject of Tragedy*, p. 67.
70 On the relationship between humanism and representations of women in sixteenth-century drama, see chapter 5 below.

PLAYING AGAINST TYPE: *GRAMMER GURTON'S NEEDLE*

1 See, for example, Charles Walters Whitworth, ed., *Three Sixteenth-Century Comedies:* Gammer Gurton's Needle, Roister Doister, The Old Wife's Tale (London: Ernest Benn Ltd., 1984), p. xxxii; see also Douglas Duncan, "*Gammer Gurton's Needle* and the Concept of Humanist Parody," *Studies in English Literature 1500–1900* (Spring 1987): 177–96, on p. 180; and F. P. Wilson, *The English Drama: 1485–1585*, ed. G. K. Hunter (New York: Oxford University Press, 1969), p. 111.
2 In the past thirty-odd years appreciation for *Gammer Gurton's Needle*'s theatrical artistry has grown, starting with R. W. Ingram, "*Gammer Gurton's Needle*: Comedy Not Quite of the Lowest Order?," *Studies in English Literature* (Spring 1967): 257–68; see also William B. Toole,

"The Aesthetics of Scatology in *Gammer Gurton's Needle*," *English Language Notes* (June 1973): 253–58; and Howard B. Norland, *Drama in Early Tudor Britain, 1485–1558* (Lincoln: University of Nebraska Press, 1995), pp. 280–91. For a recent culturally oriental study arguing that *Gammer Gurton's Needle* "erodes the difference between male/female and public/private that the Latin puberty rite upheld," see Wendy Wall, " 'Household Stuff': The Sexual Politics of Domesticity and the Advent of English Comedy," *ELH* (Spring 1998): 1–45, on p. 6.

3 Some previous critics have used the medieval and Renaissance commentaries on Terence to analyze *Gammer Gurton's Needle*. I have found Duncan's "*Gammer Gurton's Needle* and the Concept of Humanist Parody" particularly suggestive.

4 William E. Gruber, *Comic Theaters: Studies in Performance and Audience Response* (Athens: University of Georgia Press, 1986), p. 63.

5 See David Bevington, *Tudor Drama and Politics: A Critical Approach to Topical Meaning* (Cambridge, Mass.: Harvard University Press, 1968), pp. 121–24.

6 Marie Axton, ed., *Three Tudor Classical Interludes:* Thersites, Jacke Jugeler, Horestes (Cambridge: D.S. Brewer, 1982), pp. 17, 18–19.

7 J. W. Robinson argues that the play's title puns upon Girton, a village near Cambridge, the pun adding realism to the satire of village life ("The Art and Meaning of *Gammer Gurton's Needle*" in *Renaissance Drama*, Leonard Barkan, ed. [Evanston, Ill.: Northwestern University Press, 1983], pp. 45–77, on pp. 45, 48, 50–51).

8 Damian Riehl Leader, *A History of the University of Cambridge*, vol. 1: *The University to 1546* (Cambridge: Cambridge University Press, 1988), p. 283.

9 Leader, *A History of the University of Cambridge*, p. 283. See H. Rackham, *Early Statutes of Christ's College, Cambridge, With the Statutes of the Prior Foundation of God's House* (Cambridge: Fabb and Tyler, 1927), pp. 103–5, 79–81. On the background of William Stevenson, the putative author of *Gammer Gurton's Needle*, see Henry Bradley, "Critical Essay," *Representative English Comedies*, ed. Charles Mills Gayley (New York: Macmillan, 1916), p. 199.

10 Bradley, "Critical Essay," p. 204.

11 Quotations of the play follow *Gammer Gvrtons Nedle*, ed. H. F. B. Brett-Smith (Oxford: Basil Blackwell, 1920).

12 See *Respublica: An Interlude for Christmas 1553 Attributed to Nicholas Udall*, ed. W. W. Greg (London: Early English Text Society, 1952). Greg concludes that Udall authored *Respublica* (pp. viii–xviii). Udall also had an association with Christ's College drama through his translation of its *Pammachius* (1538).

13 Frederick S. Boas, *University Drama in the Tudor Age* (Oxford: Clarendon Press, 1914), p. 73.

14 On comic theory inherited from classical writers and their commen-

tators, I am indebted to Marvin T. Herrick, *Comic Theory in the Sixteenth Century* (Urbana: University of Illinois Press, 1950); and particularly to T. W. Baldwin's monumental *Shakspere's Five-Act Structure: Shakspere's Early Plays on the Background of Renaissance Theories of Five-Act Structure from 1470* (Urbana: University of Illinois Press, 1947). Baldwin provides an exhaustive and authoritative treatment of Terence, Donatus, Melanchthon, and others as they shape the Renaissance sense of drama. Following Duncan (*"Gammer Gurton's Needle* and the Concept of Humanist Parody," p. 194, n. 6), I use Baldwin's extensive translations as a primary source for the commentaries of Donatus and Melanchthon. On the rhetorical dimensions of Donatus and Melanchthon, see Joel B. Altman, *The Tudor Play of Mind: Rhetorical Inquiry and the Development of Elizabethan Drama* (Berkeley: University of California Press, 1978), pp. 130–47. On the influence of Donatus and other Terentian commentators, see also Norland, *Drama in Early Tudor Britain*, pp. 65–83.

15 Baldwin, *Shakspere's Five-Act Structure*, p. 33.

16 As Donatus says of the *Andria*, "Here is the fine-woven protasis, the tumultuous epitasis, the nearly tragic catastrophe, and yet suddenly from this disorder all comes through to tranquility" (translation mine): *"Hic protasis subtilis, epitasis tumutuosa, catastrophe pene tragica; & tamen repente ex his turbis in tranquuillum pervenit"* (*"Praefatio in Andriam Terentii"* in P. Terentius, *Comoediae Sex* [Basil, 1570]).

17 Baldwin, *Shakspere's Five-Act Structure*, p. 409. The summary in this paragraph follows Baldwin, pp. 409–10.

18 Baldwin, quoting Iodocus Willichius (1550), *Shakspere's Five-Act Structure*, p. 409.

19 On the Donatian structure of the action, see also Norland, *Drama in Early Tudor Britain*, pp. 288–91.

20 Baldwin, *Shakspere's Five-Act Structure*, p. 179. On Melanchthon, I am indebted to Baldwin, *Shakspere's Five-Act Structure*, pp. 160–251. See also Herrick, *Comic Theory in the Sixteenth Century*, pp. 72–74 and *passim*; and Altman, *The Tudor Play of Mind*, pp. 130–47.

21 Baldwin, *Shakspere's Five-Act Structure*, p. 178.

22 Baldwin, *Shakspere's Five-Act Structure*, pp. 172–73; see also Herrick, *Comic Theory in the Sixteenth Century*, p. 72.

23 The ideas of Donatus and Melanchthon are extended by Latomus (1534) and Willichius (1539); see Baldwin, *Shakspere's Five-Act Structure*, pp. 205–50. Latomus divides the epitasis into stages of increasing perturbation. Willichius localizes the epitasis in the third act, thus making the fourth act a kind of pre-catastrophe. *Gammer Gurton's Needle* reflects these influences. Its third act contains the episode of greatest conflict (III.iii), while the fourth act (the gulling of Dr. Rat) attempts to solve the dilemma of the third act and adds its own level of comic perturbation, leading to the reversal (Act v).

24 As Melanchthon says of the *Eunuchus*, " 'Here are no honest examples, no honest advice. For brothel loves are described, so that in this example young men, as in a mirror, may see the folly of this kind of loves. . . . Thraso holds the first place in the play' " (Baldwin, *Shakspere's Five-Act Structure*, p. 183).

25 Boas, *University Drama in the Tudor Age*, p. 73.

26 For examples, see the much-used 1542 volume, *The Apophthegmes of Erasmus: Translated into English by Nicolas Udall* (rpt. Boston: Robert Roberts, 1877). On *Gammer Gurton's Needle* as a play that enacts proverbs, see Robinson, "The Art and Meaning of *Gammer Gurton's Needle*," pp. 64–73.

27 Bevington, *Tudor Drama and Politics*, p. 122.

28 On theatrical "identification" and the simultaneous threat and attraction of stage figures, see Michael Goldman, *The Actor's Freedom: Toward a Theory of Drama* (New York: Viking, 1975), pp. 119–61. Because "identifying" can suggest misleadingly that spectators will recognize in a character values or attitudes that they already possess, Thomas Cartelli prefers to speak of theatrical "engagement"; *Marlowe, Shakespeare, and the Economy of Theatrical Experience* (Philadelphia: University of Pennsylvania Press, 1991), pp. 31–33.

29 Why would identification develop now, in mid-century academic drama? Beyond the argument of the present essay identification might be understood as a possibility within humanist pedagogy itself. Recent scholars of humanist education have emphasized the closeness, even bonding, that sometimes occurred between teachers and pupils; see, for example, Alan Stewart's interesting *Close Readers: Humanism and Sodomy in Early Modern England* (Princeton, N.J.: Princeton University Press, 1997); on the relationship, for example, between Roger Ascham and his pupil and bedmate John Whitney, see pp. 125–27; see also Rebecca W. Bushnell, *A Culture of Teaching: Early Modern Humanism in Theory and Practice* (Ithaca, N.Y.: Cornell University Press, 1996), e.g., pp. 23–72.

30 In an emendation proposed by J. C. Maxwell and followed by Whitworth, Diccon, slyly insulting, also links Hodge to excrement: "They gave no more hede to my talk than thou wouldst to a [turd]" (40).

31 Gail Kern Paster argues that Hodge's incontinence and his obsession with the lost phallic needle reflect the struggle of the adolescent male (or Cambridge schoolboy) to wrest control of his bodily functions away from women; see *The Body Embarrassed: Drama and the Disciplines of Shame in Early Modern England* (Ithaca, N.Y.: Cornell University Press, 1993), pp. 116–25.

32 The play does have its sexual subtext, of course. N. Lindsay McFadyen traces phallic double entendres that emphasize youthful sexual anxieties and the symbolic emasculation of boy-actors dressed as women; see "What Was Really Lost in *Gammer Gurton's Needle*?" in

Renaissance Papers 1982, A. Leigh Deneef and M. Thomas Hester eds. (Raleigh, N.C.: Southeastern Renaissance Conference, 1983), pp. 9–13. See also Paster, *The Body Embarrassed*, pp. 116–25. The play also has sodomitical overtones. The climactic thrusting of the needle into Hodge's buttocks and the emphasis upon his shameful hole treat ambivalently what appears to be a sodomitical subtext. Helpful here might be the recent interest in the relationship between Tudor humanism and homosexuality, as exemplified in Stewart's *Close Readers*.

33 Diccon suggests that Hodge also has bad breath from his lack of dainty fare (II.i.16); Hodge suffers various afflictions as a would-be lover.

34 In *Gammer Gurton's Needle*, the dialogue is unusually helpful in signalling physical action. Here Hodge says that he needs to "make a curtesie of water" (100), that he can no longer "holde it" (105), and that he must "beraye the hall" (106); Diccon asks accusingly, "be thine ars strynges brusten" (108), says he can smell the devil (110), and calls Hodge "shytten knaue" (II.ii.1). Some aural or visual indication of Hodge's incontinence seems called for theatrically.

35 At Christ's College as many as four scholars shared rooms originally meant for two; see Rackham, *Early Statutes of Christ's College*, p. vii. The list of misdemeanors from the college *Statutes* hints at the rambunctiousness of students and their correction in the manner of Master Baylye: "But in the case of other minor transgressions, as if he be a brawler, a fighter, quarrelsome, a night-walker, a vagabond by day, or extremely negligent . . . then he shall be corrected at the discretion of the Master" (p. 49).

36 Quotations from *Roister Doister* follow *Roister Doister*, ed. W. W. Greg (Oxford: Malone Society Reprints, 1934).

37 Robert Nozick, "Being More Real," *The Examined Life: Philosophical Meditations* (New York: Touchstone, 1989), pp. 128–40.

38 Nozick, *The Examined Life*, p. 130.

39 Nozick discusses how the vivid realism of mathematics, for example, can grip attention and provoke imagination (*The Examined Life*, pp. 130–31).

40 Hodge, in a comic way, epitomizes student virtue. According to the *Early Statutes of Christ's College*, "Nothing is more to be avoided by a young man than slothful idleness" (p. 107).

41 Props make up another dimension of Hodge's dramaturgical realism. In Act III, he enters with mending tools; he begins Act II with a piece of barley bread in hand and, apparently, the saucepan licked clean by Gib (II.i.26). In the fight between Gammer and Chat, he goes offstage to grab a staff. Hodge keeps introducing fragments of the village's physical facticity onto the stage.

42 Besides the offstage life discussed above, the play further embeds

Hodge in the village milieu through his references to people who never appear, Tom Tankard and his hyperthyroid cow, for example. Hodge enters with his thong, thanking Sym Glover (III.i.1), who, spying Hodge's need, had lent his awl. When Dame Chat leaves her card game in the scene before, she instructs her stand-in to "Take heed of Sim glouers wife – she hath an eie behind her" (II.ii.30). At Hodge's speech, the Glover family blossoms into imaginative life, with its watchful wife and more carefree husband. Such strokes, even when below the level of consciousness, add to Hodge's dramaturgical realism. Helen M. Whall observes of the play that "behind the visible world of the 'neutral' stage, . . . there exists a world brought into being by the mere act of suggestion" (*To Instruct and Delight: Didactic Method in Five Tudor Dramas* [New York: Garland, 1988], p. 143; see pp. 143–47).

43 In mid-century academic plays such as *Gammer Gurton's Needle, Roister Doister,* and *Thersites* the braggart soldier recurs surprisingly often. Why that stereotype then? England at that time had no special influx of soldiers home from the wars. The braggart soldier may instead reflect changes in the Tudor university student body. Oxford and Cambridge were gaining students from middle class, wealthy, or aristocratic families, students with aims other than clerical preparation. Mid-century commentary takes increasing note of quarrelling, roistering, gad-about students. The braggart soldier may point at a member of that group, the school bully.

44 For an excellent example, see Act IV, scenes vii and viii of *Roister Doister.* Act IV of Terence's *Eunuchus* culminates in the braggart soldier Thraso's march against Thais, but no combat occurs. Plautus's *Miles Gloriosus* puts the drubbing of Pygropolynices in Act V.

45 Boas, *University Drama in the Tudor Age,* p. 73.

46 See Duncan, "*Gammer Gurton's Needle* and the Concept of Humanist Parody," p. 177.

47 Margaret in *Friar Bacon and Friar Bungay* offers a later Elizabethan example of playing against a stereotype; see chapter 8.

48 Melanchthon, for example, says of the *Andria,* " 'Indeed that the disposition of Pamphilus might the more clearly be seen, and that there might be somewhat more of turbulence in the play, Charimus, very unlike Pamphilus, is contrasted with him: nothing temperate in the former, nothing of counsel; on the contrary, in the other almost all things more moderate than either age demands or love permits' " (Baldwin, *Shakspere's Five-Act Structure,* p. 181).

49 Hodge's "for a house full of gold" gives his denial an added dramatic credibility, since he has previously invoked gold pieces as a measure of how much he wants something: for example, "Gogs soule man chould giue a crown chad it but iii. stitches" (II.i.50; for other examples, see I.ii.27–28; I.iii.20; I.iv.47; II.i.52; III.iii.67; III.iv.4;

v.ii.104). The detail illustrates again Mr. S.'s dramatic sophistication.

50 Diccon's line at 254 suggests that Hodge shows a silent reaction; Diccon repeats his allusion at 292.

51 Duncan, "*Gammer Gurton's Needle* and the Concept of Humanist Parody," p. 187; see also p. 180.

52 On early Protestantism, see Horton Davies, *Worship and Theology in England: From Cranmer to Hooker 1534–1603* (Princeton, N.J.: Princeton University Press, 1970).

53 Stanley J. Kozikowski, "*Gammer Gurton's Needle*" in *Elizabethan Dramatists*, vol. 62 of *Dictionary of Literary Biography*, ed. Fredson Bowers (Detroit: Gale Publishing Co., 1987), pp. 365–68; and James C. Bryant, *Tudor Drama and Religious Controversy* (Atlanta, Ga.: Mercer University Press, 1984), pp. 85–88.

54 Quotations from Shakespeare follow *The Riverside Shakespeare*, ed. G. Blakemore Evans, assisted by J. J. M. Tobin, 2d ed. (Boston: Houghton Mifflin, 1997).

55 For example: "What deuyll can I tell man" (I.ii.39); "I know not what a deuil y" me[n]est!" (II.i.45); "What deuyll man, art afraide of nought" (II.i.98); "What Deuyll, be thine ars strynges brusten?" (II.i.108); "What deuil nede he be groping so depe in goodwife Chats he[n]s nest" (V.ii.227). Hodge uses several such interjections, but he swears more typically by God, as his early scenes emphasize: "Gogs bones" (I.ii.4), "Gods soule" (I.ii.5), "Gogs hart" (I.ii.27), "Gogs sacrament" (I.iii.27), "Gogs malison" (I.iii.38), etc.

56 Diccon's trick against Hodge enacts vintage Vice business: Jacke Jugeler, for example, promises to conjure a devil against Jenkin Careaway and looks to make Jenkin lose control of his bowels.

57 Diccon defines that response early when he describes Gammer and Tib as wringing their hands and crying "alacke and welaway" (I.i.20) over the loss of the needle, and, alternately, as sitting "as still as stones in the streite, / As though they had been take[n] with fairies or els wᵗ some il sprite" (I.ii.25–26); in Act V, Dr. Rat provides a model of irrational bafflement.

58 Mullinger describes the prevailing spirit of mid-century religious controversy and its "overwhelming current of passion, prejudice, and bigotry which was converting the universities into camps of rival schools of theology, and almost every scholar into a polemic" (James Bass Mullinger, *The University of Cambridge from the Royal Injunctions of 1535 to the Accession of Charles the First* [Cambridge: Cambridge University Press, 1884], p. 103). Recent scholarship, while acknowledging contentiousness, tends to see a dominant Protestant humanism also taking hold; see, for example, Winthrop S. Hudson, *The Cambridge Connection and the Elizabethan Settlement of 1559* (Durham, N.C.: Duke University Press, 1980). In 1545 Christ's College put on a production of

Pammachius, a Calvinist academic play caricaturing papal history and traditional religious practices. The performance landed the college in some hot water; see Mullinger, *The University of Cambridge*, pp. 72–76.

59 Of the first *Book of Common Prayer*, A. G. Dickens writes, "Though wholly in the English language, this Prayer Book remained a masterpiece of compromise, even of studied ambiguity" (*The English Reformation*, 2nd edn. [London: BT Batsford, 1989], p. 242). Instead of concentrating narrowly on abuses in Church practice and ritual, the English Reformation should, Bucer advocated, reflect more broadly on "social, ecclesiatical and economic" reform (Constance Hopf, *Martin Bucer and the English Reformation* [Oxford: Basil Blackwell, 1946], p. 99). On Bucer and the spirit of mid-century Cambridge, see H. C. Porter, *Reformation and Reaction in Tudor Cambridge* (Cambridge: Cambridge University Press, 1958), pp. 58–73.

60 That formulation wears a mid-century Protestant air, where a moralistic zeal marched side by side with salvation by faith, an attitude typical of the first generation of reformist preachers and epitomized by Hugh Latimer, the famous bishop identified with Cambridge. An approach to *Gammer Gurton's Needle* through contemporary sources, then, might support the arguments offered here. As an example of Latimer's style, see his well-known 1548 "Sermon of the Plough" in *Sermons by Hugh Latimer*, ed. Rev. George Elwes Corrie (Cambridge: Cambridge University Press, 1844), pp. 59–78. Latimer shares the roiling, alliterative rhetoric of *Gammer Gurton's Needle* (and other works), as in his railing against nonpreaching prelates: "ruffling in their rents, dancing in their dominions, burdened with ambassages, pampering of their paunches, like a monk that maketh his jubilee; munching in the mangers, and moiling in their gay manors and mansions, and so troubled with loitering in their lordships that they cannot attend to it" (p. 67). Both "Plough" and *Gammer* apply an inventive colloquial diction, as in "moil" (*Gammer*, IV.iii.23).

61 For example, Duncan, "*Gammer Gurton's Needle* and the Concept of Humanist Parody," pp. 177–93.

62 Such qualifications distinguish *Gammer Gurton's Needle* from Terence and Plautus but anticipate Shakespeare, who often leaves some matters beyond the ken of his characters, as with the love-juice left in Demetrius's eyes.

63 The paradigmatic school play of mid-century, from *Nice Wanton* (1547–53) to *Misogonus* (c. 1570), portrays the prodigal-son schoolboy succumbing to the lures of women, drinking, and dice. On prodigal-son plays, see chapter 2 above.

64 On negotiation in the English Renaissance, see Theodore B. Leinwand, "Negotiation and New Historicism," *PMLA* (May 1990): 477–90.

65 The characters of *Gammer Gurton's Needle* march offstage to celebrate

together, the conventional comic ending. Serendipitously, the play has already created an expansive offstage life, a community; and Hodge's capacity to evoke that world has been part of his theatrical realism. Here the play's thematic values and its dramaturgical virtues coincide.

66 Thomas Wilson, *The Art of Rhetoric (1560)*, ed. Peter E. Medine (University Park: Pennsylvania State University Press, 1993), p. 188. In this delightful passage, Wilson goes on to say, "The fine courtiers will speak nothing but Chaucer. The mystical wise men and poetical clerks will speak nothing but quaint proverbs and blind allegories, delighting much in their own darkness, especially when none can tell what they do say. The unlearned or foolish fantastical that smells but of learning—such fellows as have seen learned men in their days—will so Latin their tongues that the simple cannot but wonder at their talk and think surely they speak by some revelation. I know them that think rhetoric to stand wholly upon dark words, and he that can catch an inkhorn term by the tail, him they compt to be a fine Englishman and a good rhetorician" (pp. 188–89).

67 For an illuminating essay on this topic, see Thomas M. Greene, "Roger Ascham: The Perfect End of Shooting," *ELH* (December, 1969): 609–25. I am indebted to John McDiarmid for drawing my attention to the Cambridge discussion of language.

TIME, TYRANNY, AND SUSPENSE IN POLITICAL DRAMA OF THE 1560S

1 Although applying the term *tyrant* to Mary Tudor misrepresents history – since the regime's harshness involved the machinery of state and the collaboration of officials up and down the political hierarchy – the persecution of martyrs, nonetheless, deeply scarred the public consciousness. Of particular interest for resistance to "tyranny" is John Ponet's *Short Treatise of Politike Power* (Strasburg, 1556).

2 Stephen Gosson, *Playes Confuted in Fiue Actions* (1582), in Arthur F. Kinney, ed., *Markets of Bawdrie: The Dramatic Criticism of Stephen Gosson*, vol. 4, *Salzburg Studies in English Literature* (Salzburg: Institut für Englische Sprache und Literatur, Universität Salzburg: 1974), pp. 149–50.

3 Thomas Elyot, *The Boke named the Gouernour*, vol. 1, ed. Henry Herbert Stephen Croft (London: Kegan Paul, Trench and Co., 1883), Bk. I, chap. x, p. 71.

4 *A Worke of Ioannes Ferrarivs Montanus, touchynge the good orderynge of a common weale*, Englished by William Bavande (London, 1559), fol. 101ᵛ. On drama, see Bk. v, chap. 8.

5 Nicholas Grimald, Dedicatory Epistle to *Christus Redivivus* (1543), L. R. Merrill, ed. and trans., *The Life and Poems of Nicholas Grimald* (New Haven, Conn.: Yale University Press, 1925), p. 109.

6 Joel B. Altman, *The Tudor Play of Mind: Rhetorical Inquiry and the Development of Elizabethan Drama* (Berkeley: University of California Press, 1978), p. 240.
7 Bruce R. Smith, *Ancient Scripts and Modern Experience on the English Stage, 1500–1700* (Princeton, N. J.: Princeton University Press, 1988), p. 224.
8 John W. Cunliffe notes that the 1571 edition of *Damon and Pithias* includes a prologue for performances " 'either in Priuate, or open Audience,' " and concludes, "We have therefore, in this instance a play first acted at Court, then given at the University of Oxford, and finally published in a form thought suitable for any public or private performance" (*Early English Classical Tragedies* [Oxford: Clarendon Press, 1912], p. lxxii).
9 On Ambidexter's role in the play, see Bernard Spivack, *Shakespeare and the Allegory of Evil* (New York: Columbia University Press, 1958), pp. 284–91. On the play's conflict between the theatrical and the political, see Norman Rabkin, "Stumbling toward Tragedy," in *Shakespeare's "Rough Magic": Renaissance Essays in Honor of C. L. Barber*, Peter Erickson and Coppélia Kahn, eds. (Newark: University of Delaware Press, 1985), pp. 28–49, esp. pp. 31–36; and Rebecca W. Bushnell, *Tragedies of Tyrants: Political Thought and Theater in the English Renaissance* (Ithaca, N.Y.: Cornell University Press, 1990), pp. 80–103. On "ambidexterity" as a metaphor for political deceit, see Robert Carl Johnson, ed. *A Critical Edition of Thomas Preston's Cambises* (Salzburg: Institut für Englische Sprache und Literatur, Universität Salzburg, 1975), pp. 16, 21–22.
10 On the heart as a dominant image in the play, see James Phares Myers, Jr., "The Heart of King Cambises," *Studies in Philology* (October 1973): 367–76.
11 All quotations from *Cambises* follow *A Critical Edition of Thomas Preston's Cambises*, ed. Johnson.
12 Rabkin, "Stumbling toward Tragedy," p. 32; the appealing "intensity" of Cambises's villainy, Rabkin adds, leaves his characterization "at odds with or at least irrelevant to the explicit moral of the tragedy" (p. 33).
13 See Bushnell, *Tragedies of Tyrants*, pp. 80–103.
14 See Joel H. Kaplan, "Reopening King Cambises' Vein," *Essays in Theatre* (May 1987): 103–14, on p. 109.
15 Rabkin, "Stumbling toward Tragedy," p. 32.
16 *Ibid.*, p. 33.
17 Kaplan, "Reopening King Cambises' Vein," p. 110.
18 The shooting will likely be pantomimed so that the bloody heart surgery will gain shock value from the contrast. A 1968 Toronto production of *Cambises*, by the *Poculi Ludique Societas*, used "a pig's heart soaked in stage blood and glycerine" for the heart of Praxaspes's son,

one of the devices that prompted Toronto's leading theater critic to acknowledge the play's " 'luridly effective theatre' " (Kaplan, 104–05). On the Toronto production, see Joel H. Kaplan and George Shand, "The *Poculi Ludique Societas*: Medieval Drama at the University of Toronto," in *Research Opportunities in Renaissance Drama*, vol. xi, S. Schoenbaum, ed. (Evanston, Ill.: Northwestern University Press, 1968), pp. 141–61.

19 Kaplan, "Reopening King Cambises' Vein," p. 111.

20 On *Cambises* as offering an early example of stage infanticide, see Maurice Charney, "The Persuasiveness of Violence in Elizabethan Plays" in *Renaissance Drama* n.s. 2, ed. S. Schoenbaum (Evanston, Ill: Northwestern University Press, 1969), pp. 59–70, esp. pp. 63–64 and p. 66.

21 Kaplan,"Reopening King Cambises' Vein," p. 105.

22 See Gina Alexander, "Bonner and the Marian Persecutions," *History* 60 (October 1975): 374–91. The primary source for the depiction of Bonner as persecutor is Foxe's *Actes and Monuments*. From Foxe, Alexander quotes the martyr Ralph Allerton's view that Bonner represented " 'the bloody church, figured in Cain the tyrant.' " The consonance of that image with the fratricidal Cambises is striking. Likewise, consider Alexander's own language describing Bonner: "Out of his mind with rage one moment, he could show extraordinary patience and guile with a stubborn opponent the next" (391). Preston may have found in Bonner's character a more direct model for Cambises than critics have conceived.

23 For descriptions of such festivities, see A. Wigfall Green, *The Inns of Court and Early English Drama* (New Haven, Conn.: Yale University Press, 1931), pp. 40–96; and Philip J. Finkelpearl, *John Marston of the Middle Temple: An Elizabethan Dramatist in His Social Setting* (Cambridge, Mass.: Harvard University Press, 1969), pp. 32–44. For eye-witness comments on the 1561–62 revels, see William Dugdale, *Origines Juridiciales* (London, 1671), pp. 150–57, quoted in John Nichols, *The Progresses and Public Processions of Queen Elizabeth* (London: John Nichols and Son, 1823), vol. 1, pp. 130–41.

24 C. H. Conley, *The First English Translators of the Classics* (New Haven, Conn.: Yale University Press, 1927), p. 23; see pp. 18–33. See also Green, *The Inns of Court*, pp. 1–21; and Finkelpearl, *John Marston*, pp. 19–31. Jasper Heywood's preface to the first English version of Seneca's *Thyestes* (1560) celebrates a band of young translators and poets, "Minerva's men / and finest wits" who "swarm" about the Inns (83–84), two of whom he names as Sackville and Norton (Seneca, *Thyestes*, trans. Jasper Heywood [1560], ed. Joost Daalder [London: Ernest Benn, 1982]).

25 Conley, *The First English Translators*, pp. 28–54.

26 *Ibid.*, pp. 55–81.

27 *Ibid.*, p. 62. In studying the past, John Brende writes, "men may see the groundes and beginnynges of co[m]men wealthes, y[e] causes of their encrease, of their prosperous mayntenau[n]ce, and good pre-seruation : and againe by what meanes they decreased, decayed, and came to ruyne" (Quintus Curcius, *The Actes of the Greate Alexander*, trans. John Brende [London, 1553], A.ii).

28 Brende, *The Actes of the Greate Alexander*, A.ii-A.iii.

29 See Joseph M. Levine, *Humanism and History: Origins of Modern English Historiography* (Ithaca, N.Y.: Cornell University Press, 1987). On the paradox of Renaissance humanist historiography, see J. G. A. Pocock, *The Ancient Constitution and the Feudal Law* (1957; Baltimore: Johns Hopkins University Press, 1987), pp. 1–8.

30 "For in them both it shall seme to a man that he is present and hereth the counsayles and exhortations of capitaines . . . And he shall wene that he hereth the terrible dintes of sondry weapons and ordi-naunce of bataile" (Elyot, *The Gouernour*, I.xi.86–87).

31 Hugh G. Dick, ed., "Thomas Blundeville's *The true order and Methode of wryting and reading Hystories* (1574)," *The Huntington Library Quarterly*, vol. 3, no. 2 (January 1940): 149–70, on p. 149. Quotations of *The true order and Methode* will follow Dick's edition.

32 Thomas Blundeville, *Of Councils and Counsellors* (1570), ed. Karl-Ludwig Selig (Gainesville, Fl.: Scholars' Facsimiles and Reprints, 1963). *Of Councils* is a "reworking" of a 1559 Spanish treatise. In 1561 Blundeville had also published *Three Moral Treatises*, one called "The Learned Prince."

33 Blundeville, *Of Councils*, p. 15.

34 On Blundeville and Leicester, see C. H. Conley, *The First English Translators*, pp. 25–26.

35 Blundeville, *Of Councils*, p. 41. On Leicester as a reader of histories, see Blundeville, *The true order and Methode*, p. 154.

36 *Ibid.*, pp. 153–54.

37 *Ibid.*, p. 155.

38 "If many actions are to be written which do belong to one selfe ende, and are some way lynked togither one with an other, the writer ought first to bring one alone to such termes & bounds, as without feare of causing anye darcknesse or troubling the readers memorie, he may fitly staye there, vntill he hath brought euery one of the other actions to the like tearmes, and then begin againe with the first, proceeding so orderly from one to an other, vntil he hath made an ende of all" (Blundeville, *The true order and Methode*, pp. 164–65).

39 Blundeville, *The true order and Methode*, p. 165.

40 *Ibid.*, p. 167.

41 Blundeville's categories bear rough relationship to Aristotle's four causes (*Physics*, Bk. II, ch. iii): material, formal, efficient, and final. The material cause refers to the bricks and mortar out of which the

house is constructed; the formal, to the characteristics of what is being built, its form as a house; the efficient, to the builder; and the final, to the end which the house serves, shelter. Aristotle's analysis of causation was standard knowledge in the Renaissance. Aristotle and Blundeville both suggest that one's sense of causation can differ depending on where one looks: the construction material at the beginning of the task or the finished product at the end.

42 Blundeville, *The true order and Methode*, p. 167.

43 *Gorboduc* squares well with Dudley's desire to elevate his reputation, for despite his aspirations, Dudley so far "had achieved nothing concrete in terms of policy" (Alan Haynes, *The White Bear: Robert Dudley, The Elizabethan Earl of Leicester* [London: Peter Owen, 1987], p. 38). There had been hints that Elizabeth "might make him Earl of Leicester on Twelfth Night, 1561" (Robert Kendall, *Robert Dudley: Earl of Leicester* [London: Cassell, 1980], p. 37).

44 E. M. W. Tillyard, *Shakespeare's History Plays* (London: Chatto and Windus, 1948), p. 94. Sidney singles out the play for its "stately speeches and well-sounding phrases, climbing to the height of Seneca's style," words that suggest Sidney's having listened to or read *Gorboduc* aloud (*A Defence of Poetry*, ed. Jan Van Dorsten [Oxford: Oxford University Press, 1966], p. 65). Had Sidney seen a performance of *Gorboduc*?: "Our tragedies and comedies ... excepting *Gorboduc* (again, I say, of those that I have seen)" (p. 65). Attacking *Gorboduc* for violating the unities, Sidney emphasizes the play as staged (p. 65).

45 See Henry James and Greg Walker, "The Politics of *Gorboduc*," *The English Historical Review*, vol. 110, no. 435 (February 1995): 109–21; and Norman Jones and Paul Whitfield White, "*Gorboduc* and Royal Marriage Politics: An Elizabethan Playgoer's Report of the Premiere Performance," *English Literary Renaissance*, vol. 26, no. 1 (Winter 1996): 3–17. For the argument that in the 1561–62 Christmas celebrations at court, the masque *Desire and Beauty* urged Elizabeth to marry Lord Robert Dudley while *Gorboduc* chronicled the alternative horrors of unfixed succession, see Marie Axton, *The Queen's Two Bodies: Drama and the Elizabethan Succession* (London: Royal Historical Society, 1977), pp. 38–48.

46 Quoted from the courtier's account in Jones and White, "*Gorboduc* and Royal Marriage Politics," p. 4.

47 In that regard, see comments by Jones and White, "*Gorboduc* and Royal Marriage Politics," pp. 10–11.

48 On *Gorboduc*'s contribution to the succession debate, see Michael A. R. Graves, *Thomas Norton: The Parliament Man* (Oxford: Blackwell, 1994), pp. 91–99. Arguing from the play's last two speeches, Graves finds *Gorboduc* compatible with Dudley's desire to marry the queen.

49 References to *Gorboduc* follow the edition in *Early English Classical Tragedies*, ed. Cunliffe.

50 On the gods' curse, see II.ii.75–79; III.i.1–28; IV.ii.273–85. The heart in *Gorboduc* becomes, as in *Cambises*, a prime site of response, whether troubled, faithful, envious, divided, inflamed, swollen, or bloody. Another Inns play, *Gismond of Salerne*, makes particular use of heart imagery. Images of a heart cut out with a knife recur, and the play's climax involves Gismond's lover's heart brought to her in a cup, into which she pours poison to drink off suicidally.

51 *Gorboduc*'s dramaturgy of chronology is shared by other Inns of Court plays such as *Jocasta* and *Gismond of Salerne*. Although Inns of Court plays juxtapose human will and choice against implacable cosmic doom, they attribute more to human agency than do their classical antecedents. In *Gismond of Salerne* the heroine's inconstancy is faulted by the Chorus before Cupid fires her heart with love; in *Jocasta* Eteocles and Polynice seem capable of avoiding Oedipus's curse. The scope given to human agency increases the tension in the relationship between the personal and the cosmic. In *Gismond of Salerne*, for example, the heroine wishes to follow her late husband into death, but shortly thereafter she longs for a new mate. Her aunt takes up that latter cause, pleading to Gismond's father the natural desires of youth, after which the Chorus criticizes Gismond for fickleness; only subsequently does Cupid wound her. Is Gismond changeable or "natural"? Is she responsible for her affair with Guishard or is Cupid? The play offers successive judgments. No Inns of Court tragedy better employs this dramaturgy than does *Gorboduc*.

52 That opening gambit may derive from Seneca, particularly *Octavia*; likewise, Videna will show something of the passion of Seneca's *Medea*. In 1559 the first English translation of a Senecan tragedy, the *Troas*, was published by Jasper Heywood, the Inner Temple colleague of Sackville and Norton. *Medea* and *Octavia* would appear in translation in 1566.

53 Franco Moretti, " 'A Huge Eclipse': Tragic Form and the Deconsecration of Sovereignty," *Genre* (Spring–Summer 1982): 7–40, esp. pp. 8–12.

54 On *Gorboduc*'s complex, perhaps "inconsistent" presentation of Porrex, see Martha Tuck Rozett, *The Doctrine of Election and the Emergence of Elizabethan Tragedy* (Princeton, N.J.: Princeton University Press, 1984), pp. 114–17.

55 Recalling the "gaze" in cinematic theory, such moments disrupt, suspend the onrushing linear narrative. On the cinematic gaze, see Laura Mulvey, "Visual Pleasure and Narrative Cinema," *Screen* vol. 16, no. 3 (1975): 6–18.

56 Charles Lamb selects Marcella's narrative for his *Specimens of English Dramatic Poets, Who Lived about the Time of Shakespeare: With Notes* (London: Longman, 1808). He argues that "The chief beauty in the extract is of a secret nature. Marcella obscurely intimates that the murdered prince Porrex and she had been lovers" (p. 5).

57 Marcella gives *Gorboduc* an unexpected but not unprecedented dash of psychological life. In Act IV, Porrex claims that no form of grief for Ferrex's death can denote him truly: "Oh would I mought as full appeare to sight / As inward griefe doth pour it forth to me" (IV.ii.38–39), he says, and later, "to my selfe I must reserue my woe / In pining thoughtes of mine accursed fact, / Since I may not shew here my smallest griefe / Such as it is" (54–57). Unlike *Hamlet*, of course, *Gorboduc* does not build its action upon a prince's inscrutability, but the metaphor and measure of Hamlet's psychology appear some forty years earlier in *Gorboduc*. In addition, Marcella's scene may identify a certain theatrical action emerging in Elizabethan drama, one made memorable by a later isolated and elegiac stage figure, transfixed by what she has seen, the expectancy and rose of the fair state quite down.

58 On Fergus as reminiscent of Mary Stuart, see Mortimer Levine, *The Early Elizabethan Succession Question, 1558–1568* (Stanford, Ca.: Stanford University Press, 1966), pp. 30–44, esp. pp. 41–42.

59 Analyzing *Gorboduc*, Rebecca Bushnell endorses the view that English Renaissance political theory accepted continuity between the past and the present. For classically influenced Elizabethan dramatists, "tragedy was history." Bushnell sees *Gorboduc* as a play where characters "seem increasingly oppressed by time, cut off from the past, and unable to see beyond the present moment" ("Time and History in Early English Classical Drama" in *Law, Literature, and the Settlement of Regimes*, Gordon J. Schochet, ed., Vol. 2 of *Proceedings of the Folger Institute Center for the History of British Political Thought* [Washington, D.C.: The Folger Shakespeare Library, 1990], pp. 73–86, on pp. 74, 78).

60 See Barnaby Googe, *Eclogues, Epitaphs, and Sonnets* (1563), ed. Judith M. Kennedy (Toronto: University of Toronto Press, 1989), p. 86.

61 E. K. Chambers, *The Elizabethan Stage*, vol. 3 (Oxford: Clarendon Press, 1923), p. 309; Leicester Bradner, *The Life and Poems of Richard Edwards* (New Haven, Conn.: Yale University Press, 1927), pp. 57–58; D. Jerry White, "Richard Edwards," *Dictionary of Literary Biography*, vol. 62: *Elizabethan Dramatists*, ed. Fredson Bowers (Detroit: Gale Research Company, 1987), p. 75.

62 See Bradner, *Life and Poems of Richard Edwards*, pp. 22–24.

63 The text of *Palamon and Arcite* does not survive, but several records of its performance do. On the manuscripts and the performance see John R. Elliott, Jr., "Queen Elizabeth at Oxford: New Light on the Royal Plays of 1566," *English Literary Renaissance* (Spring 1988): 218–29.

64 Bradner contends that Edwards appreciated and learned from the dramatic achievement of *Gorboduc* (*The Life and Poems of Richard Edwards*, pp. 24, 60, 62).

65 See Bradner, *The Life and Poems of Richard Edwards*, pp. 58–73 and pp.

81–82. Bradner credits Edwards's plays with inventing the "dignified yet amusing" romantic comedy, introducing the popular onstage forest scene, inaugurating stage "pageantry and pomp," first allegorizing the queen, and creating English theatre's most rounded characters to date. See also Robert Weimann, *Shakespeare and the Popular Tradition in the Theater: Studies in the Social Dimension of Dramatic Form and Function*, ed. Robert Schwartz (Baltimore: Johns Hopkins University Press, 1978), pp. 105–06. On *Damon and Pithias* as a popular play, see n. 8 above.

66 All quotations of the play follow *Richard Edwards' Damon and Pithias: A Critical Old-Spelling Edition*, ed. D. Jerry White (New York: Garland, 1980).

67 White, "Richard Edwards," p. 62; see also Bradner, *Life and Poems of Richard Edwards*, p. 67.

68 On early drama's expression of economic problems, see Jean-Christophe Agnew, *Worlds Apart: The Market and the Theater in Anglo-American Thought, 1550–1750* (Cambridge: Cambridge University Press, 1986).

69 Moments later, Carisophus re-narrates the exploit to Aristippus, describing how he induced the "crafty spie" (499) to "bewray" (503) that "He was come hether to know the state of the Citie" (508). Carisophus's narrative falsifies by what it leaves out, Damon's protestations establishing his innocence. In Carisophus, Edwards gives his court audience a realistic, even irritating image of the sycophantic courtier: vicious in courtesy, deceptive in honesty, sincere in a falsehood designed to serve his interest.

70 David M. Bevington, *From Mankind to Marlowe: Growth of Structure in the Popular Drama of Tudor England* (Cambridge, Mass.: Harvard University Press, 1962), p. 136.

71 Nicholas Grimald, Dedicatory Epistle to *Christus Redivivus*, quoted from *The Life and Poems of Nicholas Grimald*, p. 109.

72 Although we are tracking the elements of suspense, we should remember that the spirit of *Damon and Pithias*, including its treatment of the two friends, is comic. Damon's last-minute entrance evokes a certain melodramatic hilarity. The New Globe production of *Damon and Pithias* in September 1996 seems to have achieved a sense of high comedy and wonder both. The play may charm in part by exploiting dramaturgical techniques such as suspense while also demonstrating humor toward them.

73 Grimald, Dedicatory Epistle to *Christus Redivivus*, pp. 109, 110.

74 About this scene, J. E. Kramer argues, "what we are given to see is the great force of moral transformation contained in true dramatic art" (p. 489); Kramer sees *Damon and Pithias* as "the first of a long line of dramas ... which investigate, often in profound ways, the relation of drama to society" (p. 476): J. E. Kramer, *"Damon and*

Pithias: An Apology for Art," *ELH*, vol. 35, no. 4 (December, 1968): 475–80.

75 See, in particular, William A. Armstrong, *"Damon and Pithias* and Renaissance Theories of Tragedy," *English Studies* (October 1958): 200–07.

HUMANISM AND THE DRAMATIZING OF WOMEN

1 The present argument undertakes to solve a problem in dramatic history without presuming that a humanist expansiveness in the stage representation of women necessarily mirrored any amelioration of women's actual social situation. It has been argued that in many regards Renaissance women came to face more rather than less restrictive conditions during the sixteenth century. Concerning "the strong female characters who wheeler-deal their way through Jacobean drama," Lisa Jardine wonders, "[h]ow are they related to their real-life sisters who were . . . increasingly constrained by an ideology of duty and obedience . . ?" (*Still Harping on Daughters: Women and Drama in the Age of Shakespeare*, 2nd edn. [New York: Columbia University Press, 1989], p. 68). Jardine asks a question that remains to be fully answered.

2 See, for example, Kathleen McLuskie, *Renaissance Dramatists* (Atlantic Highlands, N.J.: Humanities Press International, 1989); Karen Newman, *Fashioning Femininity and English Renaissance Drama* (Chicago, Ill.: University of Chicago Press, 1991); and Carol Hansen, *Women as Individuals in English Renaissance Drama: A Defiance of the Masculine Code* (New York: Peter Lang, 1993). A notable exception to the tendency to exclude early drama from discussion is Catherine Belsey, *The Subject of Tragedy: Identity and Difference in Renaissance Drama* (London: Methuen, 1985). See also Juliet Dusinberre *Shakespeare and the Nature of Women*, 2nd edn. (New York: St. Martin's Press, 1996).

3 Frances E. Dolan, *Dangerous Familiars: Representations of Domestic Crime in England, 1550–1700* (Ithaca, N.Y.: Cornell University Press, 1994), p. 139.

4 Linda Woodbridge, *Women and the English Renaissance: Literature and the Nature of Womankind, 1540–1620* (Urbana: University of Illinois Press, 1984), pp. 125–26. For background and texts concerning the *querelle de femmes*, see Katherine Usher Henderson and Barbara F. McManus, *Half Humankind: Contexts and Texts of the Controversy about Women in England, 1540–1640* (Urbana: University of Illinois Press, 1985).

5 Lynda E. Boose, *"The Taming of the Shrew*, Good Husbandry, and Enclosure," in Russ McDonald, ed., *Shakespeare Reread: The Texts in New Contexts* (Ithaca, N.Y.: Cornell University Press, 1994), pp. 193–225, on p. 196.

6 Boose, *"The Taming of the Shrew*, Good Husbandry, and Enclosure," p. 196.

7 Pamela Joseph Benson, *The Invention of Renaissance Woman: The Challenge of Female Independence in the Literature and Thought of Italy and England* (University Park: Pennsylvania State University Press, 1992). See also Constance Jordan, "Feminism and the Humanists: The Case of Sir Thomas Elyot's *Defence of Good Women*" in Margaret W. Ferguson, Maureen Quilligan, and Nancy J. Vickers, eds., *Rewriting the Renaissance: The Discourse of Sexual Difference in Early Modern Europe* (Chicago: University of Chicago Press, 1986), pp. 242–58. Jordan observes that "Humanist defenses of women generally consider three kinds of subject . . . they establish the excellence of women by referring to examples from history; they celebrate the full humanity of a wife in relation to her husband; or they argue for the humanist education of girls"; "Fascinated with examples of women who had taken part in the great drama of history, humanists compared them with men, praised their 'virility,' and entertained the possibility of a single standard for male and female virtue" (243). On humanist defenses of companionate marriage, see Wayne's introduction to Edmund Tilney, *The Flower of Friendship: A Renaissance Dialogue Contesting Marriage*, ed. Valerie Wayne (Ithaca, N.Y.: Cornell University Press, 1992).

8 Benson, *The Invention of Renaissance Woman*, pp. 2, 4. See also Constance Jordan, *Renaissance Feminism: Literary Texts and Political Models* (Ithaca, N.Y.: Cornell University Press, 1990); Retha M. Warnicke, "Women and Humanism in England" in *Humanism Beyond Italy*, vol. 2 of Albert Rabil, Jr., ed., *Renaissance Humanism: Foundations, Forms, and Legacy*, 3 vols. (Philadelphia: University of Pennsylvania Press, 1988); Retha M. Warnicke, *Women of the English Renaissance and Reformation* (Westport, Conn.: Greenwood Press, 1983); Margaret L. King, *Women of the Renaissance* (Chicago: University of Chicago Press, 1991); and (for a negative view of humanism) Jardine, *Still Harping on Daughters*, pp. 51–58.

9 On Erasmus, see S. K. Sowards, "Erasmus and the Education of Women," *The Sixteenth Century Journal*, vol. 13 (Winter, 1982): 77–89. On Salter, see Janis Butler Holm, "The Myth of a Feminist Humanism: Thomas Salter's *The Mirrhor of Modestie*" in Carole Levin and Jeanie Watson, eds., *Ambiguous Realities: Women in the Middle Ages and Renaissance* (Detroit: Wayne State University Press, 1987), pp. 197–218.

10 Holm, "The Myth of a Feminist Humanism," p. 204.

11 Benson, *The Invention of Renaissance Woman*, pp. 158, 160, 158. More's best known defense of women's education, his letter to William Gonnell (1518), appears in Elizabeth Frances Rogers, ed., *St. Thomas More: Selected Letters* (New Haven, Conn.: Yale University Press, 1961), pp. 103–07. As Warnicke puts it, "More had argued that while they were inferior beings, women could excel in scholarship,

thereby achieving intellectual equality or near equality with men" (*Women of the English Renaissance and Reformation*, p. 27).

12 More, argues Benson, "sees woman's life as offering an avenue of escape from the oppression of the state"; likewise, More "sees private female discourse as superior to male public discourse" (*The Invention of Renaissance Woman*, p. 171; see pp. 167–71). Warnicke also emphasizes More's valorizing of domestic life: "He and other humanists hoped to use their educational system to create closer spiritual and intellectual ties between husband and wife and between parents and children" ("Women and Humanism in England," p. 40). Juliet Dusinberre suggests that More did envision some role for women in public life (*Shakespeare and the Nature of Women*, pp. 205–06; see esp. pp. 199–214).

13 Benson, *The Invention of Renaissance Woman*, p. 174; on Vives as "restrictor" and "repressor," see p. 172, where Benson concludes that "the notion of an independent woman exists in Vives's book, despite Vives."

14 Benson, *The Invention of Renaissance Woman*, p. 183; see also Constance Jordan, "Feminism and the Humanists"; and Jordan, *Renaissance Feminism*, pp. 119–22.

15 Benson, *The Invention of Renaissance Woman*, pp. 205–30.

16 *Ibid.*, p. 205. On humanist exempla, see Jordan, "Feminism and the Humanists"; and Jordan, *Renaissance Feminism*, passim.

17 Benson links the "chaste, silent, and obedient" ideal to popular literature (*The Invention of Renaissance Woman*, p. 213).

18 On *Wit and Science*, see chapter 2.

19 My efforts here to distinguish humanist drama from the morality tradition notwithstanding, it would be misleading to define medieval drama by the morality plays exclusively, since mystery and miracle plays frequently offer richer roles for female characters than do the moralities.

20 Alan H. Nelson, ed., *The Plays of Henry Medwall* (Cambridge: D.S. Brewer, 1980), p. 1. Quotations from *Fulgens and Lucres* follow Nelson's edition. See also M. E. Moeslein, ed., *The Plays of Henry Medwall: A Critical Edition* (New York: Garland, 1981). For a helpful overview, see Howard B. Norland, *Drama in Early Tudor Britain, 1485–1558* (Lincoln: University of Nebraska Press, 1995), pp. 233–43.

21 On Buonaccorso's *De Vera Nobilitate* and Medwall's variations from it, see Moeslein, ed., *The Plays of Henry Medwall*, pp. 72–89; and David Bevington, *Tudor Drama and Politics: A Critical Approach to Topical Meaning* (Cambridge, Mass.: Harvard University Press, 1968), pp. 45–47.

22 Moeslein, ed., *The Plays of Henry Medwall*, p. 88.

23 Olga Horner suggests that Lucres is patterned after Lady Margaret Beaufort, Henry VII's mother ("*Fulgens and Lucres:* An Historical Perspective," *Medieval English Theatre*, 15 [1993]: 49–86, esp. pp. 65–

77). To Horner, Cornelius reflects the kind of noble who troubled Henry VII with illegal maintenance and whose armed forces and arrogation of power threatened public order.

24 Fulgens provides theatrical evidence for Debora Kuller Shuger's argument that in the English Renaissance "'father' usually does not connote authority, discipline, rationality, law, and so on, but rather forgiveness, nurturing, and tenderness" (*Habits of Thought in the English Renaissance: Religion, Politics, and the Dominant Culture* [Berkeley: University of California Press, 1990], pp. 219, 220); see pp. 218–49. For another tender-hearted father in a close-knit family, see Virginius in R. B.'s *Appius and Virginia* (*c.* 1564).

25 A sociological argument might insist that Lucres's deference demonstrates only patriarchal domination. From a different critical perspective, one could claim, however, that an act of willing submission can be liberating and is not necessarily oppressive. Viewed politically, Fulgens stands for a patriarchy not unlike Elyot's ideal of a monarchy that is both absolute and limited: the citizens are virtuous, so the just king grants them rights and governs wisely, and they reciprocate his trust with obedience; see Thomas Elyot, *The Boke named the Gouernour*, vol. 1, ed. Henry Herbert Stephen Croft (London: Kegan Paul, Trench, and Co., 1883), Bk. 1, chap. i. The analogy suggests that, despite Lucres's later demurral, her actions carry some political implications.

26 For Nelson, Lucres is superior to the male figures, "a thoroughly admirable woman – level-headed, in command of every situation, tempered by a sense of humour and an instinct for charity" (*The Plays of Henry Medwall*, p. 21).

27 Moeslein, ed., *The Plays of Henry Medwall*, pp. 88–89.

28 Catherine Belsey, *The Subject of Tragedy*, pp. 194, 195. That definition of true nobility occurs as Lucres decides between Cornelius and Gayus, a logical, careful, incremental process that, according to Joel B. Altman, makes *Fulgens and Lucres* a model of "explorative" drama structured in the form of a question (*The Tudor Play of Mind: Rhetorical Inquiry and the Development of Elizabethan Drama* [Berkeley: University of California Press, 1978], pp. 13–30, esp. pp. 25–26).

29 While Cornelius bargains with the father, Nelson observes, the audience watches a satisfyingly affectionate relationship develop between Lucres and Gayus; Gayus is also associated with the sympathetic A, Cornelius with the cynical B (*The Plays of Henry Medwall*, p. 21).

30 Lucres suggests to Gayus that she will attempt to win her father to him as her choice. Yet in her preceding dialogue with Fulgens, she has already gained his acquiescence to whomever she may choose. The scenes are not necessarily out of order; rather, Lucres's statement to Gayus can be understood in relation to her caution and her desire to make her choice emotionally acceptable.

31 Moeslein, ed., *The Plays of Henry Medwall*, p. 89.
32 Bevington, *Tudor Drama and Politics*, p. 66.
33 Quotations from Heywood follow Richard Axton and Peter Happé, eds., *The Plays of John Heywood* (Cambridge: D.S. Brewer, 1991).
34 See the discussion of *Nice Wanton* in chapter 2.
35 Noting that Custance has no counterpart in Plautine drama, Bevington cites her "feminine courage, charity, and firm maternalism"; her "patient, warm, and somewhat condescending control" of her household; and her sober good sense and loyalty (*Tudor Drama and Politics*, pp. 121–23).
36 Lois Potter notes that Custance associates herself with the besieged biblical Susanna; see "The Plays and the Playwrights" in Norman Sanders, Richard Southern, T. W. Craik, and Lois Potter, *The Revels History of Drama in English*, vol. 2, *1500–1576* (New York: Methuen, 1980), p. 219. Susanna received her own play in the 1560s and was often mentioned in the Elizabethan formal controversy about women.
37 Woodbridge, *Women and the English Renaissance*, p. 20. On the pressure applied to wealthy widows to remarry, see Jardine, *Still Harping on Daughters*, pp. 83–84.
38 Bevington, *Tudor Drama and Politics*, p. 124.
39 W. W. Greg, ed., *A New Enterlude of Godly Queene Hester* (Louvain: A Uystpruyst: 1904), pp. x, v. Quotations of the text will follow Greg's edition.
40 If, as Greg implies, *Godly Queene Hester* stands out as an early play expressing personal animosity toward Cardinal Wolsey (*A New Enterlude*, p. ix), then its political and emotional stakes are high. As a play about tyranny, *Godly Queene Hester* may be grouped with dramas such as *Cambises* and *Gorboduc*, which explore the problematic, sometimes victimized position of women in relation to politics. The 1561 publication date may celebrate the new queen Elizabeth, who might be imagined as Hester saving her people from religious persecution. For the topical implications of the play in the late 1520s, see David Bevington's analysis of Hester as a tribute to Katherine of Aragon (*Tudor Drama and Politics*, pp. 87–84). Greg Walker argues that *Godly Queene Hester* satirizes Wolsey for dispossessing certain monasteries between 1524 and 1529, but Walker says little about Hester (*Plays of Persuasion: Drama and Politics at the Court of Henry VIII* [Cambridge: Cambridge University Press, 1991], pp. 102–32).
41 The play's emphasis (e.g. 233–43) on Hester's hidden identity recalls Roman comedies such as Terence's *Andria*, where the revelation of Glycerium's parentage solves the social problems.
42 Belsey, *The Subject of Tragedy*, p. 197.
43 Benson, *The Invention of Renaissance Woman*, pp. 198–99. On Elyot's *Defence*, see also Woodbridge, *Women and the English Renaissance*, pp. 18–22.

44 Sir Thomas Elyot's *The Defence of Good Women*, ed. Edwin Johnston Howard (Oxford, Ohio: Anchor Press, 1940), p. 36; see pp. 35–40.
45 On Zenobia, see Valerie Wayne, "Zenobia in Medieval and Renaissance Literature" in Levin and Watson, *Ambiguous Realities*, pp. 48–65.
46 Woodbridge argues that "The closing segment of the *Defence* is noteworthy as one of the few Renaissance texts to view with approval the independence, assertiveness, and erudition of a widow" (*Women and the English Renaissance*, p. 20).
47 Bevington, *Tudor Drama and Politics*, p. 88. On Zenobia, see Elyot, *Defence*, pp. 62–63. Zenobia describes her proceedings: "I caused good lawes to be publyshed, obseruynge them fyrste in myne owne householde, and caused them in al other places to be well executed. I made Iustice chiefe ruler of myne affection, and in all consultations wolde I be present" (p. 62).
48 On the Marian aspects of *Respublica*, see Bevington, *Tudor Drama and Politics*, pp. 115–20. Bevington emphasizes the play's attack on the Edwardian Protestant protectorate.
49 Lois Potter calls *Respublica* a "classical" comedy with a "morality format"; see "The Plays and the Playwrights," pp. 141–257, on pp. 217–19. The attribution of *Respublica* to Nicholas Udall, favored by Greg (cited below), strengthens the play's association with humanism. Norland also notes *Respublica*'s mixture of morality and humanist drama (*Drama in Early Tudor Britain*, pp. 199–209).
50 All citations refer to W. W. Greg, ed., Respublica: *An Interlude for Christmas Attributed to Nicholas Udall* (London: Early English Text Society, 1952).
51 Woodbridge, *Women and the English Renaissance*, p. 126; she adds that "Interest in the formal controversy during the 1560s may also account for the appearance of certain other plays devoted to favorite *exempla* – Thomas Nuce's *Octavia* and John Studley's *Medea*, both translations from Seneca published in 1566, and a lost *Samson* play acted in 1567, from which Delilah cannot have been absent" (p. 126).
52 Woodbridge, *Women and the English Renaissance*, p. 49.
53 *Ibid.*, pp. 49–73. Woodbridge finds Castiglione's *The Courtier*, published in Hoby's translation in 1561, the exception, its humanist and aristocratic sensitivity toward women sometimes approaching the vision of modern feminism; see pp. 52–59.
54 On Wager's *Mary Magdalene* as illustrative of "the main thematic interests" (80) of Protestant Reformation interludes, see Paul Whitfield White, *Theatre and Reformation: Protestantism, Patronage, and Playing in Tudor England* (Cambridge: Cambridge University Press, 1993), pp. 80–88.
55 Paul Whitfield White, ed., *Reformation Biblical Drama in England:* The Life and Repentaunce of Mary Magdalene, The History of Iacob and Esau (New York: Garland, 1992), pp. xx, xxi, xxiv. Citations of Wager's *Mary Magdalene* will follow White's edition.

56 White, *Reformation Biblical Drama*, p. 146, n. 31.

57 *Learne* occurs in various forms eight times – almost once every ten lines – in the Prologue, so that the educational theme, with its humanist caste, looms large.

58 White, *Reformation Biblical Drama*, p. 148, n. 285f. *Mary Magdalene* recalls the controversies about education that stimulated humanist pedagogical drama, discussed in chapter 2.

59 On 1560s drama, see chapter 4. I am indebted to Victoria Plaza for drawing my attention to Mary's iconic power.

60 Linda Woodbridge notes that C. Pyrrye's tract of 1569, *The Praise and Dispraise of Women*, part of the pamphlet controversy about women, rails against female vanities of dress and cosmetics, including the "habit of walking about with naked breast" (*Women and the English Renaissance*, p. 60).

61 For a similar estimation, see White, *Theatre and Reformation*, p. 85.

62 The word "see" looms in the surrounding dialogue; see, for example, 1161, 1169, 1206, 1215, 1227, 1233. The language of seeing in the play's second half emphasizes transformation's visual and sensual dimension.

63 Wager retains the traditional scheme of devils or Vices taking up residence inside Mary. Thus redemption becomes possible when the Virtues replace the Vices as the internal spectacle (1305–08). Salvation triumphs as sin's visual ugliness is revealed, so that the religious problem resolves on the level of dramatic iconography. Soon Christ will cast the Vices out of Mary (1385 and s.d. at 1388).

64 Of Mary's conversion, White observes, "Where the Vices' inspired merriment had primarily appealed to the audience's sense of play, the serious, homiletic speeches of the Virtues now encourage critical detachment" (*Theatre and Reformation*, p. 86). Alan C. Dessen explores the conversion's combination "of stage business and psychological allegory" (*Elizabethan Drama and the Viewer's Eye* [Chapel Hill: University of North Carolina Press, 1977], p. 134; see pp. 134–35).

65 Mary Beth Rose, *The Expense of Spirit: Love and Sexuality in English Renaissance Drama* (Ithaca, N.Y.: Cornell University Press, 1988); see esp. pp. 93–177.

66 All textual citations refer to Ronald B. McKerrow and W. W. Greg, eds., *The Play of Patient Grissell by John Phillip* (London: Malone Society, 1909). For a recent, modernized edition of the play, see Faith Gildenhuys, ed., *A Gathering of Griseldas: Three Sixteenth-Century Texts: The Comedy of Patient and Meek Grissill*, "A Most Pleasant Ballad of Patient Grissell," *The History of Patient Grisel* (Ottawa: Dovehouse Editions, 1996).

67 For detailed discussion of these speeches, see chapter 4.

68 See also 1227–34 and the similar ritual at 1473–76 and 1518–23.

69 Gautier wrenches his children from the women of his own household

only to turn them over to another female realm. Likewise, Rebecca W. Bushnell argues, the humanist pedagogue strove to remove children from the hands of indulgent nurses and mothers but then often took on aspects of the maternal role himself (*A Culture of Teaching: Early Modern Humanism in Theory and Practice* [Ithaca, N.Y.: Cornell University Press, 1996], pp. 26–44).

70 The gender divide is not absolute: as the play advances, the male character Vulgus, who stands for the people, finds himself fed up with Gautier; others, such as Reason and Sobriete, express sympathy for Grissell.

71 Bevington, *Tudor Drama and Politics*, p. 148. Bevington also describes the early Gautier humanistically as "A model prince loved by his people, receptive to criticism" (p. 148).

72 Those thematics are not without their own problems. Catherine Belsey writes of the Renaissance Griselda plays that "Marriage as the story defines it is entirely absolutist, but the moral superiority of the wife calls into question the justice of absolutism" (*The Subject of Tragedy*, p. 167).

73 See Elyot, *The Boke named the Gouernour*, Vol. 1, Bk. 1, chap. x, e.g., p. 71.

74 John Isaac Owen, ed., *An Edition of* The Rare Triumphs of Love and Fortune (New York: Garland, 1979), p. 201; Owen cites from James Paul Brawner, ed., *The Wars of Cyrus* ([Urbana: University of Illinois Press, 1942], p. 64), whose list derives chiefly from E. K. Chambers, *The Elizabethan Stage*, vol. 4 (Oxford: Clarendon Press, 1922).

75 David M. Bevington identifies the romances structurally with the morality plays, arguing that "[f]rom the romantic saga of separation, wandering, and reunion" the romance dramatists "extracted a formula similar to the moral theme of fall from grace, temporary prosperity of evil, and divine reconciliation" (*From Mankind to Marlowe: Growth of Structure in the Popular Drama of Tudor England* [Cambridge, Mass.: Harvard University Press, 1962], p. 190; see pp. 190–98). For Bevington, the romance pattern deploys actors in "alternate, symmetrical, and sequential configuration" in the manner of the moralities (p. 190). Of the three extant romances, Bevington does not discuss *The Rare Triumphs of Love and Fortune*, which displays few elements of morality drama and more resembles John Lyly's plays. Like Bevington, Alan C. Dessen tends to group the 1570s romances with the late morality plays: *Shakespeare and the Late Moral Plays* (Lincoln: University of Nebraska Press, 1986), p. 163.

76 John Isaac Owen discovers in *Love and Fortune*'s mythological apparatus, allusions to classical writers, and in its Latinate diction the traces of humanist grammar-school education (*Rare Triumphs of Love and Fortune*, pp. 71–80). To Owen, Lucian's dialogues and the tradition of Latin debate poems may have influenced the play's debate-

among-the-gods format (pp. 83–94). *Love and Fortune*, unlike the other two romances, displays a humanist five-act structure, including a third-act crisis. The dumb show, the scene-ending music, and the gods' choric commentary also link it to other English humanist plays, such as *Gorboduc*. For its staging, *Love and Fortune* requires a cave on one side, a court setting on the other, and the gods above: the symmetry of two "houses" derives from Roman drama (on staging, see Owen, pp. 160–70).

77 See, for example, Clyomon's soliloquy, 760–85, and Clamydes's, 872–95. All quotations from *Clyomon and Clamydes* follow Betty J. Littleton, ed., Clyomon and Clamydes: *A Critical Edition* (The Hague: Mouton, 1968).

78 Stephen Gosson, *Playes Confuted in Fiue Actions* (1582), quoted from Arthur F. Kinney, ed., *Markets of Bawdrie: The Dramatic Criticism of Stephen Gosson* (Salzburg: Institut für Englische Sprache und Literatur, Universität Salzburg, 1974), p. 161.

79 Gosson recognizes as much: "paraduenture you will saye, that by these kinde of playes, the authours instruct vs how to loue with constancie, to sue with modestie, and to loth whatsoeuer is contrarie vnto this" (*Playes Confuted*, p. 161).

80 Mythological references also occur in dialogue. One seventy-odd span of lines early in *Clyomon and Clamydes* refers six times to mythology: Hercules (61), Cerberus (62), Mars (85), Hydra's head (99), Minotaur (100), and Apollo (134). Such allusions testify to the influence of humanist education. In a kind of humanist parody, Subtle Shift invokes the idea of knowledge: "I am the sonne of *Appollo*, and from his high seate I came, / But whither I go, it skils not, for Knowledge is my name: / And who so hath knowledge, what needs he to care / Which way the wind bloe, his way to prepare" (134–37).

81 Littleton, ed., *Clyomon and Clamydes*, p. 58. Littleton notes "the playwright's abundant use of the more common rhetorical devices (rhetorical question, exclamation, apostrophe, interjection and repetition) as well as some less common ones" (p. 58). Littleton also finds the author following rhetorical procedures laid out in Puttenham's *The Arte of English Poesie* (p. 60).

82 Littleton, ed., *Clyomon and Clamydes*, p. 56.

83 *Ibid.*, p. 39.

84 Littleton notes that *Clyomon and Clamydes* avoids adapting other misogynistic speeches from the prose romance source, *Perceforest* (*Clyomon and Clamydes*, p. 27).

85 In *Mucedorus*, Almadine will intervene with her father the king to save Mucedorus from execution because he had saved her life.

86 The dénouement stresses Neronis's travails on Clyomon's behalf, indicated by her quasi-formal list of labors (2192–222). When Neronis offers herself as page to Clyomon, she gives her name as Heart of Steel.

87 Hansen, *Women as Individuals in English Renaissance Drama*, p. 7.

88 See Mulcaster's chapter on educating maidens (*Positions: By Richard Mulcaster*, ed. Robert Herrick Quick [London: Longmans, Green, and Co., 1888], pp. 166–82).

89 In Anthony Munday's *The Death of Robert, Earl of Huntingdon* (pub. 1601; Oxford: Malone Society Reprints, 1965), Lord Bruce narrates how his mother, imprisoned with her son by King John, drew her own blood with her teeth and thus died in an attempt to feed her starving boy; see lines 2866–902.

90 "In early modern England . . . woman figures the human body, its corruptibility, fragility, but also its power to inspire desire, to multiply and reproduce" (Karen Newman, *Fashioning Femininity*, p. 6).

91 The staging of this act makes for interesting speculation, since it requires a baring of the breast, perhaps done with the actor's back to the audience. The bloodletting, however, must be visible to characters on stage, given the responses of Hemione and Lentulo, and Fidelia's blood must be put on a leaf and applied to Armenio's tongue and Bomelio's face.

THE CONFUSIONS OF *GALLATHEA:* JOHN LYLY AS POPULAR DRAMATIST

1 See G. K. Hunter's landmark study, *John Lyly: The Humanist as Courtier* (London: Routledge and Kegan Paul, 1962).

2 Peter Saccio selects *Gallathea* for extensive treatment as a "court comedy" in *The Court Comedies of John Lyly: A Study in Allegorical Drama* (Princeton, N.J.: Princeton University Press, 1969). The prevailing view of Lyly as a court dramatist has set a narrow range for commentary, with critics examining the plays for court issues, for allegories of court personalities, and, most frequently, for panegyrics to the queen; see Michael Pincombe, *The Plays of John Lyly: Eros and Eliza* (Manchester: Manchester University Press, 1996), pp. viii–ix. Departing from the inherited view, Pincombe finds in Lyly's plays an increasing distaste for panegyric and courtliness and locates them in the tradition not of court entertainment but of "commercial juvenile drama" (p. 18; see pp. 14–19).

3 Carter A. Daniel, *The Plays of John Lyly* (Lewisburg, Pa: Bucknell University Press, 1988), p. 22.

4 Hunter, *John Lyly*, pp. 153, 154.

5 Saccio, *Court Comedies*, pp. 1–10.

6 *Ibid.*, pp. 187–224, esp. pp. 189–90.

7 On fantasy and wish-fulfillment in playhouse drama see Thomas Cartelli, *Marlowe, Shakespeare, and the Economy of Theatrical Experience* (Philadelphia: University of Pennsylvania Press, 1991), esp. pp. 10–64.

8 See Roslyn Lander Knutson, *The Repertory of Shakespeare's Company,*

1594–1613 (Fayetteville: The University of Arkansas Press, 1991), esp. pp. 40–54.

9　Robert J. Meyer, "'Pleasure Reconciled to Virtue': The Mystery of Love in Lyly's *Gallathea*," *Studies in English Literature 1500–1900* (Spring 1981): 193–208. Saccio describes Lyly's court comedies as "almost completely static" (p. 2). Michael R. Best argues that Lyly's plays show "an almost complete lack of action" ("Lyly's Static Drama," *Renaissance Drama*, S. Schoenbaum, ed. [Evanston, Ill.: Northwestern University Press, 1968], pp. 75–86, on p. 75).

10　Mary Beth Rose, *The Expense of Spirit: Love and Sexuality in English Renaissance Drama* (Ithaca, N.Y.: Cornell University Press, 1988), p. 26.

11　Joel B. Altman, *The Tudor Play of Mind: Rhetorical Inquiry and the Development of Elizabethan Drama* (Berkeley: University of California Press, 1978), pp. 196, 97. Meyer, too, argues that *Gallathea*, "moves toward the definition of ideas rather than the resolution of dramatic conflict" ("'Pleasure Reconciled to Virtue'," p. 194).

12　Steven Mullaney, "Mourning and Misogyny: *Hamlet, The Revenger's Tragedy*, and the Final Progress of Elizabeth I, 1600–1607," *Shakespeare Quarterly* 45 (Summer 1994): 139–62.

13　All references to Lyly's plays follow R. Warwick Bond, ed., *The Complete Works of John Lyly*, 3 vols. (Oxford: Clarendon Press, 1902).

14　Daniel, "The Woman in the Moon: Afterword" in Daniel, *The Plays of John Lyly*, pp. 359–60.

15　*Woman*'s changing perspectives are amplified by its generic allusions. The setting, Utopia, brings to mind Sir Thomas More's humanist treatise. Its initiating deity, Nature, recalls, as well, the humanist More Circle drama, such as Rastell's *The Nature of the Four Elements* (*c.* 1519). Pandora's phase changes also evoke morality drama, such as *Mundus et Infans* (pub. 1522), while the device of different gods dominating each act recalls the stage romance *The Rare Triumphs of Love and Fortune* (1584).

16　See J. A. Barish's classic study, "The Prose Style of John Lyly," *ELH*, (March 1956): 14–35.

17　David M. Bevington, *From Mankind to Marlowe: Growth of Structure in the Popular Drama of Tudor England* (Cambridge, Mass.: Harvard University Press, 1962), pp. 118–19 and *passim*.

18　David M. Bergeron does examine the themes and structure of the apprentice scenes, arguing that they critique specialized learning and favor practical wisdom; see "The Education of Rafe in Lyly's *Gallathea*," *Studies in English Literature: 1500 to 1900* (Spring 1983): 197–206.

19　Robert Weimann, "Representation and Performance: The Uses of Authority in Shakespeare's Theatre," *PMLA*, 107 (May 1992): 497–510, on p. 503.

20 Vives's dialogue *"Refectio Scholastica,"* for example, contains the following exchange, between master and usher at dinner, with the typically Lylyesque movement between the philosophical and material:

USHER   So, too, the philosophers say that there are three tenses, but our art demands five, therefore our art is outside the nature of things.

MASTER   Nay, rather thou art thyself outside of the nature of things, for art is in the nature of things.

USHER   If I am outside the nature of things, how can I eat this bread and meat, which are in the nature of things?

MASTER   Thou art so much the worse to belong to another nature whilst you eat what belongs to this our nature.

In *Tudor School-Boy Life: The Dialogues of Juan Luis Vives*, trans. and intro. Foster Watson (London: J. M. Dent, 1908), p. 35.

21 Robert Y. Turner, "Some Dialogues of Love in Lyly's Comedies," *ELH* (September, 1962): 276–88, on p. 276.

22 Shakespeare pays tribute to Lyly's reinvention of stage love by recapitulating it in *Twelfth Night*, where Olivia's beauty, imaged in terms of Petrarchan portraiture, surrenders to Viola's charm, enacted as theatrical performance.

23 Anne Begor Lancashire, ed., *John Lyly:* Gallathea *and* Midas (Lincoln: University of Nebraska Press, 1969), p. xxiv.

24 For Hunter, Haebe's farewell speech evokes "the dangerous and bitter state of virginity most feelingly" (*John Lyly*, p. 203); to Saccio, Haebe's last-minute escape affords her an "astonishing" and "quite moving" "reversal" of perspective that makes her serious (*Court Comedies*, pp. 125–26, including n. 43).

25 For the Latin text with English translation, see P. Sharrat and P. G. Walsh, eds., *George Buchanan: Tragedies* (Edinburgh: Scottish Academic Press, 1983). As the sacrificial victim, Iphis passes through stages of leave taking similar to Haebe's. Then, as the slaying approaches, she blooms with blushing, eroticized beauty: "her virginal modesty spread a crimson blush over her white countenance . . . [N]ature had breathed over her a beauty more pleasing than her wont, as if she regarded the death of the noble heroine as worthy of a final gift" (pp. 92–93). Iphis calls to the god to receive her in sacrifice and commands the trembling priest to "Draw near, and remove this life . . . Discharge" (p. 94). Lyly's parody touches these elements in *Jepthes*.

26 Lyly's contemporary George Peele also made a translation of *Iphigenia*, now lost, that was praised by Lyly's Oxford classmate William Gager, the famous academic playwright, and which may have been known to Lyly. In the Christmas season of 1571–72 a play of *Iphigenia* was performed at court.

27 "The maid herself comes on with eyes in modesty cast down, but yet her face is radiant and the dying splendour of her beauty shines beyond its wont" (*Seneca in Ten Volumes*, with an English translation by Frank Justus Miller, vol. 8: *Troades* [Cambridge, Mass.: Harvard University Press, 1929], p. 219.

28 Altman, *Tudor Play of Mind*, p. 209. On Gallathea and metamorphosis, see Grace Tiffany, *Erotic Beasts and Social Monsters: Shakespeare, Jonson, and Comic Androgyny* (Newark: University of Delaware Press, 1995), pp. 49–51. On the maiden-transformation, see also Jacqueline A. Vanhoutte, "Sacrifice, Violence and the Virgin Queen in Lyly's *Gallathea,*" *Cahiers Élisabéthains* (April 1996): 1–14, on pp. 8–9.

29 Reavley Gair, The Children of Paul's: *The Story of a Theatre Company, 1553–1608* (Cambridge: Cambridge University Press, 1982), p. 106.

30 Hunter, *John Lyly*, p. 73.

31 For details of the Blackfriars venture, I am indebted to accounts by Hunter (*John Lyly*, pp. 72–76) and by Gair (*Children of Paul's*, pp. 98–112); see also Andrew Gurr, *Playgoing in Shakespeare's London*, 2nd edn. (Cambridge: Cambridge University Press, 1996), pp. 133–36.

32 Gair sees the promoters as aiming for "the best possible combination of young acting and singing talent in London" (*Children of Paul's*, p. 99).

33 Hunter, *John Lyly*, p. 75.

34 Quoted in Hunter, *John Lyly*, p. 75.

35 From Jack Roberts to Sir Roger Williams. Quoted in Hunter, *John Lyly*, p. 76.

36 For a discussion of Lyly's probable anti-Martinist play, see Gair, *Children of Paul's*, pp. 110–12.

37 Quoted in Gair, *Children of Paul's*, p. 109; also in Hunter, *John Lyly*, p. 75.

38 See Hunter, *John Lyly*, p. 82; E. K. Chambers, *The Elizabethan Stage*, vol. 3 (Oxford: Clarendon Press, 1922), pp. 416–17.

39 Michael Shapiro, *Children of the Revels: The Boy Companies of Shakespeare's Time and their Plays* (New York: Columbia University Press, 1977), p. 180.

40 Discussing the folk taste for romances, G. R. Baskervill observes that "Both simple romantic stories and mythological stories from the classics seem to have been popular in dramatic form among the folk of Elizabethan England": "Some Evidence for Early Romantic Plays in England," *Modern Philology* (August 1916 and December 1916): 229–51 and 467–512, on p. 101. See Baskervill for a comprehensive discussion of romance play history.

41 For the estimate of one half, see James Paul Brawner, ed., The Wars of Cyrus: *An Early Classical Narrative Drama of the Child Actors: Critical Edition with Introduction and Notes* (Urbana: The University of Illinois Press, 1942), p. 64; Brawner's analysis is discussed by John Issac

Owen, *An Edition of* The Rare Triumphs of Love and Fortune (New York: Garland, 1979), pp. 201–02; for the estimate of one-third, see Betty J. Littleton, ed., Clyomon and Clamydes: *A Critical Edition* (The Hague: Mouton, 1968), Appendix B, pp. 195–98. Leo Salinger also surveys the plays of 1565–84: *Shakespeare and the Traditions of Comedy* (Cambridge: Cambridge University Press, 1974), pp. 31–39.

42 Gurr, *Playgoing*, p. 120.

43 By the 1580s, argues Gurr, "There was a new middle zone of public taste, fixed in London and offering new possibilities for an urban audience somewhere between the taste of the Court and the knock-about moralising of the country market place" (*Playgoing*, p. 120).

44 Bevington treats the romances as showing "progressive" action and would generally liken them to the moralities (*From* Mankind *to* Marlowe, pp. 190–98). But the episodic action of stage romances more obviously reflects that of the older verse and prose romances, as Baskervill makes clear. We do not need the moralities to account for the stage romances.

45 Mythological figures appear not only in the romances but in such earlier popular plays as *Horestes* (1567) and *Cambises* (1561), the latter of which was performed into the 1590s. Folk and mythological figures meet in *Summer's Last Will and Testament* (1592); Robert Wilson's *The Cobbler's Prophecy* (pub. 1594) mixes clownish mortals in dialogue with Mercury, Mars, Venus, and other gods. Marlowe uses Mercury, Venus, and Cupid in his *Dido, Queen of Carthage*, and Venus makes another bow in Greene's *Alphonsus, King of Arragon* (*c.* 1587). Henslowe's Diary shows that in the 1590s the Admiral's Men at the Rose Theatre commonly enacted mythological subjects: *Hercules Part 1*, *Hercules Part 2*, *Phaeton*, and *Polyphemus*. Although they contain no classical gods (except Revenge), Kyd's *The Spanish Tragedy*, Marlowe's *Tamburlaine*, and Greene's *Friar Bacon and Friar Bungay* are drenched in mythological allusions, evidence that their enthusiastic audiences knew and took interest in mythology. In populating his plays with mythological characters, Lyly introduces figures familiar in public drama.

46 Kyd's *The Spanish Tragedy* may invoke the same stage conventions from the romances with its otherwordly onstage spectators, Revenge and Don Andrea. Peele also uses framing characters as a device, notably with Madge, Frolic, and Fantastic in *The Old Wives Tale*.

47 See, for example, John Dover Wilson, *John Lyly* (Cambridge: Macmillan and Bowes, 1905), pp. 21–43. Wilson notes the association of euphuism with the alliterative preaching style of Hugh Latimer (pp. 36–37), showing that artificial style could be popular.

48 Quotations of *The Rare Triumphs of Love and Fortune* follow the Owen edition.

49 Quotations from *Clyomon and Clamydes* follow Littleton, ed., *Clyomon and Clamydes*.

50 Littleton argues that "In fact, the play is constructed largely in rhetorical rather than dramatic units" (*Clyomon and Clamydes*, p. 58).

51 Alexander in *Campaspe* responds to the romance of Apelles and Campaspe with a magnanimity that Prince Edward echoes in *Friar Bacon and Friar Bungay; Tamburlaine*, like *Campaspe*, explores the problem of the warrior in love. For Lyly's influence on Shakespeare, see Leah Scragg, *The Metamorphosis of Gallathea: A Study in Creative Adaptation* (Washington, D.C.: University Press of America, 1982). For Jonson as Lyly's "spiritual heir," see Wilson, *John Lyly*, p. 127.

52 Jean-Christophe Agnew, *Worlds Apart: The Market and the Theatre in Anglo-American Thought, 1550–1750* (Cambridge: Cambridge University Press, 1986), p. x.

BEARING WITNESS TO *TAMBURLAINE, PART 1*

1 Richard Levin, "The Contemporary Perception of Marlowe's Tamburlaine," in J. Leeds Barroll, III, ed., *Medieval and Renaissance Drama in England*, vol. 1 (New York: AMS Press, 1984), pp. 51–70, on p. 54.

2 Quotations of *Tamburlaine* follow Fredson Bowers, ed., *The Complete Works of Christopher Marlowe*, 2nd edn., vol. 1 (Cambridge: Cambridge University Press, 1981).

3 For one claim that Marlowe condemns his hero, see Roy W. Battenhouse, *Marlowe's Tamburlaine: A Study of Renaissance Moral Philosophy* (Nashville, Tenn.: Vanderbilt University Press, 1941). On Tamburlaine's heroism as levitating him beyond moral categories, see Eugene M. Waith, *The Herculean Hero in Marlowe, Chapman, Shakespeare and Dryden* (New York: Columbia University Press, 1962).

4 See, for example, Simon Shepherd, *Marlowe and the Politics of Elizabethan Theatre* (Sussex: Harvester Press, 1986); Alan Sinfield, *Faultlines: Cultural Materialism and the Politics of Dissident Reading* (Berkeley: University of California Press, 1992), pp. 237–45; and Emily C. Bartels, "The Double Vision of the East: Imperialist Self-Construction in Marlowe's *Tamburlaine, Part One*" in Mary Beth Rose, ed., *Renaissance Drama*, n.s. 23 (Evanston, Ill.: Northwestern University Press and The Newberry Library Center for Renaissance Studies, 1992), pp. 3–24.

5 The excitement and the meaning of Marlowe's plays, argues Michael Goldman, may derive not from "our admiring or detesting the heroes" but from "our participation . . . in an experience created and sustained by acting" – in *Tamburlaine* the experience of ravishment and abandon ("Marlowe and the Histrionics of Ravishment" in Alvin Kernan, ed., *Two Renaissance Mythmakers: Christopher Marlowe and Ben Jonson* [Baltimore: Johns Hopkins University Press, 1977], pp. 22–40, on p. 39). Thomas Cartelli suggests that the play "becomes a source of transgressive pleasure for an audience whose more mun-

dane ambitions are recast in the form of heroic aspiration" *(Marlowe, Shakespeare, and the Economy of Theatrical Experience* [Philadelphia: University of Pennsylvania Press, 1991], p. 67).

6 Bartels, "The Double Vision," p. 15; see also Shepherd, *Marlowe and the Politics of Elizabethan Theatre*, p. 152.

7 See William Bavande, *A Worke of Ioannes Ferrarivs Montanus, touchynge the good orderynge of a common weale*, Englished by William Bavande (London, 1559), Bk. v, chapt. 8. See also chapter 4, above.

8 See, for example, David M. Bevington, *From* Mankind *to* Marlowe: *Growth of Structure in the Popular Drama of Tudor England* (Cambridge, Mass.: Harvard University Press, 1962), pp. 199–217.

9 I have in mind here the Aristotelian notion, familiar to Renaissance rhetoricians, that metaphor releases a sense of the immediate and palpable; see David H. Thurn, "Sights of Power in *Tamburlaine*," *English Literary Renaissance* (Winter 1989): 3–21, esp. pp. 12–13.

10 Thurn, "Sights of Power," p. 4.

11 On engagement and detachment, see Kent Cartwright, *Shakespearean Tragedy and Its Double: The Rhythms of Audience Response* (University Park: Pennsylvania State University Press, 1991).

12 Sir Thomas Elyot, *The Boke named The Gouernour*, vol. 1, ed. Henry Herbert Stephen Croft (London: Kegan Paul, Trench, and Co., 1883), p. 59.

13 Forrest G. Robinson, *The Shape of Things Known: Sidney's* Apology *in its Philosophical Tradition* (Cambridge: Harvard University Press, 1972).

14 Sir Philip Sidney, *A Defence of Poetry*, ed. Jan Van Dorsten (Oxford: Oxford University Press, 1966), pp. 27, 32, 29.

15 Geoffrey Bullough, ed., *Poems and Dramas of Fulke Greville, First Lord Brooke*, vol. 1 (Edinburgh: Oliver and Boyd, 1939), verses 12, 10, and 13.

16 J. S. Cunningham, ed., *Tamburlaine the Great* (Manchester: Manchester University Press, 1981), pp. 51–52.

17 Goldman, "Marlowe and the Histrionics of Ravishment," p. 37.

18 Stephen Gosson, *Playes Confuted in Fiue Actions* (1582) in Arthur F. Kinney, ed., *Markets of Bawdrie: The Dramatic Criticism of Stephen Gosson* (Salzburg: Institute für Englishe Sprache und Literatur, Universität Salzburg, 1974), pp. 155–56.

19 *Ibid.*, p. 164.

20 *Ibid.*, p. 186.

21 In Shakespeare's tragedies, choric characters "regulate," "orchestrate," or "guide" audience attitudes toward main characters and events; on Shakespeare's management of response, see E. A. J. Honigmann, *Shakespeare: Seven Tragedies: The Dramatist's Manipulation of Response* (London: Macmillan, 1976), p. 27; Jean E. Howard, *Shakespeare's Art of Orchestration: Stage Technique and Audience Response* (Urbana: University of Illinois Press, 1984); Robert Hapgood, *Shake-*

speare the Theatre-Poet (Oxford: Clarendon Press, 1988); and Cartwright, *Shakespearean Tragedy and Its Double*.

22 In the *Ars Poetica*, Horace declares that the chorus "should side with the good and give friendly counsel; sway the angry and cherish the righteous. It should praise the fare of a modest board, praise wholesome justice, law, and peace with her open gates; should keep secrets, and pray and beseech the gods that fortune may return to the unhappy, and depart from the proud" (*The Art of Poetry*, in *Horace: Satires, Epistles and Ars Poetica*, trans. H. Rushton Fairclough [Cambridge, Mass.: Harvard University Press, 1916], pp. 442–89, on p. 467).

23 On the use of the chorus by Watson and Christopherson, see Howard B. Norland, *Drama in Early Tudor Britain, 1485–1558* (Lincoln: University of Nebraska Press, 1595), pp. 305–06 and 317–18.

24 For a discussion of the oscillating signals for response in *Gorboduc*, see chapter 4 above.

25 Harry Levin, *The Overreacher: A Study of Christopher Marlowe* (Cambridge, Mass.: Harvard University Press, 1952).

26 Although our emphasis here is on humanist dramaturgy, it is worth noting that the play's witnessing also seems to reflect the culture of espionage and disbelief, of moveable faith and protean psychological states, in which Marlowe participated. For an exploration of that aspect of Marlowe's life and culture, see Charles Nicholl, *The Reckoning: The Murder of Christopher Marlowe* (New York: Harcourt Brace, 1992).

27 "Edward Alleyn, as Tamburlaine, . . . never looked like this description, and neither did anyone else . . . It is a direct challenge to the senses, an example of the myth-making power of words" (Lois Potter, "Seeing and Believing" in *The Arts of Performance in Elizabethan and Early Stuart Drama: Essays for G. K. Hunter*, eds., Murray Biggs, Philip Edwards, Inga-Stina Ewbank, and Eugene M. Waith [Edinburgh: Edinburgh University Press, 1991], pp. 113– 23, on p. 116).

28 Just how large was Edward Alleyn? Despite the general opinion that Alleyn was about six-and-a-half feet tall, his actual height has been estimated at "approximately 5 feet 9–10 inches," still "signficantly taller than most men of his time" (S. P. Cerasano, "Tamburlaine and Edward Alleyn's Ring" in *Shakespeare Survey*, vol. 47, Stanley Wells, ed. [Cambridge: Cambridge University Press, 1994], pp. 171– 79, on p. 178).

29 Judith Weil discounts the problem suggested above: "[T]he presentation of these qualities in images is a way of symbolizing his spirit, not of recording actual physical traits. Although the images often refer to postures of power which neither the speaker nor the audience could ever literally see, I doubt that they could produce a sharp sense of disjunction between the real and the imagined Tamburlai-

nes" (*Christopher Marlowe: Merlin's Prophet* [Cambridge: Cambridge University Press, 1977], p. 128). In rebuttal one might argue that the play keeps alive alternative visual images of Tamburlaine as either monarch or shepherd, thief, and fox.

30 Dana F. Sutton, ed. and trans., *Thomas Legge: The Complete Plays*, vol. 2 *Solymitana Clades (The Destruction of Jerusalem)* (New York: Peter Lang, 1993), p.vii. Marlowe matriculated in Corpus Christi College, Cambridge in 1581 (he entered the College in December 1580) and took his B.A. in 1584.

31 Quotations from *Richardus Tertius* refer to the Sutton edition, which provides parallel Latin and English texts. See also Robert J. Lordi, ed. and trans., *Thomas Legge's* Richardus Tertius (New York: Garland, 1979).

32 Waith, *The Herculean Hero*, p. 66.

33 Writing of *Tamburlaine*, Douglas Cole notes, "The physiological effects of *emotional* states had been reported both in early plays and in the popular romances of the 1560s, but the representation of physical suffering itself through such details [i.e., physiologically explicit details] is apparently original with Marlowe in the English drama" (*Suffering and Evil in the Plays of Christopher Marlowe* [Princeton, N.J.: Princeton University Press, 1962], pp. 90–91). As we shall see, however, Elizabethan Latin drama does provide examples of the representation of physical suffering. Concerning the romances and their humanist associations, see chapter 5, above.

34 Quotations follow Betty J. Littleton, ed., *Clyomon and Clamydes: A Critical Edition* (The Hague: Mouton, 1968).

35 All quotations of *Meleager* follow Dana F. Sutton, ed. and trans., *William Gager: The Complete Works*, vol. 1: *The Earlier Plays* (New York: Garland, 1994), pp. 127–29. The published argument of *Meleager* makes a possible allusion to *Tamburlaine*, when Gager observes, "And if somebody should think it strange that so many Greek princes came together to suppress a robber [i.e., the Caledonian boar], if he were to reflect on Viriatus of Lusitania, the gladiator Spartacus, the first Ottoman, Tamburlane the Scythian, and other notorious bandits, he would immediately cease to be amazed" (p. 43). Although first performed at Christ Church, Oxford, in 1582, *Meleager* was not published until 1593, after *Tamburlaine*'s triumph on the stage.

36 Thomas Wilson, *The Art of Rhetoric (1560)*, ed. Peter E. Medine (University Park: The Pennsylvania State University Press, 1994), p. 35.

37 *Ibid.*, pp. 35–36.

38 *Ibid.*, p. 42. Likewise, Wilson sets as one of the orator's goals that "he must persuade, and move the affections of his hearers in such wise that they shall be forced to yield unto his saying" (p. 48).

39 See, for example, Battenhouse, *Marlowe's Tamburlaine*; and Waith, *The Herculean Hero*.

40 Wilson, *The Art of Rhetoric*, p. 42.

41 Cartelli emphasizes Theridamas as a carrier of "normative" audience values; see *Marlowe, Shakespeare, and the Economy of Theatrical Experience*, pp. 75–76. A reader who tracks Theridamas through the play will note that, despite Tamburlaine's early winning of Theridamas, the danger of recidivism – and, by extension, audience resistance – attaches to the lieutenant as the play progresses, so that Theridamas, the "normative" audience-figure, must be repeatedly attended to, addressed, won again, by Tamburlaine.

42 Quotations are from *The Geneva Bible: A Facsimile of the 1560 Edition* (Madison: University of Wisconsin Press, 1969). In Deuteronomy, God gives instructions for waging war against enemy cities, including mercy toward those that surrender at the outset, killing of all men from cities that resist, and utterly annihilating all the inhabitants of cities that worship false idols.

43 Stephen Greenblatt, *Shakespearean Negotiations: The Circulation of Social Energy in Renaissance England* (Berkeley: University of California Press, 1988), p. 133. Greenblatt makes this generalization after recounting Hugh Latimer's story of how he obtained a royal pardon for a woman condemned to death, perhaps wrongly, for child murder but withheld knowledge of the pardon from the woman until moments before her presumed execution.

44 Weil, *Christopher Marlowe*, p. 131; see also J. B. Steane, *Marlowe: A Critical Study* (Cambridge: Cambridge University Press, 1964), p. 87.

ROBERT GREENE'S *FRIAR BACON AND FRIAR BUNGAY*: THE COMMONWEALTH OF THE PRESENT MOMENT

1 On Greene as a popularizing "[c]utter and paster," see Charles Hieatt, "A New Source for *Friar Bacon and Friar Bungay*," *Review of English Studies* (May 1981): 180–87, esp. pp. 182, 186.

2 The summary in this paragraph is based largely on Andrew Gurr, *Playgoing in Shakespeare's London* 2nd edn. (Cambridge: Cambridge University Press, 1996); and Andrew Gurr, *The Shakespearean Stage, 1574–1642*, 3rd edn. (Cambridge: Cambridge University Press, 1992).

3 *Ibid.*, p. 34.

4 On imitations and sequels in 1580s theatre, see Roslyn Lander Knutson, *The Repertory of Shakespeare's Company, 1594–1613* (Fayetteville: The University of Arkansas Press, 1991), esp. pp. 40–54.

5 On the humanist vision of learning and its rhetoric, see Arthur F. Kinney, *Humanist Poetics: Thought, Rhetoric, and Fiction in Sixteenth-Century England* (Amherst: The University of Massachusetts Press, 1986), pp. 3–38. On imitation, see, among others, Thomas Greene, *The Light in Troy: Imitation and Discovery in Renaissance Poetry* (New

Haven, Conn.: Yale University Press, 1982); and Jonathan Bate, *Shakespeare and Ovid* (Oxford: Clarendon Press, 1993), esp. pp. 83–117.

6 Elizabeth L. Eisenstein, *The Printing Press as an Agent of Change*, 2 vols. (Cambridge: Cambridge University Press, 1979).

7 Dana F. Sutton, "General Introduction" in *William Gager: The Complete Works*, ed. and trans. Dana F. Sutton, vol. 1: *The Earlier Plays* (New York: Garland Press, 1994), p. xxi.

8 Charles Hieatt, "A New Source for *Friar Bacon and Friar Bungay*," p. 183.

9 On John Dee's relationship to Bacon, see Barbara Howard Traister, *Heavenly Necromancers: The Magician in English Renaissance Drama* (Columbia: University of Missouri Press, 1984), pp. 82–83; and Daniel Seltzer, "Introduction," *Friar Bacon and Friar Bungay*, ed. Daniel Seltzer (Lincoln: University of Nebraska Press, 1963), p. xv. On Bruno, see James Dow McCallum, "Greene's Friar Bacon and Friar Bungay," *Modern Language Notes* (April 1920): 212–17.

10 Werner Senn argues that a major theme of *Friar Bacon and Friar Bungay* is "the education of a prince and ideal ruler of a commonweal" ("Robert Greene's Handling of Source Material in *Friar Bacon and Friar Bungay*," *English Studies* [December, 1973]: 544–53, on p. 553).

11 All citations of the text follow Robert Greene, *Friar Bacon and Friar Bungay*, 1594, ed. W. W. Greg (Oxford: Malone Society Reprints, 1926). Parenthetical citations are to scene and line numbers. References to other Greene plays follow J. Churton Collins, ed., *The Plays and Poems of Robert Greene*, 2 vols. (Oxford: Clarendon Press, 1905).

12 Seltzer refers to Edward's malcontentedness as "a formalized state of mind in Elizabethan acting" (*Friar Bacon and Friar Bungay*, p. 3n.).

13 J. A. Lavin, ed., *Friar Bacon and Friar Bungay* (London: Ernest Benn Limited, 1969), p. 5n. The green costume, meaning "as from hunting," was conventional; see Alan C. Dessen, *Elizabethan Stage Conventions and Modern Interpreters* (Cambridge: Cambridge University Press, 1984), pp. 32–33.

14 Noted by John Weld, "*Friar Bacon and Friar Bungay*," Meaning in Comedy: Studies in Elizabethan Romantic Comedy (Albany: State University of New York Press, 1975), p. 140.

15 Concerning trees, George Peele's *The Arraignment of Paris* (1581) has a tree of gold rising from the ground; Dekker's *Old Fortunatus* (1599) involves a Vice figure who brings out a golden tree with apples; Heywood's *The Brazen Age* (1611) has Hercules tearing down a tree, similar to the action in *Friar Bacon and Friar Bungay*. Ascending, descending, and attacked trees appear in *A Warning for Fair Women* (1599), *The Iron Age, Part 1* (1612), and *The Two Noble Kinsmen* (1613). I am indebted to Leslie Thomson for identifying these stage

trees. The prospective glass also occurs in John Day's *The Travels of the Three English Brothers* (1607). Concerning sword-charming, Greene returns to it in *James the Fourth*; see Lavin, *Friar Bacon and Friar Bungay*, p. 30n. As a variation on that action, characters are charmed to dumbness in *John of Bordeaux* and in *Doctor Faustus* (B-text).

16 Raphe and particularly Miles might refer to the most famous stage clown of Elizabethan drama, Richard Tarlton, who died in 1588. Miles enters the Brazen Head scene loaded down with weaponry and engages in considerable physical comedy with it, including almost impaling himself as he begins to drift off to sleep with his pike propped against his chest. That stage business may recall Tarlton, who was a skilled swordsman and was awarded his Masters of Defense in 1587. As an actor, Tarlton would have been able to combine martial and comedic skills that Miles's difficulties with his own weapons may salute and lampoon. The frontispiece to *Friar Bacon and Friar Bungay* shows Miles in the Brazen Head episode decked with drum and tabor. (The same woodcut accompanies the extant editions of Greene's prose source, *The Famous Historie*.) Miles does not use a drum and tabor in the play, but the figure of Miles in the woodcut bears a generic resemblance to the woodcut of Tarlton with drum and tabor in *Tarltons Jests* (1613) and a more distant resemblance to a figure with drum and tabor accompanying the dancing Kemp in the frontispiece of Will Kemp's *Nine Dais Wonder* (1600). Miles as visually imagined seems to resemble the kind of stage comic who might have enacted him. On the woodcuts, I am indebted to a conversation with Richard Levin.

17 Allusion-hunting is a dangerous business, as recent scholars have pointed out, for one may be tempted to see an allusion where a passage may as easily be explained as proverbial knowledge, conventional sentiment, or phrasing arising from a parallel context. On these matters, see Laurie E. Maguire, *Shakespearean Suspect Texts: The "Bad" Quartos and their Contexts* (Cambridge: Cambridge University Press, 1996), pp. 159–72. The allusions that I suggest above are based on similarities of verbal style (as with the parodies of Skeltonics or euphuism) often combined with similarly constructed dramatic actions (as with *Friar Bacon and Friar Bungay*'s resemblances to *Tamburlaine* and *Campaspe*).

18 S. K. Heninger, Jr., in Thomas Watson, The Hekatompathia; or, Passionate Centurie of Love *(1582): A Facsimile Reproduction*, intro. S. K. Heninger, Jr. (Gainesville, Fla.: Scholar's Facsimilies and Reprints, 1964), p. v.

19 Quotations from *Hekatompathia* follow Heninger's edition. Edward's perhaps idiosyncratic image of crystal skin seems to recall Watson. An examination of Elizabethan concordances suggests that Watson's use of crystal as a metaphor for skin is unusual but not unique. While

crystal is most often associated anatomically with eyes, and otherwise with glass, sky, tears, and various forms of water, crystal used to describe complexion does occur occasionally in Spenser and elsewhere.

20 Greene assuredly knew Watson's famous sonnet sequence and probably its author, since Watson had studied at Oxford and was an associate of Nash, Lyly, Peele, and Marlowe; see Mark Eccles, *Christopher Marlowe in London* (Cambridge: Harvard University Press, 1934).

21 Raphe introduces the pun on women as books, which gives a sexual cast to related words such as "learning": "Why is not the Abbot a learned man, and hath red many bookes, and thinkest thou he hath not more learning than thou to choose a bonny wench, yes I warrant thee, by his whole grammer" (i.50–53). In the second scene, Bacon reiterates the pun as he questions Burden teasingly about his mistress: "What booke studied you there on all night?" (ii.269). Bacon and others repeat that and related puns on "alchemy" and "learning" as the scene coalesces around the comic resemblance of pursuing scholarship to pursuing women (283–90, 319–20).

22 Weld, *Meaning in Comedy*, p. 147. Lavin comments on Miles's Skeltonics in scene vii and notes Greene's repetition of a phrase and a rhyme from Skelton's "Ware the Hawk"; *Friar Bacon and Friar Bungay*, p. 42n. Regarding scene vii, Collins notes that parody of Skelton's verse was a staple of the Elizabethan stage, such as in *The Death and The Downfall, of Robert Earl of Huntington; Plays and Poems*, vol. 2, p. 336n. *Fair Em* and *A Knack to Know a Knave* also contain parodies of Skeltonics.

23 Quotations of *Tamburlaine* follow Fredson Bowers, ed., *The Complete Works of Christopher Marlowe*, 2nd edn., vol. 1 (Cambridge: Cambridge University Press, 1981).

24 George Peele's *David and Bethsabe* joins *Friar Bacon and Friar Bungay* in identifying the gaze as a signal element in the post-*Tamburlaine* theatrical vocabulary. The opening of *David and Bethsabe* (*c.* 1587) displays Bethsabe bathing and singing, as "David sits above viewing her." The beauty of the titillating spectacle "scorch[es]" (i.111) David's senses and "pierce[s]" his "soul incenséd with a sudden fire" (26). Visual spectacle motivates the action, and Peele may take his cue from Tamburlaine, which brought spectacle to a new level of stage awareness. Similarly, Greene emphasizes Margaret's beauty, her brightness, and the gazing that she inspires. Citations of *David and Bethsabe* follow A. H. Bullen, ed., *The Works of George Peele*, vol. 2 (London: Ballantyne Press, 1881). On how Marlowe orchestrates spectators to "see" in his characters physical attributes that are not really there, see chapter 7.

25 Wolfgang Clemen, *English Tragedy Before Shakespeare: The Development*

of Dramatic Speech, trans. T. S. Dorsch (London: Methuen, 1961; first pub. in German 1955), p. 183.

26 See Hieatt, "A New Source for *Friar Bacon and Friar Bungay.*"

27 *Ibid.*, p. 185.

28 *Ibid.*, p. 184.

29 On the morality-play influence in *Friar Bacon and Friar Bungay*, see Lavin, *Friar Bacon and Friar Bungay*, p. xxx; on romance–narrative influences, see Senn, "Robert Greene's Handling of Source Material in *Friar Bacon and Friar Bungay*," p. 551.

30 It is possible that Greene could have written either play, although his well-known attack on *Fair Em* would seem to rule him out as its author, more frequently identified as Anthony Munday. I am inclined to doubt Greene's authorship of *John of Bordeaux*.

31 Quotations from *Fair Em* follow Standish Henning, ed., *Fair Em: A Critical Edition* (New York: Garland, 1980).

32 All citations of the play follow William Lindsay Renwick, ed., *John of Bordeaux, or The Second Part of Friar Bacon* (Oxford: Malone Society Reprints, 1936).

33 On the "middling sort" as lacking a defining class-consciousness, see Theodore B. Leinwand, "Shakespeare and the Middling Sort," *Shakespeare Quarterly* (Fall 1993): 284–303. On Margaret's popularist appeal, see David Bevington, *Tudor Drama and Politics: A Critical Approach to Topical Meaning* (Cambridge, Mass.: Harvard University Press, 1968), pp. 221–24.

34 In that regard, Margaret represents a culmination of the line of empowered women in humanist drama discussed in chapter 5.

35 The metaphor of women as books is implicit in other Tudor plays, such as *Wit and Science* (*c.* 1530–1547) and also Lewis Wager's *Mary Magdalene* (1558): "These fleshy eies . . . with their wanton lookes, / . . . They haue ben the diuels volumes and bookes" (quoted from Paul Whitfield White, ed., *Reformation Biblical Drama in England: The Life and Repentaunce of Mary Magdalene, The History of Iacob and Esau* [New York: Garland, 1992], 1797–99; see also 499–500). In George Gascoigne's *Supposes* (1566) Polynesta says that when her lover Erostrato saw her, "immediatly he cast aside both long gowne and bookes, and determined on me only to apply his study"; later the metaphor of women-as-books becomes even more explicit when Dulipo says to Erostrato, "In deede you have lost your time: for the books that you tosse now a dayes treate of smal science" (quoted from John W. Cunliffe, ed., Supposes *and* Jocasta [Boston: D. C. Heath, 1906], .i.116–18; ii.i.61–63).

36 *"Ecce quam bonum & quam iocundum, habitares libros in vnum"* (ii.174–79). The line parodies the first verse of Psalm 133: "Beholde, how good and how comelie a thi[n]g it is, brethren to dwell euen together" (*Geneva Bible*), with libros substituted for fratres (*Collins, Plays and Poems of Robert Greene* p. 327n.). The pun on women and books gives a further comic tinge to *"habitares libros in vnum."*

37 Greene's dramaturgical technique here recalls innovations of *Gammer Gurton's Needle*, where Hodge achieves theatrical impact by developing against the early stereotypes laid out for him; see chapter 3.

38 Margaret's declaration suggests her resemblance to the heroines of the stage romances, such as Neronis in *Clyomon and Clamydes* (*c.* 1576), who reveals her love to the audience before the male protagonist does. Margaret also resembles Neronis and other romance heroines in her agency and, later, in her mock-heroic offer to sacrifice herself for Lacie; see chapter 5.

39 For a well-developed argument along these lines, see Charles W. Crupi, *Robert Greene* (Boston: Twayne Publishers, 1986), pp. 126–29.

40 *Fair Em* interestingly glosses Margaret's choice of Lacie. Em dearly loves Manvile, who occupies a dramatic position parallel to Lacie's. But Manvile treats Em in an even more callow way than Lacie treats Margaret, and the action overthrows expectations by giving Em to the scorned but faithful wooer, Valingford. The divergent ending suggests that Lacie's callowness may have been as noticeable to an Elizabethan as to a modern audience.

41 Weld, *Meaning in Comedy*, p. 152; Crupi, *Robert Greene*, pp. 128–29.

42 On the Palmer in John Heywood's *The Foure PP*, see chapter 1.

43 Sandra Billington calls Raphe "Edward's substitute, or lord of misrule, playing out the disorder of Edward's behaviour" (*Mock Kings in Medieval Society and Renaissance Drama* [Oxford: Clarendon Press, 1991], p. 183). Calling Miles a "low-comic parody" and "comic extension" of Bacon, Weld concludes that "Friar Bacon's error corresponding to Edward's is his lust for glory, and the personification of his folly corresponding to Rafe is his foolish sevant Miles" (*Meaning in Comedy*, pp. 142–43).

44 A similar process occurs in Redford's *Wit and Science*; see chapter 2.

45 Miles's transportation to hell performs a variation on business apparently so familiar from the late morality plays that Samuel Harsnett ridicules it at the turn of the century: "'the old church plays, when the nimble Vice would skip up nimbly like a jackanapes into the devil's neck, and ride the devil a course, and belabour him with his wooden dagger, till he made him roar'" (*A Declaration of Egregious Popish Impostures* [London, 1603], pp. 114–15, quoted in Dessen, *Elizabethan Drama and the Viewer's Eye* [Chapel Hill: University of North Carolina Press, 1977], pp. 36–37). But Miles does not seem to have such an advantage on the devil as does the "nimble Vice," and the joke may be that what occurs as an allusion to popular "clown business" also possesses an unsettling dimension.

46 For a discussion of related qualities of openness in Lyly's dramatic endings, see chapter 6.

47 William Empson, *Some Versions of Pastoral* (London: Chatto and Windus, 1935), pp. 30–34, on p. 33.

48 Charles W. Hieatt, "Multiple Plotting in *Friar Bacon and Friar Bungay,*" *Renaissance Drama*, n.s. 16, Leonard Barkan, ed. (Evanston, Ill.: Northwestern University Press, 1985), pp. 17–34.

49 Hieatt, "Multiple Plotting," p. 22. In contrast, Traister argues that "simple moral evaluation of characters in Greene's play is impossible" (*Heavenly Necromancers*, p. 68).

50 Traister, *Heavenly Necromancers*, p. 71.

51 See Juan Luis Vives, *Vives: On Education: A Translation of the* De tradendis disciplinis, trans. and intro. by Foster Watson (Cambridge: Cambridge University Press, 1913).

52 On the play's festive quality, see Peter Mortenson, *"Friar Bacon and Friar Bungay*: Festive Comedy and 'Three-Form'd Luna,'" *English Literary Renaissance* (Spring 1972): 194–207.

53 Weld, *Meaning in Comedy*, p. 152 and p. 244, n.9.

54 Empson, *Some Versions of Pastoral*, pp. 31, 33.

Index

Coláiste Oideachais Mhuire Gan Smal Luimneach